METHODS AND STRATEGIES FOR TEACHING IN SECONDARY AND MIDDLE SCHOOLS

METHODS AND STRATEGIES FOR TEACHING IN SECONDARY AND MIDDLE SCHOOLS

KENNETH T. HENSON
Eastern Kentucky University

THIRD EDITION

Longman Publishers USA

Methods and Strategies for Teaching in Secondary and Middle Schools, Third Edition

Longman, 10 Bank Street, White Plains, N.Y. 10606

Associated companies:
Longman Group Ltd., London
Longman Cheshire Pty., Melbourne
Longman Paul Pty., Auckland
Copp Clark Longman Ltd., Toronto

This book was previously published as *Secondary Teaching Methods.*

Production editor: Ann P. Kearns
Editorial Assistant: Matt Baker
Cover design: Silvers Design
Cover art: Detail of untitled oil painting by Kenneth A. Henson (1973)
Text art: Fine Line Inc.
Production supervisor: Winston Sukhnanand
Compositor: ComCom

Photo credits: Sharon Henson, pp. 3, 23, 46, 66, 97, 205, 267, 287, 313, 379, 398; Greg Perry
(Department of Public Information, Eastern Kentucky University), pp. 97, 135, 165, 226, 339;
Tim Webb, pp. 13, 33, 55, 77, 118, 152, 184, 213, 244, 251, 277, 299, 328, 358, 389, 416

Library of Congress Cataloging-in-Publication Data

Henson, Kenneth T.
    Methods and strategies for teaching in secondary and middle
schools / Kenneth T. Henson.—3rd ed.
        p.   cm.
    Includes bibliographical references and indexes.
    ISBN 0-8013-1625-1
    1. High school teaching—United States.   2. Middle schools—United
States. I. Title.
LB1737.U6H45   1996
373.13′0973—dc20   95-9386
                                              CIP

1 2 3 4 5 6 7 8 9 10-MA-9998979695

To the hardest working and most passionate artists I know. My two sons,
Randy and Ken.

Contents

CHAPTER 13   FROM DISCIPLINE TO SELF-DISCIPLINE   339

PART SIX   TESTS AND EVALUATION   377

CHAPTER 14   EVALUATION   379

CHAPTER 15   **TEST CONSTRUCTION, ADMINISTRATION, AND SCORING**   398

Preface

Effective teaching requires the teacher to have a repertoire of strategies and to know when to use each of them. Guskey (1990, p. 12) explains, "It is only when several strategies are carefully and systematically integrated that substantial improvements in learning become possible." *Methods and Strategies for Teaching in Secondary and Middle Schools,* third edition, is designed to prepare prospective middle through senior high school teachers for their first classroom experience and to help in-service teachers improve their teaching skills.

Today's teachers have at their disposal many strategies for organizing their classes and fostering the learning process. These include cooperative learning, classroom management models, curriculum models, effective school models, effective teaching models, critical thinking, mastery learning, teacher expectations research, simulations, case studies, inquiry learning, and matching learning and teaching styles. All these strategies are discussed in this edition.

WHAT'S NEW IN THIS EDITION

Themes

The third edition has enhanced the **multicultural** theme and has added a **teachers as decision makers** theme. Both these themes run throughout the book.

Research

This revision has had over 100 research and literature entries of studies done in the past two years. These are practical studies; each provides tips that you can use to increase your effectiveness and that of your students.

Topics

Education reform is bringing changes to schools at record speeds. To keep the text absolutely current, the following topics have been added to this edition:

- A new section on Teachers as Decision Makers—Chapter 1. (This theme runs throughout the third edition.)
- A major section on constructivism—Chapter 1. (This theme also runs throughout the book.)
- A major section on teachers and research—Chapter 1.
- A new statement to guide the use of the case studies found in each chapter of this book—Chapter 2.
- A new section on outcome-based teaching.
- Four additional sample lesson plans—Chapter 4.
- Six new sections showing how to develop a lesson using each teaching strategy—Chapter 5.
- Expanded section on cooperative learning—Chapter 5.
- Totally revised (updated) section on matching teaching styles to learning styles—Chapter 7.
- New section on parent involvement—Chapter 7.
- New section on matching styles to meet the needs of gifted students—Chapter 8.
- New section on matching styles to meet the needs of underachievers—Chapter 8.
- New section on using case studies in multicultural classrooms—Chapter 8.
- New section on cognitive mapping—Chapter 10.
- New section on arts education students' attitudes toward themselves—Chapter 12.
  - Ten new tables and figures have been added to this edition, including: Constructivism versus traditional beliefs about the purposes of schools—Chapter 1
  - Constructivism versus traditional beliefs about learning—Chapter 1
  - Constructivism versus traditional beliefs about the nature and organization of schools—Chapter 1
  - The roles of constructivist teachers compared with traditional teaching roles—Chapter 1
  - Learning styles model—Chapter 7
  - Some suggestions for using some traditional forms of media in the classroom—Chapter 10
  - Some suggestions for using some newer types of media in the classroom—Chapter 10

- A comparison of formative and summative evaluation—Chapter 14
- Sample activities from the levels of Bloom's *Cognitive Taxonomy*—Chapter 15
- A major section on teachers and research

Organization

Chapters 3 and 4 have been reversed so that objectives precedes daily planing.

Chapters 8 and 9 have been reversed so that multiculturalism precedes special education.

Chapters 14 and 15 have been reversed so that evaluation precedes test construction.

Features

The third edition also has several new features designed to stimulate discussion among students. For example, students may find the President and Governors' Goals for 2000 completely unrealistic. A listing of the top discipline problems of 1940 and 1982 will amuse and shock students. Students will enjoy seeing a chart indicating the percentage of students in each of Piaget's developmental stages. I have worked to give a balanced view on controversial topics. For example, the list of pros and cons of corporal punishment should encourage all students to give their opinions.

HOW THIS TEXT IS ORGANIZED

Part One is a thorough guide to planning learning units and daily lessons. Chapter 1 examines the dynamic profession of teaching, giving a realistic but positive view. The success of American education is highlighted, and the President and Governors' Goals for 2000 are discussed. Chapter 2 introduces the reader to curriculum development, or long-range planning. Chapter 3 guides the reader in using and writing performance objectives in all domains and at all levels of the taxonomy, and Chapter 4 shows how to use objectives in daily lesson plans to achieve the goals of long-range plans.

Part Two explains how teachers can put their plans into action most effectively. Chapter 5 introduces a variety of teaching methods, ranging from the lecture to inquiry; presents the strengths and limitations of each, and tells how the teacher can incorporate each method into an overall teaching strategy. Chapter 6 explains how the teacher can use both verbal and nonverbal communications to enhance the methods and strategies.

Recognizing that learning occurs in different ways for different people, **Part Three** covers individualizing instruction, with Chapter 7 explaining how it can best be applied in normal settings. Chapter 8 focuses on students in multicultural settings, and Chapter 9 discusses students with special challenges and students with special talents.

Effective teaching requires the ability to apply technology to improve instruction, and **Part Four** is devoted to this important goal. Chapter 10 explains the role that imagery plays in learning and shows how teachers can apply media technology to improve instruction. The subject of Chapter 11 is the microcomputer, which has established itself in U.S. schools and is accepted as a permanent feature in present and future education. This chapter tells how teachers can use computers, without fear, to enhance their teaching effectiveness and the level of thinking in the classroom.

With good classroom management, motivation, and discipline skills, teachers can effectively implement their lesson plans. **Part Five** examines the research on techniques of motivation and classroom management. Chapter 12 helps teachers integrate findings from studies on motivation with their own personalities and teaching strategies to stimulate student interest. Chapter 13 examines several discipline and management models from within education and from other disciplines, with emphasis on helping teachers develop their own management and discipline strategies for the classroom.

Never before have American teachers been so accountable for their students' achievement, as shown in **Part Six.** Chapter 14 guides them to the understanding and use of evaluation techniques to promote learning, improve instruction, and assess student achievement. Chapter 15 will help teachers develop, administer, and score their own tests.

FEATURES OF THIS TEXT

Each chapter is organized to motivate the reader by direct involvement. At the beginning of each chapter, a list of **objectives** tells the reader exactly what to expect. A **Pretest** then thrusts the reader into the major concepts of each chapter, asking the reader to agree or disagree with a few pertinent statements.

From time to time boxes titled **Reflection** are incorporated within the main text. These boxes deal with important or controversial information or provide thought-provoking exercises pertinent to the subject under discussion. The boxes end with questions designed to elicit reader reactions to the statements. The main body of the chapter is followed by a **Recap of Major Ideas,** which presents a list of concise statements.

Next there is a set of **Cases** that show the major principles in the chapter in action. Each case is an experience taken from a real-life situation. The cases describe how principles were applied in classroom settings and the results of each application. At the end of each case are a few questions related to each experience and a discussion of these questions.

A college course should always be considered a beginning. This course and this book will stimulate students to go far beyond the bounds of each. A set of **Activities** follows the cases and will help students pursue further topics introduced in the chapter. Students may wish to use these activities to individualize their teaching.

Each chapter ends with a current list of **Suggested Readings** and a separate list of references. This book cites and uses information from more than 400 sources, a high proportion of which are research studies. The lists include all these references, plus many additional sources that contain further information about the content in each chapter to help students investigate topics related to the teaching profession.

INSTRUCTOR'S MANUAL

The Instructor's Manual for this book is designed to help the professor make the course more exciting and meaningful and to give ideas for drawing students into conversations that will extend their perception of the teacher's role in the 1990s. The manual is divided into seven distinct parts.

Part One: An introduction to the pedagogy used in this textbook.

Part Two: Suggested classroom approaches for introducing each chapter to students, providing transparency masters for the instructor to use to involve students with each lesson.

Part Three: Pretest responses.

Part Four: Multiple-choice test items—Approximately ten items for each chapter—conveniently arranged by chapter so that the instructor can give a test on a single chapter or on any number of chapters.

Part Five: Multiple-choice test answer key.

Part Six: Essay test items designed to inspire students to higher levels of thinking.

Part Seven: Field activities to challenge students to actively pursue topics beyond the limited information in the book and beyond the college classroom.

ACKNOWLEDGEMENTS

This book and its forerunners have been on the market for an uninterrupted 22 years. In my association with Longman, I have found the company dedicated to excellence in all areas. The production staff, the marketing and sales staff, and all in between have proved their dedication again and again. Thanks to Matt Baker who was always there and ready to help with any question or problem. His assistance made the process flow smoothly and pleasantly. As with any business, the most important quality is integrity. The Longman staff has always distinguished itself in remaining honest and straightforward in all business transactions. I thank all of the Longman staff members for their dedication and integrity and for permitting me to add over 125 new research and literature entries to this current revision. I especially want to thank my friend Laura McKenna for her commitment to this project.

Since the preparation for such a project requires a lot of word processing, I am grateful to Jennifer Martin and Mona Keaton for their help in the preparation of this manuscript. Thank you both for helping me capture my ideas in print.

I would also like to thank the following colleagues for the suggestions they contributed to this revision: Tom Dickenson, Indiana State University; Urvin Dickman, Mankato State University; Jesus Garcia, University of Illinois; and Fred Groves, Northeast Louisiana University.

Thanks to the following reviewers for their many constructive suggestions during the current revision:

Leslie Hewling Austin, Southwest Texas State University

Cathy L. Barlow, Morehead State University

Fred Groves, Northeast Louisiana University

Annette Hemmings, Southwest Missouri State University

Neil Kahn, Lasalle University

Jack Longbotham, Hardin Simmons University

Tony R. Sanchez, Indiana University Northwest

Isabelle L. Shannon, Virginia Wesleyan College

Michael L. Tanner, Northern Arizona University

REFERENCE

Guskey, T.R. (1990). Integrating innovations. *Educational Leadership, 47*(5), 11–15.

part ONE

Planning

This is an exciting time to be a teacher. Chapter 1 identifies some of the many opportunities that today's teachers have to take their students to unprecedented levels. The teacher's first priority is to help all students learn as much and as well as possible. Teachers must plan effectively to achieve this vital goal.

Although school systems and state departments of education frequently give teachers curriculum guides and courses of study, teaching is a highly autonomous profession. Ultimately you determine what to teach and what objectives to pursue. Chapter 2 will help you examine the curriculum and design units to achieve the year's goals. Chapter 3 shows you how to reach each day's objectives by selecting appropriate content and activities and by sequencing them to facilitate students' mastery of the material.

Good planning requires a working knowledge of behavioral objectives. Chapter 4 prepares you to write good objectives at all levels of all three domains of the educational taxonomies.

chapter 1

Teaching and You

If a teacher is indeed wise he does not bid you enter the house of his wisdom, but rather leads you to the threshold of your own mind.

Kahlil Gibran

OBJECTIVES

Name at least two major recommendations in the education reform reports.

Identify major strengths in the recommendations of reform reports.

Identify and criticize the major curriculum determiner in the United States.

Explain the teacher's responsibility for using research.

Give some reasons for teacher optimism.

Explain reasons for supporting the president's and governors' Goals for 2000.

Differentiate between traditionalists' and constructivists' views of (1) the purpose of education, (2) how students learn, and (3) the teacher's role in learning.

THE TEACHING PROFESSION

Congratulations! Of all the professions you might have chosen, none is more important than teaching. Whether you are just joining the profession or have been a teacher for years, this is an exciting, newly reformed profession that requires good teachers. John Steinbeck was insightful enough to realize that good teachers provide students with the motivation and skills needed to excel in all other professions. When invited to speak to the Kansas State Teachers Association, Steinbeck explained the importance of teachers:

> My eleven-year-old son came to me recently and, in a tone of patient suffering, asked, "How much longer do I have to go to school?"
>
> "About fifteen years," I said.
>
> "Oh! Lord," he said despondently. "Do I have to?"
>
> "I'm afraid so. It's terrible and I'm not going to try to tell you it isn't. But I can tell you this—if you are very lucky, you may find a teacher and this is a wonderful thing."
>
> "Did you find one?"
>
> "I found three," I said. . . .
>
> My three had these things in common—they all loved what they were doing.
>
> They did not tell—they catalyzed a burning desire to know. . . .
>
> I shall speak only of my first teacher because, in addition to other things, she was very precious.
>
> She aroused us to shouting, bookwaving discussions. She had the noisiest class in school and didn't even seem to know it. We could never stick to the subject, geometry or the chanted recitation of the memorized phyla.
>
> Our speculation ranged the world. She breathed curiosity into us so that we brought in facts or truths shielded in our hands like captured fireflies. . . .
>
> She left her signature on us, the signature of the teacher who writes on minds. I suppose that, to a large extent, I am the unsigned manuscript of that high school teacher. What deathless power lies in the hands of such a person.

I can tell my son who looks forward with horror to fifteen years of drudgery that somewhere in the dusty dark a magic may happen that will light up the years . . . if he is very lucky. . . .

I have come to believe that a great teacher is a great artist and there are as few as there are any other great artists. It might even be the greatest of the arts, since the medium is the human mind and spirit.

THE TEACHER'S ATTITUDE

As John Steinbeck so eloquently stated, good teachers can and do make a difference, but only if they possess the right skills and attitudes. You may be surprised when you read in Chapter 6 just how much a teacher's attitude can affect students' achievement. You must communicate to your students your belief that you can make a positive difference. Even the order of your actions on the first day of school communicates your competence.

Have you ever considered that students' perspectives differ greatly from those of their teachers? "They view learning only as the acquisition of knowledge" (Stefanich, 1990, p. 50). Students do not think of themselves as mastering knowledge but as working to pass a test or please a teacher. You must teach them to achieve for themselves and to demand the best from themselves. Clearly, teachers are the key to what happens in the classroom.

GOALS FOR AMERICAN SCHOOLS

Current and future teachers must understand what the Goals 2000 bill has proposed for America's schools. Lewis Carroll (1898) knew the importance of having a clear direction:

One day Alice came to a fork in the road and saw a Cheshire cat in a tree. 'Which road do I take?' she asked. 'Where do you want to go?' 'I don't know.' 'Then,' said the cat, 'it doesn't matter.'

Without goals, our schools would rush madly to unforeseen destinations. The president and governors formed the following goals for all American schools to achieve by the year 2000. This George Bush administration–created bill, originally known as America 2000, and now called Goals 2000 (National Education Goals Panel, 1991) was signed by President Clinton in 1994 (Moffett, 1994):

1. By the year 2000, all children in America will start school ready to learn (i.e., in good health, having been read to and otherwise prepared by parents).
2. By the year 2000, the high school graduation rate will increase to at least 90 percent (from the current rate of 74 percent).
3. By the year 2000, American students will leave grades 4, 8, and 12 having

demonstrated competency in challenging subject matter, including English, mathematics, science, history, and geography. In addition, every school in America will ensure that all students learn to use their minds and be prepared for responsible citizenship, further learning, and productive employment in a modern economy.

4. By the year 2000, American students will be first in the world in mathematics and science achievement.
5. By the year 2000, every adult American will be literate and will possess the skills necessary to compete in a global economy and to exercise the rights and responsibilities of citizenship.
6. By the year 2000, every school in America will be free of drugs and violence and will offer a disciplined environment conducive to learning.

What was your reaction to these goals? Do you agree with all or some of them? Try to dismiss the idea of feasibility. If they could be attained, would you want all of them or some of them for our schools? If only some, which ones?

Now, compare your assessment of these goals' relative value with the public's assessment, as shown in Table 1.1.

Reflection

Examine the Goals listed on pages 5-6 and then respond to the following questions:

1. Which goals are most feasible? Which are least feasible?
2. Which two goals do you believe are most important?
3. Which goals can you help facilitate?

As you read these goals, perhaps you questioned whether America's schools could attain them by 2000. Let us give these questions some thought using the following two categories: (1) goals most likely to be reached by 2000 and (2) goals most unlikely to be reached by 2000. The public strongly supports these goals but doubts whether they can be attained (Table 1.2).

Never before have teachers had at their disposal so much knowledge about factors that affect achievement. Yet teachers usually do not base their planning on these factors (Brown, 1990). Chapter 3 explains how effective teachers separate important information and salient information and then simplify these major concepts for their students. Less effective teachers tend to deal with more issues. Which will you do? Chapter 6 explains eight distinct advantages that accrue when teachers conduct simple classroom studies.

Do you know that teachers consider the textbook as the major and often only source of content? Yet as Chapter 2 explains, the most widely used textbooks cover as little as 8 percent of the major concepts required to master a discipline, and more than 90 percent of textbooks are written at the lowest cognitive level.

TABLE 1.1   Priority assigned each goal

Goal	Very High (%) 1991	1990	High (%) 1991	1990	Low (%) 1991	1990	Very Low (%) 1991	1990	Don't Know (%) 1991	1990
A	52	44	38	44	6	6	1	2	3	4
B	54	45	37	42	5	8	1	1	3	4
C	55	46	35	42	6	7	1	2	3	3
D	43	34	41	42	11	16	2	3	3	5
E	50	45	36	37	9	11	2	3	3	4
F	63	55	23	26	6	9	5	6	3	4

TABLE 1.2   Likelihood of goal attainment

Goal	Very Likely (%) 1991	1990	Likely (%) 1991	1990	Unlikely (%) 1991	1990	Very Unlikely (%) 1991	1990	Don't Know (%) 1991	1990
A	10	12	37	38	33	33	14	12	6	5
B	6	10	36	35	39	37	14	12	5	6
C	6	9	36	38	36	36	15	12	7	5
D	4	6	22	23	45	41	23	24	6	6
E	6	7	25	25	41	42	23	21	5	5
F	4	5	14	14	38	40	39	36	5	5

Asking questions is itself an art. Research shows that teachers can use questions to increase student achievement, yet they rarely apply this knowledge. For example, one well-known study showed that teachers can obtain 12 significant benefits simply by waiting only two seconds longer than usual for students to respond to questions. These 12 benefits are listed in Chapter 5. It is difficult to believe that after asking questions, teachers move on to other content and other students so quickly. You will be shocked to learn, in Chapter 5, how little time teachers give students to respond to their questions. Even when a teacher asks a question (e.g., before or after a lesson) can determine what students remember. Amazed that so many teachers continue to teach in traditional ways, Marshall (1991, p. 227) asked teachers why they teach as they do, that is, students in rows, quiet classrooms, teacher dominant, whole-group instruction, textbook lecture format, low or no mobility, paper and pencil. She received the following responses:

It's the way I was taught.

It's the way I learned.

It's the easiest (most expedient) way to cover the material.

Perhaps the greatest bridge we must cross to enable our schools to take advantage of reform is the willingness to change. Alexander (1994, p. 267) explains that "the greatest obstacle lurks in the basic human fear of change." The national education reports demand change, yet change requires overcoming a natural tendency to keep things constant. States, cities, and towns also have expectations for their schools. For example, in an increasingly complex world, the role of citizenship remains important. As early as 1918 citizenship was formally endorsed as an important national expectation for all schools. Moral education as well continues to be held as an important function of the schools.

Another role of the school, one that is so universally accepted that it is taken for granted, is learning. Schools have been held increasingly accountable for students' performance on standardized examinations. Because of the pressure on schools to increase the learning of all students, teachers must find ways to improve achievement in their own classrooms and throughout their schools. One way is through restructuring, a process in which all faculty redesign the total school curriculum. A second way that teachers can raise students' performance levels is through conducting research.

TEACHERS AS DECISION MAKERS

More than 400 studies were used in writing this book, and each can make you a better teacher. Unfortunately, research also shows that teachers generally fail to use such knowledge effectively, if at all. Egbert (1984, p. 14) noted that "teachers ignore research and overestimate the value of personal experience." The result is that the ordinary classroom limits what students can do.

Teachers are the main force that determines the amount of learning that occurs in their classrooms. Since teaching is an art, the combination of ingredients that are needed to produce an optimal learning environment varies with the socioculture of each school, with each group of students, and even with the same group from day to day. Teachers can improve their students' ability to learn by improving their own ability to make decisions. Teachers whose students are consistently successful at learning are good decision makers.

Teachers must make two types of decisions: proactive and reactive. Proactive decisions are needed for planning, and reactive decisions are needed to reflect on teachers' and students' behavior. Teachers must know why one method worked and another failed and why a method that succeeded yesterday failed today. Such answers are not found in their pure form; they are not found in books, nor from redesigning schools' organizational structure, nor from research, nor from using any particular method or strategy. In fact, no source can ensure that one method will be best for any lesson.

Rather, you must combine facts, intellect, and judgment to achieve academic success in your classroom. Research is a major source of information for teachers, as the following discussion shows.

CONDUCTING RESEARCH

For many years teachers have carried out research in their classrooms. Most did so as a service to researchers (Peik, 1938). As early as 1908, however, an effort was made to involve teachers in research for another purpose—to have teachers identify educational problems and investigate possible solutions (Lowery, 1908).

By the 1950s Corey (1953) and Shumsky (1958) had begun encouraging teachers to conduct studies in their classrooms. The literature shows teachers performing the role of researchers (Allen, Combs, Hendricks, Nash, & Wilson, 1988; Busching & Rowls, 1987; Copenhaver, Byrd, McIntyre, & Norris, 1982; Fischer 1988–1989; McDaniel, 1988–1989; Reading/Language in Secondary Schools Subcommittee of IRA, 1989).

But many teachers have not done research, (Olson, 1990) partially because pre-service teacher education programs have not prepared or required them to do so. Although many teachers' schedules are already full without research (Darling-Hammond, 1993), and you will probably have to use your regular planning meetings and outside time to write up the research (McLaughlin, Hall, Earle, Miller, & Wheeler, 1995), teachers should consider conducting some research in the classroom.

Many more teachers say that they would conduct research were it not for their perception of research. Some see research as too theoretical (Chattin-McNichols & Loeffler, 1989), which may be a result of their concrete, applied world (Cuban, 1992).

Using Research to Improve Teaching

Because the teacher is a strong determiner of achievement (Bellon, Bellon, & Blank, 1992; Chimes & Schmidt, 1990; Good & Brophy, 1987), teachers must develop a high level of mastery both in their teaching fields and in pedagogy (Doyle, 1990). Conducting classroom research is one route teachers can use to increase their level of mastery in these areas (Stevens, Slanton, & Bunny, 1992). Teachers who conduct research increase the variety of methods they use in the classroom (Dicker, 1990; Fullan, 1982; Santa, 1990; Santa, Isaacson, & Manning, 1987).

Such teacher-conducted research is often called action research. As defined by McLaughlin et al. (1995, p. 7), "action research is a way for teachers to gather information about what is happening in their classrooms and throughout their school, and then to take action based on their analysis of that information."

Benefits of Conducting Research

Beyond finding answers to nagging questions and discovering more effective ways to teach, conducting research offers teachers many additional benefits. For example, research projects are mentally refreshing (Chattin-McNichols & Loeffler, 1989); teachers find it invigorating (Sucher, 1990). Perhaps the most important mental change involvement with research brings to teachers is to make them more open and less defensive. Conducting research helps teachers realize that they do not have all the answers; they become lifelong learners (Boyer, 1990; Brownlie, 1990). Increased openness leads to increased confidence (Neilsen, 1990).

The next time you are in a school, compare how the teachers act. Some teachers are forever negative about everything and everyone. They will be the first to speak out against education reform in general and against any specific change in particular. Bennett (1993) reported on graduate students who were required to complete an action-research project, saying that they entered the project feeling anxious and hostile but finished it feeling positive.

Much is heard today about the need to empower teachers. Involvement with research gives teachers both a sense of mission or purpose (Marriott, 1990) and a feeling of expertness (Allan & Miller, 1990; Bennett, 1993), characteristics that empower them. The Consortium on Chicago School Research (1993) reported that increased student learning depends on increased teacher expertise.

Involvement in research makes teachers more objective and reflective (Cardelle-Elawar, 1993; Carr & Kemmis, 1986). They become more critical of their own and others' beliefs (Goswami & Stillman, 1987; Neilsen, 1990).

This has been a cursory review of teacher involvement with research. For further information, including a discussion of the benefits of collaborative research and sample collaborative models, see Henson (1996).

EDUCATIONAL REFORM REPORTS

The school reform reports have demanded excellence and have been overly critical of the schools. Their conclusions are based on student achievement test scores. Although schools do need improvement, achievement test scores have severe limitations. First, although to many people academic attainment is the major purpose of public schools, it is only one of many significant functions of American schools. For example, socialization, citizenship, and ethical character development have remained important aims for American schools over the past century. Second, American schools are the only schools in the world that have a history of commitment to educating all the nation's youth. Third, achievement tests are only one of many ways to measure the performance of American schools against the performance of the other nations' schools. Other criteria might provide a more accurate gauge of American schools' performance through the years. For example, we might use the Nobel Prizes to measure our schools against those of other nations because (1) the Nobel Prizes measure performance over a long time, (2) they recognize both the sciences and humanities, and (3) recipients are selected by an international panel. How do American schools fare when measured by this prestigious criterion? As shown in the following list, Americans have won three times as many Nobel Prizes as any other nation and have won over one third of all Nobel Prizes awarded over the past ninety-five years.

Nobel Prizes Won Since 1901

In the United States	215
In Great Britain	84
In 45 other countries	Avg. 9 each

Over the years American schools have done a highly commendable job reaching their goals. Society has changed, however, and society's goals have changed. America's schools must now meet new goals. Although schools have never existed only to prepare youth for the workplace, vocational preparation has always been a major aim of American schools. Even the nature of this aim, however, has changed as our society moved from an industrial age to an information age. Up to and during the industrial age, the workplace required people who were trained to think convergently and focus on specific, designated tasks. Since these tasks often involved solving convergent-type problems, students were taught to solve such problems as: if Car A left at 6 AM from point X traveling east at 60 miles per hour and Car B left point Y 30 miles away traveling west at 50 miles per hour, when and where would the cars meet?

The ability to solve such problems served industrial-age workers and is still useful, yet tomorrow's worker needs the ability to step back and ask why these two cars are meeting. The information age calls for workers who can explore beyond the obvious, ask different kinds of questions, and collaborate with others to generate new ideas. Perrin (1994) addressed this necessary shift from "training" people to think and act convergently to "educating" people to think and behave in divergent, creative ways.

> What is required of workers at all levels in our postindustrial society is that they be creative thinkers and problem solvers and able to work well with others or independently. Schools can no longer simply train students for specific tasks; schools must educate them in terms of broad skills, so that they will be able to function in any number of capacities. (p. 452)

A REASON FOR OPTIMISM

Many of the reform reports are flawed. Some are very narrow, reflecting only a special interest group's concerns; others make unsound recommendations such as a longer school day and a longer school week. Yet the reform movement can bring substantial improvement to American schools. Swaim (1991, pp. 47–48) states that growth in middle-level education has created a climate conducive to school reform: "Middle level education fortunately has experienced a rather positive climate for reform over the past two decades. In 1969 only two states had middle level certification. According to Alexander and McEwin (1989), "In 1989 twenty-eight states had established middle level certification and nine other states had it under consideration." Such rapid growth has created a need for priorities to give direction to middle schools.

Using the delphi technique, a group of middle-level educators identified 16 priority events for middle-level education. A look at these priorities gives a fair picture of the general status of curriculum development today (Jenkins & Jenkins, 1991, p. 29).

The goals shown in Figure 1.1 (p. 12) provide an understanding of the challenges and opportunities now facing middle- and secondary-level teachers.

HIGH SCHOOL TEACHERS' ROLE IN REFORM

The school reform movements in most states are providing high-school teachers with unprecedented opportunities to improve their schools. For example, using the findings of effective schools' research studies, several states have completely restructured their curricula. Restructuring involves examining the school's entire operations including the curricula, the administration, the testing program, and extracurricular and

Priority 1	Middle-level schools are recognized as a legitimate level of education, along with elementary and secondary schools.
Priority 2	Both curriculum and instruction become more relevant to the developmental characteristics of middle-level students.
Priority 3	Teams are organized or reorganized into interdisciplinary teams with shared responsibility for the same group of students.
Priority 4	Universities and colleges (nationwide) offer state-approved middle-level certification programs.
Priority 5	Public acceptance of the middle-school philosophy leads to a vision that supports the growth and development of middle-level schools.
Priority 6	Inservice/reeducation of existing middle-level and non-middle-level certified faculty is increased to implement and maintain knowledge of the middle-level child.
Priority 7	Cooperative learning and other heterogeneous strategies will replace current grouping and tracking strategies.
Priority 8	A majority of middle-level schools adopt interdisciplinary teaming and advisor-advisee programs.
Priority 9	State/local policy makers recognize the need for adequate funding of middle-level education.
Priority 10	Curriculum will be more integrated and interdisciplinary throughout the middle-school program.
Priority 11	Programs to develop skills in resisting peer pressures, to help form values, and to teach the causes and effects of substance abuse are increased.
Priority 12	Parents and schools form partnerships to meet the needs of the whole child.
Priority 13	Middle-level professionals are major student advocates, serving as connectors for students from elementary to middle school and from middle school to high school.
Priority 14	Collaboration and cooperative problem solving replace competition as the driving philosophy of middle-level instruction.
Priority 15	The "integrity" of the middle-school program is preserved.
Priority 16	Leaders are faced with developing plans that allow for continued growth and development of middle-level schools and the middle-school movement.

FIGURE 1.1 NMSA Delphi Report—priority events

SOURCE: From "The NMSA Delphi Report: Roadmap to the Future" by D. M. Jenkins and K. D. Jenkins, March 1991. *82 Middle School Journal, 2281*(4): p. 29. Reprinted by permission.

cocurricular programs, among other components. Restructuring involves looking at all the school's operations rather than focusing on one or two elements such as the testing program, the class schedule, or the reading program.

Although in many states teachers are excluded from reform planning, its ultimate success depends on how well teachers understand and implement each practice. As Clark and Astuto (1994, p. 520) explain, "No one can reform our schools for us. If there is to be authentic reform in American education, it must be a grassroots movement."

The teacher's role in school reform includes implementing the major reform changes called for by state legislation. Teachers must know the major elements of their state's reform program and develop the skills needed to implement these elements. Examine the major elements in Kentucky's school reform legislation, as shown in the following list:

Required Topics for Professional Development
- School-based decision making
- Performance-based student assessment

- Nongraded primary programs
- Research-based instructional practices
- Instructional uses of technology
- Effective use of education methods and materials to motivate and nurture students of diverse cultures

How proficient are you in such elements as site-based decision making, computer technology, performance evaluation, or research-based teaching? Secondary- and middle-level teachers in most states must either have or develop these skills.

Do not think of these as just new responsibilities. They are also unprecedented opportunities to improve teaching in your school. Take this time to make a difference by contributing to reform in your state. Reform can be empowering if you accept responsibility for helping shape reform in your school. Describing the relationship between power and reform, Cook (1994, p. 48) says that "this reform movement is all about power and who has it; those inside the schools or those outside."

CONSTRUCTIVISM

Constructivism is a theory about how learning occurs. Put crudely, it holds that individuals make sense of new information by connecting it to previously acquired understanding. In this sense constructivism is a set of psychological beliefs. Constructivism is also a set of philosophical beliefs that separate it from traditional education.

Many education reform reports ignore the arts.

Philosophical Beliefs

Constructivists hold a unique set of philosophical beliefs that must be understood before one can grasp the concept of constructivism. Perhaps the most basic of these beliefs is the purpose of schools. Traditionally, Americans have viewed schools as places to prepare youth for a vocation. The earliest American schools were created to prepare students for a particular profession, the ministry. By 1636, an institution of higher education (Harvard College) had been created to further this mission.

The number and diversity of professions rapidly expanded, and Benjamin Franklin's Academy quickly became the most popular type of American school because it offered such practical subjects as mathematics, engineering, and surveying. During their almost 400 years of existence, American schools have retained their focus on preparing students for a vocation.

Constructivists do not question the value of preparing youth for better adult lives, but they believe schools should do more. For example, they believe that students' quality of life in school is also important. They also believe that merely preparing students for work is an unacceptably narrow view of a school's purposes. They believe schools should do more (e.g., help students develop their creative potential). Constructivists also believe that schools should help students acquire as much knowledge as possible, not just enough to get and keep a job (Table 1.3).

Constructivists are concerned with making school and information important to students. Constructivism's ultimate goal is not simply learning but enjoying learning. Constructivists argue that maximum learning can occur only when students are intrigued by what they study. Unlike traditional teachers, who are committed to covering the broad amount of material designated for each grade level, constructivists are committed to helping students learn less information but learn it more thoroughly. Traditional schools have sought to produce more knowledgeable students. Constructivists seek to produce more creative graduates.

Psychological Beliefs

Traditionally, American educators have equated learning with acquiring information. More has been viewed as better. The classic question, "What did you learn in school today?" reflects the idea that a successful education means abundant acquired knowledge.

TABLE 1.3 Constructivist versus preconstructivist beliefs about the purpose of schools and learning

Preconstructivist Beliefs	Constructivist Beliefs
School should prepare world-class workers	School should promote creativity
School should improve the quality of adult life	School should improve students' present and adult lives.
School should produce more knowledgeable adults	School should produce better thinkers
Breadth of content coverage is most important	Depth of understanding is most important

Constructivists view learning as a process not just of acquiring information but of creating new understanding. They regard learning as a personal process requiring each individual to use newly acquired information to shape existing understanding, thus producing new insights. Constructivists believe there is a preferred way to learn each discipline. Once the structure is unlocked, learning becomes easy (Table 1.4). Successful learners have unlocked this hidden structure.

Since constructivism portrays learning as creating new insights and new understanding, knowledge itself is viewed as temporary. All knowledge is subject to error. For decades physicists believed that light traveled in waves (wave theory), but then it was discovered that light travels in particles (corpuscular theory). In fact, under certain conditions light appears to travel in particles and under other conditions light seems to travel in waves. Physicists continue to use both theories without trying to reject either; they do not see all things as having single, correct answers. They do not worry that they must adjust their current thinking to accommodate for new discoveries.

Motivation Theory

Constructivists also differ from traditionalists on how students are motivated to learn. For example, Americans have always valued competition, believing that competition among all students fosters learning. Constructivists accept that competition among classmates can be motivating and helpful when all students are of similar ability, but in most classes students vary greatly in ability. Constructivists maintain that competition is destructive to students of lower ability. Teachers can derive the motivational advantage of competition without damaging students simply by grouping students of similar ability or by establishing groups of similar students and then having the groups compete (Table 1.5).

Constructivists believe that intrinsic or internal motivation is more powerful than extrinsic or external motivation. They therefore believe learning should be made personal to each student and students helped to find ways that make material important to them.

TABLE 1.4 Constructivist versus preconstructivist beliefs about learning

Preconstructivist Beliefs	Constructivist Beliefs
Quality of learning is reflected in the amount of knowledge accumulated	Quality of learning is characterized by the learner's level of creativity
Learning is remembering existing knowledge	Learning is creating new understanding
Learning is understanding of permanent information	Learning involves shaping information
The topic of study has little effect on the way it is learned	Success in learning any discipline requires discovering that discipline's unique structure

TABLE 1.5 Constructivist versus preconstructivist beliefs about motivation

Preconstructivist Beliefs	Constructivist Beliefs
Competition is the main driving force of motivation	Cooperation is a major motivating force
Information and the learner may be unrelated	Students learn information that has personal value to them
Rewards and punishments are the main motivating forces	Discovering new relationships among concepts and developing new concepts is motivating
Good teachers are good motivators	The motivation required for learning is internal; therefore good teachers arrange conditions to invite learning
Intraclass competition is important	Interclass competition is important

Nature and Organization of Knowledge

Constructivists believe that all curricula should be designed around major content generalizations such as themes and concepts. These generalizations are the key to understanding. Instead of worrying about covering the material designated for a particular grade level, the teacher should ensure that students learn the major concepts. This does not mean the teacher "teaches" the concepts. On the contrary, students themselves should develop these concepts. Recent research shows that teachers are often unaware of the concepts their students hold and that students often hold very different understandings than those their teachers think they hold (Heckman, Confer, & Hakim, 1994) (Table 1.6).

Constructivists view all knowledge as temporary. They are less interested in students' acquiring a textbook's or teacher's knowledge and more interested in students' questioning their own understanding and discovering new understanding. All curricula should be organized so that major concepts are easily learned and new information can easily be tied to previously held information. Student interests, current events, and ease of connecting information should shape the curriculum.

TABLE 1.6 Constructivist versus preconstructivist beliefs about the nature and organization of knowledge for curriculum content

Preconstructivist Beliefs	Constructivist Beliefs
Content is often assembled into seemingly unrelated bits of information	Content is built out of large understandings called content generalizations or concepts
Knowledge is permanent	Knowledge is temporary
Like any muscle, the brain needs rigorous exercise offered only by difficult-to-learn information	Information should be organized to simplify and expedite its learning
The textbook should shape the curriculum	Student interests, current events, and ease of association should shape the curriculum

ROLE OF CONSTRUCTIVIST TEACHERS

Constructivist teachers' beliefs about school's purpose and about how students learn mean that they behave differently from traditional teachers. Constructivist teachers must use a personal approach, focusing attention on each student to make the curriculum interesting to each student. Constructivist teachers recognize that some, most, or even all students may not be interested in the curriculum. These teachers believe they must find ways to involve students with the curriculum. This may require the teacher to keep up with news and sports events. It may require the teacher to attend school sports events, clubs, and fairs. Such attendance has two major benefits: it provides opportunities to learn more about your students' interests, and it shows your students that you are interested in them as people.

Constructivist teachers must identify and understand the major concepts in their subjects. They must then find ways to lead their students to discover and develop these concepts. Instead of teaching concepts directly to their students, constructivist teachers believe that they must introduce information that will conflict with students' present understanding, creating a state of *psychological disequilibrium* (a conflict among their understandings). This requires teachers to resist the common urge to point out correct answers (Table 1.7).

How badly is this constructivist curriculum needed in today's schools? According to Gardner and Boix-Mansilla (1994, p. 14), "While students may succeed in 'parroting back' phrases from lectures and texts, they often falter when asked to apply their understandings to new situations." The news that today's students often do not clearly understand the discipline's major concepts comes as no surprise. Perkins and Blythe (1994) say:

> Teachers were all too aware that their students often did not understand the key concepts nearly as well as they might. Research affirms this perception.

TABLE 1.7   The roles of constructivist and preconstructivist teachers

Preconstructivist Teaching Roles	Constructivist Teaching Roles
The teacher:	The teacher:
Provides information	Invites students to discover information
Preidentifies important information	Invites students to identify additional content that interests them
Helps students remember information by giving clear explanations and examples	Helps students discover information
Continuously strives for clarity	Arranges for discontinuity
Keeps students quiet and on task	Encourages students to create learning; considers a reasonable amount of noise and movement necessary and acceptable
Strives to convey all information designated for the particular grade level	Strives to help students reach a deeper understanding of fewer topics
Uses threats and other punishments to motivate	Uses students' personal interests to motivate
Uses intraclass competition to motivate	Uses interclass competition to motivate

A number of studies have documented students' misconceptions about key ideas in mathematics and the sciences, their parochial views of history, their tendency to reduce complex literary works to stereotypes, and so on. (p. 4)

Constructivism offers much promise because it focuses on students' learning the major concepts in each discipline and because it personalizes learning.

A FINAL REMINDER

Hope for improving substandard schools rests more with teachers than with any other group. In fact, if the job can be done, teachers will accomplish it. Leithwood, Menzies, and Jantzi (1994, p. 40) acknowledge the important role that teachers play in school improvement: "To stand much chance of success, curriculum reforms associated with most current school restructuring efforts will require high levels of commitment to change on the part of many teachers." However, teachers must stop relying so much on personal experience and must begin using available research data. Not all solutions come easily, and some problems do not lend themselves to a single, linear application of research. As you apply the results of more studies to your lessons, you will find that results with any method may vary, just as each group of students is unique. The important thing to recognize is that teachers who have a repertoire (collection) of methods and who are aware of new findings will learn how to incorporate these resources to improve their lessons. This will also give them a number of alternatives from which to choose whenever the first method fails.

SUMMARY

The reform reports of the early 1980s make some good recommendations. These include teaching teachers to identify and teach the major concepts in their disciplines (covered in Chapter 2), teaching communications skills (Chapter 6), and learning how to motivate students (Chapter 12).

Recent studies support the claim that instruction in America's schools needs improvement. As you review the studies discussed in this book, learn how to use their findings to plan and execute lessons, motivate your students, construct tests, manage and discipline your classes, and in general become the very best teacher you can.

So, if you are among the many joining the teaching profession, welcome! You could not have found a more exciting time to join a profession that is clearly on the move and one that is improving daily. If you are already teaching, then you know the impact school reform is having. This is your opportunity to learn how to implement many changes to improve your classroom. Reform movements are introducing alternative testing, curriculum alignment, expanded educational technology, research-based teaching, and site-based decision making. And there is more good news. Teachers of the 1990s have available a knowledge base that none of their predecessors had. The opportunity to become an outstanding teacher is in every teacher's reach.

Perhaps the most exciting news produced by the 1991 Gallup Poll of the Public's Attitude toward the Schools (Elam, Rose, & Gallup, 1991) was the clear indication that Americans prize education more than ever. When asked whether they considered as very important developing (1) the best education system in the world, (2) the most efficient industrial production system in the world, or (3) the strongest military system in the world, developing the best education system was marked the most important of the three and was ranked as very important by 89 percent of the respondents, up from the previous three polls that asked this question (88 percent in 1988, 82 percent in 1984, and 84 percent in 1982). Considering the time of this poll (just after the Persian Gulf War), the finding that education excellence ranked above industrial excellence during a major recession should excite all teachers.

Since teaching is an art and not an exact science, teachers must use various means to gather data, including personal experience and self-conducted research. However, there is no blueprint for success. Teachers must combine data with their intellect and then use their judgment to make wise decisions. Good teachers make proactive decisions using their reflective skills.

Contemporary educators are accepting the constructivist view of education. This very different way of viewing education posits the purpose of school as helping each student relate newly acquired information with existing understanding to make the new information meaningful. The teacher's role is to get students interested in new information and help them discover inconsistencies between the new information and existing understanding.

REFERENCES

Alexander, J. (1994). Multicultural literature: Overcoming the hurdles to successful study. *The Clearing House, 67*(5), 266–268.

Alexander, L. (1986, November). Time for results: An overview. *Phi Delta Kappan, 68,* 202–204.

Alexander, W. M., & McEwin, C. K. (1989). *Schools in the middle: Status and progress.* Columbus, OH: National Middle School Association.

Allan, K. K., & Miller, M. S. (1990). Teacher-researcher collaborative: Cooperative professional development. *Theory Into Practice, 29*(3), 196–202.

Allen, J., Combs, J., Hendricks, M., Nash, P., & Wilson, S. (1988). Studying change: Teachers who become researchers. *Language Arts, 65*(4), 379–387.

Bellon, J. J., Bellon, E. C., & Blank, M. A. (1992). *Teaching from a research knowledge base.* New York: Merrill.

Bennett, C. K. (1993). Teacher-researchers: All dressed up and no place to go. *Educational Leadership, 51*(2), 69–70.

Boyer, E. (1990). *Scholarship reconsidered: Priorities of the professorate.* Princeton, NJ: Carnegie Foundation for the Advancement of Teaching.

Brown, D. S. (1990). Middle level teachers' perceptions of action research. *Middle School Journal, 22*(1), 30–32.

Brownlie, F. (1990). The door is open. Won't you come in? In M. W. Olson (Ed.), *Opening the door to educational research* (pp. 21–31). Newark, DE: International Reading Association.

Busching, B., & Rowls, M. (1987). Teachers: Professional partners in school reform. *Action in Teacher Education, 9*(3), 13–23.

Cardelle-Elawar, M. (1993). The teacher as researcher in the classroom. *Action in Teacher Education, 15*(1), 49–57.

Carr, W., & Kemmis, S. (1986). *Becoming critical: Education, knowledge, and action research.* London: Falmer.

Carroll, L. (1898). *Alice's adventures in wonderland.* London: Oxford University Press.

Chattin-McNichols, J., & Loeffler, M. H. (1989). Teachers as researchers: The first cycle of the teachers' research network. *Young Children, 44*(5), 20–27.

Chimes, M., & Schmidt, P. (1990). What I read over my summer vacation: Readings on cultural diversity. *The Clearing House, 64*(1), 44–46.

Clark, D. L., & Astuto, T. A. (1994). Redirecting reform: Challenges to popular assumptions about teachers and students. *Educational Leadership, 51*(7), 513–520.

Consortium on Chicago School Research. (1993). Chicago elementary school reform: A mid-term exam. *The Education Digest, 59*(3), 4–8.

Cook, A. (1994). Whose story gets told? Rethinking research on schools. *Education Week, 13*(17), 48.

Copenhaver, R. W., Byrd, D. M., McIntyre, D. J., & Norris, W. R. (1982). Synergistic public school and university research." *Action in Teacher Education, 4*(1), 41–44.

Corey, S. M. (1953). *Action research to improve school practices.* New York: Teachers College Bureau of Publications, Columbia University.

Cuban, L. (1992). Managing dilemmas while building professional communities. *Educational Researcher, 21*(1), 4–11.

Darling-Hammond, L. (1993). Reframing the school reform agenda. *Phi Delta Kappan, 74*(10), 753–761.

Dicker, M. (1990). Using action research to navigate an unfamiliar teaching assignment. *Theory Into Practice, 29*(3), 203–208.

Doyle, W. (1990). Themes in teacher education research. In W. R. Houston (Ed.), *Handbook of research on teacher education* (pp. 3–24). New York: Macmillan.

Egbert, R. L. (1984). The role of research in teacher education. In R. L. Egbert & M. M. Kluender (Eds.), *Using research to improve teacher education.* Lincoln, NE: American Association of Colleges for Teacher Education.

Elam, S. M., Rose, L. C., and Gallup, A. C. (1991). The 23rd Annual Gallup Poll of the public's attitudes toward the public schools. *Phi Delta Kappan, 73*(1), 41–56.

Fischer, R. L. (1988–1989). When schools and colleges work together. *Action in Teacher Education, 10*(4), 63–66.

Fullan, M. G. (1982). *The meaning of educational change.* New York: Teachers College.

Gardner, H., & Boix-Mansilla, V. (1994). Teaching for understanding—within and across disciplines. *Educational Leadership, 51*(5), 14–18.

Gibran, K. (1965). *The prophet.* New York: Alfred A. Knopf.

Good, T. L., & Brophy, J. E. (1987). *Looking in classrooms* (4th ed.). New York: Harper & Row.

Goswami, D., & Stillman, P. (1987). *Reclaiming the classroom: Teacher research as an agency for change.* Portsmouth, NH: Boynton Cook.

Heckman, P. E., Confer, C. B., & Hakim, D. (1994). Planting seeds: Understanding through investigation. *Educational Leadership, 51*(5), 36–39.

Henson, K. T. (1996). Teachers as researchers. In J. Sikula, T. Buttery, & E. Guyton (Eds.), Association of Teacher Educators *Handbook of Research on Teacher Education* (chap. 4) (2nd ed.). New York: Macmillan.

Jenkins, D. M., & Jenkins, K. D. (1991, March). The NMSA Delphi report: Roadmap to the future. *Middle School Journal, 22*(4), 27-36.

Leithwood, K., Menzies, T., & Jantzi, D. (1994). Earning teachers' commitment to curriculum reform. *Peabody Journal of Education, 69*(4), 38-61.

Lowery, C. D. (1908). The relation of superintendents and principals to the training and professional improvement of their teachers. In M. J. Holmes (Ed.), *Seventh yearbook of the National Society for the Scientific Study of Education, Part One.* Chicago: University of Chicago Press.

Marriott, V. (1990). *Transition.* Unpublished paper. Nova Scotia, Canada: Mount Saint Vincent University.

Marshall, C. (1991, March/April). Teachers' learning styles: How they affect student learning. *The Clearing House, 64*(4), 225-227.

McDaniel, E. (1988-1989). Collaboration for what? Sharpening the focus. *Action in Teacher Education, 10*(4), 1-8.

McLaughlin, H. J., Hall, M., Earle, K., Miller, V., & Wheeler, M. (1995). Hearing our students: Team action research in a middle school. *Middle School Journal, 26*(3), 7-12.

Moffett, J. (1994). On to the past: Wrong-headed school reform. *Phi Delta Kappan, 75*(8), 584-590.

National Education Goals Panel. (1991). *Goals report.* Washington, DC: United States Government Printing Office.

Neilsen, L. (1990). Research comes home. *Reading Teacher, 44*(1), 248-250.

Olson, M. W. (1990). The teacher as researcher: A historical perspective. In M. W. Olson (Ed.), *Opening the door to classroom research* (pp. 1-20). Newark, IN: International Reading Association.

Peik, W. E. (1938). A generation of research on the curriculum. In G. M. Whipple (Ed.), *The scientific movement in education. Thirty-seventh yearbook of the National Society for the Study of Education, Part 2* (pp. 53-66). Bloomington, IL: Public School Publishing.

Perkins, D., & Blythe, T. (1994). Putting understanding upfront. *Educational Leadership, 51*(5), 4-7.

Perrin, S. (1994). Education in the arts is an education for life. *Phi Delta Kappan, 75*(6), 452-453.

Reading/Language in Secondary Schools Subcommittee of IRA. (1989). Classroom action research: The teacher as researcher. *Journal of Reading, 33*(3), 216-218.

Santa, C. M. (1990). Teaching as research. In M. W. Olson (Ed.), *Opening the door to classroom research* (pp. 64-76). Newark, DE: International Reading Association.

Santa, C. M., Isaacson, L., & Manning, G. (1987). Changing content instruction through action research. *The Reading Teacher, 40*(4), 434-438.

Shumsky, A. (1958). *The action research way of learning.* New York: Teachers College Press.

Stevens, K. B., Slanton, D. B., & Bunny, S. (1992). A collaborative research effort between public school and university faculty members. *Teacher Education and Special Education, 15*(1), 1-8.

Sucher, F. (1990). Involving school administrators in classroom research. In M. W. Olson (Ed.), *Opening the door to classroom research* (pp. 112-125). Newark, DE: International Reading Association.

Swaim, J. H. (1991, March). Reform of teacher education implications for the middle level. *Middle School Journal, 22*(4), 47-51.

SUGGESTED READINGS

Bellon, C. B., Bellon, J. J., & Blank, M. A. (1986). *What really works: Research based instruction.* Knoxville, TN: Bellon & Associates.

Benton, S. L., & Hoyt, K. B. (1990). Education reform: Implications for educational psychologists. *Educational Psychology Review, 2*(3).

Brown, D. S. (1990, November). Middle level teachers' perceptions of action research. *Middle School Journal,* 30-32.

Brooks, J. G., & Brooks, M. G. (1993). *The case for constructivist classrooms.* Alexandria, VA: Association for Supervision and Curriculum Development.

Guskey, T. R. (1990, February). Integrating Innovations. *Educational Leadership,* 11-15.

Elkind, R. (1991). Success in American education. In R. C. Morris (Ed.), *Youth at risk.* Lancaster, PA: Technomic.

Henson, K. T. (1986, March). Reforming America's public schools. *U.S.A. Today,* pp. 75-77.

Henson, K. T. (1990). Educational reform: Implications for educational psychologists/A comment on Benton and Hoyt's study. *Educational Psychology Review, 2*(3), 271-275.

Hubbuch, S. M. (1989, April/May). The trouble with textbooks. *The High School Journal, 72*(4), 201-209.

Jenkins, D. M., & Jenkins, K. D. (1991, March). The NMSA Delphi report: Roadmap to the future. *Middle School Journal, 22*(4), 27-36.

Powell, R. R., & Garcia, J. (1991, March/April). Classrooms under the influence: Adolescents and alcoholic parents. *The Clearing House,* p. 277.

Stefanich, G. P. (1990, November). Cycles of cognition. *Middle School Journal, 22*(2), 47-52.

Stinnett, T. M., & Henson, K. T. (1982). *America's public schools in transition.* New York: Teachers College Press.

chapter 2

Long-Range Planning

Long-range planning does not deal with future decisions, but with the future of present decisions.

Peter Drucker

OBJECTIVES

List several sources for selecting curriculum content.

Give three reasons teachers should plan their own curricula and explain the student's role in curriculum development.

Describe how the teacher's philosophy affects curriculum planning.

Explain the relationship between curriculum objectives and content and between curriculum content and student activities.

List three unique characteristics of Taba's inverted curriculum model.

Develop a learning-teaching unit for a subject and grade level that you plan to teach.

Suggest some ways that teachers can help students focus on major concepts.

PRETEST

	Agree	Disagree	Uncertain
1. All teachers are responsible for determin-ing their classes' curricula.	_____	_____	_____
2. The textbook is the major source for curricula in secondary school classes.	_____	_____	_____
3. Teachers should not plan more than a few days (or at most a few weeks) in advance.	_____	_____	_____
4. Each state has curriculum guides for teachers to use.	_____	_____	_____
5. Teachers should not use textbooks to select content for courses.	_____	_____	_____
6. Principles and concepts are more important than facts in selecting curriculum content.	_____	_____	_____
7. Students do not have the expertise to become involved in curriculum planning.	_____	_____	_____
8. Because units must be kept very practical, philosophy has limited value in unit planning.	_____	_____	_____
9. Asking another teacher for advice on the curriculum is a professional mistake.	_____	_____	_____
10. Teachers must cover material so that students can progress to the next grade.	_____	_____	_____

Middle-Level Message

Middle-level teachers often have heavier and more diversified teaching assignments than high-school teachers. The increased amount of preparation required, coupled with the diversity of assignments, makes it necessary for middle-level teachers to have expertise in a range of subjects. Sometimes this leaves middle-level teachers feeling frustrated and hopeless.

One way to meet the need for expertise in a number of disciplines is to continue your formal and informal education. A 1986 survey of middle-level teachers showed that they benefit from a variety of educational experiences (Henson, Chissom, & Buttery, 1986). Middle-level teachers reported significant advantages from attending for-credit college courses and not-for-credit workshops. They also reported that they learned much about curriculum development from participating on school committees.

This chapter gives you the opportunity to learn about curriculum development. Relate each principle and each example to the grade levels and subjects you plan to teach. Appendix B will refresh your memory about middle school's nature and goals and middle-level learners' characteristics.

CURRICULUM DETERMINERS

"Could it be that most of our schools are directing their efforts toward objectives that are less relevant than they once were? Are we focusing on the wrong things in thinking about education? Do we need to rethink the whole purpose of education?" These questions, raised by Eric Oddleifson (1994, p. 447), are just a few of many questions that current and future teachers must ask themselves whenever they work on their long-term plans.

Have you ever wondered who decides what each course will cover? What will be the general goals? What experiences will be part of the course? Will there be field trips, guest speakers, or other special events? Who determines if there will be one or two units of composition in an English class? Will the geometry class spend six weeks or six months studying solid geometry or plane geometry? Is the decision based on the number of chapters devoted to each topic in the textbook? If so, who chooses the textbook? Surely not the principal or the superintendent. As you might suspect, the teacher plays a significant role in making all these important decisions. According to Joyce (1979, p. 75), most of the important decisions teachers make are long-term ones. This means that the quality of education each of your future students (and these may number in the thousands) receives will depend on your long-term planning ability.

Some teachers are willing to follow their textbooks, chapter by chapter, and bring little or no supplementary material to class. But allowing textbooks to be the sole determiners of curricula is unwise. The authors know nothing about your particular students' aspirations, strengths, and weaknesses. Furthermore, they do not know your community. Are there facilities for good field trips? Are there community members who can give excellent talks? Is there a good zoo, a museum, a park, an industry that can offer valuable learning experiences? And does the textbook content correspond to your background, so that you can use your own expertise? Or perhaps your own preparation has gaps that will prevent you from teaching textbook content that you do not understand. Teachers often overuse textbooks because they feel safe following them; they believe that as long as they cover the text, they will cover the appropriate course content. But this is a false sense of security. Textbooks do not always cover a discipline's important concepts. Textbooks also fail to cover content in depth because each year new material is added to each textbook to keep it "up to date" but material is seldom deleted. Tyson and Woodward (1989, p. 15) explain the results: "It is not surprising then, that American textbooks have become compendiums of topics, none of which are treated in depth."

Unfortunately, through the years, little attempt has been made to balance the use of textbooks with other resources; the textbook has dominated all other resources almost exclusively. Applebee, Langer, and Mullis (1987) reported that numerous studies show that textbooks structure from 75 to 90 percent of classroom instruction. Hubbuch (1989, p. 204) testifies to the importance of knowing how to use textbook structure: "A reader's assumption that a text has a structure, and his or her ability to recognize and use the cues to this structure, are central to successful reading. This frame is reflected in various units of the text, from chapters and sections to paragraphs and sentences." Yet successful teachers do much more than follow a prescribed textbook. They can be successful, however, only if they articulate a vision of the higher levels of understanding that the course can lead students to reach. Articulating a vision is not easy. Weller, Hartley, and Brown (1994, p. 298) explain the difficulty and the significance of obtaining such a vision: "Developing vision, that seemingly mystical and sometimes elusive concept, is the most important element in making any organization highly effective in promoting quality products."

Teachers, either alone or together, begin long-range planning by translating educational aims and goals into objectives. They then use these objectives to select major concepts and activities students need to attain these objectives. After they have determined the major concepts, teachers must enable students to learn these concepts.

CONCEPT DEVELOPMENT

Sometimes students need help focusing on the major concepts in a lesson. Teachers often fail to identify and understand important concepts. Perkins and Blythe (1994, p. 4) report that "our early research was energized by the fact that most teachers could testify to the importance of teaching for understanding—and to the difficulty of the enterprise. Teachers were all too aware that their students often did not understand important concepts." Before beginning a lesson, teachers should ask questions, present a simple outline, or give students a few key words to help them focus on the major concepts. Such strategies are called *advance organizers*. Snapp and Glover (1990, p. 270) found that middle-school students who read and paraphrased an advance organizer before study correctly answered more lower-order and higher-order study questions than did students not given the organizer.

This study's educational implications are straightforward. If a reasonable academic goal is to improve students' answers to study questions, advance organizers help accomplish that goal.

Harrison (1990) offers teachers the following 10 steps to help students identify and become familiar with each lesson's (or unit's) major concepts:

1. Present a nominal definition of a concept and give examples.
2. Emphasize the common attributes and ask students to name further attributes.
3. Ask students to give examples.
4. Have students give totally opposite examples.
5. Have students name metaphors to compare with and contrast to the original idea.
6. Have students review contexts in which the concept takes place.
7. Describe the concept's overt application.
8. Identify environmental factors that facilitate or hinder concept application.
9. Formulate an operational definition involving the last steps of this process.
10. Discuss consequences in terms of viable solutions to a given problem. (pp. 503–504)

Harrison (1990, p. 203) reminded teachers that to understand concepts is not enough, stating that "instruction must focus on the use of the concepts and the context in which they occur in order to ascertain their practical connotations." Teachers can use the case study method to help students apply concepts (Kowalski, Weaver, & Henson, 1994). This method enables students to separate relevant from irrelevant information. Doing so will enable them to understand concepts.

Some educators are concerned that education reform programs have emphasized pedagogical techniques rather than mastery of content. Regnier (1994, p. 82) refers to such errors as "the illusion of technique" and states that "the denigration of intellectual life has also led to a proliferation of 'interdisciplinary approaches' to instruction that blur important destinations, such as the different criteria of evidence and argument in, say, history and physics." Van Gulick (1990) believes students' performance on standardized tests has declined because of how students store information. To be able to use new information, students must see how it relates to a larger whole. Markle, Johnston, Geer, and Meichtry (1990, p. 53) say that an entire school of learning theorists (called constructivists) subscribe to this belief: "Constructivists describe learning in terms of building connections between prior knowledge and new ideas and claim that effective teaching helps students construct an organized set of concepts that relates new and old ideas."

The implications for teachers are great. "The teachers' role will no longer be to dispense 'truth' but rather to help and guide the student in the conceptual organization of certain areas of expertise" (Von Glaserfeld, 1988). Such guidance is best achieved through group assignments that require students to describe the process they use to explore new material as it relates to existing knowledge (Markle, Johnston, Geer, & Meichtry, 1990, p. 54).

Because of these limitations, most teachers choose to become involved in the long-term planning of each course they teach. Yet most teachers know how important it is to have continuity throughout the year. "More recent research has shown the increased effectiveness in learning when experiences are organized to enable students to progress from unit to unit, in which each subsequent unit builds on the preceding ones" (Tyler, 1984, p. 36). Although most teachers are not free to make all these decisions alone, they have considerable influence. Through experience, teachers can learn how to plan a greater part of their courses.

THE QUESTION OF CONTENT

At the beginning of the year you must decide what content to cover. Teachers often let their own likes and dislikes serve as the sole basis for selecting content. For example, Scheville et al. (1981) report that an elementary-school teacher who enjoyed teaching science taught 28 times more science than one who said she did not enjoy teaching science (Berliner, 1984, p. 53). Like most teachers, you will probably feel obliged to cover material that students will need as background for the next grade. But more important, you must also ensure that students gain the understanding and skills they will need throughout their lives.

How do teachers determine what students should learn in each class? Make a list of 10 ways you can determine what students must learn in a particular class. You might title it "Ways to Identify Content." No two teachers will have identical lists. Any new material chosen should relate to the existing curriculum. The curriculum components (philosophy, content, activities, aims, goals, objectives, and evaluation) should all mesh. This meshing is called *curriculum coherence.*

One logical place to begin selecting content is to check the state curriculum guide's objectives and concepts. Each state produces its own guides. These guides are important because they consider a course's content in relation to the previous year and the following years. In other words, the developers of state curriculum guides consider the total content needed by students throughout the entire K-12 school program. Another important feature of state curriculum guides is their focal points. They begin with broad goals and identify general understandings that students are expected to acquire and develop at each grade level.

A second source of information is the syllabi that local teachers of the next grade up use to teach your subject. By paying special attention to the beginning of each unit of study, you can see what students are expected to know when they leave your class. One popular source of information is textbooks. Do not let a single textbook dictate your total curriculum, but do look at several texts to remind you to incorporate important material from each. Start by examining several current texts at your own grade level and make a content-comparison chart to determine any deficiencies in your own

TABLE 2.1   Content comparison

Chapter Topics	Book A	Book B	Book C	Book D	Book E	Book F	Book G	Book H
Adolescence and learning	X	X	X	X	X			X
Planning	X	X	X	X	X	X	X	X
Classroom management	X	X	X	X	X	X	X	X
Evaluation	X	X	X	X	X	X	X	X
Teaching styles	X	X	X	X	X			X
Motivation	X	X						X
Multicultures or disadvantaged students		X		X	X			X
History and aims		X						X
Audiovisual aids		X		X				X
Teaching special pupils		X	X					X
Communications			X					X

text and to compensate for them. Table 2.1 provides an example of chapter comparison of general secondary methods texts.

Students learn best when they are involved with activities, but sometimes it is difficult to provide hands-on activities. Media offer a viable alternative. Stefanich (1990) explains:

> Teaching must occur in an arena of active manipulation of concrete hands-on experiences. When a concrete experience is impossible, semi-concrete opportunities (i.e., films, simulations, games, illustrations) must be utilized. . . . There has never been an outstanding teacher. Learning requires active participation on the part of the learner; therefore, there have only been outstanding facilitators of learning. (p. 50)

REACHING HIGHER LEVELS OF THINKING

Although making chapter comparisons is a broad and therefore crude assessment of textbook content, it is a step in the right direction. A close examination of the texts in your field can help you identify the major concepts or principles in each content area. For example, a junior-high earth science textbook should cover the following major areas of study: astronomy, geology, meteorology, oceanography, and physical geography. You may be surprised that Figure 2.1, which compares four popular texts, shows that each book contains only a small percentage of pertinent principles. Such poor coverage is not at all uncommon, however. In fact, these texts cover between 8 and 33 percent of pertinent material (Figure 2.2).

Because textbooks fail to cover all important principles and concepts, do not rely on them as your sole source to determine course content. Use them as one of many curriculum determiners. As Stefanich (1990, p. 47) said: "A strong basis of research supports the notion that the thinking of individuals from ages 10 to 14 is distinctly dif-

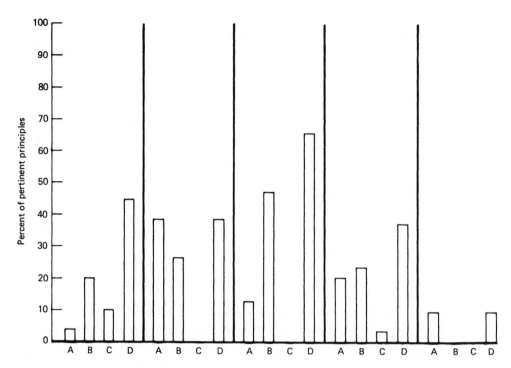

FIGURE 2.1 Variance in representation of principles among four basic science textbooks

ferent from adults, yet schools generally do not respond to these unique elements of thought when planning curriculum or guiding student decisions."

Another common weakness of textbooks is that they are geared to the lowest cognitive level. Studies by Davis and Hunkins showed that more than 85 percent of textbook content is written on the recall level (Orlich, 1980). An analysis of more than 61,000 questions in workbooks, texts, and teachers' manuals accompanying 9 world history textbooks showed that more than 95 percent of those questions were lower order (Trachtenberg, 1974, pp. 55-57).

If your students are to reach higher levels of thinking it will be not be by accident but rather the result of your purposeful planning, not by your demanding it but by your leading your students through carefully designed tasks. Stefanich (1990, p. 49) explains that "higher level thinking cannot be demanded. We must earn it through nurturing a series of successively more advanced learning tasks until the student reaches the desired level of performance." Students themselves must discover and develop some content generalizations. As Doyle (1983) explains, "Students must be given ample opportunities for direct experience with content in order to derive generalizations and invent [learning] algorithms on their own. . . . Gaps are left which students, themselves, must fill." This means that whatever sources you use, do not select material without considering your students and your intended teaching method.

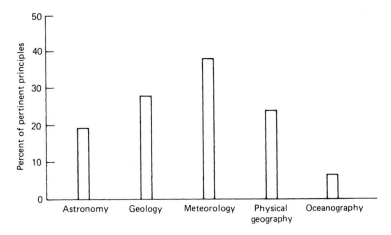

FIGURE 2.2   Mean representation of pertinent principles for each subject

Researchers at Michigan State University found more factors that influence selection of content: the effort teachers perceive as needed to teach a subject, how students perceive a subject, and whether the teacher enjoys teaching a subject (Scheville et al., 1981). Teachers' likes and dislikes often dominate selection of content. This is one reason you should involve all your students in curriculum planning. Taba (1962) developed a way to do this in the 1950s. In contrast to the other curriculum-planning models, which are developed outside the school, Taba's model is developed by teachers and their students. It is different in that it starts at the bottom—in the classroom—and moves upward, and it has come to be known as Taba's inverted model. Taba's model takes into consideration students' desires and abilities, and because you develop it, you are more likely to use it and to use it more effectively than an externally developed unit.

Another unique feature of Taba's model is that it connects curriculum with instruction. Taba achieved this by making the learning unit the center of her model. In other words, you and your students will choose major topics of study, such as astronomy or geology. Then you will develop for each topic a unit lasting from a few days to several weeks. For convenience, most units are designed to be the same length as a grading period. Since most secondary- and middle-school systems report grades every six weeks, most units are six weeks long, but there is nothing wrong with having two three-week units in a grading period.

THE UNIT PLAN

You should have a specific plan for each major objective you hope to accomplish during the year. This is the *unit plan*. For example, a teacher of junior-high earth science would probably want each student to acquire some understanding of astronomy, ecology, geology, meteorology, oceanography, paleontology, mineralogy, and physical geography. For each of these areas, the teacher would plan a unit of study lasting from a few days to a few weeks and containing the topics the teacher wants the students to learn.

Planning

Once you have selected your unit topics, you can plan each unit. Students should help plan each unit, but first you must determine your role and their role in the planning process.

Your extensive study of the subject gives you insight into what students must learn—insights your students do not have. Therefore, you must identify important ideas or concepts to develop in the unit and explain their importance to your students. Students may want to omit certain ideas or sections because they dislike them, but you must include these concepts if you deem them essential.

Give students an opportunity to include material in the unit that they want to study. Even though you may consider certain topics less important than others, remember that when students find a topic interesting it becomes relevant to them. Merely giving students more control of their education is an important, positive step (Des Dixon, 1994). Involving students in planning has another important advantage: It helps avoid the sequential approach that often limits learning. According to Hart (1983, p. 77), "Because the ordinary classroom does not provide this richness in learning and, in most instances, limits what the brain can do, students become addicted or habituated to this limited, sequential approach." Involving students can make them more interested in a subject, which enhances their ability to learn that material. According to Levy (1983), "If students are engaged [in learning activities, as opposed to remaining passive], both sides of the brain will participate in the educational process regardless of subject matter." Students learn more when they participate in lessons (Finn, 1993).

You must also help the class select activities they need to understand a unit. Activities are the vehicles through which students learn content. Doyle (1979) expressed the importance of activities when he said, "The immediate test of teaching in classrooms is that of gaining and maintaining the cooperation of students in activities that fill the available time." This does not mean that the teacher selects some of the activities and the students independently select others. When you broach the topic of selecting class activities, have a list of activities from which the class can choose. If the students want to add other feasible activities, let them. Ask yourself about each proposed activity: Is it contrary to school policy? Is it dangerous or harmful to me, to the students, or to others? Is it something I should first check with the principal? Is it worthwhile? And finally: Is it something we could try? If so, it may prove worthwhile because the students are interested in that particular activity. The significance of involving students in planning is stated well by Doll (1978, p. 393): "Despite the imperfections and general functioning one can find in instances of teacher-pupil planning, the dividends that such cooperative planning pays in pupil interest and achievement have resulted in its acceptance as a valid instructional process."

Another group you must not ignore when planning your curriculum is parents.

Students need parental encouragement.

Because of their vested interest in the schools and because they can influence students positively, effective curriculum planning includes parents. The recent popularity of school-based decision making has intensified the need to include parents in all parts of schools, especially academics. O'Neal, Earley, and Snider (1991, p. 123) stress this need: "Research has constantly indicated that parent and family involvement is critical to the academic success of many children."

Components

The learning unit (or unit plan) outlines subject material on a given topic, but it also does more. Although they vary, most unit plans contain the following parts: (1) a title; (2) a statement of philosophy, goals, objectives, and content to be covered; (3) teacher and student activities to attain the objectives; and (4) a method to evaluate students.' degree of understanding of the unit. The unit plan may also include a list of resource people (consultants) and resource materials (bibliography). Figure 2.3 illustrates a learning unit.

The statement of philosophy contains the teacher's beliefs about the school's purposes, the nature of adolescence, how adolescents learn, and the purpose of life in general. Because teachers do not reflect enough on their beliefs about these all-important issues, the statement of philosophy is the most neglected part of learning units. Yet the first question teachers often hear when beginning a new unit is "Why do we have to study this stuff?" Only by thinking through these broad issues can you answer this question intelligently.

The statement of purposes is a list of general expectations that you want the unit to achieve. For example, a tenth-grade unit in government may expect students to un-

FIGURE 2.3 Anatomy of a learning unit

Philosophy → Purposes → Content → Activities → Evaluation

derstand how a bill is introduced, to become more tolerant of others' opinions, and to appreciate democracy as a type of government. Unlike the performance objectives teachers use in daily planning, which are stated in specific, observable, and measurable terms, a unit's statement of purposes should be much more general.

Base your selection of content for any unit on three broad considerations:

1. Must students master this content to reach the general objectives?
2. Is this content important?
3. What are your students' needs and interests?

Choose activities on the same basis: select experiences that will enable students to learn content. Do not feel obligated to select one activity for each objective; some of the best activities serve multiple purposes and allow students to attain several objectives. For example, one activity for a senior English class might be to write a composition contrasting Shelley's and Lord Byron's poetry. This activity would allow students to gain writing skills and sharpen their concept of writing style. Some teachers do not believe their classes have time to achieve multiple objectives, but several objectives can be met simultaneously. Activities with multiple objectives are not necessarily inefficient. Each learning unit should contain two types of student performance and include different types of measurement, such as written tests, oral tests, debates, term projects, homework assignments, classwork, and perhaps performance in class or group discussions. This type of evaluation, which examines the quality of a product, is called *product evaluation.*

Another type of evaluation you should apply to each learning unit is called *process evaluation.* This merely describes the effectiveness of the teaching of the unit. Process evaluation analyzes various unit parts singly to determine whether the entire unit needs improvement. It also involves examining the unit as a whole to see how its parts relate. Ask yourself, Is my philosophy sound? Does it convince students that the unit is important? Are the purposes important? Is it realistic to expect these students to achieve them in the allotted time? Is the unit's content correct for the stated purposes? Will these activities help attain these objectives? Is the evaluation fair to everyone? Does it discriminate between those who have met the objectives and those who have not?

Learning units should also include certain practical information. In addition to title, subject, and grade level, they should contain a list of resources—consultants, equipment, facilities, supplies, and especially audiovisual aids—needed to teach the unit. They should also include references that students can use to pursue the topic further. Finally each unit should contain performance objectives that (1) are stated in terms of student behavior, (2) describe the conditions, and (3) specify the minimum acceptable level of performance.

Sample Unit Plans

Examine the following unit plans. Notice that the title describes the unit; the statement of purpose or objectives describes what students should accomplish; and the evaluation is stated in terms of the objectives.

Reflection

Read the following statements and respond to the questions below.

Don't Fix It If It Ain't Broke

Teacher A

Too much attention is given to instructional planning, evaluating lessons, and replanning. Some of the most effective lessons occur as spur-of-the-moment insights that teachers have on the way to class. But this can occur only when teachers are mentally free from overly structured lesson plans. In fact, the cookbook approach to teaching often results in boring the students. Anyway, aren't lessons supposed to serve the students' needs rather than the teacher's needs?

Teacher B

Don't listen to that gibberish. Those words probably come from a teacher who is too lazy to plan lessons adequately. Granted, spur-of-the-moment insights may occur, but how often does that really happen? No sensible teacher will sit around and wait for an inspiration. It's far better to overplan than underplan—if indeed one can overplan at all.

1. List some benefits of instructional planning.
2. Think about a former teacher who did little or no planning. Was this teacher able to relate to students better? Describe the amount of learning that occurred in this teacher's class.
3. Can instructional planning serve students' needs? How?
4. In Chapter 3 we will see that effective teachers can be flexible and yet return to the lesson's focus. How does planning affect teacher flexibility?

Meteorology Unit Plan: What Meteorology Means to You

I. Purpose
  A. Knowledge: To understand—
    1. The different types of weather
    2. The principles of weather formation
    3. The role of the weatherperson
    4. The names and principles of commonly used weather instruments
    5. Weather vocabulary
  B. Attitudes: To appreciate—
    1. The damage weather can do
    2. The advantage of good weather
    3. How weather affects our daily behavior

        4. The rate of accuracy of weather predictions
        5. The precision use of weather instruments
        6. The fallacies of superstitions about the weather
    C. Skills: To develop the ability to—
        1. Read and interpret weather instruments
        2. Read and interpret weather maps
        3. Predict future weather
  II. Daily Lessons
    A. Definition of weather
    B. Precipitation
        1. Different types of precipitation
        2. How each type of precipitation is formed
    C. Reading the weather map
    D. Reading weather instruments
    E. Predicting weather
    F. Effects of geographic location on weather
    G. Effects of the earth's rotation on weather
    H. Effects of the earth's tilting on weather
    I. How to change weather that can hurt you
  III. Materials
    A. Weather reports from newspapers
    B. Weather maps
    C. Equipment for making fog: air pump, water, jar
    D. Barometer, thermometer, anemometer, wind vane
    E. Graph paper for each student
  IV. Evaluation
  Tests for each section of the unit: approximately one test per week's study
  of the topic.

The above unit plan was chosen for its brevity and simplicity. This does not make it a superior plan, but such brief units are often used. Do you think the unit is too skimpy? What do you think about this format? Is the outline adequate? Figure 2.4 shows the parts commonly found in a unit. Which of the parts in Figure 2.4 are missing from the sample unit above?

Did you notice that the meteorology unit has neither a statement of philosophy nor a statement of rationale to show the unit's significance? Many educators feel that a statement of philosophy helps you clarify your own beliefs about life, school, and adolescents and how they learn. Goals and objectives should coincide and should reflect your basic beliefs. Other educators prefer to have a statement of rationale instead of a statement of philosophy. When you write a statement of rationale, you justify the unit to yourself; then you can use the rationale to convince students that the unit is worth their time and energy.

The meteorology unit has no sections titled "Teacher Activities" or "Student Activities." This is unfortunate, because at this time the teacher should be thinking about taking the class to a weather station or showing a film on meteorology. The weather

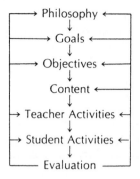

FIGURE 2.4   Diagram of a learning-teaching unit

station may need advance notice, and for field trips students must identify in advance what information they will gain from the trip. Films must be scheduled and ordered in advance, and you will need time to preview them. You can probably identify other weaknesses in this unit plan.

Below is a sample chemistry unit designed for use in an eleventh-grade class. This more comprehensive plan has fewer weaknesses (but you be the judge of that). It has most of the parts that educators consider essential to any unit, but as you study it, note both its strengths and weaknesses. Pay particular attention to the unit's overall structure and organization. Can you improve it?

Chemistry Unit Plan: The Organization of Chemistry

I. Statement of Purpose. The chapters covered in this unit are designed to introduce the beginning chemistry student to the basic background and structural knowledge needed for further studies in chemistry. Topics include atomic structure and the periodic table.

Reflection

A statement of general purpose, aims, goals, or rationale is helpful for orienting the teacher to the unit and can be used to introduce the unit to the students. The overall purpose can also include general changes in student behavior. But because the reason for teaching is to change students' behavior, a much more specific list of performance objectives is used to explain precisely what the teacher expects students to be able to do after completing the unit. Because this particular unit is built around two chapters, the following list of objectives refers to both chapters.

1. What is the statement of conditions in Objective 4, Lesson 1?
2. Which objective in Lesson 1 has the clearest statement of behavior?

II. Performance Objectives

    A. Chapter I: Atomic Theory. The eleventh-grade general chemistry student will be able to—

Lesson 1

    1. Define an atom correctly in a closed-book test.

    2. Give the size of an atom in the unit posttest.

    3. Identify the parts of an atom by name and describe them when given an unlabeled diagram of the atom. Four of five parts must be correctly labeled and described.

    4. Match the mass of the parts of the atom to the correct path when given a list of masses.

Lesson 2

    1. Define the atomic number of an atom.

    2. Define the mass number of an atom in a closed-book test.

    3. Use the concept of isotopes by correctly grouping given atoms into isotopic groups.

    4. Apply the concept of energy level shells by designating the number of electrons in each shell when given an atomic number.

Lesson 3

    1. Correctly define atomic mass in a closed-book test.

    2. Define Avogadro's number in a closed-book test.

    3. Apply the concept of a mole by the amount of a substance in a mole of a given substance.

    4. Define the atomic weight of an atom in a closed-book test.

    5. Apply the concept of atomic number, Avogadro's number, mole, and gram atomic weight in solving simple stoichiometric problems. Given the problem and required information, the student must solve for the asked-for information, correctly answering 80 percent of the problems to receive credit. (Partial credit will be given for correct setups.)

    B. Chapter 2: Periodic Table. The eleventh-grade general chemistry student will be able to—

Lesson 1

    1. List at least three of the four basic elements.

    2. Identify the common elements by symbol. This will be shown by correctly giving the elements or symbol asked for in 15 of 18 questions in two in-class quizzes.

Lesson 2

    1. Obtain atomic numbers of elements from the periodic table with an accuracy level of 80 percent.

    2. Obtain the mass number of elements from the periodic table with an accuracy level of 80 percent.

Reflection

Each performance objective should contain four parts. Check the above objectives against these criteria. It is as simple as A, B, C, D.

Audience: The student should be the subject of each objective.
Behavior: The student's behavior should be the verb of each objective.
Conditions: The objective should describe the conditions under which the student is expected to perform.
Degree: The degree or level of performance required of the students should be specified.

1. Why is it necessary to focus each objective on student behavior?
2. What assumption can be made if an objective has no statement of required level of performance?

---

   3. Obtain a given element's electron configuration from the periodic table.

Lesson 3
   1. Define periodic law.
   2. Define "group of elements."
   3. Define "period of elements."
   4. Distinguish the characteristics of families of elements by matching the correct family with the given characteristic with a minimum accuracy level of 80 percent.
   5. With 80 percent or above accuracy, match the correct family with the given element.
III. Attitudinal Objective. The eleventh-grade general chemistry student will be able to participate in class discussions. This objective will be met when 80 percent of the class answers general questions, directed to the class as a whole, during the course of the discussion.
IV. Concepts and Generalizations
   A. Topic 1: Atomic Structure

Concepts	*Generalizations*
Atomic theory	Atomic theory has been developed to support proton observations.
Atom*	
Proton*	Each subparticle composing the atom (electron, neutron, proton) has certain characteristics and is unique in energy levels or shells. Each atom has its own electrons.
Neutron*	
Electron*	

---

* Students should already be familiar with these concepts

Nucleus*
Elements
Mole
Avogadro's number arranged
Angstrom, A

B. Topic 2: Arrangement of Electrons in Atoms

Concepts	*Generalizations*
Orbitals	Quantum numbers describe the orienta-
Orbital notation	tion of an electron in an atom in terms of
Electron configuration notation	(1) distance from the nucleus, (2) shapes,
Electron dot notation	(3) position in space with respect to the
	three axes (x,y,z), and (4) direction of spin.

C. Topic 3: Periodic Table

Concepts	*Generalizations*
Periodic table	The periodic table organizes the ele-
Series (period)	ments; properties can be predicted from
Group (family)	the elements' positions.
Noble gas family	Elements with similar arrangements of
Sodium family	outer shell electrons have similar proper-
Calcium family	ties.
Nitrogen family	
Oxygen family	

Let's Talk

Now that we have identified a purpose for the unit, set down the objectives for the lesson, and selected the major concepts and content generalizations needed to achieve those objectives, it is time to plan the daily activities. These should include the teacher's activities and the activities in which the students will be involved. Chapter 3, on planning daily lessons, will cover how to involve students in meaningful ways.

RECAP OF MAJOR IDEAS

1. In selecting content, seek out generalizations that students need to understand the subject.
2. Use your own expertise but also involve students in selecting content and activities.
3. Hilda Taba's inverted curriculum model is considered superior because teachers construct it in the classroom around teaching units.

4. Learning activities are the vehicle through which students develop the generalizations they need to understand a subject.
5. Add consistency to your lesson planning by beginning each unit with a written statement of your philosophy about life, school, and learning.
6. Each part of a learning unit should relate to the other parts. This is called *coherence.*
7. When beginning a unit, consider consulting teachers at the next grade level, textbooks, curriculum guides, and students.
8. Textbooks alone are an inadequate source of information for curriculum planning.
9. Long-term planning is essential for maximum learning opportunities.
10. Maximum learning requires students to relate new concepts to existing knowledge.

INTRODUCTION TO CASES

Each of the remaining chapters in this book contains one or more case studies. These cases, which are based on actual experiences, enable the reader to see how the major principles and concepts presented in each chapter work in an actual situation. Each case also contains some superfluous information. As in real life, you must sift through this information, separate the pertinent information from the irrelevant information, and make a decision.

In most cases you will discover that the information is incomplete. You could make a better, more confident decision with more information. Although you may find this condition frustrating, it realistically reflects teachers' dilemmas; teachers rarely have all the information they need, yet they must make decisions nonetheless. This is your task with each of these cases. The intended result is to improve your decision-making skills.

The cases in each chapter are followed by questions. For about half the cases in each chapter, my responses follow the questions. My responses are not "correct" answers but are my attempts to help you tie the questions to issues in the case. I hope this practice will cause you to reflect on your own future teaching behavior.

The remaining cases in each chapter have questions without my responses. This allows different audiences to use the cases. For example, in real teaching situations, teachers must identify important issues. I hope you will have opportunities to talk with your classmates as you wrestle with identifying the issues.

CASES

This chapter focuses on the teacher's role in long-term planning. The chapter offers guidelines and suggestions for planning learning units for periods that may range from a few days to a few weeks. There are no blanket statements that dictate step-by-step planning. These guidelines and your own experience will enable you to develop a system with which you are comfortable that will allow you to teach effectively.

You will have problems and struggles, however. The following cases are examples of the dilemmas teachers can encounter as they plan teaching units.

CASE 1: SHOULD LESSON PLANNING BE SEQUENTIAL?

Bongo Nagatah was realizing his dream of attending an American university where he could learn to become a master teacher and return to his native land for a lifetime of service. Bongo applied himself totally. He had indeed mastered his chosen teaching field, mathematics, which he enjoyed for its preciseness and structure, and he had done equally well in his professional education courses. Despite all this, however, he ran into problems. Ironically, much of his frustration resulted from his love of structure.

When his methods course began developing learning units, Bongo looked for guidelines or rules that would help him develop a learning unit. First, he wrote a brief statement of philosophy for the unit but was not sure about the next step. The professor had instructed the class to follow the statement with a list of general goals for the unit, but Bongo felt that he was leaving out some important content and that perhaps he should make a content outline before identifying the goals. Later, when he began identifying content and activities, the same dilemma emerged: If he selected the activities first, how could he be sure that content was being adequately covered, but if he selected the content first, how could he take advantage of opportunities that he wanted to offer his students—field trips, speakers, and civic activities? He especially wanted to encourage his students to enter projects in the regional science and mathematics fair.

Discussion

1. Is there a definite sequence for developing a unit?

In a general sense there is. Write your statement of philosophy first. The goals should precede the behavioral objectives, and the objectives should precede the selection of content and activities. Most teachers find this sequence helpful, but many believe that following it in all situations is restrictive and could even damage their units.

2. How can you ensure complete content coverage and also take advantage of opportunities to involve students in valuable learning experiences?

Because a general sequence of design can be helpful, you may prefer to follow the accepted sequence until you have a specific reason for changing it. Many teachers find that skipping a step and going back to it later can be useful in some situations.

CASE 2: A PRINCIPAL REQUIRES SIX MONTHS' ADVANCE PLANNING

When I moved from teaching in a rural school to my first urban school, I learned the true meaning of planning. In the smaller, rural school lesson planning had never been mentioned, but during my first faculty meeting at the urban school the principal handed each teacher a 300-page spiral book for entering lesson plans for the following six months. Because I had never planned for more than a week or two in advance, I was overwhelmed, but my fellow faculty members accepted the principal's request without question.

After the meeting, I asked whether the principal ever actually checked the plans to see if they were completed so far in advance and was told that there would probably be a surprise check once or twice a year. In addition, my lesson plan book would have to be left in the office in case I were absent, so a substitute teacher could use it.

The other teachers assured me that there was no required length for each lesson and suggested that I list only the name or title of each lesson without attempting to describe it. Because even this would consume several hours and appeared to be a waste of time, I decided to take a chance and enter only two weeks of plans in advance. I followed this procedure throughout the year. My hunch was correct. The lesson plan book was never checked, and fortunately I was not absent. The following year no mention was made of the six-month policy.

Discussion Questions
1. How far in advance should teachers plan?
2. What are some reasons teachers should not be required to plan months in advance?
3. Why did my principal "misuse" lesson plans?
4. Was my decision to disregard the rules justified?

ACTIVITIES

The objectives at the beginning of this chapter promised that you would learn how to develop a complete learning unit. If you are ready for this challenge, select a topic in one of your teaching fields and apply your skills as follows:

1. Write a brief statement of your philosophy of education. Include your beliefs about the general purpose of secondary schools, the nature of adolescence, and the nature of learning.
2. Write at least three broad goals for a unit of three to six weeks.
3. For each goal, write a few behavioral objectives.
4. Outline the major content generalizations for the unit.
5. Select some teacher activities and student activities to facilitate attainment of these objectives.
6. Design a grading system and a system for evaluating unit effectiveness. Consider whether it has all the essential parts; also check the sequence of these parts.

REFERENCES

Applebee, A. N., Langer, J. A., & Mullis, I. V. S. (1987). *The nation's report card: Literature and U.S. history.* Princeton, NJ: Educational Testing Service.
Berliner, D. C. (1984). The half-full glass: A review of research on teaching. In P. A. Hosford (Ed.),

Using what we know about teaching. Alexandria, VA: Association for Supervision and Curriculum Development.

Des Dixon, R. G. (1994). Future schools and how to get there from here. *Phi Delta Kappan, 75*(5), 360-365.

Doll, R. C. (1978). *Curriculum improvement: Decision making and process* (4th ed.). Boston: Allyn & Bacon.

Doyle, W. (1979). Making managerial decisions in classrooms. In D. L. Duke (Ed.), *Classroom management, 78th Yearbook of the National Association for the Study of Education, part II.* Chicago: University of Chicago Press.

Doyle, W. (1983). Academic work. Review of Educational Research. Washington, DC: *American Educational Research Association, 53*(2), 176-177.

Finn, J. D. (1993). *School engagement and students at risk.* Washington, DC: National Center for Education Statistics, U.S. Department of Education.

Harrison, C. J. (1990). Concepts, operational definitions, and case studies in instruction. *Education, 110*(4), 502-505.

Hart, L. A. (1983). *How the brain works.* New York: Basic Books.

Henson, K. T., Chissom, B., and Buttery, T. J. (1986). Improving instruction in middle schools by attending to teachers' needs. *American Middle School Education, 2,* 2-7.

Hubbuch, S. M. (1989, April-May). The trouble with textbooks. *The High School Journal, 72*(4), 203-209.

Joyce, B. (1979). Toward a theory of information processing in teaching. *Educational Research Quarterly, 3,* 66-77.

Kowalski, T. J., Weaver, R. A., & Henson, K. T. (1994). *Case studies on beginning teachers.* White Plains, NY: Longman.

Levy, J. (1983). Research synthesis on right and left hemispheres: We think with both sides of the brain. *Educational Leadership, 40,* 66-71.

Markle, G., Johnston, J. H., Geer, C., & Meichtry, Y. (1990, November). Teaching for understanding. *Middle School Journal, 22*(2), 53-57.

Oddleifson, E. (1994). What do we want our schools to do? *Phi Delta Kappan, 75*(6), 446-453.

O'Neal, M., Earley, B., & Snider, M. (1991). Addressing the needs of at-risk students: A local school program that works. In R. C. Morris (Ed.), *Youth at risk* (pp. 122-125). Lancaster, PA: Tecnomic Publishing Co.

Orlich, D. C. (1980). *Teaching strategies: A guide to better instruction.* Lexington, MA: D. C. Heath.

Perkins, D., & Blythe, T. (1994). Putting understanding up front. *Educational Leadership, 51*(5), 4-7.

Regnier, P. (1994). The illusion of technique and the intellectual life of schools. *Phi Delta Kappan, 76*(1), 82-83.

Scheville, J., Porter, A., Billi, G., Flooden, R., Freeman, D., Knappan, L., Kuhs, F., & Schmidt, W. (1981). Teachers as policy brokers in the content of elementary school mathematics. National Institute of Education Contract No. P-80-0127. East Lansing: Institute for Research on Teaching, Michigan State University.

Snapp, J. C., & Glover, J. A. (1990). Advance organizers and study questions. *The Journal of Educational Research, 83*(5), 266-271.

Stefanich, G. P. (1990, November). Cycles of cognition. *Middle School Journal, 22*(2), 47-52.

Taba, H. (1962). *Curriculum development: Theory and practice.* Orlando, FL: Harcourt Brace Jovanovich.

Trachtenberg, D. (1974). Student tasks in text material: What cognitive skills do they tap? *Peabody Journal of Education, 52,* 54-57.

Tyler, R. W. (1984). Curriculum development and research. In P. A. Hosford (Ed.), *Using what we know about teaching.* Alexandria, VA: Association for Supervision and Curriculum Development.

Tyson, H., & Woodward, A. (1989, November). Why students aren't learning very much from textbooks. *Educational Leadership,* 14–17.

Van Gulick, R. (1990). Functionalism, information, and content. In W. G. Lylcan (Ed.), *Mind and cognition.* Cambridge, MA: Basil Blackwell.

Von Glaserfeld, E. (1988). *Environment and communication.* Paper presented at Sixth International Congress on Mathematics Education, Budapest.

Weller, L. D., Jr., Hartley, S. H., & Brown, C. L. (1994). Principles and TMQ: Developing vision. *The Clearing House, 67*(5), 298–301.

SUGGESTED READINGS

Bugler, K., & Fraser, B. (1990). *Windows into science classrooms: Problems with higher level cognitive learning.* New York: Falmer Press.

Ciscell, R. E. (1990). A matter of minutes: Making better use of teacher time. *The Clearing House, 63*(5), 217–218.

Drucker, P. F. (1954). *The Practice of Management.* New York: Harper & Bros.

Henson, K. T. (1995). *Curriculum development for education reform.* New York: Harper-Collins.

Oliva, P. F. (1992). *Developing the curriculum* (2nd ed). New York: HarperCollins.

Trump, J. L., & Miller. D. F. (1979). *Secondary school curriculum improvement: Meeting challenges of the times* (3rd ed.). Boston: Allyn & Bacon.

Van Horn, R. (1994). Power tools: Building high-teach schools. *Phi Delta Kappan, 76*(1), 90–91.

chapter **3**

Using Performance Objectives

The more we proceed by plan the more effectively we may hit by accident.
Fredrich Durrenmatt

OBJECTIVES

Explain three advantages of using objectives in daily planning.

Differentiate educational aims, goals, and objectives.

Discuss the three domains of educational objectives.

Write an objective for each level of each domain.

List three criteria essential to all performance objectives.

Explain how performance objectives and daily lessons fit into the total curriculum.

Give an example of a well-known educational aim, and explain why aims are needed.

Write one goal appropriate for the subject and grade level you plan to teach.

List three ways to involve students in curriculum planning.

PRETEST

	Agree	Disagree	Uncertain
1. Generally, teachers have both the freedom and the responsibility to plan their own lessons.	_____	_____	_____
2. The terms *aims, goals,* and *objectives* mean the same thing when used in education as they do elsewhere.	_____	_____	_____
3. The more concise and precise an objective, the better it will be.	_____	_____	_____
4. Every lesson should include some written objectives that involve students' attitudes.	_____	_____	_____
5. Every lesson should contain objectives written at all levels of the taxonomy.	_____	_____	_____
6. An objective should help you communicate to students exactly what you expect of them.	_____	_____	_____
7. At the end of any lesson, students should be able to do some things they could not do at the beginning of the period.	_____	_____	_____
8. Objectives can be used to raise the level of thinking in a classroom.	_____	_____	_____
9. Classroom discussions usually remain at the lowest level of thinking.	_____	_____	_____

10. Every lesson plan should include some questions from all three educational domains.

     _____   _____   _____

Middle-Level Message

Middle-level students enjoy discussion because discussion allows them to be active; these students need opportunities to work off their energy. But there is another reason middle-level students like discussion: Discussion gives them room to express their opinions. However, middle-level students should use discussion to absorb more information, not merely to express their opinions. When conducting middle-level discussions, press students to give examples to support what they say. Because some middle-level students tend to dominate a discussion and others remain passive, try to involve every student in the discussion.

One of your first decisions as a classroom teacher involves deciding what content to cover in each class. Some school systems regulate content so closely that they virtually dictate what each teacher will teach. By providing externally designed curriculum plans, guides, and syllabi, they may even specify what material teachers must cover each day. Curriculum directors, supervisors, assistant superintendents, and assistant principals in charge of curricula may periodically visit classes to make sure that each class is studying the prescribed lessons. Even within such dictatorial systems, however, you have flexibility in how you teach the lessons.

At the opposite extreme are the many school systems that do no more than provide general guidelines. In fact, some teachers are not given anything more than a textbook from which to design their curricula. Fortunately, most school systems operate somewhere between these two extremes. They realize that teachers need suggestions and guidelines, but they also realize that teachers must be free to select content and plan their curricula according to their students' needs and interests and the community's desires and resources.

The question "How do teachers plan?" is quite different from the question "How should teachers plan?" Most education programs and professional literature advise teachers to use the curriculum planning model introduced by Ralph Tyler (1949). Tyler's model is often called the *ends-means model* because it encourages teachers to identify desired learning outcomes (objectives) before selecting instructional methods or activities.

Unfortunately, "most teachers [ignore this model and] begin the planning process by determining the content to be covered and then design or select learning activities for students" (Walter, 1984, p. 55). Walter adds, "Once teachers begin lessons for groups of students, they are very reluctant to change those lessons, even when things are going poorly" (p. 60). Beginning teachers should be assisted in developing high-quality tasks for their initial lessons. According to Walter, teachers need help to develop a repertoire of learning activities so that if one technique is ineffective in a particular class, teachers have other options (Walter, 1984).

OUTCOME-BASED EDUCATION

This chapter is about objectives. A popular term today is *outcome-based education* (OBE). Buschee and Baron (1994, p. 193) say that "outcome-based education is a student-centered, results-oriented design based on the belief that all individuals can learn." Objectives can give students direction and add meaning to education. Clarifying expected outcomes for students also allows students to be more involved with their assignments (Unger, 1994). If teachers choose the activities wisely, students' involvement can give them a better understanding of their own reasoning. Woods (1994, p. 35) explains that "helping [students] understand the basis of their own reasoning and test it against the real world has become for me a fundamental curriculum practice."

As with most practices, OBE has not been universally accepted. Not all educators agree with stating anticipated outcomes. Some believe that setting outcomes may not help all students and may even hinder some. For example, Towers (1994, p. 627) says that "to a degree OBE may be allowing our best and brightest future teachers to go unchallenged, drifting aimlessly from one undemanding task to the next. In short, minimum competency levels are stressed—not maximum learning expectations."

Connecticut, the first state to adopt state-wide goals, has had an increase in graduate rate, percentage of students going to college, and average reading and math scores. But even Connecticut has been criticized for using OBE. Zlatos (1994, p. 28) summarized the effects of OBE in Connecticut: "Up until now, the consensus is that opponents have been winning the skirmish on OBE."

EDUCATIONAL EXPECTATIONS: AIMS, GOALS, OBJECTIVES

To some degree you will be responsible for developing the curriculum. Because the curriculum should address what the school, the community, and you the teacher want to achieve, you should examine these expectations at various levels. Educational expectations—aims, goals, and objectives—have different degrees of immediacy and specificity. The following discussion begins with aims, the broadest and most general expectations, and progress toward objectives, the most immediate and specific expectations.

Aims

Educational aims are the most general expectations of all. In fact, they are so distant and so general that they can never be fully achieved. A good example of educational aims is the list of the "Seven Cardinal Principles of Secondary Education":

1. Health
2. Development of moral character
3. Worthy home membership
4. Citizenship
5. Worthy use of leisure time
6. Vocational efficiency
7. Development of the fundamental processes

Each of these expectations can never be completely fulfilled or attained (e.g., people must work all their lives to preserve their health, develop their morality, and be good citizens), and the same is true of all educational aims. They provide long-term direction, but no one can attain them completely.

Goals

Educational goals are expectations that take weeks, months, or even years to attain. A particular high school may have as one of its goals that all students will be literate by the time they graduate. Every student may not attain this goal, but probably most will achieve it. Goals can spark a class's interest. Unger (1994, p. 9), reporting on a class that had been introduced to a unit's goals, said: "Because they know the goals, Kendall's students became more involved in their projects and felt more at ease in exploring and assessing their achievement of the goals."

But a goal need not take 6 or 12 years to reach. For example, a biology teacher may set a goal that all students will appreciate all forms of life by the end of the school year (a year-long goal). Or the teacher whose students spend six weeks studying endocrines may set the following goal: Students will understand reproduction, transportation, and respiration. Students thus can attain an educational goal, although some may not. The goal can require several days to several years to attain. Students usually have a set time to reach a goal, such as a semester or a six-week grading period.

Several factors facilitate goal attainment. Students are more likely to attain clearly stated, challenging yet attainable, and meaningful goals (Leithwood, Menzies, & Jantzi, 1994, pp. 43–44).

Objectives

This book uses the term *objectives* to refer precisely to what is expected of students daily. We might think of these as performance objectives, because each refers to students' ability to perform selected tasks in one or more specific ways. As Wulf and Schane (1994, p. 117) have said, when objectives are used "there are no unexpected or surprise results, since both parties have agreed upon the end product." Because performance objectives are the most specific of all educational expectations, they must be written in great detail. The following sections explain how to write performance objectives.

CRITERIA FOR WRITING PERFORMANCE OBJECTIVES

Each professor of education has a particular way of teaching students to write objectives. Most authorities agree, however, that all statements of performance objectives must meet at least three criteria:

1. Objectives must be stated in terms of expected student (not teacher) behavior.
2. Objectives must specify the conditions under which students are expected to perform.
3. Objectives must specify the minimum acceptable level of performance.

Look again at the first of three criteria for writing objectives. Stating objectives in terms of expected student behavior is important because all teaching is directed toward students. The lesson's success is defined by the students' response. To be more precise, school exists to improve students' mental, physical, social, emotional, and moral behavior. When you state objectives in terms of desired student performance and use observable and measurable specifics, you and your students will better understand what you expect of them and if they are meeting these expectations. Figure 3.1 (p. 52) shows verbs that describe specific, observable, and measurable actions (see the Yes column) and verbs that are too vague to be accurately observed and measured (see the No column).

Because students can grasp only a limited number of major ideas in a class period of 45 or 50 minutes, the daily lesson plan should contain only four or five major ideas. Suppose you are an English teacher who wants to teach composition writing. You could select four or five of the most important ideas about capturing and holding readers' attention. These will become the content for the first day's lesson in a unit titled "Composition Writing." You may determine that five ideas are essential to capturing the readers' attention and that four ideas are essential to holding it, once captured. If so, you could plan one lesson on how to capture the reader's attention and a subsequent lesson on how to hold the reader's attention.

Write your objectives in terms of desired student behavior. Emphasize not "Today I'll teach" but "As a result of the lesson, each student will be able to. . . ." Second, state the conditions under which students are expected to perform ("When given a list containing vertebrates and invertebrates. . . ."). Third, state the expected level of performance ("with 80 percent accuracy" or "without error"). Finally, avoid using verbs that cannot be observed or measured, such as learn, know, and understand. Instead, use specific, action-oriented verbs such as identify, list, explain, name, describe, and compare.

PERFORMANCE OBJECTIVES IN THE THREE DOMAINS

Some of education's aims and goals deal with thinking (e.g., command of fundamental processes), others involve attitude (e.g., development of moral character), and still others focus on physical skills (e.g., physical education). You should establish perfor-

Yes	No
Build	Appreciate
Classify	Consider
Contrast	Desire
Demonstrate	Feel
Distinguish	Find interesting
Evaluate	Have insight into
Identify	Know
Interpret	Learn
Label	Like to
List	Love to
Match	Really like to
Measure	Recognize
Name	Remember
Remove	See that
Select	Think
State	Understand
Write	Want to

FIGURE 3.1   Performance terms: Specific and measurable (yes); vague, not measurable (no)

mance objectives in each of these domains (cognitive, affective, and psychomotor) for each class.

Writing Objectives in the Cognitive Domain

The first real systematic approach to helping teachers write objectives at specified levels came in 1956 when Benjamin S. Bloom and a group of students at the University of Chicago developed a taxonomy of educational objectives in the cognitive domain that include six levels (Bloom, 1956):

Level 1: Knowledge

Level 2: Comprehension

Level 3: Application

Level 4: Analysis

Level 5: Synthesis

Level 6: Evaluation

To involve students in tasks that require them to function at these six levels, you must be able to write objectives for each level.

Level 1: Knowledge.   The simplest and least demanding objectives are those that merely require students to memorize facts. Before students can move on to more advanced tasks, they must first know basic facts. For example, many secondary mathematics problems require students to multiply. The multiplication tables are probably best learned by memorization. Unfortunately, many secondary classes fail to go beyond this most elementary level. There is nothing dishonorable about introducing assignments or tasks at the knowledge level, as long as such assignments have a purpose and do not dominate the curriculum.

An example of an objective written at the knowledge level would be: "When given a list of 10 elements and a list of atomic weights, the student will be able to correctly match 8 of the 10 elements with their correct atomic weights." Another example is: "When given a list containing 10 vertebrates and 10 invertebrates, the student will correctly identify 8 of the 10 invertebrates."

Notice that both objectives begin with a statement of the conditions under which students should perform the task ("When given. . . .") and define the desired student performance ("the student will. . . ."). In addition, both objectives contain measurable, action-oriented verbs ("match," "identify") and state the minimum acceptable level of performance ("8 of the 10").

Level 2: Comprehension.   Objectives at the comprehension level require students to do more than memorize. Students must translate, interpret, or predict a continuation of trends (Bloom, 1956). For example, an English teacher who wants students to learn the difference between phrases and clauses may set the following objective: "When given a paragraph containing two clauses and three phrases, the student will correctly underscore the phrases using a single line and underscore the clauses using double lines." What is the minimum acceptable level of performance for this objective? Because no acceptable level is stated, assume that students are expected to perform with 100 percent accuracy.

See if you can write one objective in your teaching field at the comprehension level that requires the students to translate, one objective that requires them to interpret, and one that requires them to predict. (Hint: You may want to use charts, maps, graphs, or tables.)

Level 3: Application.   Objectives written at the application level require students to use principles or generalizations to solve a concrete problem. For example, a mathematics teacher might write the following objective for geometry students: "Given the lengths of both legs of a right triangle, the student will use the Pythagorean theorem to solve the length of the hypotenuse." Or an English teacher might write the following objective: "Given the beats and measures in iambic pentameter, the student will write a five-verse poem in iambic pentameter without missing more than one beat per verse."

The advantage of writing objectives at this level is that once students learn to apply a principle to one situation, they can apply it to multiple situations to solve many other problems.

Level 4: Analysis.   Like the application level objectives, analysis level objectives require students to work with principles, concepts, and broad generalizations—but students must do this themselves. Students are required to break down the concepts and principles to understand them better, and to do this they must understand not only the content but also its structural form.

For example, a government teacher might write the following objective for a class studying how a bill becomes a law: "Given a particular law, students will trace its development from its introduction as a bill, listing every major step without missing any."

A teacher of auto mechanics might write the following objective for a group of students studying the automotive electrical system: "Starting with the positive battery terminal, the student will trace the current throughout the automobile until it returns to the negative battery terminal, stating what happens in the coil, alternator, distributor, and condenser without getting more than one of these steps out of sequence." A biology teacher might ask students to trace the circulatory system.

Suppose you are teaching the circulatory system to a biology class. See if you can write an objective that will enable students to understand the sequence in which the blood travels throughout the body. (Hint: You may want to designate one of the heart's chambers as a beginning point.)

Check your objective to see whether it includes the three designated criteria: Is it written in terms of expected student performance? If so, underline the part of the objective that identifies both the performer and the performance. Does the verb you used express action? Can it be observed or measured? Is your statement of conditions clear? Circle it. Does it accurately describe the conditions under which you expect students to perform? Did you begin the objective with a statement such as "Given. . . ." or "When given. . . ." (This is an easy way to be sure you have included a statement of conditions in each objective.) Is your statement very general, such as "When given a test" or "following a lesson"? Can you make it more specific? Can you think of a way to alter the task, making it easier to perform, simply by changing the conditons?

Finally, examine your objective to see whether it states a minimum acceptable level of performance. Draw a box around this statement. Does it tell the student exactly how accurately to perform the task for it to be acceptable? Does it contain a percentage or fraction, such as "with 80 percent accuracy" or "four out of five times"? Can you express your concept of minimum acceptable level of performance without using percentages or fractions?

By now you probably would like to start over and rewrite your original objective, improving each part.

Level 5: Synthesis.   In a way, the synthesis level objective is the opposite of the analysis level objective because it requires the student to take several parts and put them together. The synthesis level objective is more demanding, however, because it requires students to form a new whole. Unlike analysis level objectives, synthesis level objectives require students to use divergent thinking and creativity.

The student's attitude is especially important at the synthesis level. Synthesis requires experimentation—investigating the new. Furthermore, students must understand that there is not a definite solution or preconceived notion to reach.

For example, a history teacher who wants students to understand problems the early settlers experienced might preface the unit with the following objective: "Suppose you are on a team of explorers that is going to another inhabited planet to start a new colony. List at least 10 rules you would propose to guide the new nationals, making sure that at least five of the rules would serve to protect the interests of all the native inhabitants."

Because they require creative thinking, synthesis level questions are difficult to write. You may need practice before you feel comfortable writing objectives at this level.

Suppose you are an art teacher. In your class, you have studied such concepts as cubism (using cubes to form objects) and pointillism (using points to form shapes). Can you write an objective at the synthesis level? (Hint: Begin by identifying a particular effect you want your students to achieve using cubism and pointillism; this might be a specific feeling or mood.)

One example of such an objective is as follows: "While looking at cubism in Picasso's paintings and at pointillism in Seraut's paintings, the student will combine these two techniques and a new technique to create at least three of the following feelings: happiness, surprise, sadness, anger, love." At the synthesis level, be sure to provide enough structure to make the assignment meaningful and yet allow students enough freedom to put themselves into the work.

Level 6: Evaluation.   The highest level in Bloom's cognitive domain is the evaluation level. Here the student is required to make judgments based on definite criteria, not just on opinions. Evaluation level objectives contain various combinations of elements in the first five levels.

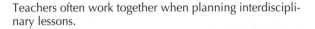

Teachers often work together when planning interdisciplinary lessons.

A speech teacher might use the following objective with students who are studying diplomatic and persuasive techniqies: "While viewing a video recording of a president's two most recent public addresses, each student will rate the speeches in terms of tact and persuasion, pinpointing in each address at least three areas of strength and three areas of weakness."

A physical education instructor who is teaching bowling may want to write an objective that involves the starting position, delivery, and follow-through. Can you help this teacher by writing an objective at the evaluation level? If you do not bowl, you may substitute another activity that involves the same three steps, such as golf or diving.

Now examine your evaluation level objective. Must judgment be based on supportive data or on internal or external standards?

The ability to write objectives at each cognitive level is crucial, since this is the only way to ensure that your students will learn to develop intellectual skills at each level. Because teaching students to make judgments is vital, you must be able to state objectives clearly. You may want a classmate to critique a few of your objectives for clarity.

Not all educators agree that such distinct steps represent students' actual development, however. One skeptic is Donald Orlich (1991), who says:

> For over a quarter of a century, I have assumed and taught my students that the four upper levels of the taxonomy had to be taught in a sequence. But the more that I observed young students in hands-on classes . . . the less support I found for the linear assumption. . . . I can no longer assume a linear connection to the four upper levels of the cognitive taxonomy. Nor can I support the idea of hierarchical arrangement of the entire model! (p. 160)

Orlich uses the following quote from John Goodlad's 1984 book, *A Place Called School,* to alert readers that other educators also have concerns over the levels of objectives represented in high-school curricula:

> Only rarely did we find evidence to suggest instruction (in reading and math) likely to go much beyond merely possession of information to a level of understanding its implications and either applying it or exploring its possible applications. Nor did we see activities likely to arouse students' curiosity or to involve them in seeking a solution to some problem not already laid bare by teachers or textbook. . . . And it appears that this preoccupation with the lower intellectual processes pervades social studies and science as well. An analysis of topics studied and materials used gives not an impression of students studying human adaptations and exploration, but of facts to be learned. (p. 236)

When you accept your first teaching position, one of the first challenges you will face is to raise the thinking levels of your students. Good planning on your part will enable students to reach higher levels of the taxonomy, since students cannot function beyond their level of development.

Writing Objectives in the Affective Domain

Educators have recently become more concerned with the effect of schooling on the attitudes of students. This concern has been stimulated in part by the students' own acknowledgment of the difference between their attitudes and values and those of "the system." Such differences began to show up in the 1950s with the beatniks, who were rebelling against the material wealth syndrome that was sweeping the nation. Everyone seemed determined to get ahead of the Joneses by building a larger house and owning a larger car or boat. The youth of the 1960s expressed their dissatisfaction about U.S. involvement in Vietnam by burning draft cards and holding moratoriums and demonstrations. Further dissent was expressed in civil rights marches.

Status.   In recent years the community at large has begun to blame schools for everything from pollution to destruction of natural resources to economic recession. The greatest accusation currently aimed at schools is that they are failing to teach students basic skills (cognitive domain) as well as failing to discipline students (affective domain).

Society's interest in having schools address the affective domain is shown by the 1994 Gallup Poll (Elam, Rose, & Gallup, 1994, p. 50), which found that over 90 percent of Americans favor teaching respect for others, hard work, fairness, compassion, and politeness. Furthermore, two thirds of Americans favor nondevotional instruction about various world religions in their local public schools. Although schools will never rid society of all ills, they must play a major role in shaping students' views on such important issues as equality, world peace, honesty, integrity, and the value of life itself.

But what exactly *is* the school's role in shaping students' values? Does a teacher have the right to influence students' values? First, you cannot avoid influencing your students' values. Second, all teachers should stress such values as honesty, fairness, and good citizenship. On the other hand, do not try to persuade students to accept your religious, political, and cultural beliefs.

Schools should help students become aware of their own values, question these values, and discover whether their values are factual and logical or prejudiced and illogical.

David R. Krathwohl helped develop a system to categorize values. The outcome was a hierarchy of objectives in the affective domain (Krathwohl, Bloom, & Masia, 1964):

Level 1: Receiving
Level 2: Responding
Level 3: Valuing
Level 4: Organization
Level 5: Characterization

Level 1: Receiving.   Receiving refers to students' being aware or alert to new information or experiences. Students receive information in varying degrees. In a single class, some may not receive the information at all, while others attend or receive at a low level of awareness. Still others may be very selective, attending only to what they find meaningful. Of course, teachers can help students develop attention skills.

All teachers want their students to listen carefully to their lessons and to be aware of their peers' feelings. Can you write an objective that enables you to measure how well students pay attention to a lesson? Now examine your objective. Does it include a statement of the conditions under which you want the students to perform? Does it specify a minimum acceptable level of performance? Is it observable and measurable? An example might be: "When participating in a group discussion, the student will ask every other student at least one question."

Can you write an objective at the receiving level for a ninth-grade art class taking a field trip to a local art museum?

Level 2: Responding.   At the responding level, students react to whatever has attracted their attention. This requires physical behavior. Responses may be overt or purposeful or simple and automatic. A student who becomes involved at the responding level might, at the teacher's request or even voluntarily, go to the library and research an issue further. Or the student may obey the rules set forth in the class. Can you write an objective at the responding level? Try a responding objective for a homework assignment. You choose the subject and grade level.

Examine your objective to determine whether it involves active student participation. Does it reflect the student's attitude(s)? It should. Specifically, a student who performs this objective shows a commitment to the homework assignment that a student who does not complete the objective might not have.

Level 3: Valuing.   A value is demonstrated when someone prizes a behavior enough to perform it even in the face of alternatives. (A person who reacts without having had time to think does not necessarily demonstrate a value.) If people really value a behavior, they are likely to perform it even though they know the results it may bring, and they will do so repeatedly (Simon, Howe, & Kirschenbaum, 1972).

For example, a mathematics teacher whose students are learning to use simulation games might write the following valuing objective: "When given free time next week at the end of each period to read, play simulation games, talk to friends, or sleep, each student will choose to play simulation games at least two out of the five days." Note that the objective asks students to choose individually of their own free will and to repeat that choice. Also note that students can choose alternatives.

One of the most valued qualities of American life is our freedom to be unique, and a basic strength of America results from its tradition of welcoming peoples of all cultures. Ironically, this orientation toward embracing all people makes the teacher's role in working with values, morals, and religions challenging. Teachers must make a special effort in multicultural classrooms to ensure that all students and the teacher understand values and morals that differ from their own. Unfortunately, there is no one way to do this. In fact, no one process ensures any success at all. Perhaps the best approach any teacher can take is a heart-centered one that begins by establishing and maintaining a classroom climate of mutual respect by all and for all class members and the teacher.

Teachers of multicultural classes should learn more about their students' cultures and encourage all students to do likewise. Including affective objectives in each lesson is a good start toward achieving this goal.

Level 4: Organization.   The organization level of behavior requires individuals to join different values to build a value system. Whenever two or more of their values conflict, they must resolve the conflict. For example, secondary and middle-school students constantly encounter friends' and parents' conflicting expectations. As students mature, it is hoped that they will not always react to peer pressure but will learn to listen to their own beliefs and values. At this level students may change their behavior or defend it.

For example, a teacher might assign students to defend opposing positions on a controversial issue. By defending both sides, each student will compare the two points of view and may even learn to compromise between the two extremes.

A teacher of a class in U.S. government might introduce a hypothetical bill and have students form two teams, one composed of those who favor the bill and one of those who oppose it. The objective might read: "After having had the opportunity to support the bill, and the opportunity to try to defeat it, students will combine all the information and write a statement that expresses their feelings for and against the bill. Given the opportunity, the students will choose to modify the bill to make it fit better with their own value systems."

Level 5: Characterization by a Value or a Value Complex.   At the characterization level, students have already developed their own value systems. They are so consistent in the way they behave that they are predictable. At this level, students also demonstrate a degree of individuality and self-reliance.

An example of an objective written at the characterization level is: "Each student will bring one newspaper article or news report to class and explain at least two ways in which the article caused the student to change his or her mind from a previously held position on a controversial issue." Does this objective prove that the student really has changed values? What if the student just says so? Right now the student may believe this, but what about a week from now or a year from now? Can you rewrite this objective to remove or reduce this doubt?

Writing Objectives in the Psychomotor Domain

The psychomotor domain involves developing physical skills that require coordination of mind and body. It is especially relevant to physical education, art, drama, music, and vocational courses, but all subjects provide many opportunities to develop psychomotor skills.

Although this domain was the last to have a taxonomy developed for it, at least two scales have now been developed. The following taxonomy is based on a scale developed by E. J. Simpson (1972):

Level 1: Perception

Level 2: Set

Level 3: Guided response

Level 4: Mechanism

Level 5: Complex overt response

Level 6: Adaptation

Level 7: Origination

Level 1: Perception.   Purposeful motor activity begins in the brain, where phenomena received act as guides to motor activity. The performer must first become aware of a stimulus, pick up on cues for action, and then act on these cues. For example, a writer discovers that she is separating her subjects and verbs, thus diluting the impact of her themes. A baseball batter notices himself flinching and taking short steps away from the plate when striking, causing him to miss the ball. A piano student becomes aware of failing to reduce the interval between double notes.

A sample objective at the perception level would be: "Following a demonstration, a geometry student who has been confusing x and y axes in plotting graphs will notice that the x axis always runs horizontally and the y axis always runs vertically."

Level 2: Set.   In the psychomotor domain, set refers to an individual's readiness to act. It includes both mental readiness and physical and emotional readiness. For example, a diver always pauses before a dive to get a psychological, emotional, and physical set. Emotionally she must feel confident about her ability to make a safe and accurate dive. Psychologically, although she may have performed the same dive hundreds of times, she still takes the time to think through the sequence of steps before each dive. Physically, she must ready her muscles to respond quickly and accurately. On a less dramatic scale, students preparing to take notes or do a writing assignment may be seen flexing their fingers or rubbing their eyes—in short, getting set to perform at their best.

An example of a psychomotor objective at this level for piano students is: "At the signal 'ready,' each student will assume proper posture and place all fingers in correct keyboard position." Is there a minimum level of performance specified in this objective? Can you rewrite this objective to assign a more meaningful type of behavior? Take a minute to think about this objective. List two ways you can establish minimum levels of performance.

Does either of your objectives explain what is meant by "correct posture" or "correct keyboard position"? Do both of your suggested changes help make the act measurable?

Level 3: Guided Response.   Once students see the need to act and ready themselves to act, they may find that they need guidance for acts involving complex skills. For example, students in the photography club may need verbal guidance as they process their first negatives. An example of an objective to enhance the development of these skills would be: "When given step-by-step directions in the darkroom, each student will open the film cylinder, remove the film, and, without touching the surface of the film, wind it on a spool so that the surface of each round does not touch previous rounds."

Level 4: Mechanism. This level involves performing an act somewhat automatically without having to pause to think through each separate step. For example, the photography teacher might want students to be able to perform the entire sequence of development operations while simultaneously counting the number of seconds required to wait between each step. A chemistry teacher might write the following objective at the mechanism level: "Given a series of compounds to analyze, the student will operate the electron microscope without having to pause even once to think about the sequence involved in mounting the slide, focusing the projector, and changing the lens size."

Level 5: Complex Overt Response. The level of complex overt response is an extension of the previous level, but it involves more complicated tasks. For example, a driver education teacher may write an objective at this level such as: "When given an unexpected and abrupt command to stop, the student will immediately respond by applying the correct amount of pressure to the brakes, giving the correct signal, and gradually pulling off the road."

Level 6: Adaptation. At the adaptation level the student is required to adjust performance as different situations dictate. For example, to allow for an icy surface the driver would adjust brake pressure and swerve. The cook would adjust the timing when going from an electric stove to a gas stove. A boxer would alter his style to adjust for a left-handed opponent. An example of a psychomotor objective at the adaptation level is: "When planning a budget vacation, the student (without being reminded of the gas shortage and cost increase) will eliminate unnecessary automobile travel and substitute gas-saving strategies."

Level 7: Origination. At the origination level, the highest level of the psychomotor domain, the student creates new movement patterns to fit the particular situation. For example, chefs add their own touch of genius, and the pianists alter their style or the music itself. An art teacher might write the following objective: "Given a mixture of powders and compounds of varying textures, the student will use these to accentuate the feeling being communicated in an oil painting."

RECAP OF MAJOR IDEAS

1. Well-written objectives will help clarify the teacher's expectations.
2. Objectives should be precise and concise.
3. Verbs used in objectives should express action that can be observed and measured.
4. Objectives can be used to raise the level of thinking in the classroom.
5. Use textbooks as one of several sources of information.
6. In planning, first determine the desired ends (aims, goals, and objectives) and then choose the means (content and activities) accordingly.
7. Each objective should be stated in terms of student (not teacher) behavior,

describe the conditions under which students are expected to perform, and specify the minimum acceptable level of performance.

8. For each lesson plan, identify objectives at varying levels of all three domains. However, a lesson probably will not have objectives at all levels of all domains.

9. Use a multitude of planning strategies in lessons, including discussion, field trips, oral reports, projects, and homework assignments.

CASES

This chapter covers techniques for writing behavioral objectives. As you read the following cases, consider how often you will use objectives in your future lesson planning.

CASE 1: A PRINCIPAL MISUSES OBJECTIVES

Lincoln High School had the reputation of being one of the most innovative, experimental, and advanced schools in the district. The large number of oil wells in the area made financing one of the least of the principal's worries. When Sondra Bell became principal last year, she promised the board that, with their support, she would lead the school to even greater heights.

As the principal planned her annual report, she realized that the board had delivered their part of the bargain, but she wondered whether they felt as positive about her. The report contained two parts, "In Retrospect" and "In Prospect." Because she thought that the first part looked a little weak, Sondra decided to compensate by planning an impressive "In Prospect" section.

She began spelling out her objectives for the coming year. Could she impress the board by planning everything for the coming year around those performance objectives that she would set for the students? It seemed logical, so she pulled out a taxonomy of educational objectives from the notes in her methods course. For each daily lesson, she wrote an objective at each level of the cognitive domain. But when she began writing objectives for all levels of the affective domain, her task became more difficult. Although she had initially planned to write objectives that represented all levels of all three domains, Sondra gave up in despair long before the task was completed.

Rather than admit failure, Sondra appointed a committee consisting of the department heads and one or two members of each department. She assigned them exactly the same task—to write sample objectives at all levels in all domains for each subject in the entire school curriculum. The faculty was not at all happy with this request. Most teachers were already using objectives in planning their lessons, but they thought this was going too far.

Discussion

1. Was this principal wrong to require her faculty to use objectives in their planning?

The mistake she made was more in the degree of the requirement than in the decision to require the use of objectives. Certainly all teachers should use objectives to help clarify their expectations of students and to organize their lessons better, but taken to this extreme the objectives could become a nightmare for teachers and for students.

2. Why did Sondra have trouble writing objectives at all levels in all domains?

It is almost impossible to write so many objectives in all levels for all subjects. The goal itself is admirable, because sample objectives can be very helpful to teachers who do not have extensive experience writing objectives.

3. If you were a teacher at Lincoln High, how would you respond to this requirement?

CASE 2: MARSHALL MIDDLE SCHOOL FACES GOALS 2000

Marshall Middle School has earned a reputation as a school for the children of yuppies. Located in an upper-class suburban district of a major city, this school has received support that is unequaled in many districts. At a time when other schools are working to devise ways to increase attendance to benefit from the additional revenue, this fortunate school's principal Ms. Ann Grimes convinced the parent-teacher association leaders to support the hiring of a assistant principal for instruction. Soon afterward, Mr. James Upchurch, a Phi Beta Phi graduate from one of the nation's most prestigious universities, was hired to help. Marshall retained its position as one of the nation's most innovative and academic elite schools.

During his interview, Mr. Upchurch was given a clear charge. Told that the mission of Marshall was to remain the state's premier middle-level academic institution, he was further notified that he was to make Marshall the state's leader in education reform. This was no minor task because this state led the nation in education reform.

Mr. Upchurch knew that the demands were great and that to succeed he must arrive at his new position with a plan in hand. After giving this task his total attention during the two months between his interview and his first day on the job, Mr. Upchurch arrived with his plan complete. He wasted no time introducing his new strategy. At the first chairs' meeting, he revealed the following plan. Marshall's curriculum included grades 6 through 8. Each grade had a designated department chair. Mr. Upchurch explained the following assignment to the three department chairs:

> I am pleased and honored to receive this academic post at such a distinguished institution as Marshall Middle School, and I accept the responsibility for keeping this school's reputation. I'm sure that all of you know that the nation is headed toward a national curriculum. It has already begun with the Goals 2000. Here is a list of these six goals for your review. Each department has been designated two of these goals. It will be your responsibility to see that the entire school reaches your two designated goals. Grade six will take goals 1 and 2; grade seven, goals 3 and 4; and grade eight, goals 5 and 6. Your first assignment is to use the two days of designated inservice planning to lead your faculty as they break your two goals down into performance objectives. You are responsible

for ensuring that these objectives are clear to all and that adhering to them will mean success on your two Goals 2000.

At the beginning of the first designated in-service planning day, each department chair recounted the instructions given at the chair's meeting. Like all faculties, the Marshall Middle School faculty had some natural leaders who were eager to take charge of the job at hand. But as they read their goals, they began to realize that these were no ordinary goals.

Discussion Questions

1. Which of the six goals would be the easiest to translate into performance objectives? Why?
2. In which domain of the educational taxonomies would most of these performance objectives be written?
3. What is one affective objective that could be written for one of these goals?

ACTIVITIES

Most teachers today recognize that carefully written, specific behavioral objectives will help them reach their broader goals.

1. Each teacher has different aspirations for students. Consider your subject and write one broad goal that you believe is essential for students to understand. Write several specific behavioral objectives to help your students reach this goal.
2. Think about the problems that characterize modern society. Write a general attitudinal goal to eliminate or minimize one of these problems. Now write a few specific behavioral objectives to help students attain this goal.
3. Have you any opinion(s) about the use of objectives that you are willing to share with your classmates? If so, write these down and get another student to listen to your opinion(s). Of course, do the same for your partner.
4. Choose a topic for class discussion. Write five objectives for the discussion and select a reading for all members. Now identify at least one or two related sources that give information not contained in the student assignment.
5. Plan a field trip for a learning unit in your major field. Start by listing five objectives. Now construct a short questionnaire to evaluate the trip's degree of success.

REFERENCES

Bloom, B. S. (1956). *Taxonomy of educational objectives: The classification of educational goals, Handbook I: Cognitive domain.* New York: McKay.

Buschee, F., & Baron, M. A. (1994). OBE: Some answers for the uninitiated. *The Clearing House,* *67*(4), 193–196.

Elam, S. M., Rose, L. C., & Gallup, A. M. (1994). The 26th Annual Phi Delta Kappan/Gallup Poll of the Public's Attitudes Toward the Public School. *Phi Delta Kappan, 76*(1), 41-56.

Goodlad, J. J. (1984). *A place called school.* New York: McGraw-Hill.

Krathwohl, D. R., Bloom, B. S., & Masia, B. B. (1964). *Taxonomy of educational objectives: The classification of educational goals, Handbook II: Affective domain.* New York: McKay.

Leithwood, K., Menzies, T., & Jantzi, D. (1994). Earning teachers' commitment to curriculum reform. *Peabody Journal of Education, 69*(4), 38-61.

Orlich, D. C. (1991, January/February). A new analogue for the cognitive taxonomy. *The Clearing House, 64*(3), 159-161.

Simon, S. B., Howe, L. W., & Kirschenbaum, H. (1972). *Values clarification.* New York: Hart.

Simpson, E. J. (1972). *The classification of educational objectives in the psychomotor domain. The psychomotor domain (Vol. 3).* Washington, DC: Gryphon House.

Towers, J. M. (1994). The perils of outcome-based teacher education. *Phi Delta Kappan, 75*(8), 624-627.

Tyler, R. W. (1949). *Basic principles of curriculum and instruction.* Chicago: Chicago University Press.

Unger, C. (1994). What teaching for understanding looks like. *Educational Leadership, 51*(5), 8-10.

Walter, L. J. (1984, March). A synthesis of research findings on teacher planning and decision making. In R. L. Egbert & M. M. Kluender (Eds.), *Using research to improve teacher education.* Lincoln, NE: Clearinghouse on Teacher Education.

Woods, R. K. (1994). A close-up look at how children learn science. *Educational Leadership, 51*(5), 33-35.

Wulf, K. M., & Schane, B. (1984). *Curriculum design.* Glenview, IL: Scott, Foresman.

Zlatos, B. (1994). Outcomes-based outrage runs both ways. *Education Digest, 59*(5), 26-29.

SUGGESTED READINGS

Burns, D. E. (1990). The effects of group training activities on students' initiation of creative investigations. *Gifted Child Quarterly, 34*(1), 31-36.

Cooper, H. (1990). Synthesis of research on homework. *Educational Leadership, 47*(3), 85-91.

Phelps, P. H. (1991, March-April). Helping teachers excel as classroom managers. *The Clearing House, 64*(3), 241-242.

Solomon, S. (1989). Homework: The great reinforcer. *The Clearing House, 63*(2), 63.

Towers, J. M. (1994). The perils of outcome-based teacher education. *Phi Delta Kappan, 75*(8), 624-627.

chapter 4

Planning Daily Lessons

A journey of a thousand miles must begin with a single step.
Lao Tzu

OBJECTIVES

Define and differentiate between a daily lesson plan and a unit plan.

Describe four major steps in developing a unit plan.

Write a unit plan in your area of specialty.

List four essential qualities of a behavioral objective and write five behavioral objectives.

List in order six pertinent parts of a daily lesson plan.

Write a plan for each of two daily lessons.

Develop a strategy for more efficient use of classroom time.

Explain how teachers can help students connect new information with existing knowledge.

PRETEST

	Agree	Disagree	Uncertain
1. All lesson plans should begin with a list of the subject content to be learned.	——	——	——
2. A lesson plan that works well with one group may not work well with another group.	——	——	——
3. The best lesson plans are those drawn up by outside experts (as opposed to teacher-made plans).	——	——	——
4. To be effective, a lesson must cause students to change their behavior.	——	——	——
5. A lesson is a failure unless it gives students new skills.	——	——	——
6. Student activities are essential to all lesson plans.	——	——	——
7. Most teachers begin planning by identifying goals and objectives.	——	——	——
8. Most changes in teaching-student interaction are based on lesson objectives.	——	——	——

Chapter 2 discussed how important planning is to teaching. You learned to begin each year by identifying the goals you hope to achieve and to select content accordingly. You also learned how to design learning units through which your students and you could achieve these goals. As essential as they are, however, goals alone remain no more than elusive generalities. To enable students to attain them, you must design daily lesson plans that include goals but can also be translated into more specific terms. Each daily lesson plan should cover a particular part of the unit; in fact, most units contain a series of daily lesson plans.

Middle-Level Message

This chapter shows that the amount of time teachers allocate to a subject does not mean students will learn it; however, the amount of time students are engaged with a subject does. This can hinder middle-level classes because their energy level is so high that keeping them on task is difficult. You must use their high energy level as a positive learning force, since the time they spend developing concepts (instead of just studying concepts) correlates positively with their achievement.

Remember, do *not* try to suppress these students' high activity level; rather, channel their energy toward developing the concepts that comprise their chosen disciplines.

THE DAILY LESSON PLAN

Strategies

Because the teaching unit is usually content oriented, you must develop daily strategies to help students move nearer to the unit goals. For most teachers, this is the daily lesson plan. A teacher who attempts to teach without a lesson plan is like a pilot taking off for an unknown destination without a map. Like a map, a lesson plan provides direction toward the lesson objectives. If the lesson begins to stray, the lesson plan brings it back on course. Teaching can be difficult without a lesson plan. According to Walter (1984), however, despite the emphasis teacher education places on the "ends-means" approach, data now show that experienced teachers do not begin the planning process by determining objectives. They begin by determining what content to cover and then design or select learning activities for students (Zahorik, 1975; Walter, 1979; Shavelson & Stern, 1981). One study, which examined planning in middle-level laboratories, found that teachers spend most of their planning time with content, a moderate amount of time selecting strategies, and the smallest amount of time on objectives (Peterson, Marx, & Clark, 1978). Furthermore, even when teachers modify their teaching approach, they seldom consider the lesson objectives (Clark & Peterson, 1986). You should choose strategies that work with the content (Acheson & Gall, 1992) and feel right for you (Walker & Chance, 1994–1995).

Factors Affecting Achievement

Other recent data provide a framework for developing daily lesson plans. Romberg and Carpenter (1986) reviewed studies of mathematics classes and discovered three significant variables associated with student achievement. First, instead of teaching the concepts students need to understand a subject, teachers of the same subject and grade level may cover very different materials. This unfortunately reduces the time students spend studying important concepts, and "classes in which less time is allocated to mathematics instruction (or instruction in any subject) are likely to have relatively poorer achievement in the subject" (Romberg, 1983, p. 60). Yet as we saw in Chapter 2, the most frequent determiner of content—the textbook—usually does a poor job covering concepts that students need to understand a discipline. In a similar study of content coverage by textbooks, Schville et al. (1983) examined the three most commonly used fifth-grade math textbooks and learned that there was very little content that all the authors considered significant; more than half the 290 topics common to one or more books were unique to a single book.

A second factor in daily lesson planning is the amount of engaged time teachers spend on a topic or concept compared with the time allocated for the subject. For example, during a 50-minute period, one class may spend 20 minutes on the day's lesson (engaged time), while another class may spend 40 minutes on the lesson and is likely to achieve more. Plan each lesson so that it engages students with that subject's important concepts and skills.

A third factor that affects achievement is the time students spend developing particular concepts, as opposed to the time they spend just studying the concepts. In the developmental portion of a lesson, students spend time discussing such issues as why the concept is true, how skills or concepts are interrelated, and how to use these broader relationships to estimate answers to problems. In other words, developmental time puts the important concepts and skills in a broader context to help students understand those ideas.

Class size has been studied for more than 50 years to determine its effect on student achievement. Carson and Badarack (1989, p. 9) reported that "studies of the achievement effects of substantial reductions in class size indicate that smaller classes do have more positive effects than large ones, but the effects are small to moderate." Although data show smaller classes' positive effects to be minimal, Carson and Badarack (1989) argue that over time the cumulative effect may be significant. Johnston (1990) reported that one advantage of smaller classes is improved teacher morale. Nye, Achilles, Boyd-Zaharias, Fulton, and Wallenhorst (1994, p. 9), who have been conducting research on class size for several years at the Tennessee Center for Excellence: Basic Skills, reported that "small is far better."

APPLYING CONSTRUCTIVISM TO DAILY PLANNING

A continuing decline in student performance on the Scholastic Aptitude Test (SAT) is evidence that U.S. students are not learning how information fits together. Van Gulick (1990) believes that the lower scores on the SATs result from how students store information. To be able to use new information, students must see how it relates to a larger whole as they learn it. Markle, Johnston, Geer, and Meichtry (1990, p. 53) say that an entire school of learning theory (called constructivism) subscribes to this belief: "Constructivists describe learning in terms of building connections between prior knowledge and new ideas and claim that effective teaching helps students construct an organized set of concepts that relates new and old ideas." The implications for teachers are great. Markle, Johnston, Geer, and Meichtry quote von Glaserfeld (1988, p. 53) as saying: "The teachers' role will no longer be to dispense 'truth' but rather to help and guide the student in the conceptual organization of certain areas of expertise."

Such guidance is best achieved through group assignments that require students to describe the process they use to connect new information to existing knowledge (Markle, Johnston, Geer, & Meichtry, 1990).

Traditionally, teachers have not based their planning on factors affecting student achievement (Carnahan, 1980). Furthermore, clear concepts in each discipline, and effective models and strategies for teaching them, have not been available because they were not identified. As Armento (1986, pp. 948–949) stated, "Methodological advances have outpaced conceptual advances in the last 10 years." Although Armento was referring to the field of social studies, the same is true of all disciplines. But more studies are identifying important concepts, and metacognitive studies have increased, which will help determine more effective ways to teach students to analyze how they process new information. For now, you should seek out the concepts and skills your students need to achieve each lesson's objectives and plan to use them as focal points for studying. Make these concepts and principles the content portion of each lesson plan. There are two ways to learn concepts: by observation or by definition (Slavin, 1994).

Planning Lessons for Multicultural Classes

Teachers with multicultural students and teachers in inner-city schools often plan fewer concepts into each lesson, providing more engaged time and more opportunities (activities) for students to be involved with these concepts. Constructivist teachers support the use of fewer concepts because they perceive it as a trade-off; covering fewer concepts allows students to understand these concepts more deeply. In other words, they believe that students should learn a few concepts in depth rather than have a shallow understanding of many concepts.

What Makes a Lesson Plan Good?

Lesson plans come in many sizes and varieties. Length or style does not make one plan better than another. A good lesson plan can be a formally worded comprehensive outline, neatly typed on bond paper, and enclosed in a plastic binder, or it can be a brief outline written in pencil on three-by-five-inch cards. The styles of good lesson plans vary as much as their length. A good lesson plan contains material that will challenge students throughout the class period and activities that involve every student. The format should be easy to follow with only a glance, and you should not have to stop the lesson to read the lesson plan.

Arguing about types of lesson plans is a waste of time. Think of the lesson as a tool; like any tool, it is only as effective as the person using it. However, a worker who has good machinery has an advantage over a worker who has faulty equipment. You must develop and correctly use a lesson plan that works for you.

Setting Objectives

Research on schools in which achievement is high has shown that when the teacher sets clear expectations for the class, students achieve more (Walker & Chance, 1994–1995). Begin planning a daily lesson by thinking: How do I want this lesson to change my students? Or, what will this lesson enable them to do? State these proposals at the beginning to give direction to daily activities.

Organizing Materials

Now that you have decided what material to include in the lesson, you must decide on a sequence to present the material. Sometimes a subject dictates its own sequence, so check the major ideas you want to cover to see if a natural sequence exists.

For example, a physical education teacher who wants to teach students to drive a golf ball will think, "What ideas are important to understanding this process?" The answer is: "Addressing the ball, the backswing, the downswing, and the follow-through." The sequence is obvious because a natural process is involved. Another example is the home economics teacher planning a lesson on how to bake a chiffon cake. Again, the process dictates the sequence. A history teacher preparing lessons would follow events' chronological order.

If the four or five objectives of the day's lesson have no natural order, try to determine whether a particular sequence would help students understand the lesson. For instance, a chemistry teacher would probably not teach students a compound's formula until they had learned to recognize the elements' symbols.

THE CURRICULUM

The word *curriculum* comes from a Latin word meaning "race course" (Zais, 1976), but the concept of curriculum has changed considerably. At first, curriculum meant "program of studies." It was merely a list of the courses being offered. Later the meaning of the word changed to denote course content. Today many educators define the word in terms of learning experiences. One such contemporary definition is: "the formal and informal content and process by which learners gain knowledge and understanding, develop skills and alter attitudes, appreciations, and values under the auspices of the school" (Doll, 1978, p. 6).

In other words, most contemporary educators view the curriculum as the content and experiences the school plans for students. It can mean either the plan (the document) itself or the actual functioning curriculum (Beauchamp, 1975). This text regards the curriculum as the purposefully planned content and experiences you select to help students achieve goals and objectives.

Generally, experience is now emphasized more than content, because today's educators recognize that experiences are major avenues for learning (Finn, 1993). A lesson plan must therefore describe what experiences you expect to use to teach the content. Students often complain that their lessons have no relevance, so educators tell us that we must provide meaningful experiences. How can you make experiences meaningful so that your classes will be relevant? And because students should not engage in an activity without knowing what they are trying to accomplish, how will you plan their involvement?

Review the partially completed lesson plan. You have stated how you wanted the lesson to change the students (i.e., the lesson's objectives). Little (1985) found that objectives can be used as advance organizers to improve student achievement. You have also selected and organized some major ideas you want to develop. Now you are ready to plan involvement by assigning a task that will require students to use each of the major ideas in the lesson.

The English teacher who is planning a lesson on "How to Capture the Reader's Attention" would assign tasks that make students use what they have just learned. Presented with several compositions, students could be asked to identify the principles of capturing the reader's attention each time they occur. Later in the hour, each student will write the lead paragraph of a composition, employing the five techniques of capturing the reader's attention introduced earlier in the hour.

The physical education teacher who wants to teach the correct procedure for driving a golf ball may demonstrate each step and ask students to identify mistakes that the teacher deliberately makes in each phase. Eventually, students go through the process themselves while other students critique them.

Note that each experience is an assigned task. Students must have mastered the content to carry out the procedure correctly.

Reflection

It is time to begin building your own lesson plan. Choose a subject you plan to teach. Use the following template to assemble the essential parts of your plan.

Objectives
1.
2.
3.
Teacher Activities
1.
2.
Student Activities
1.
2.
Major concepts or essential ideas to develop
1.
2.
3.
4.

IMPLEMENTING THE LESSON PLAN

A lesson will probably be no better than the daily lesson plan, yet a lesson plan does not guarantee that students will learn. Even the best plans may need modification as students interact with the materials and activities (Green & Smith, 1982). In summarizing several studies on planning, Shavelson (1984) suggests that prolific planning may be counterproductive if you become single-minded and do not adapt the lesson to your students' needs. As you develop planning skills, consider ways to alter your plans if they are not effective with a particular group at a particular time.

Managing Your Time

Ciscell (1990) explains why teachers must manage their time effectively:

> Teachers' inefficient use of their professional time recently has become the focus of much attention within the educational community. What started out as simple efforts to measure the amount of on-task behavior have resulted in somewhat alarming reports concerning the ways elementary and secondary teachers manage the school day. In the last decade, educational time has taken on a vocabulary all its own: Researchers now talk in terms of allotted time, engaged time, and academic learning time. Almost inevitably, teachers' use of classroom time has been blamed for declining achievement in America's schools. (p. 217)

Ciscell goes on to suggest that teachers can better use their time by delegating some responsibilities and by letting others know that you are time-conscious. He suggests the following steps to achieve this goal:

> Keep an appointment calendar
> Always be on time for meetings and appointments
> Start and end meetings on time and follow an agenda
> Limit time spent on idle teacher-lounge chit chat
> Keep your classroom door closed to avoid spontaneous walk-ins by colleagues
> Organize and manage your classroom efficiently
> Forget trying to work in the teacher's workroom—find a place to hide. (p. 218)

A final way to manage time is to learn to say no. When you are asked to fill in for a friend on a committee or assignment, say "I'm sorry but I'm tied up at that time" or negotiate—"I'll be happy to if you will take my place selling football tickets Friday night." With practice, these strategies will become natural and easy, and your colleagues will learn to find an easy target elsewhere. "Benefits accrue not only for teachers themselves but also for students as they take on the responsibility and challenge of a well-planned assignment" (Ciscell, 1990, p. 218).

Effective teachers separate important information and salient information (Corno, 1981) and simplify these major concepts for their own students; less-effective teachers attempt to deal more with issues (Morine & Vallance, 1975). Because beginning teachers often cannot simplify and make sense of classroom events (Calderhead, 1981), make a wise investment by identifying your discipline's major principles and concepts.

Summarizing the Daily Lesson

End your lesson plan with a review of the main ideas you have covered. Do not review every detail in the lesson or merely list the lesson's main parts. Harrison (1990, p. 503) makes an excellent suggestion for ending a lesson summary or review: "Have students name analogies and metaphors, and compare and contrast these with the original idea." The review should show the relationships among the major ideas and tie together the lesson's parts.

For example, the physical education teacher planning a lesson on how to drive a golf ball would include in the review each of the major ideas—the address, the backswing, the downswing, and the follow-through—and review the major issues related to each. The review would begin with the first idea, how to address the golf ball, and include the major points involved in the proper address as they were mentioned in the lesson. Likewise, the English lesson on "How to Capture the Reader's Attention" would include each point and its development.

Reflection

Hunter's Design for Effective Teaching

Madeline Hunter (1984) offered the following seven-step approach to designing lessons. After reading the steps, respond to the questions below.

1. Anticipatory set. The teacher causes students to focus on the lesson before the lesson begins. Example: "Look at the paragraph on the board. What part do you think is most important to remember?"
2. Objective and purpose. The teacher states explicitly what students will learn and how it will be useful. Example: "Sometimes you find it difficult to know what to study and hard to remember the important parts. Today, we're going to learn ways to identify what's important, and then we'll practice ways we can use to remember important things."
3. Input. Students must acquire new information about the knowledge, process, or skill they are to achieve. The teacher must have analyzed by task the final objective to identify needed knowledge and skills.

4. Modeling. To enhance creativity, several examples should be a routine part of most lessons. These might include live or filmed demonstrations of process and products.
5. Checking for understanding. Check that students understand the tasks before they become involved in lesson activities. You may check before or during student activity.
6. Guided practice. Students practice their new knowledge or skill under teacher supervision. New learning is like wet cement: it is easily damaged. An error that "sets" can be hard to eradicate.
7. Independent practice. Assign independent practice only after you are reasonably sure the students will not make serious errors.

1. How do you know which lesson parts are most important? List two or three criteria for judging the importance of content and skills.
2. Describe two different ways to establish anticipatory set.
3. Name one important concept in your discipline, list all the tasks that you need to teach this concept, and name some understandings and skills students must develop before mastering the concept.

LEARNING CYCLE THEORY

Another instructional theory is called the learning cycle theory. Lawson, Abraham, and Renner (1989) introduce a learning cycle approach to instruction to help students move through the levels of understanding. The program has three parts: exploration, concept introduction, and application. The hands-on introduction enables students to develop descriptive and qualitative understandings. The concept introduction lets them talk about their experiences, either with the teacher or in cooperative learning groups. The teacher guides the discussion. During the application phase, students are given assignments to apply the concepts in different ways.

Markle, Johnston, Geer, and Meichtry (1990) caution teachers against making unwarranted assumptions about what students know. They advise teachers to provide procedural structure that tells students in advance what they are going to do, what the key points are, and what they should know when the lesson is completed.

SAMPLE DAILY LESSON PLANS

Following are some sample daily lesson plans. They differ in style, but each contains a few major ideas and is arranged in a sequence that facilities learning. Note that each major idea is followed by an assigned task that requires students to use the idea. Note also that each sample lesson ends with a review that ties together the lesson's major ideas.

The parts of a plan (statement of purpose, introduction, student activities, and summary) vary among plans. Make a list of all the parts you find in these plans. Put an asterisk next to the parts you believe will be helpful when you teach. Use the results as an outline to make a lesson plan in your subject area.

Lesson Plan 1

Physical Education: Grade 9

    I. Purpose: To develop the ability to score a complete bowling game

    II. Materials: Scoresheet and lead pencil with eraser for each student

    III. Equipment: Overhead projector

    IV. Main ideas

        A. How to score and add an open frame

        B. How to score and add a spare

        C. How to score and add a strike

        D. How to score and add the last frame

    V. Procedure

        A. Five-minute explanation of each concept

        B. Demonstration of scoring a game

    VI. Assignment: Students are to score and add the following games at their desks.

```
|4-2 |4-/| 8 /| 9 /|  X|  X|4 /|  X|  X| 2-3| 4/| 2 |
|___|___|___|___|___|___|___|___|___|___|___|___|___|
```

    VII. Summary: The teacher will show a transparency of the game on the overhead screen and use questions to lead the class in filling out each step in the game.

Discussion of Lesson Plan 1.   Do you like the lesson plan? Is it clear? Among its strongest assets are its initial statement of purpose telling immediately what the lesson should do for the student, its clear statement of the ideas being taught, and its summary. The task is also stated clearly. Notice that the teacher selected as an example a game that starts with the simplest ideas and moves to progressively more complex ideas until it covers everything one must know to score a bowling game. Note also that because the game contains all the essential ideas of scoring, it provides a satisfactory review of the whole lesson.

    How could you improve this plan? Note the procedures. Would the plan be easier to follow if time limits were stated alongside the activities? Can you think of other ways to improve it?

Lesson planning often requires library research.

Lesson Plan 2

Mr. Hulsey   *Class: Tenth-grade Business*
Date: December 2

I. Descriptive Title: "How to Prepare a Balance Sheet"
II. Concepts in Logical Sequence
    A. The balance sheet tells what is owned, what is owed, and what the owner is worth on a specific date.
    B. Assets and liabilities determine owner's equity.
    C. Assets are entered in the left column, and liabilities and owner's equity are entered in the right column.
    D. The totals of both columns must be equal. If they do not balance, an error exists.
III. Presentation: Discussion will be used to present the concepts as a sample balance sheet is worked through on the board.
IV. Assign task: Each student will prepare a balance sheet to determine what the student owns, owes, and is worth.
V. Summary: Go back over the four concepts, having students check to be sure they have followed these concepts in preparing their balance sheets.

Discussion of Lesson Plan 2.   Compare the format of this plan with Lesson Plan 1. Which is easier to follow? Notice that this plan has no time indicated for any part of the lesson. Is that good, or would you need time limits to determine how long you should spend on each part?

Lesson Plan 3

Mr. Alfred Harding   ***Class: Speech, Grade 12***

1. Title: "How to Use Time When Reading with Expression." Establish set by reading a poem ("Richard Cory") aloud as monotonously and ineffectively as possible, with no pauses or variation in speed.
2. The essential concepts of time: pause, rate, duration. Introduce these concepts (pause, rate, and duration) in that order because we go from time where no words are involved to time that involves several words down to time that involves just one word.
3. (a) Pause—the pregnant space of time when no sound is uttered, the dramatic pause after a heavy statement—give an example; the anticipating pause—slight hesitation before key word, often used both in dramatic and comedy punch line—give an example. (b) Duration—the amount of time spent on just one word. Used for emphasis and imagery. Show how one can stretch out a single word and how it highlights the meaning of a passage.
4. Assignment: Go around the room and have each student say "Give me liberty, or give me death" using the three concepts of time for more expression.
5. Summary: Read the same poem ("Richard Cory") as in beginning, only read it well and with expression. Then ask class if they've heard it before. Tell and then show how important the proper use of those three concepts is for effective communication. In the second reading, demonstrate how those three concepts worked.

Discussion of Lesson Plan 3.   What is your major criticism of this plan? Do you find the format complicated and involved? This lesson plan has some definite assets. Can you recognize them? The introduction would be effective in almost any class. The lesson content is divided into three clear categories, so the class would not be overwhelmed with too much content. The summary is very good because it allows students to compare and actually see the value in the main ideas developed—pause, rate, and duration. Can you think of ways to improve this lesson plan?

Lesson Plan 4

Mrs. Grace Bishop   ***Class: English, Grade 9***

I. Objective:	The student should understand the importance of using proper grammar.
II. Objective:	Teach students to identify nouns and know their classes.
(5 min.)	A. Introduce subject: Grammar.
	1. Give a brief outline of the plan of study.
	2. Announce the noun as the first part of speech you will study.
(10 min.)	B. Present the idea that proper use of grammar is important.
	1. Give one example.

2. Ask students for other examples.

(15 min.)   **C.** Give the definition of nouns and explain classes.

    1. Common.

    2. Proper.

    3. Abstract.

    4. Concrete.

      Give an example of each on the board.

      Ask students to give other examples and add to list.

(15 min.)   **D.** Have each student make a list of 15 nouns naming objects seen in the classroom (3 min.).

    1. List the four classes on the board.

    2. Call on students for nouns and have them designate the proper list of each case.

(5 min.)   **E.** Summary

    1. Conduct a brief questioning period reviewing the definition and classes of nouns.

    2. Evaluate the effectiveness of the lesson by the response of the students. Did they understand the various classes? Could they easily choose the appropriate list for each noun?

Discussion of Lesson Plan 4.   What is your reaction to the time indicators in this plan? Would they help you teach this lesson, or would they make you uncomfortable? Perhaps they are too restrictive. The teacher's activities and the students' activities are listed in steps. Do you like this? Notice the objective stated in the beginning. How could it be improved? There is no written evaluation at the end. Would this make it difficult to evaluate accomplishment of the stated objective, "To understand the importance of using proper grammar?" Can you rewrite the objective, stating it in performance terms?

Lesson Plan 5

November 16th 1995
Bells 3, 4, 6, and 7

Class: United States History
Grade: 11th
Unit: The Progressive Era
Topic: Woodrow Wilson won sweeping reforms

SWBAT: List and evaluate the reforms accomplished by the first Wilson administration.

Anticipatory set: Ask students for whom were most of the progressive reforms made. Most were made for white, middle-class people. Few reforms were made for immigrants, blacks, and Native Americans. Tell the students that the Wilson administration initiated many reforms to help these people.

(10 min.)

Input: Wilson launched his New Freedom-Underwood Tariff. Wilson established powerful controls over banking and the trusts—Federal Reserve Act, Federal Trade Commission Act, Clayton Antitrust Act. Use advanced organizer to reinforce learning.

(15 min.)

Check for understanding: Ask students random questions about the material and Wilson's reforms. Ask students to tell the instructor what they think of the reforms and how they could have been made better. Write answers on the overhead.

(8 min.)

Guided practice: Have students complete the worksheets on Section 5. Go over answers in class and if need be have students use their books to make corrections. Tell them that they can use these to study for the tests.

(12 min.)

Closures: Remind students that some of the existing examples of the progressive legacy: national parks, conservation programs, direct primaries, safe food and drugs, and the federal banking system. Ask students if these are a good ideas, Why or Why not???

(5 min.)

Independent Practice: Study for the test!!!

Evaluation:

Discussion of Lesson Plan 5.   This plan clearly identifies each of several pedagogical strategies: Anticipatory set, input, check for understanding, guided practice, closure, and independent practice. Do you think this is a good algorithm for designing a lesson? Why or why not?

Lesson Plan 6

CHPT. 1 pg. 12–13
Bell 3–7Y
Date: Mon. Sept. 16

UNIT:	Adding and Subtracting Whole Numbers
TOPIC:	Estimating Sums & Differences
OBJECTIVES:	To estimate sums & differences To inform students of my Ps & Qs (Rules)
KEY TERMS:	Estimate, Sums, Differences

ANTICIPATORY SET:	*You and your friends have been planning a day out.

T.Q.) What might you girls plan?

S.A.) <u>Girls Plan</u>— Shopping, eating, movie.
& (You will use your money
Prompts) you've saved from babysit-
ting, chores, etc.)

PRAISE ALL ANSWERS & EFFORTS	

T.Q.) What might you guys plan?

S.A.) <u>Guys Plan</u>—Play video game, get some-
& thing to eat, see a movie.
Prompts)

T.Q.) How much money should you bring?

S.A.) Answers will vary

T.Q.) How did you arrive at dollar amount needed?

S.A.) Give response

T.Q.) GREAT—you <u>estimated</u> in your head the amount
needed. Based on previous trips to mall, movies, ar-
cade, etc., you <u>ESTIMATED</u> monies needed.

LESSON PURPOSE & INSTRUCTIONAL INPUT	Estimating <u>Sums & Differences</u> is topic of today's lesson. Ob-viously we use this concept every day. You proved it by your above examples.

T.Q.) What is a <u>SUM?</u>   S.A.) Numbers added together.

T.Q.) What is a <u>DIFFERENCE?</u>   S.A.) Numbers being sub-
tracted.

Before we jump into the lesson, let's quickly review a needed concept: <u>ROUNDING</u>

MODELING
<u>Height in feet</u>

Mt. McKinley in Alaska

	TENS	HUNDREDS	THOUSANDS
1) 20,320	(20,320;	20,300;	20,000)
2) 1,456	(1,460;	1,500	1,000)

T.Q.) <u>Any questions on the ROUNDING??</u>

*To estimate the sum or difference <u>round</u> each number to the greatest <u>(largest) place value of the greatest</u> (largest) number. Then add or subtract.

EX 1) We are going to take a trip.

Day 1 Billings, Mont.		Rounds to
to Casper, Wy.	287 miles	300 miles
Day 2 Casper, Wy.		
to Denver, Co.	277 miles	300 miles
Day 3 Denver, Co.		
to Pueblo, Co.	112 miles	+100 miles
		700 miles

T.Q.) In our example, what is the greatest place value of the greatest number?

S.A.) Hundreds

*In order to estimate a <u>SUM,</u> add the individually rounded numbers.

*In our first example, 300 + 300 + 100 = 700 miles estimated.

EX 2) Let's round the following numbers and estimate the sum.

		Rounds to
Richmond, VA to Wash., D.C.	106	100
Wash., D.C., to New York, N.Y.	233 miles	200
New York, N.Y. to Boston, Mass.	206 miles	+200

T.Q.) What is the greatest place value of the greatest number?

S.A.) HUNDREDS

In EX. 2, 100 miles + 200 miles + 200 miles = 500 miles estimated

EX. 3) Let's estimate the <u>sum</u> of the following numbers.

	Rounds to	
1,988	2,000	*T.Q.) What is the greatest
1,359	1,000	place value of the
2,467	+2,000	greatest number?
	5,000	S.A.) THOUSANDS

EX. 4)

	Rounds to	
13,321	10,000	*T.Q.) What is the greatest
10,950	10,000	place value of the
17,289	+20,000	greatest number?
	40,000	S.A.) 10-THOUSANDS

EX. 5)

	Rounds to
133,421	100,000
159,950	200,000
+173,289	+200,000
	500,000

*T.Q.) What is the greatest place value of the greatest value of the greatest number?

S.A.) 100-THOUSAND

T.Q.)   Any questions up to this point???

CHECK UNDERSTANDING

Estimate the sum of the following numbers:

1)	637	600	2)	1,448	1,000
	885	900		2,756	3,000
	+241	+200		+1,313	+1,000
		1,700			5,000

3)	25	30	4)	25,436	30,000
	89	90		17,189	20,000
	+67	+70		+31,201	+30,000
		190			80,000

5)	276,953	300,000
	484,848	500,000
	+137,999	+100,000
		900,000

MORE MODELING

Let's look at estimating a difference

T.Q.)   What is a difference?

S.Q.)   Subtracting two numbers.

T.)   IN ORDER TO ESTIMATE A DIFFERENCE, WE ROUND EACH NUMBER TO THE GREATEST PLACE VALUE OF THE GREATEST (LARGEST) NUMBER, THEN SUBTRACT.)

PRAISE ALL ANSWERS & EFFORTS

EX. 1)

Estimate   8,115
                            −1,643

T.Q.)   What is the greatest place value of the greatest number?

S.A.)   THOUSANDS

	Rounds to
8,115	8,000
−1,643	−2,000
	6,000

EX. 2)

Let's Estimate

$$
\begin{array}{r}
679 \\
-145 \\
\end{array}
$$

T.Q.) What is the greatest place value of the greatest number?

S.A.) Hundreds

	Rounds to
679	700
−145	−100
	600

EX. 3)

	Rounds to
48,529	50,000
−9,769	−10,000
	40,000

PRAISE ALL
ANSWERS &
EFFORTS

T.Q.) What is the greatest place value of the greatest number?

S.A.) 10-THOUSANDS

EX. 4)

	Rounds to
89	90
−23	−20
	70

*T.Q.) What is the greatest place value of the greatest number?

S.A.) Tens

CHECK
UNDERSTANDING:

T.Q.) Any questions estimating sums and differences?

Estimate the following differences:

1)
458	500
−219	−200
	300

2)
8,765	9,000
−4,321	−4,000
	5,000

3)
69	70
−34	−30
	40

4)
15,828	20,000
−9,761	−10,000
	10,000

5)
912	900
−854	−900
	0

GUIDED PRACTICE:

Worksheet—Group work
(Attached)

HOMEWORK: None

CLOSURE: *Recap OBJ.
                       *What's a Sum, Difference, Estimate?
                       *What is rule for estimating?
                       *Praise for hard work.
                       *What are my Ps & Qs?

TIMING:

TOO LONG: May have too many examples

TOO SHORT:

EVALUATION:

Discussion of Lesson Plan 6. This lesson is much longer than the other sample plans. Is it too long? Is the topics column helpful? This lesson plan specifies the teacher's behavior at each step throughout the lesson. Do you find this helpful? Why or why not?

Lesson Plan 7

SPANISH 1: 7:35–8:25
2/24/96 Thursday

Objective: Review voc. 5A, review possessive adjectives, review forms of estar, introduce new voc., monologues
Student will be able to:

1. Repasar mi, tu, su
2. Tomar prueba, mi, tu, su
3. Repasar/usar estar
4. Identificar nuevo vocabulary
5. Hacer los monólogos
1. Create sentences with estar
2. Sentences using estar
3. Identify new vocabulary
4. Create monologues

Warm up: Vocabulary-transparency
A. Pairs: Students to create sentences with vocabulary using the verb estar (S to S)
   *Model: La camera está en la maleta
B. Feedback: Students to share sentences with class (S to C/T)

Content:

I. Review possessive adj: mi, tu, su
  A. Pairs: Students to create sentences with mi, tu, su.
  B. Feedback: Students to share sentences with class.

II. Quiz #2, mi, tu, su

III. Homework check: libro: p 138 ej A7–8, MA: p 58, ej 3
  A. Book: Student to be "professor" and review hw orally with class calling on volunteers
    *teacher circulates the room and checks homework
  B. Workbook: Students to share answers with class.

IV. Introduce new vocabulary—transparency
  A. Teacher to model/point out new works on trans.
  B. Students to listen and repeat after teacher.
  C. Individual students to identify words.
  D. Pairs: Students to create sentences with new voc.
  E. Feedback: Students to share sentences with class.

V. Monologues
  A. Paris: Students to form pairs and practice for monologue.
  B. Class: to form a circle and student to give monologue with other students making comments or questions.

Closure: Review new voc. and homework

Guided practice: The class will be conducted in whole class form and in groups to practice what they are learning.

Homework: Libro: p 139. ej A10 leer; Ej A12; escriban 5 oraciones usando estar.

Evaluation:
_____ dialogues, monologues, skits
_____ quiz/test
_____ student oral responses
_____ paired/group oral practice
_____ homework check
_____ teacher observation

Materials/Equipment:

_____ overhead/transparencies	_____ visuals
_____ language lab/cassette tapes	_____ flash cards
_____ quiz/test	_____ text/workbook/activity wkbk
_____ other	_____ video/film

Discussion of Lesson Plan 7.   This lesson plan begins with a list of objectives. Is this helpful? Notice that this lesson requires individual work and work in pairs as well as teacher-directed activities. Should teachers strive to include such variety in all lessons?

Lesson Plan 8

Claudia D. Tate Indian River High School
DAILY LESSON PLAN
Subject: Trig Date: 12–3 Monday
Bells: 2 and 3
Topic: STATISTICS

Objective(s): Students will be able to:

1. graph a line plot.
2. define mean, median, mode, outliers, cluster, gaps, range.
3. graph a stem & leaf plot.
4. compare and contrast the line and stem & leaf plots.

Procedures and/or activities:

A. Set: Each student is given a box of raisins and must count the raisins. A line plot will be set up on the overhead, and each student's number will be plotted on the line plot.

B. Input: Using the set, define mean (average), median (middle), mode (most), outlier, cluster, gap, range. Have the students find and discuss the above numbers.

Using the ages of U.S. Presidents at the time of inauguration, graph a stem and leaf plot. Find through coaching and questioning the mean, median, mode, outlier, cluster, gap, range.

As students fill in their advanced organizers, present the reasons for using the line or stem & leaf plots.

Independent practice: HW to be started in class, time permitting.

Closure: Compare and Contrast the plot graphs.

Reference: *The World Almanac 1989.* "Statistics is for Everyone"—a presentation by John R. Dunham.

Assignment: Complete glossary and adv. org., complete line plot and stem and leaf plot worksheets in notebook.

Evaluation: Notebook worksheets, guided practice, and test.

Material: Reference books, overhead; worksheets, advanced organizer, glossary.

Discussion of Lesson Plan 8.   This subject of this lesson plan is Statistics. Educators realize teachers must conduct research, and statistics is an important subject for teachers as well as for their students. Can you think of other lesson topics that can serve both your students and your own progress and needs? Could you make a computer assignment for this lesson that you might offer for extra credit?

RECAP OF MAJOR IDEAS

1. Daily lesson plans are essential for students to attain the expectations set forth in units.
2. Do not become so enslaved to lesson plans that you read them step-by-step to students. On the other hand, do not ignore the value that planning offers in giving necessary direction as each lesson progresses.
3. Like any other tool, the value of a lesson plan depends on how it is used.
4. Begin lesson plan design by identifying desirable changes in student behavior.
5. All lesson plans should contain activities to involve students.
6. Organize content according to natural sequences, simple to complex, or sequences that facilitate students' understanding of the material.
7. End each lesson plan with a review of the lesson's major concepts.
8. Teachers seldom use objectives when beginning lesson planning and when changing their approaches.
9. Constructivists advise teachers to tie newly introduced concepts to students' existing knowledge.

CASES

The quality of planning is as important as the act of planning. Poor planning, overstructuring, and lessons that are too short or too long can lead to serious problems. The following cases are examples of problems caused by inadequate planning.

CASE 1: A TEACHER ATTEMPTS TO BE DEMOCRATIC IN PLANNING

It was a year to remember: 1976, the nation's bicentennial. Mr. Henry, a first-year teacher, was dedicated to establishing a completely democratic classroom atmosphere. Although he was young and inexperienced, he was determined to give each student a feeling of freedom so that everyone could better understand the true meaning of democracy.

Mr. Henry's approach to creating this atmosphere was sensible. From the first day, he incorporated democratic machinery into his tenth-grade democracy classes. Every controversial idea was put to a vote. The majority's opinion always determined the class's direction and behavior. To say that the students enjoyed his classes is an understatement, at least throughout the first term.

The students decided to determine subject content on a completely individual basis. Some of the more studious quickly identified their areas of interest and immediately began their projects. Some of the slower students did not reach definite decisions for several days, but they did not worry about it. Mr. Henry was patient and helpful when asked.

All was well, and everyone was happy as the term got underway. Many students were thrilled with this new approach and the complete freedom it provided—something they had not experienced in other classes. The first students to become concerned—and later doubtful—about whether the approach was "right for them" were the high-performing students. Since most members of this group were planning to attend college and would take courses in American democracy, they began to wonder if they were getting the foundation they would need for college. Mr. Henry told them not to worry because they would probably be even more adequately prepared than other students. He brought to his classes some studies showing that several nondirective and open-ended mathematics and science classes had prepared students so well that they outscored their counterparts in traditional classes on standardized college entrance examinations. This pacified some of the students, but it failed to erase their doubts.

As the end of the first grading period approached, the students who had been concerned began worrying again. When they asked how their grades would be determined, Mr. Henry replied, "How do you want your grade to be determined?" They soon realized that the competitive examinations to which they were accustomed were not adequate to test the content in this class. When Mr. Henry proposed that the students provide evidence of their academic progress and let class members determine their appropriate grades, the students rejected the proposal.

The class appeared to be in trouble, and so did the teacher. This approach had not produced the uniformity of content found in traditional classes. Mr. Henry wondered how he could have democratic classes and yet avoid these problems.

Discussion

1. How much freedom should a secondary school class have in selecting content?

   The idea of providing complete freedom for any group of people (youth or adults) is a misguided one. People who have guidelines are the freest of all—far more so than people who have no rules to follow. Individuals who have no regulations find themselves wandering aimlessly without purpose or direction. The teacher who attempts to give a class absolute freedom of choice and behavior usually finds that the students do not appreciate such a completely unstructured approach. From professional education courses and practical experience, teachers can learn to identify certain information that students need to prepare for the future. By sharing essential experiences, which is the teacher's right and responsibility, the teacher can help students select other content and experiences.

2. Should Mr. Henry discontinue using democratic procedures in the classroom and teach the principles of democracy as content rather than as practice?

   Definitely not. Democracy should be practiced in all classes. Teaching the rules of democracy is essential, but the best way to do this is to have the students practice them. Aristotle once said, "We learn virtue by being virtuous." Democracy is a way of treating others as you want them to treat you. This cannot be achieved through learning rules, principles, and definitions.

3. How can Mr. Henry retain structure in the class and yet involve students in planning?

   Your role is to guide students in selecting appropriate content. One method would be first to discuss with your students the objectives that you expect them to achieve, showing them why each objective is needed. Then you can let the students decide how they want to achieve these objectives. What content you cover is less important than developing students' understanding. If Mr. Henry is more concerned with the class's ultimate goals—and he should be—he will not worry so much about content but will concentrate on objectives and planned experiences that will keep his students working toward those goals. You can probably think of other ways to let students share the planning responsibility.

4. What can you say about when the evaluation system was determined?

Mr. Henry waited too long to decide how grades would be determined. Students should know this from the beginning so that they can direct their activities and prepare for evaluations.

CASE 2: A TEACHER USES NOTE CARDS FOR PLANNING

Every student in the school liked Mr. Little, the teacher who supervised my student teaching experience. Mr. Little's classes were both entertaining and successful. Students seemed to learn automatically in his classes. During the three months I spent in his classes, I never once saw a detailed lesson plan.

During class, Mr. Little—who coincidentally was small in stature—always sat in front of the room perched on a high stool. As he talked, joked, and laughed with his students, he continually shuffled a few three-by-five cards, glancing at them while carrying on a dialogue with the students. After his introductory lesson on rocks and minerals, I examined Mr. Little's note cards (Figure 4.1).

Although the cards were not detailed or impressive, they did structure the lesson. Each item was mentioned briefly. The cards contained key words and phrases

Rocks & Minerals

1. Why study rocks
2. Joke about igneous rocks
3. Basic types of rocks
    A. Sedimentary
    B. Igneous
    C. Metamorphic
4. Rock collecting

FIGURE 4.1   Three-by-five-inch card used for planning

rather than complete sentences. This system enabled Mr. Little to glance at his notes without taking his attention away from the students, and I believe it contributed significantly to his unusually effective teaching.

Discussion

1. What are some advantages of brief lesson plans?

   When lesson plans are brief, you are less likely to "read" the lesson to the class. Brief plans also leave room for flexibility: You have time to let students pursue both planned topics and any related topics and materials that interest them. A brief plan also leaves time for students to become involved.

2. What are some dangers in too-brief lesson plans?

   If a lesson plan is too brief, you may run short of material and have time left with nothing planned. In addition, a brief lesson may be "shallow"; it may not challenge students to think.

3. Can a lesson be too highly structured?

   Yes, if you mean too detailed. When a lesson is too detailed, you are likely to dominate the class, leaving students no opportunity to ask questions and to comment on the lesson. If you interpret this question literally and answer no, I agree with you. The more structure (not detail) a lesson has, the more likely students will reach set goals. Although educators often stress the value of pupil-centered discovery approaches, this method cannot succeed without much planning and hidden structure. Although pupil-centered classes may appear to have little structure, the successful ones are usually more highly structured in terms of objectives and activities than are traditional classes.

CASE 3: A TEACHER FAILS TO USE OBJECTIVES

Our college biology teacher had a style of her own. Each hour Mrs. Woods promptly opened her notebook and began the lesson. She wrote everything she said on the board in perfect outline form. Her speaking speed was equaled only by her writing speed; she did not waste a minute during the hour. Students were amazed by how neat, organized, and professional her approach to every lesson was.

Mrs. Woods always kept to the day's objectives. Once when she was absent, her husband, who was also a biology teacher, took over for the day. Having specified no objectives, he kept students wondering when he was going to get into the lesson. They complained that his remarks had nothing to do with the topic being studied. Mr. Woods understood biology, but his lecture seemed to confuse students.

Some of the best students in school got their lowest marks in Mrs. Woods' classes. Furthermore, they said they learned very little about biology. Students were surprised that they had benefited so little in the class of a teacher who was not only brilliant in her subject but also extremely well prepared for every lesson.

Discussion Questions

    1. Did Mrs. Woods' lessons lack structure?

    2. Why did the students feel so lost in Mr. Woods' class?

CASE 4: A TEACHER GETS LOST IN HIS OWN LESSONS

Each day, when students came to my class after their music class, they complained to me about their music homework assignments. I heard complaints like "This assignment has nothing to do with what we studied in class today," "I don't see the value in this," and "Why does Mr. Marshall make us do this?" I reminded them that they should not direct their criticisms to me, because it would be unprofessional and unethical for me to discuss the issue with them. I refused to comment, but I continued to hear complaints: "Mr. Marshall rambles," "He skips around with the material so much that it doesn't make sense."

    Finally, the complaints reached administrators, who spoke with Mr. Marshall about the issue. I do not know what was said during the meeting, but it apparently produced a change in Mr. Marshall's teaching because the complaints were fewer and fewer. I always wondered how Mr. Marshall managed to change so quickly and to improve his teaching so effectively.

Discussion Questions

    1. Teachers of special subjects, such as music, art, and physical education, are usually assigned to teach several sections of the same class. This often contributes to a teacher's forgetting just what was covered with each group, which was apparently what happened to Mr. Marshall. What would you do if you ever found yourself forgetting where you ended the previous class and exactly what you had covered in it?

    2. When teaching multiple sections of the same class, should you make separate lesson plans for each section?

    3. Should you ever stray from the planned lesson?

    4. Does a teacher's ability to plan improve with experience?

ACTIVITIES

    1. Develop a daily plan in your own major teaching field. Specify the subject and grade level and include performance objectives, content generalizations, activities to help students attain the objectives, and a summary of the most significant ideas in the lesson.

    2. Write a unit plan in your area of specialty. Begin by writing a brief statement of your philosophy of education. For each curriculum component, write one sentence to explain how your particular philosophy should affect each component.

    3. Identify a topic you might select for a lesson. Now write several student activities to use during the hour. Finally, order these in the best sequence possible. Explain why you put each activity in its selected sequence.

4. Examine all the sample lesson plans in this chapter. For each plan, select one or more features you would change if you were using the plan in your classes. Explain your reason for making each change.

REFERENCES

Acheson, K. A., & Gall, M. (1992). *Techniques in the clinical supervision of teachers.* White Plains, NY: Longman.

Armento, B. J. (1986). Research on teaching social studies. In M. C. Wittrock (Ed.), *Handbook of research on teaching* (3rd ed.). New York: Macmillan.

Beauchamp, G. A. (1975). *Curriculum theory* (3rd ed.). Wilmette, IL: Kagg.

Calderhead, J. (1981). *Research into teachers' and student teachers' cognitions: Exploring the nature of classroom practice.* Paper presented at the annual meeting of the American Educational Research Association, Montreal, Canada.

Carnahan, R. S. (1980). *The effects of teacher planning on classroom processes.* Unpublished doctoral dissertation, University of Wisconsin at Madison.

Carson, M. D., & Badarack, G. (1989). *How changing class size affects classrooms and students.* Riverside, CA: University of California at Riverside, California Educational Research Cooperative.

Ciscell, R. E. (1990). A matter of minutes: Making better use of teacher time. *The Clearing House, 63*(5), 217–218.

Clark, C. M., & Peterson, P. L. (1986). Teachers' thought processes. In M. C. Whittrock (Ed.), *Handbook of research on teaching* (3rd ed.). New York: Macmillan.

Corno, L. (1981). Cognitive organizing classrooms. *Curriculum Inquiry, 11,* 359–377.

Doll, R. C. (1978). *Curriculum improvement: Decision making and process* (4th ed.). Boston: Allyn & Bacon.

Finn, J. D. (1993). *School engagement and students at risk.* Washington, D.C.: National Center for Education Statistics, U.S. Department of Education.

Green, J., & Smith, D. (1982). *Teaching and learning: A linguistic perspective.* Paper presented at the Conference on Research and Teaching, Airlie House, VA.

Harrison, C. J. (1990). Concepts, operational definitions, and case studies in instruction. *Education, 110*(4), 502–505.

Hunter, M. (1984). Knowing, teaching and supervising. In P. L. Hosford (Ed.), *Using what we know about teaching* (pp. 175–176). Alexandria, VA: Association for Supervision and Curriculum Development. Abstracted with the author's permission.

Johnston, J. M. (1990, April). *What are teachers' perceptions of teaching in different classroom contexts?* Paper presented at the annual convention of the American Educational Research Association, Boston, MA.

Lawson, A. E., Abraham, M. R., & Renner, J. W. (1989). A theory of instruction: Using the learning cycle to teach science concepts and thinking skills (NARST Monograph No. 1). Cincinnati, OH: University of Cincinnati, National Association for Research in Science Teaching.

Little, D. (1985). An investigation of cooperative small-group instruction and the use of advance organizers on the self-concept and social studies achievement of third-grade students. Doctoral dissertation, University of Alabama.

Markle, G., Johnston, J. H., Geer, C., & Meichtry, Y. (1990, November). Teaching for understanding. *Middle School Journal, 22*(2), 53–57.

Morine, G., & Vallance, E. (1975). Special study B: A study of teacher and pupil perceptions of classroom instruction (Technical Report No. 75-11-6). San Francisco: Far West Laboratory.

Nye, B. A., Achilles, C. M., Boyd-Zaharias, J., Fulton, B. D., & Wallenhorst, M. P. (1994). Small is far better. *Research in the Schools, 1*(1), 9–20.

Peterson, P. L., Marx, R. W., & Clark, C. M. (1978). Teacher planning, teacher behavior, and student achievement. *American Educational Research Journal, 15,* 555–565.

Romberg, T. A. (1983). *Allocated time and content covered in mathematics.* Paper presented at the annual meeting of the American Educational Research Association, Montreal, Canada.

Romberg, T. A., & Carpenter, T. P. (1986). Research on teaching mathematics: Two disciplines of scientific inquiry. In M. C. Wittrock (Ed.), *Handbook of research on teaching* (3rd ed.). New York: Macmillan.

Schville, J., Porter, A., Billi, G., Floden, R., Freeman, D., Knappan, L., Kuhs, T., & Schmidt, W. (1983). Teachers as policy brokers in the content of elementary school mathematics. In L. S. Schulman & E. G. Sykes (Eds.), *Handbook of teaching and policy.* New York: Longman.

Shavelson, R. J. (1984). Review of research on teachers' pedagogical judgments, plans, and decisions. Los Angeles: Rand Corporation and University of California. In R. L. Egbert & M. M. Kluender (Eds.), *Using research to improve teacher education* (pp. 132–133). Lincoln, NE: American Association of Colleges for Teacher Education/Teachers College, University of Nebraska-Lincoln.

Shavelson, R. J., & Stern, P. (1981). Research on teachers' pedagogical thoughts, judgments, decisions, and behavior. *Review of Educational Research, 51,* 455–498.

Slavin, R. E. (1994). *Educational psychology: Theory and practice* (4th ed.). Needham Heights, MA: Allyn & Bacon.

Van Gulick, R. (1990). Functionalism, information, and content. In W. G. Lylcan (Ed.), *Mind and cognition.* Cambridge, MA: Basil Blackwell.

von Glasersfeld, E. (1988). *Environment and communication.* Paper presented at the Sixth International Congress on Mathematics Education, Budapest. As cited by Tobin, K., Bugler, K., & Fraser, B. (1990). *Windows into science classrooms: Problems with higher-level cognitive learning.* New York: Falmer.

Walker, V. N., & Chance, E. W. (1994–1995). National award winning teachers' exemplary instructional techniques and activities. *National Forum of Teacher Education Journal, 5*(1), 11–24.

Walter, L. J. (1979). How teachers plan for curriculum and instruction. *Catalyst, 2,* 3.

Walter, L. J. (1984). A synthesis of research findings on teaching, planning, and decision making. In R. L. Egbert & M. M. Kluender (Eds.), *Using research to improve teacher education.* Lincoln, NE: American Association of Colleges for Teacher Education/Teachers College, University of Nebraska-Lincoln.

Zahorik, J. A. (1975). Teacher planning models. *Educational Leadership, 33,* 134–139.

Zais, R. S. (1976). *Curriculum: Principles and foundations.* New York: Crowell.

SUGGESTED READING

Snapp, J. C., & Glover, J. A. (1990). "Advance organizers and study questions." *The Journal of Educational Research, 8*(5), 266–271.

part TWO

Teaching Strategies and Communications

Effective teachers take a definite approach to teaching each lesson. They select specific methods and develop them into more general and complex strategies. To do this well, a teacher must have a repertoire of methods from which to choose. Chapter 5 presents a variety of teaching methods. To help you select the most appropriate method for each lesson, the strengths and limitations of each method are discussed. To be effective, you must make strategies and methods come to life in the classroom. You do this by communicating effectively. Chapter 6 presents several verbal and nonverbal techniques to prepare you to communicate effectively.

chapter 5

Teaching Strategies

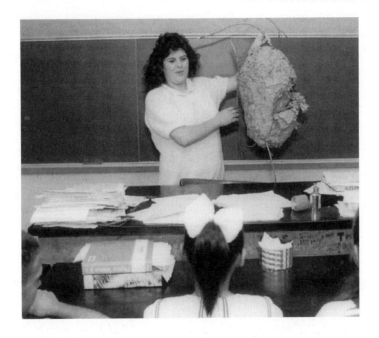

It is only when several strategies are carefully and systematically integrated that substantial improvements in learning become possible.

T. R. Guskey

OBJECTIVES

Differentiate between questioning and the Socratic method.

List three unique strengths of simulation gaming.

List two teaching strategies that are good motivators.

List two guidelines for teachers who use questions in classroom instruction.

Give three suggestions to help teachers improve their lectures.

Define inquiry learning.

Name one major advantage and one major limitation of inquiry learning.

List three advantages of the lecture.

Explain how using case studies can help students develop important concepts.

Justify the use of cooperative learning.

PRETEST

	Agree	Disagree	Uncertain
1. Teaching methods are unimportant because good students learn in any setting and poor students do poorly regardless of the teaching method.	____	____	____
2. Some methods are best for some students; others are best for other students.	____	____	____
3. The way a teacher implements a teaching method is more important than which method is selected.	____	____	____
4. The lecture has no place in secondary schools because other methods are superior in every way.	____	____	____
5. Use rhetorical questions only when you have informed students that they are not expected to answer.	____	____	____
6. Games the teacher and students develop are usually superior to commercial learning games.	____	____	____
7. Inquiry learning is the same as discovery learning.	____	____	____
8. Questions' effectiveness is enhanced when teachers give students more time to respond, help students reach acceptable answers, and encourage students to ask questions.	____	____	____

9. Simulation-type games are good motiva-
   tors and lead to increased retention.   _____   _____   _____
10. Case studies enable students to study
    concepts in context.   _____   _____   _____

Middle-Level Message

The success of any lesson hinges on the teacher's ability to get the students' attention. At the middle level this can be a real challenge. This chapter introduces advance organizers that can help you get students' attention at the beginning of the period and hold it throughout the period as you introduce new concepts.

This chapter also introduces a variety of teaching methods. All teachers need a repertoire of methods from which to choose. Because of the transescent's need for socialization opportunities, middle-level teachers should pay especially close attention to discussions, simulations, and games as teaching methods. Learn when to use each of these methods and how to use them to achieve each method's full potential. Appendix C gives an overview of the middle level teacher's role.

DEVELOPING LESSONS

Not long ago, teachers could be described according to their particular teaching style. Prospective teachers spent many hours wondering what their own teaching style would be. Would they use mainly expository teaching—something like the many lectures they had listened to in college? Or would they use an entirely different approach, which would lead students to discover for themselves the important truths of a discipline?

Today's education majors are asking different questions because they recognize that there are many teaching methods—expository, inquiry, questioning, discovery, and simulation gaming. The old question "Which one should I use?" has given way to a new one: "Which ones should I use for what purposes?" Education students know that certain methods work best with certain objectives.

This chapter looks at several teaching methods and helps you develop the skills you need to select and use each to achieve particular goals. "Particular" is emphasized because if the stated goals are too broad, any one method has no particular advantage over another. For example, suppose your goal is to select and use the method that will produce maximum learning or understanding. "Of eighty-eight comparisons between traditional lecture and traditional discussion methods, as reported in thirty-six experimental studies, 51 percent favored the lecture method and 49 percent favored the discussion method" (Berliner & Gage, 1975). In other words, 51 percent of the studies found that the lecture method was superior to the discussion method for effective learning; 49 percent found the discussion method superior to the lecture.

This does not mean that teaching methods are unimportant; it does mean that they are contextual. A method's success depends on your ability to relate it to the overall instructional program in a particular classroom with a particular group of students. In fact, hundreds of studies show that, if correctly used, each style can produce certain specific results.

As you study each method, keep these questions in mind: What are this method's unique potentials? How can I best implement this method? If I decide to experiment using this method, what precautions should I take? Can I learn to implement this method effectively, along with other approaches, to develop overall instructional strategies that will enable students to achieve my course objectives?

THE LECTURE

The lecture has been the teaching method used most frequently in U.S. classrooms and in most other countries. Although contemporary educators have criticized the lecture, it has survived because it does have value as a teaching method.

When to Use the Lecture

When deciding whether to use the lecture, keep your students in mind. Are your classes college preparatory, elective, or remedial? If they are composed of students whose potential is limited, the lecture is a poor choice because it requires students to take notes; most students are not good note takers. In fact, under ideal conditions, even college students are able to capture only 52 percent of a lecture's important ideas (Maddox & Hoole, 1975). King (1990) says:

> Researchers have found that when students take notes during a lecture they are far more likely to record bits and pieces of the lecture verbatim or simply paraphrase information rather than organize the lecture material into some sort of conceptual framework or relate the new information to what they already know. (p. 131)

The lecture's success also depends on whether students are self-motivated, because the lecture itself is a poor motivator. So before you decide whether to use the lecture, consider your students' interest level. Many students prefer the lecture because it demands little direct participation and involvement. Less-capable students tend to favor the lecture over other modes of instruction that place more responsibility on them. Teachers should not lecture frequently to groups of low performers.

Weaknesses

Although students may learn well with a well-planned and well-executed lecture, they often say that lectures are boring, do not involve them, are poorly organized, focus on the lowest level of cognition, and do not recognize individual differences. Lectures also make students anxious, more so than other teaching methods. Many teachers use the lecture to show off their own knowledge. Feeding their egos, these teachers tend to be too formal, too authoritative, and too structured. They often stress technical points instead of interpreting or relating information, and they may not be receptive to students' questions. Such domination of students is an example of gross misuse of the lecture.

The lecture, when properly planned and executed, works best for capable, motivated students. The lecture is most appropriate when all students have similar abilities and backgrounds (Rothstein, 1990). But is it best for teaching a certain subject? Is it best for communicating in general? No. In fact, a review of 91 surveys covering four decades of research on comparative teaching methods found no difference between the effectiveness of the lecture and other methods of teaching (Voth, 1975). The lecture is superior only for certain objectives; it is inferior for others. For example, the lecture generally does not stimulate interest, promote creativity, or help students develop responsibility or imagination, nor does it help students synthesize, internalize, or express themselves. Compared with educational games, the lecture is equally as effective for immediate cognitive gain and significantly less effective for retention over three weeks or longer.

Strengths

The lecture does have several unique attributes. It is an extremely effective way to introduce a unit or build a frame of reference. It is also a superior technique for demonstrating models and clarifying matters that may confuse students. A short lecture can effectively introduce and summarize a lesson's major concepts. It allows the teacher to collect related information and assemble it into a meaningful and intellectually manageable framework.

Implementing the Lecture

Why are some lectures good and some bad? Why are some teachers stimulating and others boring? Not all lectures are the same. How do they differ, and how can you make them more interesting and informative?

Most successful lectures are relatively short. Few people can concentrate for a long time, so even the best lecturers should limit their lectures to short periods, occasionally changing to activities that involve students. The next section presents some effective ways to improve the lecture through correct planning and delivery and by combining the lecture with other instructional approaches.

Improving the Lecture

Instructional Objectives.   Much attention has recently been given to instructional objectives. Do they really affect learning? If so, how? Should you introduce them before or after the lesson?

Instructional objectives do affect students' reactions to the lecture. Those introduced at the beginning of the lecture tend to increase intentional learning (i.e., the learning that teaching seeks to stimulate); those used after the lesson affect students' incidental learning. To ensure that students will learn a lesson's most important concepts, always introduce the objectives before the lecture. In this way the objectives become advance organizers, giving learners a basis for new concepts. In addition, many teachers lecture above their students' cognitive level. Such lessons fail. Stefanich (1990, p. 49) says that this practice leads to failure: "In order to be successful teachers, we must be prepared to lower the level of instruction to the point at which the student can become a successful learner."

Tempo.   One important variable in any lecture is the tempo, or pace. When the pace of a lecture is too slow, students become bored; when it is too fast, their inability to keep up with and understand the lesson discourages them. The pall level—a state of physical, program-related fatigue—is reached when students lose interest because the concept is too simple or too difficult or when the steps in its presentation are too short or too long. In both cases, students tend to respond by generating their own discussions. Lectures that move at a moderate pace produce less noise than those that move at a slow or fast pace. Studies show that most studio-recorded presentations are too slow and that students would learn more if the lecturer increased the speed by as much as three times. If the lecture is too fast, however, students feel rushed and begin to reject the speaker.

Stimulus Variation.   Certain actions during a lecture help prevent student boredom, especially among secondary school students. Stimulus variation—such as your moving through the class or gesturing and pausing—correlates positively with student recall of lectures. At the elementary level, however, stimulus variation actually lowers student performance on lecture tests; excessive teacher movement distracts younger students from the lecture content.

With a little imagination and effort, teachers can vary their evaluation activities in much the same way as they vary their other classroom teaching activities (Parsons & Jones, 1990). Varying instructional methods can help teachers reach the underachievers in their classes. O'Neal, Earley, and Snider (1991, p. 122) stress the need for instructional variety: "Research indicates that while many underachieving students have poorer auditory and visual skills, their kinesthetic and tactile capabilities are high. Implications are that teachers may need to use a greater variety of instructional methods."

Structure.   Most lectures can be vastly improved and simplified by (1) organizing the content into only a few (three to five) major concepts, (2) ordering the concepts in a logical or natural sequence, (3) limiting the lecture to 10 or 15 minutes, (4) providing tasks that require all students to use the concepts, and (5) summarizing the major concepts. English teachers often outline the major concepts in a story and put them in a definite sequence; history teachers may use events and dates. Identification and ordering of concepts is equally important in math, science, and social studies.

Titus (1974) presents the following list of steps for preparing a good lecture:

1. Organization is vital.
2. Stick to a limited number of concepts.
3. Limit time.
4. Use humor.
5. Avoid tangents.
6. Watch your language.
7. Listen to yourself.

Vocabulary. Titus' concern for language is especially warranted. Too many lectures are loaded with jargon, technical vocabulary, or other unfamiliar language that confuses students.

Audiovisual Aids. Commonwealth and Gootnick (1974) express the attitude of many educators that visual aids should accompany all lectures. The overhead projector seems to have replaced the chalkboard as the most popular visual aid in today's classroom. The most effective use of either tool occurs when the lesson is not predeveloped but built up in front of the students, who help develop the concepts by working the problems or by responding to the teacher's questions as the lesson develops. In other words, the most effective delivery depends on student participation in developing the ideas set out by the lesson plan.

Histrionics. The high anxiety level that is common among students during lectures can be reduced if the teacher tells jokes. It is interesting to note that students for whom a lecture is appropriate (high-ability, low-anxiety students) also benefit most from humor, whereas their counterparts—the slow, anxious students—retain less from humorous lectures. In some instances, humor does not affect students' immediate cognitive gains, but several weeks later students find that they have retained significantly more concepts from lectures containing humor. Humor also serves those students who are socially isolated from their classmates. It can become a method of reuniting these students with their peers. Barth (1990, p. 515) addresses this potential of humor. He says "humor can be the glue that binds an assorted group of individuals into a community."

Altering the Lecture Method. In addition to improving the lecture itself and its delivery, teachers can greatly improve lectures by combining them with tutorials and student discussions. When tutorials were added to lectures in an eleventh-grade class, the combination increased immediate cognitive gains and retention measured over an 11-week interval (Rowsey & Mason, 1975). The individualizing effect seems to be of special benefit to lower-ability and lower-achievement students, whereas increasing emphasis on recitation and problem solving benefits higher-ability and higher-achieving students. Adding modeling demonstrations to the lecture tends to increase both immediate and long-term learning and also improves student attitudes toward the lesson. Social learning theorists contend that social reinforcers, such as modeling, are critical to the learning process (Eller & Henson, in press).

For lecture blending to be effective with students, they must be exposed to nonlecture teaching styles at early ages. By seventh grade, many students are already conditioned to the lecture method, and alternatives should be used earlier. For students who are accustomed to the straight lecture, combining lectures with student discussion produces little difference in cognitive gain among seventh-graders and may actually damage their attitude toward the lesson. For this reason, teachers should balance their selection of learning methods to improve student achievement and attitude.

Developing Lessons

Although the knowledge base in teacher education is rapidly growing, there is currently no comprehensive theory of education. This means that teaching remains an art. For each situation you face as a teacher, you must make a separate decision. You must call on your knowledge of many areas and descriptions including learning theory, human development, and social theory; on your knowledge of the particular situation and the particular student(s) involved; and even on your understanding of yourself, including your philosophical beliefs and knowledge of your strengths and weaknesses.

That is how you must prepare each lesson. You must use all your knowledge in all these areas. Although there is no sure-fire way to determine the best way to approach any particular lesson or to plan to use each method or strategy, sometimes novice teachers can benefit from a suggested way to plan a lesson. A beginning teacher might ask, "Just show me one way to plan a lesson using each strategy." Therefore, the discussion of each method presented in this chapter is followed by a suggestion of one possible way to plan a lesson using that method.

Developing a Lecture

There are limitless ways to develop a lecture. First you must determine your own philosophy. For example, suppose, like John Locke, Col. Francis Parker, and John Dewey, you believe that learning is the result of experience and that the only way students learn is by tying new information to existing knowledge. And suppose, like these constructivists, you believe that to understand any discipline you must develop the major concepts that hold that discipline together.

Given this constructivist view, a logical place to begin developing a lesson would be to identify a few major concepts the class will learn during one class period. Don't get overzealous. *A few* means six or fewer, maybe only three or four. For each concept, you might develop a transparency. Each transparency might be a visual drawing. To add interest, you might make some or all of the concept transparencies humorous.

Next, build into each lesson one or more student activities. Vary the activities so that some are independent tasks, some pair students together, and some involve small groups (three to five students). If your class periods are an hour or less, do only one or two activities.

Next, reconsider your objectives for this lesson. In addition to wanting students to understand the lesson's major concepts, what else would you want them to learn from this lesson? Do not forget the affective and psychomotor domains. For each additional objective (e.g., attitude or psychomotor skill), develop at least one transparency.

You now have a stack of transparencies. Arrange them in the order that you believe easiest for your students to learn. Next, make a list of these concepts and make a transparency of the list. This list will become the first transparency on the stack. Use it to present an overview at the beginning of the lesson. You may wish to make a second copy to use near the end of the period to review the lesson. You may wish to embellish this lesson by planning questions through out the lesson to focus students' attention and to involve students.

Do not forget that variety itself is motivating and the number of ways a lecture can be developed is limitless. This is just one of many ways to develop a lecture.

THE CASE STUDY METHOD

For several decades the case study method has been popular in schools of business and in law schools. For example, in the Harvard Business School curriculum the case study method has been a prominent feature for over 60 years. "The case method refers to the use of cases as educational vehicles to give students an opportunity to put themselves in the decision making or problem solver's shoes" (Leenders & Ersking, 1978).

Strengths

Case studies involve students in what they are studying (Kowalski, Henson, & Weaver, 1990) through repeated personal analysis, peer discussion, definition of problems, identification of alternatives, statement of objectives and decision criteria, choice of action, and plan for implementation; they also enable students to develop analytical planning skills in a laboratory setting (Leenders & Ersking, 1978).

Because good cases are realistic and because the case study method involves students, it is highly motivating. Because it usually requires group work, the case study method fosters development of good social skills.

Limitations

Success with the case study method depends on the availability of quality cases. Armchair cases (contrived cases) can be as effective as real events, but students must perceive both types as plausible. Good cases must contain an ample amount of pertinent information, but, as in real life, the problem solver never has all the information needed. Good cases must also contain some irrelevant information. (The importance of this will become evident in the following section.) Paget (1988) explains:

> A case report is a description of a factual situation that must be realistic and not obviously contrived or artificial. It must reflect the kind of situation en-

countered naturally in the conduct of the discipline concerned. It must be of practical and immediate importance to have relevance as an illustrative example. (p. 175)

Teachers must understand the case study method's potential and limitations. They must give students the time and guidance needed to explore alternatives and help them to accept the less-than-perfect conditions that always describe real problems.

Methodology

When using the case study method, remember that its purpose is not to enable students to find the one right choice but to enhance their ability to make judicious decisions.

Using Case Studies to Develop Concepts

Case studies can be used to reinforce a lesson's major concepts. Case studies can complement on-site observation and hands-on experience to help students grasp the practical significance of concepts. However, simply understanding concepts is not enough. "Instruction must also focus on the use of the concepts and the context in which they occur in order to ascertain their practice connotations" (Harrison, 1990, p. 503).
Harrison (1990, pp. 503–504) uses 10 steps to teach a concept:

1. Present a concept and give examples.
2. Emphasize the common attributes and ask students to identify further attributes.
3. Ask students to generate examples.
4. Have students give opposite examples or nonexamples.
5. Have students name analogies and metaphors and compare these with the original idea.
6. Have students review contexts in which the concept takes place.
7. Have students describe the overt behavior in identifying the concept.
8. Have students identify environmental factors that facilitate or hinder application of the concept.
9. Help students write an operational definition involving the elements of these last steps.
10. Discuss the consequences or how viable the definition really is.

Developing a Case Study Lesson

From the discussion of ways to develop a lecture, we learned that one strategy to develop any type of lesson is to begin by examining your own philosophy. This enables you to build on your own strengths. Another strategy for developing any type of lesson is to begin by examining the strengths of the case study method. For example, one of the case study's major strengths is its power to motivate. Therefore, you might begin by writing a case that you believe your students will enjoy. Suppose you are a middle-level teacher. You know that this age group has a vivid imagination. When you studied poisonous snakes, several students became excited and offered stories that their parents, grandparents, or older siblings told them. You watched their eyes (and a few of their mouths) open wide as they embellished the tales they told. You will want to use this knowledge about your students in developing your case. Be sure to include some information that especially interests this age group.

Next, you also know that a good case study includes irrelevant information that students must sift through (Kowalski, Weaver, & Henson, 1994). So include such information; load your case with high-interest but irrelevant information.

Consider recording your case. A simple audio recording can add interest to the lesson and can enable you to monitor student reactions and learn what type of stimuli work best for your age group. Adding different sound effects can make the lesson more interesting. If you do not have time to develop a recording you can also use a written copy of the case.

The case study method invites creativity. Plan your lesson so that students can use their imagination. Give them opportunities to explore their own ideas by asking questions that have no "correct" answers. For example, "What would have happened if. . . ."

Summarize the lesson by listing the major problem(s) in the case, the major issues in the case, and the major conclusions. List these items on the chalkboard or on an overhead transparency so that all students can see them and become involved in developing the summary.

An alternative method for using the case study is to have students role play the characters in the case and follow my discussion questions. You may also want students to write their own cases to present to the class.

TUTORING

The act of tutoring dates back many centuries. In England it has been a major, if not the major, teaching strategy for many years. It derives its strength from being a one-on-one process that gives the student personal, individual attention. The student receiving the help (the tutee) receives immediate feedback and has continuous opportunity to ask questions.

But tutoring has limitations. It requires much time from the tutor, and because most teachers cannot give so much time to each student, students are often used as tutors. Students selected to tutor other students are usually the brightest and highest achievers in their classes. Some say these high-achieving students are giving up time they could spend pursuing their own learning. Others say that having high-achieving students tutor lower-achieving students lowers the self-esteem of the latter and makes the former arrogant.

After many years of experience directing the tutoring program at the University of Wisconsin in Madison, Klausmeier (1980) concluded that tutoring probably does little psychological damage to the tutors because they tutor for unselfish reasons. They want to help others, and tutoring makes them feel needed. Klausmeier suggests that to be fair to the students, tutors should be volunteers who can stop whenever they wish.

Ross MacDonald (1991) states that:

> Tutoring has four primary benefits. First, one-on-one instruction motivates students by demonstrating a personal interest in their learning. A teacher who expresses interest in a child will be rewarded by a student more interested in the subject matter and more attentive to what the teacher has to say. Second, tutoring is an effective intervention for a student struggling with a particular lesson, especially if it is begun before a student falls dangerously behind. Third, tutoring provides an effective means to fill gaps in students' knowledge. . . . Finally, our nation's agenda for social change can be advanced by one-on-one instruction. A disproportionate number of students who fall behind are minorities. Extra efforts, such as tutoring, are sometimes necessary to prevent past educational inequities from being continued in current classrooms. Of particular importance to any instruction is a teacher's sensitivity to cultural differences between the expectations of students and their home environments and the expectations of the teacher and the school environment (p. 25).

Combining Tutoring and Grouping

Research has focused on how tutoring affects student achievement. Studies have reported varying results. Tutoring alone does not always increase learning, so some educators have begun combining tutoring with other teaching strategies. Of notable repute is the work of Benjamin Bloom at the University of Chicago. According to Bloom (1984, p. 6) the most striking finding was that with tutoring, the best possible learning condition, "the average student is two stigmas above the average control student taught under conventional group methods of instruction." This is powerful testimony for tutoring. First, it says that one-on-one tutoring is the very best learning condition we can devise. Second, it says that, on average, students who are tutored outscore their counterparts by two stigmas, or two standard deviations. Another way to express this is to say that the average tutored student outperformed 98 percent of the students in the control class. Bloom (1984, p. 17) offers the following suggestions for all schools and teachers:

1. Improve how students process information by using the mastery learning feedback-corrective process or enhance the initial cognitive prerequisites for sequential courses.
2. Improve the tools of instruction by selecting a curriculum, textbook, or other instructional material that has proved effective.
3. Improve parental involvement in student learning by beginning a dialogue between the school and the home.
4. Improve instruction by providing favorable classroom conditions for all students and by emphasizing better learning skills for all students.

As you study instructional strategies and ways to individualize instruction, identify techniques that you can combine with tutoring to make tutoring more effective in your classroom.

Developing a Tutoring Lesson

Since tutoring does not always guarantee increased learning, design lessons that use tutoring to achieve multiple benefits. For example, tutoring can help at-risk students fill in educational gaps. One approach to developing tutoring lessons is to identify gaps that otherwise might go unnoticed. You might assign all students to write a brief essay, using the topic the next unit will cover. While tutors are tutoring, you can focus on those students who need the most help. Using their essay as a guide, you can clarify misunderstandings and fill in gaps. This approach also allows you to give students your individual attention.

Make sure the directions for writing the essay tell students to focus on the major concepts you want them to understand. In a multicultural class, include objectives to help students to learn to work harmoniously with members of other cultures.

Reflection

Read the following statement and respond to the questions below.

Another Bandwagon

Tutoring is not new. In fact, it's the most primitive type of education, even predating civilization. Today's educators seem to get excited over every bandwagon that comes along. Some of the bandwagons simply don't produce music worth the price of the players, and tutoring is an excellent example. The students who tutor don't need the ego trip they get from being the leader. The tutees already know that they are below-average students—they don't need the additional humiliation. Bright students should not waste their time helping slower students. Instead, the program should be challenging the bright students to achieve even higher goals, but in tutoring they give valuable learning time to do the teacher's job. And if this isn't enough, not all studies agree that the tutee achieves more with tutoring.

1. Do you think that tutees experience lower self-esteem? What evidence can you give to support your answer?
2. Do you think that receiving tutorial help exposes a student's performance level, or do students already know their peers' general achievement level? When you were in secondary or middle school, did you know your peers' performance level? Has this changed in recent years?

INQUIRY LEARNING

Inquiry learning, a familiar and popular concept in education today, is student-centered instruction. The student's role is to question, explore, and discover. The teacher's role is to question and guide students toward understanding; therefore, inquiry learning is often called *guided discovery learning.*

At all levels and in all subjects, inquiry learning is recognized as a viable teaching strategy. Despite its popularity and prestige, however, confusion exists over exactly what inquiry learning is. When we consider that inquiry is itself a most complicated style of learning, this comes as no surprise. Furthermore, inquiry is closely related to other similar learning approaches that are often confused with it.

Basic to the complexity of inquiry learning is its paradoxical nature. Inquiry learning is concerned with solving problems, but it does not require solutions. It involves a flexible yet systematic approach to solutions—systematic in that a set of activities is used, yet highly flexible in that the sequence of the activities, and other activities, can be changed or substituted at any time. The success derived from inquiry learning does not necessarily depend on solving the problems at hand. In fact, identifying and defining problems may be as important as solving problems. Eller and Henson (in press) explain: "Problem finding is important in scientific discovery." Einstein and Infeld (1938) comment:

> Galileo formulated the problem of determining the velocity of light, but he did not solve it. The formulation of a problem is often more essential than its solution, which may be merely a matter of mathematical or experimental skill. To raise new questions, new possibilities, to regard old problems from new angles, requires creative imagination and marks real advance in science. (Eller & Henson, in press)

A special panel for the National Center for Education Statistics (Special Study Panel on Education Indicators to the Acting Commissioner of Education Statistics, 1991) says that students need the ability to integrate information from all disciplines and use integrative reasoning to solve problems:

> Integrative reasoning is essential in modern life and today's workplace. It represents not the ability to recall bits and pieces of information but the "things" one can demonstrate one can do. These include communication, using technology and information effectively, and proficiency in working in a problem-solving capacity either alone or in teams. (p. 65)

Advantages

Inquiry learning involves all those who participate in the process. This is by no means unique to inquiry learning, because many other teaching-learning styles (such as simulation gaming, individualized instruction, discovery learning, and problem solving) offer participants an equal amount of involvement. But inquiry offers involvement that is more meaningful. It is characterized by early and continuous involvement. In true inquiry learning, the student must be involved from the very beginning, even in setting up the problems.

Another major advantage of inquiry learning is its flexibility. In attempting to understand their environment, people have fallen into a trap of trying to systematize everything within human awareness. For example, for years U.S. schools required students to learn a certain set of behaviors and were led to believe that this was the "method" scientists used to discover, invent, and find solutions to all problems. Yet studies failed to show that any specific pattern of thought exists to any reliable degree in problem solving. Inquiry is somewhat systematic, without being as rigid as the "scientific method." Instead of just answering questions, students are also involved in asking questions. Instead of just verifying the truth, students are actually seeking the truth.

The absence of a single, predetermined correct answer in inquiry learning is another advantage, because it frees the investigator to explore diverse, multiple possibilities and because it frees the psyche from fear of failing to achieve what is expected. On the contrary, inquiry learners are motivated positively and by the strongest type of motivation—internal motivation. They learn to work for the joy of learning. Involvement in inquiry learning improves students' attitudes toward the subject and, more important, toward school in general. Students in inquiry learning often become so aroused that they return to class on other days eager to continue pursuing the concepts.

The nature of inquiry enhances the development of creative potential. True inquiry learning provides freedom and encouragement in using the imagination, and the learner is responsible for determining what information to gather and then determining how important it is. These are essential conditions for creative thinking.

The teacher-student relationship in inquiry classes must remain positive. Although you must give students the freedom to develop their own hypotheses or hunches, your role is nevertheless important. In fact, no learner can develop critical thoughts alone, but students can be taught in a way that develops critical and inquiry-oriented thinking. An interesting thing happens to the total perspective and behavior pattern of teachers who use the inquiry approach in their classes: They become student-oriented rather than subject-oriented. Students also become more cooperative, whereas students in textbook-oriented classes tend to be more competitive.

For those who are concerned primarily with cognitive gains, note that the relative retention rate of inquiry learning (as opposed to lecture, for example) is extremely high. The highly personal experience involved in inquiry adds meaning to the learning. As Abraham Maslow (1973) explains, true learning is very personal; the most valuable learning always involves our emotions.

Disadvantages

Like all other teaching strategies, inquiry learning has its share of disadvantages. First, it is a slow process for exposing students to material. Teachers who feel obligated to cover certain amounts of content (e.g., to get through a textbook) may find the process inefficient for their goal. A more critical disadvantage of inquiry learning is that it requires teachers to have a unique type of expertise that most cannot acquire without special training. Today's teachers need more training in inquiry activity.

The Teacher's Role

Because inquiry learning is a flexible process, you may want to set the stage in different ways. Taxey (1975) suggests using heterogeneous subgroups within a classroom to capitalize on unique personalities, interests, and skills so that each student can contribute to the task at hand. In inquiry learning lessons, your major role is that of a catalyst. You must give students the freedom to investigate in their own ways. Students must be allowed to develop their own ideas and to discover ways to explain what they observe. The questions and problems they form are theirs, not yours. You passively provide direction by selecting objects, activities, events, problems, or questions. You can provide much closer direction by giving cues and supportive feedback. Don't be tempted to give information before it is necessary, and avoid making nonverbal communications, such as grimacing.

The student of inquiry should not have to worry about pleasing the teacher. In fact, learners must not be dominated by others. The most impressive precondition for inquiry undoubtedly is the learner's autonomy. Encourage students to form hypotheses and test them on their own initiative. Also encourage students to recognize that a problem can have many aspects and solutions. Students who participate in inquiry must not be afraid to make mistakes. You must encourage each student to make bold conjectures and then to test them. Students should pursue any hypothesis that seems at all probable.

Participants in inquiry learning are self-motivated. They must learn to work for the joy of learning, even in the absence of feedback—which students in traditional classes get from test scores and grades. Inquiry is a cooperative process, not a competitive one. Even the teacher who becomes involved with inquiry soon becomes student-oriented rather than subject-oriented. Students' independence and separate responsibility, coupled with the opportunity to pursue learning for the joy of it, produce a high level of motivation. For this reason, inquiry learning's retention rate is superior to most other teaching strategies and offsets its disadvantage of being slow in content coverage.

Effective inquiry learning does, however, require certain special skills that some teachers simply do not have. You must be able to match personalities, interests, and skills to get the most out of each student. Perhaps most of all, you must learn to give students enough freedom to investigate in their own ways. Do not give information before it is necessary. The student of inquiry must treasure diversity, and the teacher must be able to encourage and reinforce students who take risks, make bold conjectures, and then explore a variety of aspects and solutions.

Developing Inquiry Lessons

Inquiry lessons are one of the most exciting types of lessons to plan because of the suspense that inquiry always involves. Examine the photo that opens this chapter. This teacher is holding up a hornet's nest. Hornets are intriguing because most students have never seen a hornet, yet most have heard of their powerful stings. A nest this size would contain hundreds of deadly hornets.

Hornets are also highly social animals. Like ants, they are highly organized. Further, they have a unique system for determining their direction. Most adults who encounter hornets during their childhood harbor feelings of excitement over their youthful encounters with hornets.

So, when a teacher holds up a dried-out, empty hornets' nest it may mean little to the unaware student. However, by providing just enough information to whet their imagination a teacher can stimulate a line of inquiry. A good prelude to such a lesson would be to assign students to ask their parents, grandparents, or any senior citizen for stories about the topic of study.

Like any type of lesson, successful inquiry requires some purposeful objectives. Your role is to intervene only enough to guide students to discover the concepts that you expect them to gain from the lesson.

QUESTIONING

Chapter 6 examines in depth the role that questioning plays in communications. Here we will look at questioning in a much broader context, that is, at the many ways teachers can use questions in various phases of their teaching methods.

When we think of using questions to teach, Socrates usually comes to mind. One of the greatest teachers of all time, Socrates used a variety of instructional techniques. A master of the art of questioning, he used questions to lead his students down a treacherous path of contradictions. Tricky? Of course. But his students respected and admired him. Socrates knew the importance of self-analysis and of discovering one's own errors.

The Socratic method—that is, teaching by asking questions and thus leading the audience into a logical contradiction—is one style of questioning. Many other questioning strategies are in use today. As a teaching style, questioning is second in popularity and in common use only to lecturing, but the technique of questioning is grossly misused. It is helpful to identify several valid uses of questioning and several ways that teachers can improve their questioning skills.

How Teachers Should Use Questions

Although the textbook is the major curriculum determiner in most classes, most textbooks do not stimulate advanced levels of thinking. The Wisconsin School Improvement Program found that 90 percent of all textbooks are written at the knowledge (recall and memory) level. Therefore, if students' thinking is to climb to higher cognitive levels, you must find other ways to stimulate it. Studies that use interaction analysis show that most teachers never achieve this goal and that most thinking in the classroom remains at the recall level (Chaudhari, 1975). Of course, some knowledge-level questions can be desirable, as long as they are complemented with higher-level questions. Teachers who ask more higher-order questions have students who achieve considerably more (Redfield & Rousseau, 1981). Chaudhari (1975) suggests the following three-step model:

Phase 1: Encourage students to ask questions.

Phase 2: Emphasize questions requiring convergent thinking (application and analysis).

Phase 3: Emphasize questions requiring divergent thinking (synthesis and evaluation).

Miller and Vinocur (1973) provide the following suggestions for moving up to higher levels of thinking. Miller suggests that the teacher move from such recall level words as state, name, identify, list, describe, relate, tell, call, give, and locate to such evaluation-producing words as judge, compare, analyze, contrast, measure, appraise, estimate, and differentiate, and then move on to creative and stimulating words such as make, design, create, construct, speculate, invent, devise, predict, and hypothesize.

Teachers can use students' names to increase students' response; teachers should pause after each question to give students time to think about it. Studies by Santieslebau (1976) and Rowe (1974) show that there are a number of advantages to waiting at least three seconds after each question is asked. Sund (1971, p.) lists 12:

1. The length of students' responses increases.
2. The number of unsolicited but appropriate responses increases.
3. Failure to respond decreases.
4. Students' confidence increases.
5. The incidence of speculative creative thinking increases.
6. Teacher-centered teaching decreases.
7. Pupils give more evidence before and after inference statements.
8. The number of questions pupils ask increases.
9. The number of activities students propose increases.
10. Slow students contribute more.
11. The variety of types of responses increases.
12. Students react more to each other.

Santieslebau (1976) found that as wait time increased to at least three seconds the confidence of the slow students increased, speculative thinking increased, the number of experiments by students increased, and observation and classification skills improved. The price for these advantages appears to be cheap. Just by pausing and doing nothing, the teacher can stimulate these results. However, a study by Rowe (1974) found that the average wait time in the public school classroom is only one second.

Another common mistake teachers make is to overuse questions. Teachers begin many lessons with a series of cognitive questions, but research shows that it is far more effective to wait until a knowledge base has been established before initiating questioning. For example, a short lecture is far more efficient for building this necessary framework. Furthermore, too many questions turn students' attention from one subject to another (Santieslebau, 1976).

Classroom questions that seek cognitive feedback often lack specificity. For example, the question "What was the cause of the Civil War?" is impossible to answer. In posing such a question just to create an entry into the lesson, the teacher rejects some correct responses—and there are many for that question—in hopes that a student will finally guess the particular desired response. The session proceeds as follows:

Q: What was the cause of the Civil War?

A: Slavery.

Q: Okay, but that's not what I'm looking for.

A: Economics? [*This time the student is less certain.*]

Q: What about economics? [*Another broad question.*]

A: The North's economics.

Q: What about it?

A: It was different from the South's.

Q: But what about the North's economy? [*etc., etc.*]

In addition to increasing the lesson's efficiency and preventing student embarrassment, the teacher's specificity will enhance student recall of related material. Shiman and Mash (1974) suggest that instead of using a series of fact-seeking questions, teachers should move back and forth among the factual, conceptual, and contextual modes. Factual questions elicit only recall level information; conceptual questions probe, analyze, compare, and generalize; and contextual questions promote judgment. To help increase the number and quality of responses to each question in these categories, teachers should tape or write their questions, testing themselves for the answers. This will remove much ambiguity and generate more specific and precise questions.

Some experts believe that students are becoming less curious and less inquisitive—less eager to ask questions. Describing this as a decay of students' minds, Sutton (1977) suggests that teachers work together to reverse this trend. Far too often a student attempts to answer a question only to hear the response "Yes, but" or a murmured "Uh-huh" as the teacher looks quickly to another student for the "correct" answer. To improve students' attitude toward answering questions, the teacher should help the faltering student with an "Oh, that's interesting. I hadn't thought of it that way" or "Oh, yes, I see what you mean" or "Are you saying . . . ?" Further reinforcement can be provided by returning later to quote the student. For example, "John, what you're saying now seems to agree (or disagree) with Debbie's earlier comment that. . . ." This tells John, Debbie, and everyone else in the class that you do listen to other people's comments.

This does not suggest that all teacher questions should seek to provoke student responses. Rhetorical questions increase motivation and enhance learning and recall of facts among audiences with low motivation. Yet teachers must resist the temptation to answer all their questions and should let students know, by calling on students by name, when they expect an answer.

Questions can also be used effectively before and after a lesson. Bull and Dizney (1973) found that asking questions before a reading assignment can stimulate students to remember relevant information. In a similar study, Sanders (1973) found that students questioned after they read a paragraph retained both relevant and irrelevant material, while students questioned before reading showed increased retention of relevant material only. Teachers can apply this knowledge about questioning to reading assignments, field trips, laboratory exercises, and such audiovisual materials as the tape recorder, filmstrips, and films. Students also must learn to ask productive questions.

Reciprocal Peer-Questioning

King (1990) presents another questioning strategy, which she recommends using to enrich the lecture:

> Reciprocal peer-questioning is a strategy that can be used with any lecture regardless of subject matter and is appropriate for fourth grade to university students. With this strategy, a form of guided group questioning in conjunction with classroom lecture is used. Students are given a set of generic questions and trained to use those questions as a guide for generating their own specific questions on the lecture content. During the self-questioning step of the procedure, students usually make up two or three thought-provoking questions. Those questions may or may not be ones that they themselves are able to answer. Following the self-questioning, they engage in peer-questioning. Working in groups of three or four, students pose their questions to their group and then take turns answering each other's questions. . . . Students who were trained to use this strategy demonstrated lecture comprehension superior to students who used other comprehension strategies, such as group discussion or independent review. (p. 131)

Irving Sigel found that children's ability to move from the concrete to symbolic level requires distancing themselves from the present (Ellsworth & Sindt, 1994). Combining higher-order questions with drawing can help students make this necessary time transit (Phillips, Phillips, Melton, & Moore, 1994). Ramsey, Gabbard, Clawson, Lee, and Henson (1990) give the following guidelines to help teachers improve their use of questions:

1. Ask knowledge-level questions when assessing students' ability to recall, recognize, or repeat information as it was learned.
2. When assessing students' higher-level thinking, use terms such as how, why, and what if to encourage deeper thought.
3. Prepare questions in advance.
4. Ask questions in a logical sequence.
5. Ask specific questions that students can answer silently.
6. As direct questions are asked, sprinkle the questioning with direct statements.
7. Request that students repeat the teacher's question before answering.
8. When a specific student is asked a question, have another student repeat the question before allowing a response.
9. Allow students to converse with each other in a directed manner after a question is asked or answered.

10. Request that students express their own questions fully and specifically.
11. Name specific students in a random order to respond to questions.
12. Provide adequate waiting time after naming a respondent. Rowe (1974, pp. 421–422) found that waiting approximately three to five seconds after naming a respondent before eliciting a response brought better responses from more students.

Building Lessons around Questions

Perhaps the most common mistake teachers make when building a lesson around questions is starting the lesson with questions and continuing throughout the period with questions. A far better approach is to introduce some information to build a common knowledge base. Discussions can then draw on this well of knowledge, thus preventing a mere sharing of ignorance.

As with other methods, a lesson built on questions will likely be no more productive than the degree to which a teacher sets specific objectives and plans. So, as with other types of lessons, preface a lesson built on questions with a few clearly stated objectives.

The Socratic method is one of many effective strategies that use questions. Since it requires special skills and charisma, it is not the best type of lesson for a novice teacher. A better approach would be to (1) write a few objectives (perhaps between three and six), (2) give the class a few basic concepts (by a short reading assignment, a short audio or video recording, or a short written assignment), (3) write a few questions for each group to answer, (4) have each group report its response to the group, and (5) summarize the lesson.

DISCOVERY LEARNING

What is discovery learning? Chances are you have some understanding of, and faith in, the discovery process. Most contemporary students have experienced this approach. The following paragraphs define discovery learning, list its advantages and disadvantages, and provide suggestions for teachers who want to try discovery learning for the first time or improve their skills with planning and implementing discovery learning.

Definition

Most of the literature on discovery learning does not define it; this leaves the reader feeling embarrassed about not knowing exactly what it is and probably ashamed to ask. Discovery learning is not easy to define. There is no single clear-cut definition, just as there is no single process of discovery learning; in fact, there are many. Each experience is unique, ranging from guided to open discovery. Furthermore, each type of discovery has its own advantages, and the management of each is unique. Weimer (1975) lists six types of discovery learning: (1) discovery, (2) discovery teaching, (3) inductive discovery, (4) semiinductive discovery, (5) unguided or pure discovery, and

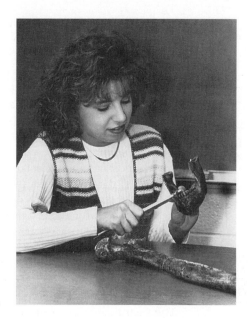

Discovery learning is a strong motivator.

(6) guided discovery. Notice that these six types are actually degrees in which discovery is controlled.

The term *discovery learning* is frequently but erroneously used interchangeably with two other terms: *inquiry* and *problem solving.* Actually, each of these other terms is, or can refer to, a specific type of discovery learning. The educational process called inquiry is more accurately defined as guided discovery—that is, during an inquiry lesson the teacher carefully guides the student(s) toward a specific discovery or generalization. Discovery learning and problem solving are synonymous when a solution to the problem is discovered. In other words, by definition, problem solving must involve the solving of problems. A good working definition of discovery learning is intentional learning through problem solving and under teacher supervision. In other words, individuals can sometimes solve problems without any leadership, guidance, or supervision: they can also make discoveries quite accidentally. Neither of these activities is discovery learning, which must be intentional and supervised. At one extreme, it may be carefully guided (inquiry learning); at the other extreme, it is very casually supervised (free discovery). In fact, your main function may be to supply a stimulus, or it may be to organize or arrange tasks (or problems) to make the result obvious. In inquiry learning, the students themselves are involved in setting up the problem as well as in seeking its solution.

Advantages

Discovery learning has advantages other instructional approaches share. For example, the high degree of student involvement is a strong motivator for most students, especially students who find it difficult to remain quiet and passive. Discovery learning appears to be appropriate for almost all students. Only about one-third of today's college students are able to reason in an abstract, logical way. An even smaller percentage of secondary and middle school students is able to profit from abstracting. Can most students benefit from discovery learning? Yes. The Contemporary Cambridge Conference states that anyone can take part in and create experiences in generalizing, testing conjectures, discarding or modifying false hypotheses, and forming rules or theorems. A study involving junior-high math students (Vance, 1974) found the discovery approach to be a superior motivator in traditional math classes and inferior only to an experimental laboratory setting.

When students are more motivated, they learn and retain knowledge more effectively. However, discovery learning has another advantage. The correlation between a student's knowledge and later success in life is constantly diminishing. Far more important are one's understanding of broad concepts and principles and one's ability to get along with other people. In fact, the Manpower Development Act of 1960 found that as early as 1960 fewer than 15 percent of all jobs lost in the United States were lost from inability to perform adequately and that more than 85 percent were lost from inability to get along with supervisors and coworkers. When discovery learning involves group work, the socialization is itself a worthy goal.

The discovery process is superior to lecture-type lessons because it offers students an opportunity to focus on major concepts and principles and to develop positive social skills. Discovery learning is a cooperative process. Vance (1974) found no significant difference in the ability of junior-high math students in discovery, laboratory, and traditional lessons to score on an examination administered just after learning. However, students in the discovery classes scored highest on a special examination designed to measure high-level thinking and problem solving. Another test designed to measure divergent thinking showed that the students in the discovery classes could better relate the new set of materials to their study of mathematics. Students also preferred a learning style that permitted them to work at their own rate and without a teacher always telling them what to do.

Disadvantages

It may be difficult to believe that a learning system with so many advantages also has inherent disadvantages, but it does. First, unlike the lecture (which requires little more of students than their attention and an ability to take notes), the discovery method demands more of students and teachers. Probably its greatest demand is that both teacher and students understand and adjust to the nature of discovery. At the beginning, teachers and students are uncomfortable because the discovery approach has no constant feedback to show them how well they are progressing. The lack of competition in discovery learning also upsets students. Discovery learning is ideally a cooperative process, not a competitive one. The competition is between the student and the task.

At its best, discovery learning is an inefficient system because it is not a good way to cover large amounts of material. Students and teachers are usually highly concerned about completing the amount of material they are expected to cover in a particular course. College preparatory classes are especially concerned with this limitation of the discovery learning approach.

Reflection

Football quarterback Jay Barker is known by football audiences as the quarterback who has no special talent; he is said *not* to be a strong runner and he is said *not* to have a good throwing arm. But anyone who knows anything about him will tell you that he does one thing consistently well. That one thing is win. As a University of Alabama college quarterback, this athlete held the enviable record of 35 wins, 2 losses, and 1 tie. How can this incongruence be explained? To be candid, not very well. But failure to explain the phenomenon that surrounds such a leader does not negate its existence.

On closer observation, Jay Barker has three strengths: an unwavering awareness at all times of what is happening on the playing field, an excellent sense of timing, and a coolness under pressure.

1. What similarities can you see between the roles of a quarterback and a teacher?
2. Each classroom seems to have its own character. How does this character affect the teacher's role?

Methodology

As with any instructional approach, the degree to which discovery learning is successful is determined by the teacher's ability to plan and execute effectively, that is, manage and supervise the lesson. Sickling (1975) has suggested that the teacher's task is to organize or arrange tasks (or problems). Rebrova and Svetlova (1976) explain the problem situation as a dilemma, deliberately created by the teacher, which forces students to think, analyze, draw conclusions, and make generalizations. In other words, the teacher's role is to provide a situation that allows students to see a contradiction between what they already know and newly discovered knowledge. Sobel (1975) suggests the following guidelines:

1. Make use of contemporary materials (e.g., daily newspaper, comic strips).
2. Use topics from the history (of the subject).
3. Introduce applications (of the subject).
4. Provide opportunity for guessing.
5. Provide for laboratory experiences.
6. Introduce new topics with innovative teaching strategy.
7. Make frequent use of visual aids.
8. Set the stage for student discovery.
9. Use motivation.
10. Teach with enthusiasm.

Two suggestions can help the teacher in discovery learning. First, the teacher and the textbooks must use unambiguous terms. Second, the student must be allowed to discover generalizations. This suggests that teachers should learn to put more trust in their students and to refrain from interfering with students' work. The many interdisciplinary programs of the 1960s and 1970s stimulated by the Woods Hole Conference (1959) were based on generalizations, and the more recent study reported by Goodlad (1984) in *A Place Called School* reiterated the important role that principles and generalizations play in learning.

Overview

Like all teaching-learning approaches, the discovery method has advantages and disadvantages. Although discovery learning and traditional lessons both enable students to learn, discovery learning is better at motivating students toward learning broad concepts and principles and developing social skills. Its main disadvantages are that it is not a good way to cover large amounts of material and that it fails to provide constant feedback. Discovery learning is most effective when students are involved in planning the lesson and making their own discoveries, conclusions, and generalizations and when teachers combine it with visual aids and contemporary, easy-to-read materials.

SIMULATION GAMES

Games have always played a significant role in children's learning; children are quick to mimic adults and to invent games that allow them to assume adultlike roles. The records credit a nineteenth-century schoolteacher, Maria Montessori, with being the first person to realize the potential of games for purposeful use in the school curriculum. By watching children play, Montessori learned to devise games based on children's natural behavior. Such natural curricula reflected the philosophy of John Locke, Jean Jacques Rousseau, and John Dewey, who believed that children should be actively involved in the curriculum. Today, simulations and games are used extensively in industry and in schools to train and educate. A simulation is a technique that teaches some aspect of the world or environment by imitation or replication (Alessi & Trollip, 1991).

The use of games in schools is actually world-wide. For example, more than one-third of all schools in England and Wales now include games in their syllabi. The most popular type of game used in educational settings is the simulation game, which allows players to experience a variety of roles that are common in life. By definition, a simulation game must imitate some reality and give players the opportunity to compete in a real-life role, yet the emphasis on competition must be kept in perspective. Winning is not the major object of a simulation game. On the contrary, because games offer great socializing potential, use them to help students learn to empathize with others. Every player should have a chance to win. Above all, the game should be fun. Games using machines tend to become dehumanizing and require special effort by the teacher to counterbalance this with a high level of personal contact with students.

But this does not imply that games are effective only for developing social skills.

On the contrary, a good simulation-type game can provide a sound and interesting learning experience. Simulation games can:

1. Actively involve students.
2. Create a high degree of interest and enthusiasm.
3. Make abstract concepts meaningful for students.
4. Provide immediate feedback to students.
5. Allow students to experiment with concepts and new skills without feeling they must be correct at all times.
6. Give students the opportunity to evaluate their mistakes.
7. Allow students to practice communication skills.

Basic to the learning potential for any strategy is motivation. When using a simulation game based on the stock market, Watman (1973) found that by having students work together in small groups and allowing them to discover strategies for playing the game, low achievers and students with discipline problems became more motivated. Shy students became involved, and all students considered the activity relevant. As for academic achievement, students quickly mastered the new math concepts, and their work became neater and more accurate.

Simulation games offer special opportunities to learners. Hostrop (1972) found that American history students who used a simulation on the impeachment proceedings of Andrew Johnson learned far more effectively than had they listened to a lecture. Simulation games enable students to interact at their own level and learn how to compete and cooperate with others. But exactly how effective are games compared with more traditional modes of instruction? Wylie (1974) reports on a study in which a simulation game is compared with a programmed text in social studies. After the material was introduced by these two methods, a test showed no significant difference between learning in the two groups. Two weeks later, however, the same two groups retook the test, and students who played the game outscored the control group. Simulation gaming is apparently equal to traditional methods in producing learning and superior in producing retention. Lucas, Postma, and Thompson (1975) found that, compared with the lecture, simulation games used to teach mathematics had similar learning and retention results for up to five weeks, but after 10 weeks students using the simulation had a significantly higher retention rate. Kelly (1970) says that games are especially effective for use with slow learners. Learning itself can be increased during simulations when students work in small groups, when they are permitted to evaluate their own mistakes, and when the vocabulary level is kept simple.

But the question "Is simulation gaming more effective than a textbook?" may not be an appropriate question, because simulation games can be used to supplement the text. Simulations can make the abstract material in a textbook more real and vivid. Taylor (1976) lists the advantages of developing your own simulation:

1. You are able to pick the precise subject matter.
2. You know best your students' ability level.

3. Time constraints are not a problem.

4. You can change or alter the game if necessary.

Implementing Simulations

Of course, any simulation's success depends on its design and implementation. To help teachers design their own simulation games, Taylor (1976) gives the following suggestions:

1. Identify your objectives.

2. Decide on a problem or simulation.

3. Define the simulation's scope.

4. Construct the rules.

5. Identify the participants' goals.

6. Write rules and teacher instructions.

7. Design any additional parts.

8. Develop a debriefing.

When designing simulation games, consider how to teach the simulation and your students' ability. Simulation games are valid only if they teach the desired ideas, values, and facts. The best game development involves students. Students who help develop a game are more involved in playing the game and have a more positive attitude.

How you use the simulation also determines its success. In fact, many teachers shun simulations because they are afraid they might not work. Heyman (1976) gives four rules for directing a simulation game:

1. Say no more than the few words necessary.

2. Run the simulation, not the students.

3. Run the game; do not teach.

4. Do not tell students how to behave.

Good classroom management and rapport with students are necessary for good gaming. Anyone adapting a game for classroom use should keep the rules simple, keep the game shorter than one class period, and attain a balance of risk, chance, skill, and knowledge in determining victory.

When correctly designed and implemented, simulation games are an effective mode of instruction. Games enable students to develop generalizations, which take students to higher levels of the educational taxonomy. Parsons and Jones (1990, p. 18) testify to this advantage: "Games in the classroom lend themselves easily to learning facts, generalizations, and concepts."

In addition to being a sound method for learning, simulation gaming is a good motivator and therefore can increase retention. Games can also promote development of social skills. Some of the best simulation games were designed by teachers who themselves can select, relate, and adjust the game to their own students. When using a simulation game, be sure all students will enjoy it and resist the temptation to interfere with the students. Appendix D is a directory of sources.

Developing a Simulation/Gaming Lesson

Simulations and games are among the most enjoyable lessons to develop. By joining the two and forming a simulation (or lifelike) game you can give your lesson a sense of realism and a sense of competition.

A simple yet remarkably stimulating simulation game—baseball—is appropriate for all levels of middle and high school. If you understand the real game of baseball, designing such a lesson is quite simple: Identify the concepts that you wish your students to understand. Then write questions to help students learn these concepts. Next, assign a value to each question ranging from one to four points depending on the level of complexity of each question. You will need at least 2 or 3 dozen questions. Write each on a strip of paper, fold the strips, and put them in a hat or box.

Next, divide the class in half, assigning the most capable students equally between the two teams. Let each team choose a captain. Start by flipping a coin to see which team bats first. Give each team an alphabetized list of its members. This list determines the batting order. Let the person at the top of the list on the team that wins the toss pick a question. Unfold the question and announce whether the ball will be a single, double, triple, or homerun (4-point question). Read the question or ask the captain of the opposing team to read it. The batter gets to continue until he or she misses a question. One missed question constitutes an out. Scores are kept, and when a team misses a total of three questions, it must retire to the field and let the opposing team bat. The game should continue until all questions are asked. Should time run out, the team captains should note who is up to bat when the next lesson resumes, how many outs there are, and the running score. Be sure to let the students resume the game during the first available period. If you do not understand the scoring of baseball, you may choose to develop a game based on a television quiz show.

COOPERATIVE LEARNING

Throughout the history of our schools, teachers have permitted students to work together in groups. By the turn of the twentieth century, Col. Francis Parker had introduced student-centered curricula in the Quincy, Massachusetts, school system (Campbell, 1967). Indiana (The Gary Plan) and Illinois (The Winnetka Plan) had begun experimenting with student-centered programs. By the mid 1920s the Progressive Education Era was underway with John Dewey proclaiming that "learning is doing." By mid-century, an Illinois superintendent, Lloyd Trump, introduced the Trump Plan, which designated 20 percent of students' time to be spent in working in small groups and 40 percent to be spent in large groups.

Twentieth-century American education is characterized by student activities, and these activities have often been pursued by students working together. By the layperson's definition students working together to pursue assignments is a type of cooperative learning. But the cooperative learning emphasized today is distinctly different than this loose definition. The following discussion focuses on this more modern view of cooperative learning.

Cooperative learning involves two or more students working toward a common goal. Distinct goals are set for the group to reach. All students in the group help attain their group goal(s). Because students differ in their abilities, differentiated assignments may be required to allow all students to contribute to attaining the group goal. Unlike the groupwork used in student-centered curricula during the first half of the century, today's cooperative learning programs require all group members to succeed. Performance is based on total group success, because it prompts all group members to help their fellow group members and because the group's success depends on all its members' success.

Team performance in contemporary cooperative learning programs is generally evaluated differently than in the past. Then, the success of any group was determined by how well that team competed with other teams. Today, team success is often determined by comparing the team's performance with earlier performance of the team (Slavin, 1995). Today, cooperative learning groups compete with themselves. This self-competition has a distinct advantage. Cooperative learning definitions vary. Linblad (1994) says that:

> In its purest form, cooperative learning is merely a few people getting together to study something and produce a single product. (p. 291)
>
> Thus, because self-reliance is every bit as important a skill to master as cooperative relationships, good teachers will continue to emphasize the importance of individual effort and accountability at the same time that they use cooperative learning techniques. (p. 292)

The future of America and of the world will require not so much a spirit of competition but a spirit of cooperation. Manning and Lucking (1991) explain:

> The need for people to interact cooperatively and work toward group goals undoubtedly will increase during the 1990s. Yet, American education traditionally has emphasized individual competition and achievement, an approach that results in winners and losers and sometimes produces outright hostility among learners. (p. 152)

Although cooperative learning programs seem especially suited for low achievers, most studies show that high, average, and low achievers gain equally from cooperative learning experiences (Manning & Lucking, 1991). Spencer Kagan (1989–1990, p. 9), a former professor at the University of California–Riverside who has researched effective learning for 25 years, reports that "both behavioral and paper-and-pencil measures in over 20 published research studies document that cooperative learning leads to a more pro-social orientation among students."

Augustine, Gruber, and Hanson (1989–1990, p. 4) report on their collective 23 years of experience in using cooperative learning strategies. Their conclusion was "we

are confident that cooperation works: it promotes higher achievement, develops social skills, and puts the responsibility for learning on the learner."

For cooperative learning to be effective, students must get to know one another,
communicate accurately and unambiguously, accept and support one another, and resolve conflict. These skills should be taught just as systematically as subject content.
Several research studies have concluded that cooperative learning teams increase students' self-esteem (Manning & Lucking, 1991, p. 155). But these authors quickly remind their readers that "emphasizing cooperation over competition requires teachers
to change their teaching roles from a power figure or conveyor of knowledge to a guide
of learning events or to a resource person."

Johnson and Johnson (1989) also view cooperative learning much more specifically than the loose definition given at the beginning of this section. They say that all
real cooperative learning has five basic elements: (1) positive interdependence, (2) face-
to-face interaction, (3) individual accountability, (4) collaborative skills, and (5) group
processing. Positive interdependence means that each student's success (grade) depends on a group grade. The converse of this principle is also true; the group's success depends on each member's mastering the material being tested (individual accountability).

But not all students automatically know how to work together, or cooperate, so
Johnson and Johnson (1989) provide an organized set of activities to help students develop the social and collaborative skills needed to contribute to and benefit from
group learning. They refer to the group's discussing and assessing their progress as
group processing.

Advantages

Traditionally, a distinguishing characteristic of graduate education has been the seminar. Educators have long recognized that graduate students can contribute to the class.
Interestingly, even at this level of maturity, students are often extremely uncomfortable during the first few seminars. This level of discomfort is intensified when the professor pauses to think and to give students time to think about issues. Ironically, even
in school—a place designated for learning—students are made uncomfortable by
pauses, even though those pauses give them time to think.

Equally unusual is educators' failure from kindergarten through college to recognize that students of all levels can contribute to the learning process and can help
others learn. Cooperative learning welcomes students to benefit from their classmates'
knowledge and thoughts. Currently American schools are experiencing a paradigm
shift in the way learning is perceived to occur. As discussed in Chapter 1, constructivism is a dominating learning theory that recognizes that knowledge is temporary
and that each student can construct knowledge. Cooperative learning theory also recognizes that each student can not only learn but can help classmates learn.

Cooperative learning also removes competition between and among students.
Some of the harmful effects of such competition are discussed in Chapter 14. Some
teachers believe that competition with all classmates is necessary to motivate students
to perform at their best. The assessment used with cooperative learning motivates students yet protects less capable students from impossible challenges.

A closely related strength of cooperative learning is that it teaches students to co-operate with others. Since the team's score is a sum of the team members' scores, each participant is encouraged to help fellow team members. Most adult jobs, like daily living, require cooperation.

Another advantage of cooperative learning is that this method is motivational. Unlike such traditional images as the "bookworm" and the "gentlemen's C," which have militated against academic success, cooperative learning encourages all students to do their best. It is uncertain whether these terms were purposefully developed to discourage maximum academic success, but the fact that they have this effect is certain. In contrast to traditional classrooms, where each student knows that the teacher is likely to distribute an allotted number of As and that each classmate's star performance reduces others' chance to earn an A, discovery learning students actually want their classmates to succeed (Hulten & DeVries, 1976; Madden & Slavin, 1983; Slavin, 1978). Furthermore, several studies have found that students in cooperative groups who improved academically gained in peer status (Slavin, 1975; Slavin, DeVries, & Hulten, 1975).

Developing a Cooperative Learning Lesson: The Teacher's Role

As with all teaching strategies, how you use cooperative learning determines its success. Lindblad (1994) cautions teachers not to interfere with group work:

> Too often the traditional teacher feels the need to be part of everything going on in the class. Let students handle their own team progress. When the teacher stays removed from minor discord, the team members are forced to deal with those problems themselves. (p. 293)

Heckman, Confer, and Hakim (1994, p. 39) say that "children's own questions are the most powerful source of curriculum topics and investigation."

Alfke (1974) explains that such questions develop skills in learning how to learn, to inquire, and to conceptualize. Teachers can achieve this by asking fewer but better questions and by requiring students to pose more productive questions. Data suggest that all teachers should:

1. Avoid using questions to introduce lessons.
2. Delay questions about content until a knowledge base has been established.
3. Use a combination of levels of questions, extending from recall to evaluation.
4. Pause for at least three seconds following each question.
5. Not expect students to be able to guess what you mean.
6. Address questions to individual students, using students' names.
7. Keep content-oriented questions specific.
8. Help students by modifying their inaccurate answers until they become acceptable.
9. Encourage students to ask questions.

10. Help students develop skills in asking questions.

11. Listen carefully to students' questions and respond using their content.

12. Before assigning reading, showing a film, or taking a field trip, ask questions about that experience's major concepts or objectives.

Cooperative learning is more than just letting students work together. Begin developing your lesson by developing a short assignment. You can use the same variety of media as used to build a knowledge base in a questioning lesson (i.e., recordings, minilecture, introduction). Remember that in cooperative learning the competition is between or among groups, not individuals. Assign students to groups of about four members each. Designate membership so that each group has about the same potential as the other groups.

Advise all students that at a designated time you will administer a test on the lesson they are studying and that each member's success depends on the group's success. Explain that it is to each student's advantage to help the other group members understand the lesson's major concepts.

A strategy that can be combined with most of these methods is team-teaching. Its primary benefit is its potential for letting teachers use their expertise more extensively than when teaching a self-contained class. Teaming is often effective when used with large groups of students. Alexander (1995) recommends this combination of team-teaching and large groups in the new middle school, combining one or two science and math teachers with one or two language arts and social studies teachers and one fine arts or language teacher.

The number of teaching methods this chapter discusses may seem a little overwhelming. One way to understand these methods is to think about the sizes of groups in which they are used (Figure 5.1). For example, you will generally use a lecture, simulation game, and case study method with the entire class. Individual students generally pursue inquiry and discovery learning independently. Tutoring involves two stu-

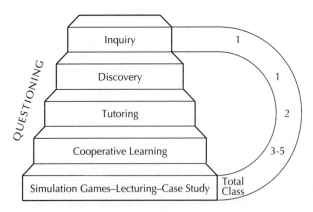

FIGURE 5.1 Relative group size of teaching methods

dents, and cooperative learning involves between three and five students. Questioning is used with all of these methods, so the class size may vary from one to everyone.

RECAP OF MAJOR IDEAS

1. Use the lecture with highly motivated students who can take good notes. Most students do not have this ability.
2. The lecture is an effective means of introducing a unit, building a frame of reference, clarifying confusing issues, and summarizing major concepts in a lesson. It is not usually a good motivator, and it does not stimulate imagination and creativity.
3. Begin most lectures with a clear statement of objectives, keep them short and simple, and proceed briskly. A lecture should contain only a few major concepts and should provide activities that require students to apply the concepts.
4. Supplement lectures with audiovisual aids, gesturing, joking, and modeling.
5. Tutoring usually helps both the tutor and the tutee. It is more effective when used with other approaches, such as mastery learning.
6. Inquiry lessons offer students opportunities to cultivate their creative talents when they have freedom and flexibility. The absence of continuous feedback and frequent grades in inquiry learning makes self-motivated students a must.
7. You enhance the effectiveness of questioning by giving students more time to respond, helping students provide acceptable answers, and encouraging students to ask questions.
8. Simulation games are good motivators and lead to increased retention. Used appropriately, they emphasize cooperation, not competition.
9. Cases enable students to study concepts in the context in which they occur.
10. Students learn more and develop their social skills during cooperative learning.

CASES

You may have already begun to choose your own teaching strategies. The following cases will give you some opportunities to refine your ideas.

CASE 1: A METHODS COURSE EMPHASIZES STRATEGIES

Carole Harman had enjoyed her introductory course in education. She had also taken an exploratory course in education that provided interesting field experiences. These courses made her feel certain that she wanted to be a teacher.

The next year Carole took two courses in her major (chemistry), two in math, and a general secondary methods course. But after only two weeks she felt lost in the education course. Her professor had begun talking about educational research and teaching strategies and the relationships between the two. Carole was uncomfortable because she had never taken a course in research methodology and did not have any background in teaching strategies.

Almost from the start the professor began making such comments as "When selecting your strategies" or "You can apply your favorite strategy." Carole had never before thought about teaching strategies, which sounded like unnecessary educational jargon. She wondered whether other class members felt the same way, until one of them nearby mumbled, "How can you have a favorite strategy if you don't know what one is?"

Discussion

1. Why might an education professor assume that students in a general methods course have knowledge of teaching strategies?

    Teachers often get so close to their subjects that they expect their students to have more knowledge of and enthusiasm about the subject than they actually do. College professors are just as likely to make this mistake. After all, educational strategies are this teacher's major subject.

2. Why is it important that teachers be familiar with many teaching strategies?

    Many teachers believe they need a good repertoire of methods to function in the classroom. What works with one group of students may not stimulate another group. The teacher who is familiar with various methods can shift quickly among them when the class's level of interest drops. (This is only one advantage of having a repertoire of methods. Perhaps you can think of others.)

3. What should the teacher know about each teaching strategy?

    To get the most benefit from each strategy, teachers must know the purposes that each method serves best, and the age levels for which it is most appropriate. Besides knowing how to use a strategy, teachers should recognize its strengths and limitations. What else will you want to know about methods that you might use? (You could consider their practicality, cost, and effects on other teachers.)

CASE 2: SHOULD TEACHING IN SECONDARY AND MIDDLE SCHOOLS BE FUN?

Louis Martinez was the most interesting math teacher ever to come to Jackson High. Before he arrived, three years ago, not enough students were interested in math to offer more than the very basic general mathematics, geometry, and first-year algebra. But when school opened this fall, Mr. Martinez had so many students requesting Algebra II that two sections were necessary. In addition, 27 students had signed up for trigonometry, and 15 others wanted a class in first-year calculus. For a school as small as Jackson High, this degree of interest in any single subject was incredible. Happy to see that so many of his students were sharing his enjoyment of mathematics, Mr. Martinez became even more enthusiastic, and his lessons became even more exciting.

The students enjoyed his classes for many different reasons. For one, they never knew what to expect from one day to the next; they just knew it would be different. Most of the lessons involved every student, and usually in a number of ways. Moreover, Mr. Martinez had a great collection of props, audiovisual materials, and games.

Then some of the other teachers began complaining about him. His classes were noisier than most, and although he had more equipment than most of his colleagues, his students were running all over the school borrowing other paraphernalia to use in math class. Basically, though, the other teachers' complaints stemmed from jealousy. Although they would never admit it, they would have tolerated the noise and other minor irritants if they could have their students become that enthusiastic about their classes.

Unfortunately, the complaints reached Mr. Martinez only after they had spread through the school and the community. The principal called him in to discuss the complaints and remind him how important it was not to alienate other teachers. Mr. Martinez was perplexed to learn that his successful teaching strategies had begun to cause trouble for him.

Discussion Questions

1. Is having a repertoire of teaching methods likely to get a teacher into trouble?
2. How might Mr. Martinez react to such an accusation?
3. How should Mr. Martinez deal with complaints from other teachers?

ACTIVITY

Make a list of your best teachers' best qualities. Review the effective schools research and the effective teachers research found in this book. Now, add the qualities found here to your own list.

REFERENCES

Alessi, S. M., & Trollip, S. R. (1991). *Computer-based instruction, methods, and development.* Englewood Cliffs, N.J.: Prentice-Hall.

Alexander, W. M. (1995). The junior high school: A changing view. *Middle School Journal, 26* (3), 21-24.

Alfke, D. (1974). Asking operational questions. *Science and Children,* 11, 18-19.

Augustine, D. K., Gruber, K. D., & Hanson, L. R. (1989-1990, December/January). Cooperation works! *Educational Leadership, 47*(4), 4-11.

Barth, R. S. (1990). A personal vision of a good school. *Phi Delta Kappan, 71,* 512-516.

Berliner, D. C., & Gage, N. L. (1975). The psychology of teaching methods. In N. L. Gage (Ed.), *The psychology of teaching methods.* Chicago: National Society for the Study of Education.

Bloom, B. S. (1984). The search for methods of group instruction as effective as one-to-one tutoring. *Educational Leadership, 41,* 4–17.

Bull, S. G., & Dizney, H. F. (1973). Epistemic—curiosity—arousing pre-questions: Their effect on long-term retention. *Journal of Educational Psychology, 65,* 45–49.

Chaudhari, U. S. (1975, January). Questioning and creative thinking: A research perspective. *Journal of Creative Behavior,* pp. 30–34.

Commonwealth, V., & Gootnick, D. M. (1974). Electrifying the classroom with the overhead projector. *Business Education Forum, 28,* 3–4.

Einstein, A., & Infield, L. P. (1938). *Evolution of physics: Growth of ideas from early concepts to relativity and quanta.* New York: Simon & Schuster.

Eller, B. F., & Henson, K. T. (in press). *Educational psychology for effective teaching.* Atlanta: West Publishing Co.

Ellsworth, P.C., & Sindt, V.G. (1994). Helping "Aha" to happen: The contributions of Irving Sigel. *Educational Leadership, 51*(5), 40–44.

Goodlad, J. I. (1984). *A place called school.* New York: McGraw-Hill.

Harrison, C. J. (1990, Summer). Concepts, operational definitions and case studies in instruction. *Education,* 502–505.

Heckman, P. E., Confer, C. B., & Hakim, D. C. (1994). Planting seeds: Understanding through investigation. *Educational Leadership, 51*(5), 36–39.

Heyman, M. (1976). How to direct a simulation. *Phi Delta Kappan, 16,* 17–19.

Hulten, B. H., & DeVries, D. L. (1976). *Team competition and group practice: Effects on students' achievement and attitudes.* (Report No. 212). Baltimore: Johns Hopkins University Center for Social Organization of Schools.

Johnson, D. W., & Johnson, R. (1989). *Cooperation and competition: Theory and research.* Edina, Minn: Interaction Book Company.

Johnson, D. W., & Johnson, R. T. (1989–1990). Social skills for successful group work. *Educational Leadership, 47*(4), 29–33.

Jones, P. (1970). Discovery teaching from Socrates to modernity. *Mathematics Teacher, 63,* 501–510.

Kagan, S. (1989–1990, December/January). The structural approach to cooperative learning. *Educational Leadership, 47*(4), 12–15.

Kelly, W. H. (1970, November). Are educational games effective in teaching? *Agricultural Education Magazine, 43,* 117.

King, A. (1990, November/December). Reciprocal questioning: A strategy for teaching students how to learn from lectures. *The Clearing House, 64*(2), 131–135.

Klausmeier, H. J. (1980). Tutoring to increase achievement and motivation. *Theory into Practice, 19*(1), 51–57.

Kowalski, T. J., Weaver, R. A. & Henson, K. T., (1990). *Case studies on teaching.* White Plains, NY: Longman.

Kowalski, T. J., Weaver, R.A., & Henson, K.T. (1994). *Case studies of beginning teachers.* White Plains, N.Y.: Longman.

Leenders, M., & Ersking, J. (1978). *Case research: The case writing process* (2nd ed.). London, Canada: University of Western Ontario School of Business Administration.

Lindblad, A. H., Jr. (1994). You can avoid the traps of cooperative learning. *The Clearing House, 67*(5), 291–293.

Lucas, L. A., Postma, C. H., & Thompson, J. C. (1975, July). Comparative study of cognitive retention used in simulation gaming as opposed to lecture: Discussion techniques. *Peabody Journal of Education, 52,* 261.

MacDonald, R. (1991, Fall). Tutoring: An effective teaching tool. *Kappa Delta Pi Record, 28*(1), 25–28.

Maddin, N. A., & Slavin, R. E. (1983). Effects of cooperative learning on the social acceptance of main streamed academically handicapped students. *Journal of Special Education, 17,* 171–182.

Maddox, H., & Hoole, E. (1975). Performance decrement in the lecture. *Educational Review, 28,* 17–30.

Manning, M. L., & Lucking, R. (1991, January/February). The what, why, and how of cooperative learning. *The Clearing House, 64*(3), 152–156.

Maslow, A. (1973). What is a taoistic teacher? In L. Rubin (Ed.), *Faces and feelings in the classroom.* New York: Viking.

Miller, H. G., & Vinocur, S. M. (1973). How to ask classroom questions. *School and Community, 59,* 10.

O'Neal, M., Earley, B., & Snider, M. (1991). Addressing the needs of at-risk students: A local school program that works. In Robert C. Morris (Ed.), *Youth at risk.* Lancaster, PA: Tecnomic, 122–125.

Paget, N. (1988, January). Using case methods effectively. *Journal of Education and Business, 63,* 175–180.

Parsons, J., & Jones, C. (1990, September/October). Not another test. *The Clearing House, 64*(1), 17–20.

Phillips, D.R., Phillips, D.G., Melton, G., & Moore, P. (1994). Beans, blocks, and buttons: Developing thinking. *Educational Leadership, 51*(5), 50–53.

Ramsey, I., Gabbard, C., Clawson, K., Lee, L., & Henson, K. T. (1990). Questioning: An effective teaching method. *The Clearing House, 63*(9), 420–422.

Rebrova, L. V., & Svetlova, P. R. (1976). The problem-solving approach: A way to insure solid and thorough learning. *Soviet Education, 18,* 75–84.

Redfield, D. L., & Rousseau, E. W. (1981). A meta-analysis of experimental research on teacher questioning behavior. *Review of Educational Research, 51,* 237–245.

Rothstein, P. R. (1990). *Educational psychology.* New York: McGraw-Hill.

Rowe, M. B. (1974). Wait-time and rewards as instructional variable: Their influence on language, logic, and fate control, Part one. *Journal of Research in Science Teaching, 11,* 81–94.

Rowsey, R., & Mason, W. H. (1975). Immediate achievement and retention in audio tutorial vs. conventional lecture-laboratory instruction. *Journal of Research in Science Teaching, 12,* 393–397.

Sanders, J. R. (1973). Retention effects of adjunct questions in written and oral discourse. *Journal of Educational Psychology, 65,* 181–186.

Santieslebau, A. J. (1976). Teacher questioning performance and student affective outcomes. *Journal of Research and Science Teaching, 13,* 553–557.

Shiman, D. A., & Mash, R. J. (1974). Questioning: Another view. *Peabody Journal of Education, 51,* 246–253.

Slavin, R.E. (1975). *Classroom reward structure: Effects on academic performance, social connectedness and peer norms.* Doctoral dissertation, Johns Hopkins University.

Slavin, R.E. (1978). Student teams and comparison among equals: Effects on academic performance and student attitudes. *Journal of Educational Psychology, 70,* 532–538.

Slavin, R.E. (1995). *Cooperative learning* (2nd ed.). Needham Heights, MA: Allyn & Bacon.

Slavin, R.E., DeVries, D.L., & Hulten, B.H. (1975). *Individual vs. team competition: The interpersonal consequences of academic performance* (Report No. 188). Baltimore, MD: Johns Hopkins University Center for Social Organization of Schools.

Sobel, M. A. (1975, October). Junior high school mathematics: Motivation vs. monotony. *Mathematics Teacher, 68,* 479–485.

Special Study Panel on Education Indicators for the National Center for Education Statistics (1991, September). Education Counts. Washington, DC: U.S. Department of Education, p. 67.

Stefanich, G. P. (1990, November). Cycles of cognition. *Middle School Journal, 22*(2), 47–52.

Sund, R. B. (1971). Growing through sensitive listening and questioning. *Childhood Education, 51,* 68-71.

Sutton, R. M. (1977). On asking and answering questions. *Physics Teacher, 15,* 94-95.

Taxey, P. J. (1975). Heterogeneous subgroups within a classroom. *American Biology Teacher, 37,* 165-167.

Taylor, A. J. R. (1976). Developing your own simulation for teaching. *The Clearing House, 50,* 104-107.

Titus, C. (1974, February). The uses of the lecture. *The Clearing House,* pp. 383-384.

Vance, J. H. (1974, February). Mathematics laboratories—More than fun? *School Science and Mathematics, 72,* 617-623.

Voth, R. (1975). On lecturing. *Social Studies, 66,* 247-248.

Weimer, R. C. (1975). An analysis of discovery. *Educational Technology, 15,* 45-48.

Woods Hole Conference (1959). Woods Hole, MA.

SUGGESTED READINGS

Birkel, L. F. (1973). The lecture method: Villain or victim? *Peabody Journal of Education, 50,* 298-301.

Brown, D. S. (1990, November). Middle level teachers' perceptions of action research. *Middle School Journal, 22*(2), 30-32.

Campbell, J. (1967). *Colonel Francis Parker: Crusader for children.* New York: Columbia University Teachers College Press.

Einstein, A. Quoted in B.F. Eller and K.T. Henson (in press). *Educational psychology for effective teaching.* Atlanta: West Publishing Co.

Erasmus, C.C. (1989). Ways with stories: Listening to stories aboriginal people tell. *Language Arts, 66*(3), 267-75.

Guskey, T.R. (1990, February). Integrating innovations. *Educational Leadership, 48,* 11-15.

Sickling, F.P. (1976). Patterns in integers. *Mathematics Teacher, 68,* 290-292.

chapter **6**

Communications

We must learn to listen and listen to learn.
Erasmus

OBJECTIVES

List three voice qualities important to teaching, and explain how to improve each one.

Give one suggestion for helping a teacher improve the quality of classroom questions.

Define set induction, and describe two techniques for establishing it in the classroom.

Explain how teacher efficacy affects student achievement.

Describe the difference in communication behavior of effective teachers and less-effective teachers.

Respond appropriately to an incorrect response, a correct confident response, and a correct doubtful response.

Describe how to use review at the beginning and end of a lesson.

Give an example of how the hidden curriculum can communicate positively (usefully) and an example of how it can communicate negatively.

Plan one research study you can conduct in your classroom to address a major concern of yours.

PRETEST

	Agree	Disagree	Uncertain
1. Most beginning teachers talk too fast.	___	___	___
2. Teachers should avoid using personal examples in their lessons.	___	___	___
3. Students tend to emulate their teachers' behavior.	___	___	___
4. Teachers tend to pause too long after asking a question, which bores many students.	___	___	___
5. A teacher's nonverbal communication is more important than what the teacher says.	___	___	___
6. The meaning that results from communication is context specific (depends on the context in which it is used).	___	___	___
7. Teachers seldom explain what a lesson expects from the students.	___	___	___
8. Effective teachers (those whose students exceed in achievement) spend less time introducing new topics, giving exam-			

ples, and giving students opportunities
for guided practice than do less-effective
teachers.

9. When students respond correctly but
doubtfully to teacher questions, the
teacher should explain the process used
to derive the answer.

10. More than 95 percent of the questions
in textbooks and similar materials are
lower order.

11. Most student responses to higher-order
questions are higher order.

12. Teachers should not direct questions to
individual students because many students find this embarrassing.

Middle-Level Message

During transescence, that awkward time between childhood and adolescence,
young people are often confused. Just when they get it together, it comes apart.
They may feel that nobody understands them. Too often, they cannot effectively
communicate their feelings. This leads to further frustration, exacerbating the
problems. When asked to do a chore at home and being later called to task for
not completing the job satisfactorily, their common response is "Oh, I thought
you meant. . . ."

Teachers of this age-group must clearly communicate what they expect of
their students. Students of this age have no criteria to help them decide which
concepts are academically important. But when teachers explain how each activity fits into the lesson's goals or structure, students are no longer at a loss.

Students often have teachers who fail to follow their own advice. If students
are advised to behave one way and teachers behave differently, this further confuses these students. This chapter shows how verbal and nonverbal communication strategies can help in the classroom.

THE NEED FOR COMMUNICATION SKILLS

The Lesson: Exciting or Boring?

Students are slow to arrive at Ms. Simms's history class. As the tardy bell rings, there
are usually a few still coming in and walking casually to their desks. Equally predictable
is the way Ms. Simms will present the lesson. She always begins by mumbling a few
words about yesterday's lesson, even while the latecomers are ambling in. Early in the
year these students got the impression that Ms. Simms did not really care whether they

learned the subject. They still do not know if it is because her knowledge of history is inadequate or she is merely unable to communicate.

The scene in Miss Armstrong's class is different. There, students arrive quickly, find their seats, and open their books and notepads. The students recognize Miss Armstrong's expertise in her subject. She begins each lesson promptly and assertively. She presents many concepts, but she does this clearly, and it is obvious that she wants her students to understand. Furthermore, she seems to know when even one student is confused. Right away she gives an example that clarifies the matter. By the end of the period, she has given a clear picture of the subject under study; the personalities involved have come to life.

Why are some teachers confusing and boring while others are clear and interesting? The difference may be not how well teachers know their subjects but how well they communicate what they know. The teacher who communicates well can make a subject interesting and easy to learn; a poor communicator is apt to make lessons boring and confusing.

This chapter will help you focus on your own communication skills. Before you read further, take a few minutes to list your own strengths in communicating, along with any limitations that may need attention. Consider such things as your voice, vocabulary, repertoire of examples and jokes, ability to ask questions, ability to listen to students, and ability to use expression and movements to show others how you feel. Include both verbal and nonverbal skills, because both are necessary for effective communication. Because teaching is a complex process, teachers must have good communication skills. In Chapter 1 we learned that in the past teachers have not made full use of research findings. Buckner and Bickel (1991, p. 29) address the relationship between teachers' communication skills and their failure to use research: "A major barrier to bridging the gap between research and practice in most instructional settings has been communication."

Because teaching is a complex set of activities, teachers are expected to perform an increasing number of varied roles; their primary responsibility, however, is to ensure that students learn. This role—regardless of teaching techniques or strategies used—requires communicating. Today's teachers' many other roles also require communicating. Indeed, conversation affects students' thought processes and therefore what they learn (Cazden, 1986).

Your ability to teach your students depends on your ability to communicate. Teachers who are stimulating and exciting communicate more effectively than teachers who bore their students. Moreover, classroom communication is not merely a line between the teacher and student. Figure 6.1 shows the pattern of communication in the classroom. Although the figure may make your role seem complex, it is accurate. Effective teachers seem to develop a sixth sense that picks up and responds to students' many comments.

Research shows that teachers may engage in more than 1,000 interpersonal exchanges with students in a single day (Jackson, 1968). Managing such complex processes requires teachers to be acutely alert to students. Teachers also learn to address a number of expressed (and even unexpressed) concerns simultaneously. In addition to talking, teachers learn to communicate nonverbally. As you read this chap-

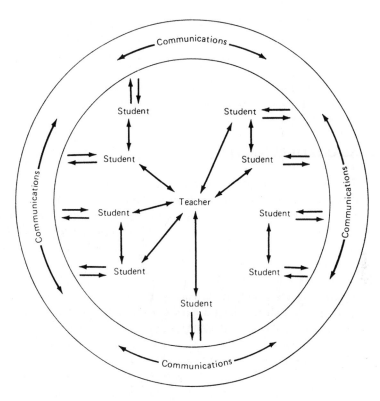

FIGURE 6.1   Classroom communications

ter, see how many new verbal and nonverbal communication skills you can add to the list you made earlier.

Communicating in Multicultural Classrooms

Multicultural classes often offer special challenges for overt and covert reasons. For example, in many classes, language barriers alone almost ensure misunderstanding. The same words often carry different meanings to students of different cultures. Gestures, hand signals, facial expressions, and other body language may carry very different meanings as well.

For example, the hand sign North Americans use to ask someone to come closer means goodbye in Trinidad, and the bowed head that North Americans recognize as a sign of shame or even guilt is a sign of high respect in some cultures. The teacher who expects eye contact is expecting behavior that some students may consider insulting or disrespectful.

Through group assignments, teachers can help students begin to understand their culturally different peers. You can provide special opportunities (activities) to help students learn more about other students' cultures. As you work to understand and help students learn about other cultures, remember to help minority students understand their mainstream classmates.

You can enhance your ability to improve communication in the classroom by getting involved in the school's curriculum. For example, organize a cultural fair to celebrate the different cultures at your school. Any effort that helps students understand other cultures is likely to improve communication in the classroom.

MESSAGES TO COMMUNICATE

An unprecedented number of recent studies reveals several categories of messages that you must communicate for students to achieve maximum learning. Keep these in mind as you read the rest of this chapter. Think about ways to communicate these messages effectively.

A Sense of Efficacy

An important factor affecting learner achievement is teachers' confidence in their ability to cause students to learn. Fuller (1982) referred to this when he said, "Efficacy— the individual's perceived expectancy of obtaining valued outcomes through personal effort—appears to yield a variety of important effects in school organizations." Secondary and middle-level students must know that their teachers are able and determined to lead them to attain class goals.

But how do you achieve this confident image? By setting clear goals for the class, by asserting the leadership needed to get students on task quickly each period, and by managing all phases of the classroom environment toward these ends. Good and Brophy (1995, p. 378) encourage teachers to uphold students' expectations for success:

> Therefore, whatever their ability, the motivation of all students, even the most discouraged, can be reshaped by their teachers. Empty reassurances or a few words of encouragement will not do the job, but a combination of appropriately challenging demands with systematic socialization designed to make the student see that success can be achieved with reasonable effort should be effective.

Efficacy begins with an attitude—a positive belief in your students' ability and a belief in your ability to make students succeed. It also involves a determination that says if you do not succeed the first time, do not give up—we have just started. Teachers who display efficacy do not give excuses. If the necessary materials are not available, the efficacious teacher finds or makes other materials. Such teachers are invaluable to schools and to students. While getting the job done, they silently communicate to students that anything is possible as long as they believe in themselves.

Teachers can increase their levels of efficacy through several strategies. Leithwood, Menzies, and Jantzi (1994) explain:

Success raises one's appraisal of one's efficacy, although such appraisals are shaped by task difficulty, effort, effort expended, amount of help received, and other circumstances. Teachers who actually try out new practices in their classrooms, with sufficient on-site assistance to ensure success, will possess this kind of information. (p. 47)

Establishing a definite sequence for your own activities can contribute to a positive teacher image. Brooks (1985) examined videotapes of seventh-grade math classes on the first day of school and concluded that the sequence of activities on that day was a critical factor in communicating teacher competence. He recommends that teachers follow this sequence: Call class to order, take roll, explain rules and procedures, introduce course content, solicit student information, talk about yourself, and preview tomorrow's lesson.

Classroom environment affects the types of communications that are appropriate and, consequently, the messages communicated. Green (1983) drew the following conclusions about communications:

1. Face-to-face interaction, between teacher and students and among students, is governed by context-specific rules.
2. Rules for participating in classroom activities are implicit and are learned through the action itself.
3. The meaning that results from communications is context specific.
4. Over time, frames of reference are developed.
5. The diversity of classrooms makes communications complex and demanding for teachers and students.

A Sense of Meaning

Too often students go through the motions of learning without really understanding what they are doing and why they are doing it. According to Good (1984), "It is essential that direct instruction include explicit attention to meaning, not simply focus on engagement as an end in itself." All students need help in deciding what information is important. You should not assume that children have the necessary criteria to decide which are academically important concepts and which are unimportant. Your explanation of how each activity fits into the goals or structures of the lesson can help illuminate the lesson and make it meaningful to students. According to Fisher (1980, p. 26), students "pay attention more when the teacher spends time discussing the goals or structure of the lesson and/or giving directions about what students are to do." But teachers seldom clearly explain what is expected of the students (Bruner, 1981).

Expectations

Several researchers have conducted studies to determine how teacher expectations affect students' learning. The expectation literature is consistently (although not unanimously) interpreted to show that teachers who communicate their goals for performance to their students have a powerful effect. Unfortunately, students and teachers may not appreciate the value of goals. Content goals often appear to have little salience for either students or teachers. Students do not think of themselves as mastering knowledge but rather as achieving what the teacher or test requires. As capsuled by Stake and Easley (1978, p. 29), "Teachers are the key to what happens in the classroom."

The Role of Emotions

Since Aristotle, communication scholars have viewed communication as something one does to an audience; the message is something one transfers to the other (Gronbeck, McKerron, Ehninger, & Monroe, 1994). But communications are more complex than a simple action between two individuals.

Communication also involves more than the physical exchange of ideas. Often our emotions affect our ability to receive a message. Gronbeck, McKerron, Ehninger, and Monroe (1994) stress the effect of emotions on communications:

> Even when a message is completely clear and understandable, we often don't like it. Problems in "meaning" or "meaningfulness" often aren't a matter of comprehension but of reaction; of agreement; of shared concepts, belief, attitudes, values. (p. 501)

These writers are not alone in recognizing the complexity of communications. Communications experts who prepare communicators are among those who acknowledge the complexity of communications. Rudick (1994) says:

> The premise that individual behavior is a part of a system rather than a characteristic of individuals provides an expanded view of the training process. . . . The trainee is seen as one system immersed in and inseparable from a larger ecological framework of systems. . . . it is impossible to separate the client, the trainer, the setting, the community.

VERBAL COMMUNICATION SKILLS

Teachers can develop and refine several technical skills to improve their ability to communicate with students.

Voice Control

Volume.   Some teachers have such weak voices that most students cannot hear them. Their valuable planning is thus largely wasted. How can you ensure everyone will hear you? The obvious answer is to speak louder, but this may not be so easy. One way to increase your volume is to look at and talk to the students in the back of the room during the lesson. Even when you answer a question from a student in the front row, let students in the back row know that you are not ignoring them. Just because a student in the front row asks the question, do not assume the rest of the class knows the answer.

A common mistake all teachers make is attempting to drown out talkative students. Grubaugh (1989, p. 38) discusses an effective alternative: "For a teacher, it is best to time one's remarks at the trough of a wave of sound in the classroom so as to begin speaking in a softer voice to set a more quiet tone."

Another way to help yourself be heard is to reduce sound interference—for example, close the windows and doors to keep distracting sounds out. But if your school does not have air conditioning, you will sometimes need to keep windows and doors open for ventilation. Traffic noises and other unavoidable interference will always require you to speak more loudly.

Tone. Once you have adequate volume, examine your voice to see whether it is monotonous. Listen to yourself. When you do, you will feel obligated to speak louder, more clearly, and in a more interesting manner. If possible, have one of your lessons videotaped or make an audiotape of your classes. A videotape will help you improve your eye contact.

Clarity. An equally common voice problem is lack of clarity, frequently caused by speaking too fast. Remember to speak slowly enough to give students time to absorb the message. Because of nervous tension, almost all beginning teachers talk too fast, leaving behind confused and discouraged students.

Pauses. At times you should pause for a minute, to give students time to think. When you introduce an important idea, stop for a minute, then continue. Also, after you ask a question, give students time to collect and organize their answers. Research shows that the most productive time lapse following a question is three seconds, but teachers usually are uncomfortable with silence and rush on after pausing for only one second (Rowe, 1978). Finally, if a student directs a question to you, pause for an instant to think before answering. A poor answer blurted out immediately is still a poor answer; a good answer is worth a moment's wait.

Even now, in your education courses, you may want to tape a short lesson given to a class of your peers. Try to have a minimum of 10 or 12 students spaced throughout the room. Do not be ashamed to let others help you critique your lesson. You might ask one group to observe your voice and another to observe your eye contact.

Be aware of how you appear to students. Teachers who cannot speak in an interesting way cannot expect students to learn much. Take the time and make the effort to improve voice inflection.

Set Induction

A major difference between the beginning teacher's and the experienced teacher's classes is often the amount of attention that students give the teacher at the start of the period. The experienced teacher may refuse to begin a lesson until all students give their undivided attention. You must get students to be quiet because you will generally begin a lesson with an explanation. This could describe what you have planned or be directions for the students. In either case, teachers prefer to give an introduction or directions one time only.

Teachers' strategies for getting students' attention on the lesson are collectively known as *set induction*. How do you get the whole class's attention? One approach is to face the class silently, looking at those whose attention you must capture. If you begin talking before the others are quiet, the noisy students usually get louder. Once things are quiet, you might say, "It took us a little while to get started. Is there a topic that we should discuss before we begin?" Frequently, there is, and a few minutes discussing it will be a good investment.

Another method for getting total class attention is to begin the lesson with a subject the group finds vital. It may not even be related to the day's lesson or to the subject. By listening to class conversation, you can determine what students' current interest is and begin the lesson with a discussion of that topic. Do not feel obligated to lead the discussion. Just remark, "Tom, you seem awfully interested in something. How about letting the rest of us in on it?"

Teachers have tricks for getting students' attention. Some teachers begin the period by talking very low, then raise their voice to normal when students get quiet. Students recognize the signal, and with some groups it is effective all year long.

There is merit in relating the attention getters to the cognitive aspects of the day's lesson. Studies have shown that by involving students cognitively, teachers can elevate students achievement. In secondary school science classes, Riban (1976, p. 10) found that having students define their own problems for investigation, discuss their problem with the teacher, and organize the collection of information, dividing responsibilities among themselves, resulted in increased student achievement that "exceeded any reasonable expectations."

A few days of experience will alert you to times when catching class attention will be difficult. For example, a drastic change in the weather from hot to cold or rainy to fair, or vice versa, is an indicator of forthcoming boisterousness among middle-level students. An important high school event will often have this effect too. By keeping up with the local news, school news, and the weather, you can plan an appropriate entry into the day's lesson, for example, "Who went to the basketball game last night?" Or "Did you hear on the local news . . . ?" Once you let students express their opinions about the topic that holds their interest, they will become free to concentrate on other topics, and then you can introduce the day's planned lesson. Keep such set induction exercises brief.

Another effective method for achieving set induction is suspense. Begin the class by letting students guess what a diagram on the board represents, or begin by introducing a hypothetical case that will lead into the lesson. Perhaps you have a model that you can place so all can see it, or you may do a demonstration for the class. Such practices capture attention. You can increase effectiveness by using a few students, or perhaps the entire class, in the demonstration.

Using Examples

Examples can help clarify the lesson and make it a personal experience for each student, if the students can see how they relate to the lesson. Of course the amount students learn depends on how clear the lesson is, but the influence of examples may be far greater than expected. One study of the effect of teacher clarity on learning found that this one variable accounted for 52 percent of the variance in mean class achievement (Hines, Cruickshank, & Kennedy, 1982).

Research shows that examples help achieve clarity. For example, effective mathematics teachers spend more time on presenting new material and guided practice than do less-effective teachers (Evertson, Anderson, Anderson, & Brophy, 1980; Good & Grouws, 1979). According to Rosenshine (1986), "The effective teachers used this additional presentation time to give additional explanations and many examples." To be sure students understand the example, begin with simple examples and move to more complex ones.

Middle-level students tend to enjoy lessons that involve the teachers' previous experiences, especially when the examples involve activities that are most interesting to the specific age-group. Ask students to give examples from time to time. By asking them for examples of the principle just introduced, you can determine how well they understand the lesson. Too often teachers follow information with the question "Does everyone understand?" Students' admitting they do not understand is admitting a weakness that might be embarrassing. By asking an average achiever to give an example, you can gauge how clearly you have presented the lesson.

Using Repetition

Students admire and respect the teacher who takes the time and has enough patience to help those who have difficulty grasping a concept. This frequently requires repetitions. When and what should you repeat? Never refuse a serious request to repeat, but do not make the repetition verbatim. Explain the concept in different words. Saying the same thing, word for word, may elicit "I still don't get it."

Repetition is not only for the student who does not seem to understand. Full comprehension seldom comes when a concept is first introduced. All students benefit from repetition that varies from the introduction. Some classes have students who can restate what you have said well enough to help other students comprehend.

Because some students are reluctant to speak up when they are unsure, teachers may overlook the need for repetition. Because repeating everything would be boring, repeat only important points unless students request otherwise.

Providing Variety

Variety is a key element in good teaching. Every class session should contain several different experiences for each student. Do not lecture (teacher talk) or read to students for more than 10 or 15 minutes; invite students to contribute immediately afterward.

Variety is also needed from day to day. If most of today's lesson involves lecturing (heaven forbid), build tomorrow's lesson around group work, a field trip, a film, assignments at the chalkboard, or another totally different activity. Do not use a film or a group discussion for two consecutive days. Vary the activities daily or, better yet, within the period.

Using Questions

Students often become bored with lessons that are more teacher talk than student activities. Goodlad (1984) found that, on the average, only 75 percent of class time is devoted to instruction, and most of that time the teacher is giving students information. Goodlad encourages teachers to teach the major principles and generalizations in their subject(s). Much of the information pertinent to any lesson is general and already known to students. To prevent monotony, intersperse questions with talking.

Do not always ask simple and basic questions, because questions can make students think. Good questions do not ask students to state a rule or quote a definition. Instead, they ask students to apply the rule. A good classroom question prompts students to use ideas rather than just remember them. Using this type of question is a simple operation. You need only remember to ask the student for more information: "Why?" "How do you know that?" "How do you feel about that?" Direct questions to a particular student; otherwise the questions may go unanswered or the same few students may answer them all. But when teachers use questions they seldom use them in a way that promotes depth in understanding. Ellsworth and Sindt (1994) explain:

> When many teachers question students, they often move from student to student, asking each one only one or two questions so as to involve as many students as possible. Sigel and his colleagues found that this practice results in very little distancing, and it is not, therefore, the best way to develop representational compliance. (p. 43)

A better approach to achieving depth of understanding through questioning requires staying with a student with a succession of questions, requiring the student to explain, clarify, and justify the answer given.

Is it fair to embarrass students with direct questions? Suppose you direct a question to a student who cannot provide the correct answer. Once you direct a question to a student, you are obligated to help that student find an acceptable answer. This is not difficult if you remember to (1) pause to give time for organization of thoughts, (2) modify the answer until it is acceptable, and (3) provide hints for getting started. When used in this manner, questioning becomes a form of guided discovery. One former teacher recognizes that at times student answers will be incorrect or at best tangential and that in either case the teacher is obligated to protect the students' integrity (Mosston, 1972). He gives an example of how the teacher can respond effectively to an incorrect or tangential answer: "My question was not clear. Let me try this one. . . ."

Mosston, an expert on guided discovery, used diagrams (Figure 6.2) to show how a series of carefully selected questions can guide students to discover relationships. Note that in Figure 6.2 the size of the steps of progress are not always equal, and neither are the sizes or frequencies of the reinforcements. To some extent the subject affects these variables, as does the learner's ability to follow a line of pursuit, and especially the teacher's skill to guide and reinforce students until they reach their goal. Mosston reminds us that in guided discovery the teacher, never the student, is the cause of failure.

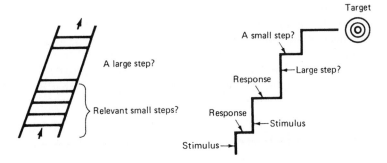

FIGURE 6.2   Using questions to guide learning

From *Teaching: From command to Discovery* (p. 124) by M. Mosston, 1972. Belmont, CA: Wadsworth. Used with permission

This figure reminds the teacher that it is essential to remain alert to the size of the cognitive steps that are being dealt with. The size of the step determines the pace of the progress. Large steps may require large reinforcements with long intervals, whereas smaller steps may require reinforcements of less magnitude.

When students respond correctly and confidently, you can simply ask another question or give a short statement of praise while maintaining the lesson's momentum (Rosenshine, 1986). However, if the student's response is correct but the student appears doubtful, give process feedback that explains the process used to derive the correct answer. For example, "Yes, Paul, you're correct because. . . ."

CLASSIFYING QUESTIONS

Teachers use questions to achieve very different types of objectives, so we do not rank them in higher and lower levels or from good to poor. Teachers who ask many higher-order questions (i.e., questions that seek to stimulate responses at the upper levels of the cognitive domain) have students whose attainment is higher than average (Redfield & Rousseau, 1981). But generally teachers do not use higher-order questions well.

Considering the level of questions in the most widely used resource, the textbook, this is not surprising. By analyzing over 61,000 questions in textbooks, manuals, workbooks, and tests, Trachtenberg (1974) found that more than 95 percent of the questions were lower order. Even when teachers do ask higher-order questions, their students seldom recognize that the questions are higher order. In fact, Mills, Rice, Berliner, and Rousseau (1980) found that analysis, synthesis, and application questions elicit responses at these levels only 50 percent of the time. After reviewing the research of Mills and colleagues, Berliner (1984, p. 64) concluded that "teachers need experience in learning to classify questions." In his book *Strategic Questioning*, Ronald Hyman (1979) classifies questions according to cognitive process and other considerations.

We categorize questions to make them understandable. Because no one can design a system to improve the use of questions in the classroom by studying every imaginable question, we must reduce the number of elements under study by establishing categories of questions. But the number of categories possible is also staggering, so we need to limit the number of categories. You could categorize questions according to number of words in a question or number of words required to answer a question, but such a system would be pointless. A more effective approach is to group questions according to the mental processes involved—that is, according to cognitive processes.

Cognitive Process Questions

Three main types of cognitive process questions are used regularly in classrooms: definitional questions, empirical questions, and evaluative questions. No one type is necessarily of a higher order than the others—that is, no hierarchy is implied.

Definitional Questions. Definitional questions require students (or teachers) to define a word, term, or phrase. The following are examples of definitional questions:

1. What is a tornado?
2. Give an example of a verse in iambic pentameter.
3. What does it mean to play "piano"?

Notice that definitional questions search for exact answers or "true" feelings. In other words, you either know the correct answer or you don't.

Empirical Questions. Unlike definitional questions, which ask for a definite, specific answer, empirical questions give respondents an opportunity to express their perceptions of the world. These questions may ask for facts, generalizations, comparisons, explanations, conclusions, or inferences. For example:

1. Who wrote the play Hamlet? (Fact)
2. What generalizations can you make about the lifestyle in Great Britain? (Generalization)
3. How are American football and European football similar? Different? (Comparison)
4. What did the poet mean by the lines "Oh, what tangled webs we weave when first we practice to deceive"? (Explanation)
5. What conclusions can you draw when you know that the number of lives lost in traffic accidents decreased by 50 percent following enactment of the 55 mph national speed law? (Conclusion)
6. On any day of the year, the number of drownings in the state of New York correlates significantly with the total sales of ice cream in the state. What do you infer from these data? (Inference)

Each of these empirical questions prompts us to observe the world around us to find answers and proof that our answers are correct.

Evaluative Questions. Evaluative questions ask students to express their opinions or values. They ask the respondent either to express an opinion or to justify one. For example:

1. Who is the greatest living fiction writer? (Opinion)
2. Why do you say that the Rolls Royce is the best car ever made? (Justification of opinion)

Now we will expand the three major types of cognitive process questions into a set of five categories:

1. Definitional
    a. Definitions
2. Empirical
    b. Facts
    c. Relationships of facts (generalizations, comparisons, explanations, conclusions, or inference)
3. Evaluative
    d. Opinions
    e. Justification of opinions

Using these five categories, write your categorizing number to the left of each question.

_____ 1. Which is worse—a tornado or a hurricane?
_____ 2. What is a sonnet?
_____ 3. You said that the Edsel was actually a very good car. How do you know this?
_____ 4. In what year did the Revolutionary War end?
_____ 5. What do you think is the major difference between the Democratic party and the Republican party?
_____ 6. Who is the greatest U.S. president of the century?
_____ 7. How fast does light travel?
_____ 8. What did Patrick Henry mean by "Give me liberty or give me death!"
_____ 9. What is a decibel?
_____ 10. When did the stock market first crash?

Other Types of Questions

We have seen that questions used in the classroom can be effective when they are selected, analyzed, and grouped according to the cognitive processes that they provoke. But there are other considerations. For example, what demands does the question place on students? Does it require them to reproduce information given in class, or does it demand that they assemble information to produce their own answers? Another consideration might be the kind of mental activity or process the question requires. Except for rhetorical questions, which are not intended to draw a response, all questions must tell students what behavior is expected of them. A third consideration is the type of cue, if any, that the question gives to help clarify the expected answer.

Productive versus Reproductive Questions.   A productive question asks students either to produce their own information (a productive question) or to reproduce an answer given earlier by another source, such as the textbook or teacher (a reproductive question). The context of the question determines whether it is productive or reproductive. For instance, if the question "Why did the issue of Russian military forces in Cuba resurface in 1979?" had been discussed in class, or if you refer to a certain cause given by specific media, the question is reproductive. If the issue has not been previously discussed, students create their own explanations, making the question productive.

Information-Process Activity Questions.   A second comparison is the information-process activity that you want the student to perform. There are three general ways you may expect students to perform: yes/no, selection, and construction. An example of a yes/no question is: "In the 1992 presidential election, did President Clinton carry the state of New York?" Selection questions require the respondent to select from two or more given alternatives—for example, "Is lonely an adjective or an adverb?" Construction questions require students to construct their own response: "Explain your position on abortion."

Response-Clue Questions.   There are five types of response-clue questions, which give clues to the type of response desired: Wh-words, parallel terms, cited terms, excluded terms, and questions that lead the respondent.

> Questions with Wh-words, such as when, why, what, who, and how, may clue the student to answer in terms of time, reasons, things, people, and number.
>
> Questions with parallel terms ask the student to provide more information about the same topic: "Can you give another reason?" "And then what happened?" "Who else was involved?"
>
> Questions with cited terms offer a framework for the response—for example, "Which is the best college football team this year, in terms of cooperative teamwork?" "What were the major causes of the American Revolution, including social, economic, and political?"
>
> Questions with excluded terms tell the respondent what not to include in answering—for example, "Other than its cost, why is electricity an undesirable source for heating homes?" "Besides earning good grades, why do you believe it is necessary to learn all you can?"
>
> Questions that lead or guide the respondent to a yes or no response—for example, "Don't you agree?" "It's rather humid, isn't it?" "Most American cars aren't subcompacts, are they?"

THE QUESTIONING GRID

The questioning grid shown in Figure 6.3 can be used as an observation instrument in the classroom to record and classify questions as they are asked. For this purpose you may wish to record a T in the appropriate cells for all questions you ask and an S in the appropriate cells for each question students ask. Next to each question, list its type. Consider the following sample questions and their classifications:

Practice Questions	*Question Type*
1. To convert from centimeters to millimeters, do you divide?	Yes/no; reproduction
2. What is the symbol for silver—Ag or Si?	Selection: Wh-productive
3. What is the best gas to burn in a lawnmower?	Selection: Wh-reproductive
4. Is Athens the capital of Greece?	Construction-reproductive
5. If we exhaust our petroleum, will we turn to using coal?	Yes/no; productive
6. What are the basic differences between the Democratic and Republican parties?	Constructive: Wh-productive

REINFORCEMENT

You frequently can elicit desired pupil behavior by using reinforcement. All students want to be able to answer questions and perform assigned classroom tasks; they also want to believe that the teacher looks on them favorably. Some students do not believe they can benefit from school because they feel incapable of "fitting in." Such special cases are discussed later. Here we will look at how a teacher can affect a student's attitude through reinforcement.

FIGURE 6.3 The questioning grid

From *Strategic Questioning* (p. 29) by Ronald Hyman, Englewood Cliffs, N.J.: Prentice-Hall. Reprinted by permission.

			Production Type		Information-Process Activity			Response Clue				
			Productive	Reproductive	Yes/No	Selection	Construction	Wh-Interrogative Words	Parallel Terms	Cited Terms	Excluded Terms	Leading the Respondent
Short Set		Expanded Set										
Cognitive Process	Definitional	Definitions										
	Empirical	Facts										
		Relations between facts										
	Evaluative	Opinions										
		Justifications										

Too often the teacher responds to a student with "You're right, but that's not the answer I wanted," leaving the student confused and discouraged. Why not reverse this response, make the correction, and leave the student feeling correct? For example, "Your answer is not what I was looking for, but you are absolutely correct" or "That's interesting. I was expecting you to say . . . but you didn't. You gave an answer I had not even thought about."

To be effective, be sincere and address specific achievements. Too often teachers get into a rut and use the same reinforcement for every student. For example, they tend to overuse such general expressions as "good" and "okay," making the reward routine and ineffective. Other teachers overemphasize or overdramatize reward; sensing insincerity, students become skeptical of the teacher.

How can you judge how much emphasis to place on rewarding? The best guide is to consider the age-group and give rewards only when students have earned them. Overpraising can easily embarrass students from junior-high age upward and produce negative results. The key is to allow each student to feel successful at least one time every day. For some students this will require teacher concentration, but with experience you will learn to create opportunities for students to experience success.

REVIEW

Review is needed at least twice within each lesson—at the beginning and at the end. Between one day and the next, many things can intervene and distort students' memories of the previous lesson. By beginning each lesson with a brief review of the previous day's high points, you can tune students back into the topic under study.

According to Rosenshine (1986, p. 64):

Teachers should praise correct answers.

Effective teachers begin a lesson with a five to eight minute review of previous material, correction of homework, and review of relevant prior knowledge. To make sure that students possess the prerequisite skills for the day's lesson, the teacher can review concepts and necessary skills to do the next day's homework; have students correct each other's papers; ask about items where the students had difficulty or made errors; and review or provide additional practice on facts and skills that need reteaching.

Review at the end of the period can reemphasize the major points covered during the lesson, clarify the lesson, remove any misconceptions, and give students a feeling of accomplishment. Make a special effort to include material that will resurface at a later date. "Daily review is particularly important for teaching material that will be used in subsequent learning, for example, math facts, reading sight words, and grammar and skills such as math computation, math factoring, or solving chemical equations" (Rosenshine, 1986, pp. 64–65).

When reviewing, carefully select and clarify the major concepts developed during a period. Encourage students to ask questions about concepts they do not understand. This enables them to correct misconceptions and to process further the information they have gained. MacKenzie and White (1982) found that eighth- and ninth-grade students retained information gathered on a geography field trip when the trip was followed by such review activities as small-group discussions, sketching, and tasting leaves they had collected. Review also contributes to student achievement because it raises the level of students' interaction or involvement with the lesson. Correctly used, reviewing involves explicit instruction. During "explicit" instruction in well-structured areas, the teacher initially takes full responsibility for performing a task but, to increase students' alertness, gradually involves them in this part of the lesson.

NONVERBAL COMMUNICATION SKILLS

According to Galloway (1984), educators often overlook the relationship of setting and context to individual behavior and the influence of nonverbal expressions on teacher-student relationships. Students are turned on more by how we say things than by what we say. They constantly watch for excitement or enthusiasm in the teacher's expression. Even when you are not instructing verbally, students are getting information about how you feel. You communicate your attitudes, likes, dislikes, approval, and disapproval through facial expressions and other body language.

Whether they realize it or not, some teachers use their desks as walls for protection from their students; others use them as a symbol of authority. Thus the desk can become a nonverbal psychological barrier to good teacher-student communications. Until the teacher moves from behind it, true communication is not likely to occur.

The next time you are a classroom observer, take notes on the teacher's nonverbal communication. See how many different ways this teacher communicates nonverbally. If before you graduate you have an opportunity to peer-teach a lesson or to teach a lesson to public school students, near the end of the lesson you might ask your students what different ways they believed you were communicating nonverbally with them. Ask how they felt about what you did and about how you did it. Today's students tend to be honest and say what they feel, so you can learn much from them.

Feedback

While students receive nonverbal communication from you, you can simultaneously receive feedback from them. Alert teachers watch their students' movements and emotions and use what they see to adjust their teaching methods. For example, suppose several students begin yawning while you are teaching. You might open a window or lower the room thermostat. If the drowsiness continues, you might change your teaching style to include more inflection in your voice. Unless you are dealing with students who come from very poor homes—and therefore have poor nutrition and inadequate sleeping facilities—or with students who have night jobs, the yawning can probably be attributed to something you are or are not doing. Again, be aware of any clues students give you regarding a communication breakdown.

Another way to obtain feedback is to change the bulletin board to let students give their impressions of you. For example, at the end of each lesson or each day, middle-level students might be given a positive "thumbs-up tab" or a negative "purple-shaft tab" to attach to the board to show how the teacher left them feeling on that particular day. High-school teachers may prefer to use a closed suggestion box. You should use this information to improve your teaching style. For best results, let the student put the symbols on the board anonymously, lest some respond the way they think you want them to.

Eye Contact

An important nonverbal teaching skill is eye contact. Teaching should be a multi-channeled dialogue. Beginning teachers, usually because of insecurity, avoid direct eye contact with students and instead look at their notes. To prevent this, try using fewer notes. A list of the major ideas—or at most a broad outline of the lesson—may work better than a detailed lesson plan. Focus on a few individuals in each conversation. Public school teaching is not lecturing. It is a multicommunicative process between teacher and students and among students.

We all know people who, when they talk to us, look over our shoulders, above us, or anywhere but directly at us. A little disconcerting, isn't it? We may become so distracted by this annoying behavior that we miss what they are saying. It's no different in the classroom. Without eye contact, teachers experience a communication breakdown and the learning environment becomes far from optimal.

Other Nonverbal Teacher Behaviors

Much of what a teacher does can be characterized as a combination of verbal and non-verbal behaviors. When you ask a student to settle down, you are communicating verbally. At the same time, however, you may be gesturing with your hands or giving a look that is actually more effective in getting your point across. Here are a few examples of such verbal and nonverbal communication (addressing mainly the nonverbal):

1. You have asked a question to which the student has responded incorrectly. Smiling, you indicate in a nice way that you were seeking a different answer. Your smile alone says, "That's all right. Nobody's perfect."
2. While you are talking, you see a student poking his pencil at a classmate. You pause, tilt your head downward, and look over the top of your glasses. The foolishness stops immediately.

These are examples of occasions when your nonverbal behavior can play an extremely important role in teacher-student relationships. With verbal reprimands only, these relationships would tend to weaken.

Body Movement

The time when teachers hid behind a desk is, we hope, long gone. You must circulate among your students so you can communicate with each one. Because talking to individual students often disturbs the others, much of the communication must be done nonverbally. Walk throughout the room, pause momentarily, or give a smile and nod your head to give your students confidence in you. Older students prefer nods, winks, and hand signals to excessive touching. Even more important, this type of individual recognition can help build self-confidence. Students feel good about themselves when they know their teacher is pleased with them.

Using Silence

Most teachers talk too much. After studying teachers for eight years, Goodlad (1984) reported that, on average, teachers talk 75 percent of each class period, leaving little opportunity for pupil participation. Learning to remain quiet requires self-discipline.

When advised by her supervisor that she talked too much, a first-year teacher made tapes of her classes and kept a daily log of her experiences. Over time she was able to analyze, record, and evaluate her progress. However, she did more. On her desk, she put a sign that said in Swedish "Shut up." The teacher explained that she had a tendency to answer her own questions before the students could. She then noted, "The uncomfortable quiet can actually be a time for thinking . . . and if the teacher outwaits the students, one of the latter will begin speaking."

How much silence can you tolerate? How much can you refrain from talking? Instead of feeling obligated to respond to student comments, encourage other students to respond. Try to lead rather than dominate the discussions.

You will be asked many questions for which you will not have an answer. To bluff is pure folly, because it can misguide students and destroy your credibility. Do not feel obligated to know all the answers. Admitting your limitations will not show weakness if you show a willingness to seek the answers.

The Hidden Curriculum

The total process of communicating nonverbally, intentionally or not, has a considerable effect on students. Sometimes the effects are positive, and sometimes they are negative. Nonverbal communication is part of the hidden curriculum. Michael Radz (1978) states the significance of the hidden curriculum:

> One should not underestimate the knowledge, skills, and attitudes that are acquired through the informal culture of the school. Indeed, the hidden curriculum can reinforce classroom learning or make it a gross hypocrisy. It can promote the development of individual self-esteem or it can crush a fragile self-concept. It can make learning a meaningless experience in gamesmanship." (p. 6)

Teachers can use the hidden curriculum to communicate positive, constructive messages. For example, an orderly, task-oriented classroom routine can socialize students to the world of work (Doyle, 1986). The energy needed to communicate positive constructives can come from various sources, but it cannot come from nowhere. One possible energy source for helping at-risk students become more positive and self-confident is arts education. According to Sautter (1994):

> The arts promote the "hidden curriculum" of social behavior to improve self-discipline, self-motivation, self-esteem, and social interaction. These are all necessary characteristics contained within the spirit of thwarts. (p. 436)

For further discussion on the significance of the hidden curriculum see Henson (1995).

Detecting Boredom

Another group of nonverbal signals that teachers must learn to recognize are those that show boredom. Nierenberg's *How to Read a Person Like a Book* (1971) includes in this group: resting head in hands, giving a blank stare, and doodling. Other clear indicators of boredom are squirming (because it involves movement of the entire body as one shifts weight from hip to hip while simultaneously repositioning arms, legs, feet, and hands) and yawning, which adds the dimension of sound. Squirming might carry other messages, such as a need to use the restroom, and yawning may indicate a physical need for sleep, but what they probably mean is that communications are breaking down.

Students are also frequently seen resting their heads in their hands. They may or may not be aware that this gesture also symbolizes boredom. By the time they reach high school, most know that such actions are not polite and have begun substituting more subtle expressions, such as giving a blank stare or silently doodling. A few highly creative individuals do express their creativity through doodling, and a few great thinkers are glassy-eyed when they engage in deep thought, but these are a minority and their wisdom can be detected by examining their drawings or pursuing their thoughts with questions. Sometimes students offer fake, hollow stares to trick the teacher, but most students today are quite open, both verbally and nonverbally.

EFFECTIVE SCHOOLS RESEARCH

The effective schools research has provided additional insights that teachers can use to improve communications in the classroom. After reviewing approximately two decades of school effectiveness, Ornstein and Levine (1990) offer guidelines for implementing six multischool projects to generate more effective elementary and secondary schools.

1. Enforce discipline; the school must be safe and orderly.
2. Establish remedial and tutoring programs.
3. Teachers must assign and properly check homework. Students must be held accountable for homework; teachers must explain and discuss homework.
4. Improvement goals must be sharply focused to avoid teacher and school overload.
5. Instructional teachers must avoid elaborate schemes to train all staff and must focus on a particular instructional technique.
6. Significant technical assistance must be available to faculty.
7. Effective school projects should be data-driven.
8. Effective schools must avoid reliance on bureaucratic implementation that stresses forms and checklists.
9. Effective schools should seek out and consider using materials, methods, and approaches that have been successful elsewhere.
10. The success of an effective school's project depends on a judicious mixture of autonomy among participating faculties and a mixture of autonomy among the faculties and directives from the central office, a kind of "directed autonomy."

RECAP OF MAJOR IDEAS

1. Teacher efficacy is essential for maximum learning and is established by setting clear goals and objectives, quickly getting all students on task, and keeping them on task until the goals and objectives are attained.
2. Teachers must communicate to students how each class's activities relate to class goals. Otherwise, students will not know the purpose of the activities they are doing.
3. By communicating high but realistic levels of expectations to students, teachers can increase the amount of learning in each class.
4. Teacher educators have failed to impress on prospective teachers the im-

portance of research for classroom teaching. As new information is discovered, teachers can use it to improve their teaching in ways that are currently unknown.

5. Teachers usually give students only one second to respond to questions. By giving them three seconds, they can significantly improve the learning process.
6. By listening to students, teachers can identify topics that prove to be excellent channels of communication.
7. Do not begin or continue a lesson without all students' attention.
8. Choose examples that relate to adolescent experiences rather than those that relate to your experiences.
9. When directing a question to a student, help the student respond favorably.
10. Nonverbal teacher behaviors communicate important messages to students. Improve your nonverbal communication skills by observing and critiquing yourself.
11. Get involved with research studies to improve your observational skills, instructional decision-making skills, and lesson planning skills.

CASES

Chapter 13 will portray the teacher as a manager of students, equipment, space, and activities. Chapter 6 has purposely omitted communications because an entire chapter was needed to explore the teacher's role in managing the complex communications in the classroom. The following experiences give you an opportunity to see how important good communications are in instruction.

CASE 1: A NEED FOR TACT IN QUESTIONING

Jack Cobb was a good biology teacher who planned thoroughly. Each day's lesson was highly content oriented but there was room for student participation. Jack claimed to be student centered, but he was not very patient when he asked questions. In one particular class period he damaged the self-esteem of three students considered slow learners. In each case he had asked a question to which the student responded incorrectly. His response was "That's wrong. Who knows the answer?"

Discussion

1. How can students be made to feel successful when responding incorrectly to a question?

    This chapter makes it clear that the teacher has both the opportunity and the responsibility for making a student feel successful. No matter how incorrect a response, a resourceful teacher can guide the student out of despair or embarrassment. Some techniques for doing this have been discussed, but here is another possibility:

Jack Cobb did not realize, or did not care, that his remarks left students feeling inadequate. He could have said, "I don't believe you're totally correct. Would you like some help?" The student would surely have said yes. Then he could ask for volunteers. When the correct answer was given, Jack could go back to the original student and say, "Do you think that's right?"

This type of response will let a student know that he or she was incorrect but will not exclude that student from the discussion. The student makes the decision to seek assistance and has the final comment, since the teacher returns to him or her for verification of the correct response. A teacher who treats students humanely will earn the entire class's respect.

2. Should slow learners be asked questions in class?

All students should have an opportunity to respond to questions or to originate questions of their own, but the teacher should be selective in matching questions to students. Unfortunately, too many questions require short answers of merely yes or no, but this may be the best type of question to ask a student with low achievement. Although shallow questions and responses result in little additional knowledge, they do give the student a chance to be successful.

But slow students should not receive only low-level questions. When a student volunteers to respond to a question that appears too difficult, the student deserves a chance to try. If correct, the student will be pleased and so will you. The experience might provide the encouragement needed for accepting other challenges.

CASE 2: TEACHING STUDENTS, NOT SUBJECTS

When Sue began teaching in high school, her students were amazed at how smart she was. She seemed to have the facts, names, and dates all memorized, and she could give from memory every detail of any war. But Sue never tried to show off. She was in fact a borderline introvert. When the beginning bell rang for each period, she seemed to lack the courage necessary to start the lesson. After calling the roll, she would mumble about the homework assignment for several minutes without looking up from her book. A typical lesson started like this:

> (Looking down at her text): All right, class, what did we learn yesterday? What did we say was the cause of World War II? What did we learn about Germany's economic status at the time? Why did the United States stay out of the war for so long?

Discussion Questions

1. Why do you think Sue talked to her book instead of to her students?
2. How could Sue improve her questioning?

ACTIVITIES

Good teaching requires good communication, but this does not always happen automatically. Some teachers depend mostly on verbal communications; others, who are less verbal, use more nonverbal strategies to communicate. Every teacher should combine verbal and nonverbal strategies to improve two-way communications in the classroom. The following activities may challenge you to relate these strategies to your own behavior style.

1. How much do you talk? When you are in a one-on-one conversation with a colleague, who dominates the discussion? Think about it. Do you tend to talk too much? Too little? Devise a plan for helping yourself reach a balance.
2. Now that you are aware of a number of effective nonverbal strategies for communicating, relate this knowledge to teaching. Consider your unique attributes and explain how you can use nonverbal communication techniques in your classroom.
3. From your own experience as a student, can you list any techniques not included in this book that could be effective for classroom application?
4. Check the library for additional recent books and articles on business and speech communications. Try to relate each to teaching, altering it to serve teachers better.

REFERENCES

Alessi, S. M., & Trollip, S. R. (1991). *Computer-based instruction, methods, and development.* Englewood Cliffs, NJ: Prentice Hall.

Berliner, D. C. (1990, March). Creating the right environment for learning. *Instructor, 99,* 16–17.

Brooks, D. M. (1985). Beginning the year in junior high: The first day of school. *Educational Leadership, 42,* 76–78.

Bruner, J.S. (1981). On instructability. Paper presented at the meeting of the American Psychological Association, Los Angeles.

Buckner, J. H., and Bickel, F. (1991, January). If you want to know effective teaching, why not ask your middle school kids? *Middle School Journal, 22*(3), 26–29.

Cazden, C. (1986). Classroom discourse. In M. C. Wittrock (Ed.), *Handbook of research on teaching methods* (3rd ed.). New York: Macmillan.

Doyle, W. (1986). Classroom organization and management. In M. C. Wittrock (Ed.), *Handbook of research on teaching* (3rd ed.). New York: Macmillan.

Ellsworth, P.C., & Sindt, V.G. (1994). Helping "Aha" to Happen: The Contributions of Irving Sigel. *Educational Leadership, 51*(5), 40–44.

Evertson, C. C., Anderson, G., Anderson, L., & Brophy, J. (1980). Relationships between classroom behaviors and student outcomes in junior high mathematics and English classes. *American Educational Research Journal, 17,* 43–60.

Fisher, C. W. (1980). Teaching behavior, academic learning time, and student achievement: An overview. In C. Denham & A. Lieberman (Eds.), *Time to learn* (p. 26). Washington, DC: U.S. Department of Education, National Institute of Education.

Fuller, B. (1982). The organizational context of individual efficacy. *Review of Educational Research.* Washington DC: *American Educational Research Association, 52*(1), 7-30.

Galloway, C. M. (Ed.) (1984). Nonverbal and teacher-student relationships: An intercultural perspective. *Theory into Practice, 16*(3), 129-133.

Good, T. L. (1984, August). Paper presented at the First Annual Conference for Relating Research and Practice. East Lansing, MI: Michigan State University.

Good, T. L., & Brophy, J. E. (1984). *Looking in classrooms* (3rd ed.). New York: Harper & Row.

Good, T.L., & Brophy, J. (1995). *Contemporary educational psychology* (5th ed). White Plains, NY: Longman.

Good, T. L., & Grouws, D. A. (1979). The Missouri mathematics effectiveness project. *Journal of Educational Psychology, 71,* 143-155.

Goodlad, J. I. (1984). *A place called school.* New York: McGraw Hill.

Green, J. L. (1983). A study of schooling: Some findings and hypotheses. *Phi Delta Kappan, 64,* 465-470.

Gronbeck, B. E., McKerron, R. E., Ehninger, R. D., & Monroe, A. H. (1994). *Principles and types of speech communication* (12th ed). New York: HarperCollins.

Grubaugh, S. (1989). Nonverbal language techniques for better classroom management and discipline. *High School Journal, 73,* 34-40.

Hines, C. V., Cruickshank, D. R., & Kennedy, J. J. (1982, March). Measures of teacher clarity and their relationships to student achievement and satisfaction. Paper presented at the annual meeting of the American Educational Research Association, New York.

Hyman, R. T. (1979). *Strategic Questioning.* Englewood Cliffs, N.J.: Prentice-Hall.

Leithwood, K., Menzies, T., and Jantzi, D. (1994). Earning teachers' commitment to curriculum reform. *Peabody Journal of Education, 69*(4), 38-61.

MacKenzie, A. A., & White, R. T. (1982). Fieldwork in geography and long-term memory structures. *American Educational Research Journal, 19,* 623-632.

Mills, S. R., Rice, C. T., Berliner, D. C., & Rousseau, E. W. (1980). The correspondence between teacher questions and student answers in classroom discourse. *Journal of Experiential Education, 48,* 194-209.

Mosston, M. (1972). *From command to discovery.* Belmont, CA: Wadsworth.

Nirenberg, G. I. (1971). *How to read a person like a book.* New York: Pocket Books.

Ornstein, A. C., & Levine, D. U. (1990, November/December). School effectiveness and reform: Guidelines for action. *The Clearing House, 64*(2), 115-118.

Radz, M. A. (1978). Responsibility, education, and the early adolescent. In C. H. Sweat (Ed.), *Responsibility of education in the junior high middle school* (p. 6). Danville, IL: Interstate.

Redfield, D. L., & Rousseau, E. W. (1981). A meta-analysis of experimental research on teacher questioning behavior. *Review of Educational Research, 51,* 237-245.

Riban, D. M. (1976). Examination of a model for field studies in science. *Science Education, 60,* 1-11.

Rosenshine, B. V. (1986). Synthesis of research on explicit teaching. *Educational Leadership, 43,* 60-69.

Rowe, M. B. (1978, March). Wait, wait, wait. *School Science and Mathematics, 78,* 207-216.

Rudick, K. L. (1994). *Training and the transactional view.* Unpublished manuscript, Eastern Kentucky University, Richmond, KY.

Sautter, R. C. (1994). An arts education school reform strategy. *Phi Delta Kappan, 75*(6), 432-437.

Stake, R. E., & Easley, J. A. (Eds.) (1978). Case studies in science education (Vol. 1, p. 29). Urbana, IL: Center for Instructional Research and Curriculum Evaluation.

Trachtenberg, D. (1974). Student tasks in text material: What cognitive skills do they tap? *Peabody Journal of Education, 52,* 54-57.

SUGGESTED READINGS

Berliner, D. C. (1984). A half-full glass: A review of research on teaching. In P. A. Hosford (Ed.), *Using what we know about teaching* (p. 66). Alexandria, VA: Association for Supervision and Curriculum Development.

Brown, D. S. (1990, November). Middle level teachers' perceptions of action research. *Middle School Journal, 22*(2), 30-32.

Egbert, R. L. (1984). The role of research in teacher education. In R. L. Egbert & M. M. Kluender (Eds.), *Using research to improve teacher education.* Lincoln, NE: American Association of Colleges for Teacher Education.

Erasmus, C. C. (1989). Ways with Stories: Listen to the stories aboriginal people tell. *Language Arts, 66*(3), 267-275.

Henson, K. T. (1995). *Curriculum development for education reform.* New York: Harper Collins.

Smith, B. O. (1980). A design for a school pedagogy. Washington, DC: U.S. Government Printing Office.

part THREE

Providing for Individual Differences

Early in their programs, most prospective teachers learn that to be successful and enable students to attain a high level of achievement, they must meet all students' needs and interests. They quickly ask how this can be done in a class of 30 or so students whose needs and interests are so different. All teachers face this dilemma. Chapter 7 provides general information to help you develop an individualized approach to instruction. Chapter 8 will help you meet the needs of students with exceptional limitations and those who are exceptionally gifted. Chapter 9 acquaints you with the responsibilities and roles of teachers whose students come from different ethnic and cultural backgrounds.

Individualizing Instruction

If students do not learn the way we teach them, then we must teach them the way they learn

Carol Marshall

OBJECTIVES

List at least four approaches commonly used to meet individual learning differences.

Differentiate between two major categories of ability grouping.

Describe ways to avoid common problems that result from ability grouping.

Describe ways instruction for low-ability groups should differ from instruction for average groups.

Name the elements on which mastery learning hinges.

Design a contingency contract.

Differentiate between teacher-paced and group-paced instruction and between group-based and individual-based instruction.

List categories of learner preferences used to determine learning styles.

Discuss strengths and weaknesses of matching learner and teacher styles.

Describe one way that you can make your classroom environment more personal.

PRETEST

	Agree	Disagree	Uncertain
1. Individualizing instruction is contextual, which means that the success of a particular approach may vary as the situation changes.	____	____	____
2. The simple act of grouping students according to ability usually increases learning.	____	____	____
3. When using ability grouping, teachers should spend more time with the less-capable students.	____	____	____
4. Ability grouping can be psychologically destructive to both high achievers and low achievers.	____	____	____
5. Intraclass grouping produces more competition than interclass grouping.	____	____	____
6. Recent studies show that, given adequate time, motivation, and presentation of material, at least 90 to 95 percent of all high-school students can master all the curriculum objectives.	____	____	____
7. Teaching style has little effect on students' ability to learn.	____	____	____
8. Teachers should use only the teaching styles their students prefer.	____	____	____

9. In many ways learning is an individual
   experience.   _____   _____   _____
10. As many as one-third of all students are
    at risk.   _____   _____   _____

Middle-Level Message

One question prospective teachers usually have is how to plan and teach so that each lesson meets the needs of 20 to 30 students whose abilities range from educationally handicapped to gifted. By the time such a diverse class reaches the senior grades, many of the poor performers drop out of school, and some mediocre performers find themselves and become serious students. But at the middle level this narrowing process has not yet occurred. At this level the teacher must face the very difficult challenge of meeting a wide range of needs. Bradley and Fisher (1995, p. 13) have said that "students in middle school vary in as many ways as imaginable, including physically, emotionally, intellectually, and socially." This is true for all secondary students.

Although there is no guaranteed solution to this problem, one approach to meeting individual needs is ability grouping. But sometimes this approach produces disastrous results because teachers mismanage the groups. Chapter 7 explains how grouping can and should be used and identifies common mistakes that teachers make when using groups. Because transescents' general lack of self-confidence makes them especially vulnerable to the psychological damage ability grouping produces, you must learn how to avoid these common effects of the approach.

THE NEED TO INDIVIDUALIZE

As prospective teachers begin their involvement in public school classrooms, they quickly are introduced to classes that contain students with a wide range of abilities. They can be overwhelmed by the challenge of designing instruction for students who have not only a broad range of abilities but also different levels of motivation (Bradley & Fisher, 1995).

Chapter 8 suggests ways to plan instruction to meet the needs of students who vary so much from the average that they require special, individualized lesson plans. Chapter 9 discusses special techniques for teaching students of varying ethnic groups and cultures. This chapter looks at ways to meet the instructional needs of all students in secondary and middle school classrooms, but you can use many of the strategies presented in this chapter in special and multicultural classes.

Individualized instruction can be defined as instruction that meets all students' needs. Its existence is based on the premise that students are different—indeed, that each student is different and therefore has unique learning needs that each teacher must make special efforts to meet. When teachers do not consider the variety of student needs, at least two things happen: Some students become bored because they are inadequately challenged, and others become discouraged because too much is expected of them.

Although educators recognize the need to individualize instruction, few agree on how to do so. This chapter looks at some common approaches that schools and teachers use to individualize instruction. The approaches discussed are far from all-inclusive, however. Every day new approaches are being applied. Some of the more successful innovations may never get beyond the immediate classroom walls; others are studied and tested, and the results are disseminated through the professional literature. This is the case with the approaches described in this chapter.

As you read about each innovation, consider its potential for your future classes. Make a list of ways to improve each method, and think of ways to modify these approaches to make them more useful for you with your own future students. Remember that most of these approaches began in the minds of a few teachers who believed they needed a certain method to reach particular students. Explore your own mind, the minds of other educators with whom you come into contact, and the ideas of those who have done research and shared their findings in journals and books.

IN-CLASS ABILITY GROUPING

A common approach to reducing the task of teaching 30 or so students of varying abilities and needs is to form subgroups of students who share abilities and interests. Simple arithmetic would suggest that dividing a class of 30 students into five groups of six students each would reduce the range to which the instruction must be adapted to one-fifth the original range. But to conclude that this maneuver would improve the level of performance by a similar margin is wrong. The results of ability grouping are not usually so monumental. Yet ability grouping does tend to improve student learning. An analysis of more than 40 studies of ability grouping found that grouping improves students' ability to learn slightly and improves their motivation level greatly (Julik, 1981).

Grouping

But ability grouping may not be appropriate for all students. Lindbald (1994, p. 292) explains that "students with poor self-images and those with over-inflated egos can create group conflict that is difficult to resolve." This suggests that when students with extremely weak or extremely strong self-image are grouped, teachers may need to increase the level of supervision.

Individualizing Instruction

How effectively ability grouping improves learning depends on how you adjust the instruction to each group. We do know that, in general, less-capable students need more concrete material and examples of ways to apply newly learned concepts to real-world experiences and that more-capable students need greater challenges. But the challenges must be of different types. For example, a teacher of ability-grouped math students should not merely assign the upper group a much larger number of the same type of problems given to less-capable groups. Instead, the upper group might receive more creative challenges that require divergent thinking. Advanced groups might even be assigned to develop problems instead of solutions or to find a variety of solutions to a problem.

Expect to spend more time with the less-capable students, especially after the more-capable groups get on task, when you use ability grouping. Slower students may require more careful monitoring and guidance. Good, Reys, Grouws, and Molyran (1990–1991) say that when working in groups, higher-ability students tend to dominate the group or to work alone. Furthermore, low-ability students perform less well in school when placed with other low-ability students (Calfee & Brown, 1979). This is probably partly because teachers usually spend less time with the lower groups. A review of the literature found that the amount of time teachers devote to direct instruction is directly related to student achievement (Centra & Potter, 1980).

Unintentional Differential Treatment

Ability grouping requires different treatment for different groups at different levels, but you must avoid unintentional differential treatment. For example, although it is realistic to expect high-ability students to cover more material faster than lower groups, teachers often make unrealistic demands. Shavelson (1983) found that high-ability groups were paced as much as 15 times faster than lower-ability groups, increasing dramatically the difference in amount of material the two groups covered.

Teachers tend to treat students for whom they hold low expectations in several different ways. For example, Brophy (1983, p. 274) reports that teachers treat these students in the following unique ways. The teacher will:

1. Wait less time for lows to answer questions.
2. Give lows the answer or call on someone else.
3. Provide inappropriate reinforcement.
4. Criticize lows more than highs for failure.
5. Praise lows less than highs for success.
6. Fail to give lows feedback on their public responses.
7. Interact with lows less and pay less attention to them overall.
8. Call on lows less often in class.
9. Ask for lower performance levels from lows.
10. Smile less, have less eye contact, have fewer attentive postures toward lows.

Differences in Evaluation

You may want to devise nontraditional ways to evaluate advanced students. For example, objective tests may not be able to measure the kinds of growth anticipated for this group. You may choose oral discussions or one-on-one questioning to discover the depth of insight these students have developed. Term projects may be preferable to examinations. For example, the teacher of a student who writes a computer program to breed plants may find that the resulting product—that is, the computer program—is itself the best measure of success for this assignment.

Precautions

Whenever students are grouped by ability, you must take certain precautions. There is a certain prestige in being affiliated with the upper group(s), while a certain disgrace befalls students who are assigned to the lower group(s). Attempts to disguise the ranking or ordering of groups usually fail. Indeed, students often know the level to which they are assigned even before their teachers know it.

Do not make comments that allow comparisons among ability groups, and do not allow students to make judgmental or derogatory comments about any group. Sometimes teachers contribute to the caste problem without even realizing their error. Mrs. Bentley's Typing I class had about 30 girls and 10 boys, none of whom had previously taken typing. She had a unique system for reporting individual grades. Along one wall she posted a white sheet of paper with a landscape scene. It had a fence in the foreground and a blue sky above the fence. Higher up were beautiful, fluffy cumulus clouds. On the fence sat about 40 bluebirds. Each had the name of a student.

The namesake of the bird called "James" lived in one of the city's worst ghettos. As each student developed the ability to type 25 words a minute, the namesake bird would leave the fence and begin to ascend. Right away, several birds made their departures. These represented students who owned a typewriter and had been familiar with typing at the beginning of the class. This frustrated James because he was still learning the keys when others were typing more than 25 words per minute.

Each day he found himself trying a little harder and making more mistakes (each mistake carried a five-word penalty). By the end of the year, some of the bluebirds were flying into the clouds. James's bluebird was still sitting on the fence.

Peer approval is important to students in middle and high school, and its absence can reinforce the emotional damage resulting from ability grouping. Also, upper-level groups tend to become snobbish and condescending toward members of lower groups. Make a list of at least five ways teachers can limit the amount of psychological damage that ability grouping might cause.

INTERCLASS ABILITY GROUPING

In some schools, ability grouping is done independently of teachers—standardized intelligence tests determine student placement in groups. Under these circumstances, teachers are still responsible for protecting the lower groups from ridicule.

Interclass and intraclass (within the class) grouping produce different types of competition. When students are grouped within the same class, they are forced to compete with classmates, but when the grouping is done externally the competition is between two or more classes.

For several centuries schools in England have had "houses." A house is a group of students whose abilities are heterogeneous. In other words, each group (or house) contains students that have a wide range of abilities. The houses frequently compete in oral debates. This encourages cooperation, not competition, among members of a group.

Other schools choose homogeneous ability grouping. For example, five groups of students with similar abilities may be formed, producing five "tracks," each track representing a different level of general ability. Here is an example.

Reflection

Read the following description and respond to the questions below.

A School District Uses Systematic Grouping

You walk into a seventh-grade classroom and see several groups of students throughout the room. On closer observation, you notice that Group A is collecting weather data, using a weather vane, thermometer, and hygrometer; Group B is constructing a U.S. map with a weather symbols key at the bottom, and Group C is shading the map to show general rainfalls, altitudes, and temperatures. Groups D and E are competing vigorously, developing new ways of forecasting the weather one year into the future. On the wall are color-coded charts that show at a glance the group level to which any student belongs.

You notice that Bobby Burns belongs to Group A in English, Group B in social studies and science, Group C in mathematics, and Group D in spelling. A small square is added above Bobby's name as he completes a unit in the appropriate subject. It doesn't seem to bother Bobby that he belongs to groups of different academics levels; his rate of performance in each group appears to be more important to him.

If you were teaching in a school system that was contemplating using a similar approach, and if you had an opportunity to vote for or against a tracking program, how would you vote? Why?

This example is typical of a classroom in one of the nation's largest and most progressive school systems; all 185 schools use the approach found in this classroom. Several similar approaches to cooperative learning have been developed. One system, called Teams-Games-Tournaments (TGT), has heterogeneous groups competing for academic awards (Slavin, 1980). It enables low-ability and high-ability students to contribute the same number of points to the team. TGT has been used in more than 2,000 schools. Group games arrange for each group member to have some of the information needed to solve a problem, ensuring that everyone is responsible for group success (Sharon, 1980).

GRADE CONTRACTS

Grade contracting is a method that recognizes that students are more highly motivated by some topics than others. It permits a student to place more emphasis on certain topics. Here is how it works.

At the beginning of each unit of study, students are issued contracts. According to the student's ability and interest in the topic, the student agrees to perform a certain amount of work to earn a certain grade. Sample contracts are shown in Figure 7.3 (p. 175) and figure 12.3 (p. 327). As shown in Chapter 12, grade contracts can be powerful motivators. In addition to contracting for specific grades, students can contract to earn free time and other rewards.

USING INSTRUCTIONAL MODELS

Another way to organize lessons is to use the formats provided by instructional models. An advantage to using models is that models have been examined and tested and have been proven theoretically and practically sound. Lewellen (1990, p. 63) says that a model should be "systematic, descriptive, explanatory, and widely applicable." Some examples of instructional models include direct instruction, scientific inquiry, concept attainment, and the Socratic questioning model. Reyes (1990) endorses the use of such models to plan lessons:

> Models provide a convenient organizer for teaching the precepts of effective teaching or for teaching the steps of lesson planning. For the teacher in the classroom at any level, models of instruction can structure his or her decision making. For example, the teacher's choice of classroom questions, homework assignments, introductions to lessons, and so on are typically influenced by the instructional model being used as an organizer. (p. 214)

Information Processing Model

A popular contemporary way to examine and describe learning is by viewing it mechanically, as you might describe the process that computers use to store and retrieve information. Using the five senses to gather information (Figure 7.1), humans immediately decide which information to store. A perceptual screen is used to filter out unwanted information (Figure 7.2).

Information selected for keeping is stored in one of two places. Information that is to be used immediately or in the near future is stored in the working memory; other information is stored in the long-term memory. Van Gulick (1990) believes that students cannot possess information unless it is stored in a manner that allows them to use it. He stresses the need for interconnections.

As you introduce new information to students you can use advance organizers to point students toward the most important information, thus affecting the information they retain. Then, by helping them relate this new information to existing knowledge, you can help your students get meaning from otherwise meaningless information.

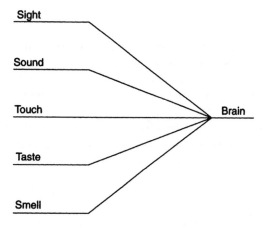

FIGURE 7.1 Our five senses act as receptors

Historically, teachers have generally taught subject matter without emphasizing—indeed often without even addressing—the question of how we know what we know. When the "how" has been addressed, our teachers have taught us that we learn through our senses and through applying logic. Notice that these channels are cognitive. In recent years, we have learned to directly study our minds (metacognition) to discover how they operate. Note, too, that this emphasis has also been restricted to cognition.

What our teachers have failed to teach us is that we also learn through our emotions. Since a major way that we express our emotions is through the arts, should we not also explore the role that the arts play in our learning? Are there not many other

FIGURE 7.2 Information is stored in either short-term or long-term memory

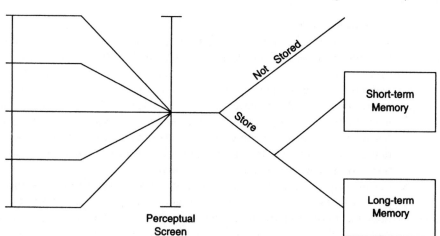

ways that our feelings and perceptions affect our learning? Should we also be studying how our feelings help us learn?

Oddliefson (1994) tells us that several prominent scientists, including Einstein, have stressed the inextricable link between the sciences and the senses and that Einstein said that the aim of science is to comprehend the sense experiences in their full diversity. Through the arts, we can and do grasp meanings that we might otherwise never have. Unfortunately, those who hold the education pursestrings seem to lack an appreciation for the perceptual arts. Considering the arts as frills in education (Perrin, 1994), less than 1% of the U.S. Department of Education's budget is devoted to arts education, and when local school districts are forced to trim their budgets the arts are usually first to go.

As you continue to study long-term curriculum planning, consider the need for balance among the arts and sciences. As you select activities, consider the power that each has for providing insights into our perceptions.

MASTERY LEARNING

In 1963 a professor at Harvard University wrote an article titled "A Model of School Learning" in which he challenged the then-accepted belief that students' intelligence quotients (IQs) are a major factor in determining academic success (Carroll, 1963). Carroll hypothesized that if three conditions were met, at least 90 to 95 percent of all high school students could master class objectives. The three conditions were (1) the student must be given all the time he or she needed, (2) each student must be properly motivated, and (3) the subject matter must be presented in a manner compatible with the individual student's learning style. (See Figure 7.3.)

Using Carroll's model, Benjamin S. Bloom and his students at the University of Chicago developed an education system called Learning for Mastery (LFM) (Block & Henson, 1986). This is a teacher-paced and group-based system. In other words, the teacher leads the lessons and the class as a group follows. Most mastery learning programs, however, are student paced (i.e., the students set the pace) and individually based. Each student pursues learning individually—at that student's own preferred pace (Guskey & Gates, 1986).

All mastery learning programs have several important characteristics in common. First, they provide students with different lengths of time to master each topic. Second, they give students opportunities to remediate or restudy material that proves difficult and then to retest without penalty. Third, all mastery learning programs use formative evaluations—evaluation designed to promote learning, not to be computed in the grading system. Short daily or weekly tests are given to diagnose learning weaknesses and teaching weaknesses; teachers and learners then adjust to improve the resulting learning. Finally, all mastery learning uses criterion-based evaluation. This means that the criteria essential for success are revealed before the study unit begins. (For further discussion of formative evaluation and criterion-based evaluation, see Chapter 15.)

Finally, with mastery learning programs, as with all other programs, the success depends on how it is used. Cunningham (1991) explains:

There are two essential elements of the mastery learning process. The first is an extremely close congruence between the material being taught, the teaching strategies employed, and the content measured. The second essential element is the provision of formative assessment, opportunities for students followed by feedback, corrective and enrichment activities. (p. 84)

How effective is mastery learning compared with traditional programs? Burns (1979) examined results from 157 mastery learning studies and discovered that 107 studies found that mastery learning students significantly outscored their traditionally

FIGURE 7.3 Twelfth-grade English six-week writing unit contract

Grade of B*

The grade of B can be earned through attending the class meetings and contributing to class discussions—especially those that involve critiquing the manuscripts of other participants and preparing a folder containing the following:

1. One query letter with all required criteria clearly marked as such
2. One cover letter with all required criteria clearly marked as such
3. A list of at least three journals selected for this manuscript, with a description of the following characteristics of each journal:
   a. audience
   b. average reading level
   c. average minimum-to-maximum manuscript pages, using an average of 300 words per manuscript page
   d. guidelines for submitting manuscripts
   e. name and address of editor.
4. A list of ideas for topics
5. A list of your personal writing requirements including preferred time of day, length of writing sessions, physical conditions, and materials and equipment
6. A description of at least two strategies that will help you deal with rejection.

Grade of A*

Complete all assignments for the grade of B and

1. Submit a second article on this topic rewritten to fit another type of journal, using the same cover-page format as on the first article.
2. Explain how this manuscript is more suited to this new audience in terms of the readership and the requirements of this journal.
3. Submit a system for tracking your manuscripts.
4. In one page, explain how this course has helped you to
   a. improve your writing skills (style)
   b. improve your chance of getting manuscripts accepted.

*All assignments are due and must be submitted on or before the last class session. All materials should be submitted typed and bound in a folder. Part I should contain the B-level assignments; Part II, the A-level assignments. Inexpensive cardboard folders with metal tabs inside are preferred.

taught counterparts, while 47 of the studies showed no significant differences. Only three of the 157 studies reported traditionally taught students outscoring mastery learning students. Burn's (1979) study of mastery learning over 15 years in 3,000 schools concluded that mastery learning was consistently more effective than traditional curriculums (Hyman & Cohen, 1979). Guskey and Gates (1986) reviewed 25 studies of group-based and teacher-paced mastery learning in elementary and secondary schools. In all 25 studies, the students in the mastery learning groups outlearned their counterpart control groups.

But mastery learning is not without its critics and criticisms. In a 1984 review of studies on mastery learning, Arlin (1984) reports some of the more popular criticisms. According to this report, some critics claim that the ability of mastery learning to equalize students' learning abilities is an overstatement. Some critics describe mastery learning as a "psychological trap": many claim that it does not have a proper conceptual base. Some even label mastery learning as a Robin Hood phenomenon that takes from the advanced students and give to the poor students. Arlin himself argues that studies that find all students equally capable should be interpreted more cautiously. Slavin (1989, p. 79) says that "if school districts expect that by introducing group-based mastery learning or Madeline Hunter's methods they can measurably increase their students' achievement, there is little evidence to support them."

When you read professional journal articles, remember that any innovation may experience either astounding success or total failure, depending on the conditions of the moment. The old adage "Never believe anything you hear, and believe only half of what you see" is good advice as an admonition to proceed with caution as you continue to learn more about your chosen profession.

MATCHING STUDENTS' LEARNING STYLES AND TEACHERS' TEACHING STYLES

How individuals concentrate on, process, internalize, and remember new and difficult academic information is called their *learning style* (Dunn & Dunn, 1992; Dunn, Dunn, & Perrin, 1994). Approximately three-fifths of learning style is biologically determined; the remaining two-fifths develops as an outgrowth of life experiences (Thies, 1979).

Dunn and Dunn (1992, 1993) describe learning styles as each person's:

1. Environmental (quiet versus sound, warm versus cool, bright versus soft illumination, and formal versus informal seating);
2. Emotional (motivation, persistence, responsibility, and internal versus external structure);
3. Sociological (learning alone, learning with peers, learning with adults present, learning in varied ways versus in patterns or routines; being motivated by a teacher; or being motivated by a parent);
4. Physiological (auditory, visual, tactual, or kinesthetic perceptual memory preferences, intake, energy highs and lows, and mobility versus passivity);
5. Psychological (global versus analytic and reflective versus impulsive) preferences (see Figure 7.4).

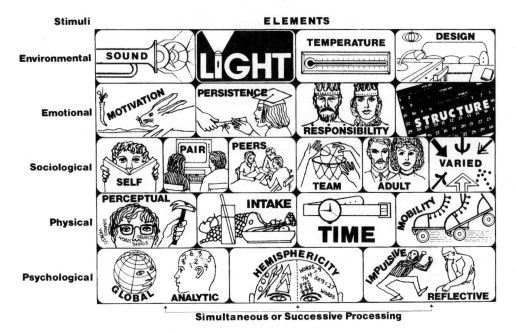

FIGURE 7.4 Learning styles model

From *Teaching secondary students through their individual learning styles* (p. 4) by R. Dunn and K. Dunn, 1993. Boston: Allyn and Bacon. Reprinted by permission.

Designed by Dr. Rita Dunn and Dr. Kenneth Dunn.

Research has demonstrated that teachers are able to identify only a few elements of their students' learning styles through observation; other elements are only identifiable through administration of reliable and valid tests (Beaty, 1986; Dunn, Dunn, & Price, 1977; Marcus, 1977). Keefe (1982) reported that the *Learning Style Inventory* (LSI) (Dunn & Dunn, 1978) is the most widely used instrument to identify the learning styles of K through 12 students.

Although learning style changes with age and maturity, in every family: (1) mothers and fathers invariably have opposite styles; (2) siblings learn differently from each other; and (3) offspring tend to learn differently from at least one or both of their parents (Dunn, Beasley, & Buchanan, 1994). Some learning-style differences exist between students from different cultures, but more have been shown among students within the same culture (Milgram, Dunn, & Price, 1993; Dunn & Griggs, 1995).

Research conducted at more than 100 institutions of higher education indicates widespread and growing interest in this construct (Research on the Dunn and Dunn Learning Styles Model, 1994). No learning style appears to be better or worse than another. Crucial to academic success is the matching of each student's learning style with either a complementary teaching style or instructional approaches that match students learning styles. Statistically higher standardized reading and mathematics achievement test scores were reported for elementary (Andrews, 1990, 1991; Lemmon, 1985; Stone, 1992) students and significantly higher grade-point averages were reported for secondary (Elliot, 1991) and college (Clark-Thayer, 1987) students. These data were confirmed in a meta-analysis of 42 experimental studies with the Dunn and Dunn Learning Styles Model conducted at many universities between 1980 and 1990. (Dunn, Griggs, Olson, Gorman, & Beasley, in press). In addition, practitioners reported impressive standardized achievement test gains among average students and underachievers (Andrews, 1991) and for special education students (Quinn, 1993).

For example, under the supervision of a team of researchers from the State University of Buffalo, classified learning disabled (LD) and emotionally handicapped (EH) students (K through 6) in the Buffalo City Schools were randomly selected and randomly assigned to two groups. The learning styles of the students in the experimental group were identified, and complementary methods and resources were used to teach them through their learning-style strengths and to teach themselves and each other with tactual and kinesthetic resources. The control group was taught with conventional lectures, discussions, readings, and writing assignments by their experienced special education teachers. Results at the end of two years revealed that the experimental group achieved statistically higher test scores than the control group in both reading and mathematics on two different standardized achievement tests—the *Woodcock-Johnson* (WJ) and the *California Tests of Basic Skills* (CTBS). In contrast, the control group evidenced academic losses between the pretest and posttest (Quinn, 1993) (Figure 7.5).

These findings revealed that LD and EH students whose instruction was not responsive to their learning styles achieved significantly less well than LD and EH students whose instruction was responsive to their learning styles. Buffalo's special education population was composed of multiculturally diverse students who had not been achieving well with conventional instruction. Improvement in the students' test scores suggested that their teachers' traditional teaching styles had been inappropriate for them. Significant improvement was also revealed in students' behavior and at-

FIGURE 7.5   Report from the Independent Research Team from the University of Buffalo

WJ: Woodcock-Johnson
CTBS: California Test of Basic Skills

Results of Standardized Achievement Test Scores in Reading and Mathematics for Students in the Buffalo City Schools' Learning Style Program (Experimental Group) in Contrast with the Results for Students in its Nonlearning Styles Program (Control Group) for the First Two Years of Program Implementation

Test Name	Group	Pretest	Posttest	Net Difference
WJ Reading	Exper.	72.38	79.1	+ 6.72
	Control	76.48	71.52	− 4.96 (loss)
WJ Math	Exper.	69.67	84.2	+ 14.53
	Control	73.52	69.09	− 4.43
CTBS Reading	Exper.	18.76	31.33	+ 12.57
	Control	24.83	21.25	− 3.58
CTBS Math	Exper.	15.83	18.61	+ 2.78
	Control	23.44	16.95	− 6.49

titude test scores (Kyriacou & Dunn, 1994). Buffalo, which normally reported a minimum 3 percent suspension rate, reported no suspensions at all during the entire two-year period in which the LD and EH students were involved in learning-styles instruction.

The Learning Styles of Gifted and Talented Adolescents in Nine Diverse Cultures

Recently, the learning styles of gifted versus nongifted adolescents in nine different cultures were examined. The populations included Brazilian, Canadian, Egyptian, Greek, Guatemalan, Israeli, Korean, Mayan, Filipino, and United States' adolescents diagnosed with the LSI (Dunn, Dunn, & Price, 1989). The learning-style preferences of students with high versus low levels of creative accomplishment in eight domains assessed by the *Tel Aviv Activities Inventory* were examined. Those domains were athletics, art, dance, leadership skills, literature, mathematics, and music.

1. Although significant differences existed among the nine culturally diverse groups, there were as many differences within each group as between groups. Despite some similarities among cultures, there were clear cross-cultural differences in both learning style and creative activity.
2. Gifted and nongifted students revealed significantly different learning style characteristics. Thus, instruction provided for one group is unlikely to be beneficial, and is likely to be detrimental, to other groups.
3. Gifted adolescents who comprised the population for the Milgram, Dunn, and Price (1993) investigation were highly motivated with strong preferences for kinesthetic or tactual—as opposed to visual and auditory—instruction. A meta-analysis of experimental research conducted in the United States between 1980 and 1990 revealed that students' learning-style preferences were the traits through which they most easily mastered new and difficult information (Dunn, Griggs, Olson, Gorman, & Beasley, in press).
4. Although gifted students prefer kinesthetic (active) and tactual (hands-on) instruction, they are able to learn auditorially or visually, although less easily or enjoyably. On the other hand, underachieving students, who also prefer kinesthetic or tactual learning, can only master difficult information through those modalities. It is not unusual for slow learners to have either only one or no perceptual strength.
5. Despite cultural background, students gifted in a particular domain had essentially similar learning styles, which differed significantly from the styles of the gifted in other talent domains. Thus, the gifted in each talent domain—art, dance, drama, leadership, literature, mathematics, music, or sports—reported learning through styles that were significantly different from the characteristics of the gifted in other talent domains and from those of nongifted.
6. The gifted adolescents from nine diverse cultures preferred to learn either by themselves or with an authoritative teacher. Cooperative learning and

small-group instructional strategies should not be imposed on gifted students because few of them learn best with classmates. When permitted to learn alone, with peers, or with a teacher based on their identified learning-style preference, even highly achieving students in grades 1 through 12 consistently obtained significantly higher achievement and attitude test scores through their preferred—rather than their nonpreferred—sociological styles (Dunn, Dunn, & Perrin, 1994).

7. Although some of the gifted adolescents in this study learned well in the morning, many more preferred late morning, afternoon, or evening as their best time for learning. Previous research documented the influence of time-of-day energy patterns on achievement (Dunn, Dunn, & Perrin, 1994). Conventional schooling practices that require early-morning testing appear to be unresponsive to the majority of gifted adolescents, whose best time of day frequently is not early morning. At best, conventional school schedules are responsive to only a minority of K through 12 learners, because no single period during the day was preferred by more than 40 percent of school-age learners (Dunn, Dunn, & Perrin, 1994).

8. Of the gifted and talented in this population who were tested for processing style, 18.5 percent were analytic, 26 percent were global, and 55.5 percent were integrated processors who functioned in either processing style when interested in the content. These results demonstrate that both global and analytic students can be gifted students. However, instructional incongruence may be the rule in schools because both textbooks and teacher training tend to promote analytic rather than global lesson planning and delivery. The revived emphasis on a thematic approach to curriculum (Dunn & Dunn, 1992) may be responsive to global students, but the handicap then may be transferred to those who are analytic. Until we either teach each group of processors differently, or teach students to teach themselves through their strengths, education will continue to help some and not help others.

Strategies For Matching Learning and Teaching Styles

Most educators recognize differences in how students learn but lack the knowledge about which methods are effective for which students and the skills for individualizing instruction. Teachers must experiment with:

1. Electroboards, learning circles, task cards (and other essentially tactual/visual resources that students can create themselves) for tactually strong learners;
2. Floor games or experientially based activities for kinesthetic students;
3. Contract activity packages, which permit choices of objectives, resources, activities, and student interactions, for motivated, perceptually strong, and/or nonconforming students;
4. Programmed learning sequences, designed with global subtitles and introductions and many tactual resources built into the frames, for students who need structure; and

5. Multisensory instructional packages for unmotivated, perceptually poor, unconventional learners (Dunn, Dunn, & Perrin, 1994).

Reflection

Read the following paragraph and respond to the questions below.

The Matching-Learning-and-Teaching-Styles Movement

The movement to match learning styles with teaching styles is a fluke that several educators dreamed up to get attention. Little quality research had been conducted in this area, and some of the limited studies on matching styles found little or no difference in learning. Some studies suggest that teachers should expose students to several styles, but teachers naturally tend to alter their approaches according to student responses. So matching teaching and learning styles is nothing new—it is the same old wine in a new bottle. To quote Shakespeare, it is "much ado about nothing."

1. How consistent must research findings be to be considered conclusive? In other words, must all studies produce the same answer before the answer can be considered factual?
2. Choose one of your favorite teachers. Does this teacher use different teaching styles? List three or four of this teacher's styles.
3. Do you have a single preferred style? To reach an intelligent answer to this question, draw a vertical line down the middle of a sheet of paper. On the left side list variables that enhance learning for you. On the right list variables that impede learning for you.

USING MICROCOMPUTERS TO INDIVIDUALIZE

Microcomputers offer teachers unprecedented opportunities to individualize instruction. As Magney (1990) so aptly notes:

> Computer games can be a window [through] which students can enter many academic realities. . . . Prior to the microcomputer, computers were used primarily to give rules and other information to players but now the computer often makes decisions for the players. Unlike most of the older games, and simulations, which focus on group work, those computerized activities can be easily designed for individual use. (pp. 55–56)

Computers and other technology can also be used to empower students. Edinger (1994, p. 58) prepared fourth graders to use computers in a writing workshop to achieve this goal. As she explains, "The children decide what to write about, how much revision to do, and when and how to publish their work."

PROGRAMS FOR AT-RISK STUDENTS

Much attention is being given to increasing the success of at-risk students. These are the millions of students with a greater-than-average likelihood of dropping out. These students often come from poor families or have no family at all. The characteristics that identify at-risk students are well documented. They include low achievement, retention in grade, behavior problems, poor attendance, low socioeconomic status, and attendance at schools with large numbers of poor students (Morris, 1991). These factors are stress related; they ultimately affect classroom performance.

According to Levin (1987) approximately one-third of secondary school students are at risk of dropping out of school. Other reports estimate that the percentage of secondary students who are at risk is even higher, perhaps approaching 50 percent (Aksamit, 1990).

Several societal conditions have contributed to the larger number of at-risk students. For example, one-half of American families in all social groups will at some time become involved in dangerous behavior; the United States leads the entire industrialized world in its rate of adolescent pregnancy; 1 million children run away from home every year; adolescents are the only age group in the United States for which the statistics for suicide, obesity, sexually transmitted diseases, drug and alcohol abuse, and violent death keep increasing (Banks, Kopassi, & Wilson, 1991).

Even the schools conduct several activities that seem to work against students' best interests. For example, a *Phi Delta Kappan* study of at-risk students found that failure to promote students is clearly harmful because it increases the likelihood that students will drop out and diminishes the probability that they will raise their achievement levels (Frymier & Gansneder, 1989). Many at-risk students are vulnerable to failure of any kind because they do not have the assurance lent by academic success; therefore, their blossoming depends on a supportive, warm, confidence-building environment (Blumenthal, Holmes, & Pound, 1991).

A study at Florida State University found that arts education has considerable potential for helping at-risk students improve their levels of self-confidence. Sautter (1994) reported:

> The Florida researchers also discovered that students in the arts learned to take criticism from peers, teachers, parents, and audiences. The constructive use of criticism, they said, built confidence in at-risk students. It helped the students come to value themselves and their achievements. (p. 436)

As Perrin (1994, p. 453) has said, "Artists take risks and learn from their mistakes."

At-risk students have developed counterproductive behaviors. Wellington and Perlin (1991, p. 88) say, "We need innovations for 'unteaching' counterproductive behavior." Alternative learning styles also can contribute to programs for at-risk students. One program director (Friedman, 1991, p. 89) says, "We respect the fact that individuals learn differently and we empower our students to accept responsibility for maximizing their learning potential."

Other appropriate qualities for at-risk curricula include high involvement, high reinforcement, and personalization. But each program must be designed or altered to meet students' particular needs. Elkind (1991) cautions that making programs more rigorous is an oversimplistic view that is both mindless and destructive.

Today, educators realize that to meet the needs of at-risk students, schools must begin addressing them early in their school experiences, preferably even in preschool. Karweit (1987) found that full-day kindergarten programs, as opposed to half-day programs, improved the performance of at-risk students. The additional time is required for attitude changes. These children must develop self-confidence. But students don't outgrow this problem, and secondary teachers have a big role to play in educating at-risk students.

Successful programs for at-risk students have several common characteristics. Most have close relationships among the schools, other community agencies, and the homes. Successful classrooms for at-risk students also have several common characteristics, including:

Using a minimum of clearly stated classroom rules

Setting clear expectations

Monitoring student behavior

Because many at-risk students do not have anyone who can have a conversation with them, one program for at-risk students provided students at least 30 minutes each day to discuss whatever they wanted to talk about (Blumenthal, Holmes, & Pound, 1991).

In response to the isolation that at-risk students experience in our society, most programs for these students require them to work cooperatively with their classmates. For example, in a program called "Writing Roulette," one participant identifies a problem in writing, another writer suggests ways for solving the problem, and a third concludes by solving the problem. This cooperative approach encourages persons who may be reluctant to express their ideas in writing (Lile, Lile, & Jefferies, 1991). Because at-risk students are often isolated and alienated from the mainstream in our society, successful at-risk programs tend to be personal, requiring one-on-one attention (Coleman, 1991).

OTHER WAYS TO INVOLVE STUDENTS

In addition to varying your lesson plans, you also must use a variety of learning avenues, such as textbooks, discussions, field trips, oral reports, term projects, and homework. We now turn to the use of these and your role in each.

Textbooks

Throughout the history of education in the United States, one type of textbook or another has dominated the curriculum. At first, the textbook determined the content to be studied. There were virtually no experiences other than rote memorization and recitation, which often resulted in a boring, irrelevant curriculum. To a large extent, this is still true: "Teachers consider the textbook as the major (and usually only) source of content" (Walter, 1984, p. 58). Although the twentieth century is changing the textbook's role as sole determiner of content, the textbook can still play an effective role in today's planning.

One common way to use a textbook is to build the curriculum around it. The textbook may be the center of the curriculum, but it is supported by other textbooks, journals, magazines, and newspapers. This approach is probably a good choice in communities or school systems that press for traditional education and in schools with very limited resources. But it is much more likely to succeed if you include some contemporary problems and help students apply their acquired knowledge toward solving them.

Another approach is to use the textbook along with other materials. Instead of letting the textbook lead your students and you in the selection of content and experiences, take the lead in designing the curriculum. For example, determine the sequence of topics, instead of following the textbook organization from chapter 1 to chapter 2. Perhaps some chapters are not worth including in your curriculum. Teachers are becoming increasingly competent in curriculum development, and more and more teachers insist on having the freedom to shape the curricula in their classes as they see fit.

But not all school systems provide teachers with such freedom to develop their

All teachers should individualize and personalize.

own curricula. Concern that students may not "cover" all the content needed for the following year or for college is always present. Such concern is legitimate. School administrators know that they are responsible for seeing that the total school curricula do not have major content gaps. Many larger secondary schools hire a curriculum director, a curriculum supervisor, or an assistant principal who is directly responsible for that. You should work with the curriculum leader and other teachers to avoid curriculum redundancy and gaps.

Other teachers make even less use of the textbook, almost totally avoiding it. They substitute current problems, learning activity packages, or learning units they developed themselves. Of course, these teachers are in school systems that permit an unusually high degree of teacher freedom. Such systems are not typical.

Some school districts are beginning to take money designated for buying textbooks and spending it on computers and other information technology. Many districts are using these funds to help students learn how to use the Internet. Whatever freedom your system permits you in using the textbook, be sure you do not spend most of the class period reading the text or requiring the students to read it. It is much better to assign a chapter as homework the evening before a lesson and use class time to discuss what students read.

Discussions

Today's students want to be involved. They feel that their own opinions and judgments are worthwhile, and they want to share them. For this reason the discussion has increased in popularity. A good discussion involves all participants. Everyone has an opportunity to relate the topic to his or her own experiences. This sharing of various perspectives can enrich individual participants' knowledge and understanding. Avoid discussions that are merely rambling gossip sessions and that do no more than share ignorance.

Plan discussions carefully. First, to encourage total participation, group students according to their interest in the topic. Achieve this by letting students choose discussion topics. Second, avoid assigning both very passive students and aggressive students to the same groups. By putting the reserved students together, you will force one or more to assume leadership, and by placing aggressive students in the same group, some will be forced to learn to yield the floor to others. By assigning roles, such as "discussion moderator" and "recorder," and then varying these roles, you will prompt all group members to participate even further.

Select topics that have answers, although there may be multiple answers depending on individual perspective. Letting students know that you expect a definite outcome gives them a sense of purpose and responsibility.

If the moderator fails to keep group discussion progressing and on target, you may want to intervene, but too much interference will cause a group to become dependent on your leadership. Take care, also, to ensure that the group moderator does not dominate the discussion. In addition, the discussion must reflect the belief that all serious comments are worth hearing, regardless of how inaccurate or insignificant others may consider them.

A free-flowing discussion provides a valuable opportunity to develop social skills, which is in itself an important goal for secondary and middle-level students. It also helps students identify with their peers. All adolescents need to belong, and all need positive recognition and approval from peers. Group discussions should help fill these needs.

Participants must know that each person has a definite role in every discussion. First, each participant is obligated to read the assignment so the discussion will begin from a common base. Second, each person is responsible for contributing additional information to the discussion. Opinions and contributions of knowledge are prized only when the participants can present evidence or knowledge to support them. Third, each participant is responsible for listening to others and, when possible, for referring others' specific comments. This assures all participants that their comments are being considered.

You, the teacher, are responsible for seeing that the environment remains informal, pleasant, and nonthreatening. You are also a facilitator, helping students to locate adequate resources and to plan their discussion. When the discussion is over, you can help them evaluate discussion techniques and redesign their strategies for future discussions.

Field Trips

Like many fine inventions of the past, the field trip has become almost prematurely moribund, even though it still has many unique advantages. The reasons for its loss of popularity are many. First, there has been a growing trend of more lawsuits against schools, and the courts have begun to find more schools liable as charged. Because administrators and teachers can also be found liable, many of them are reluctant to encourage field trips, which are perceived as unnecessary risks.

This is unfortunate, because field trips still have unique potentials. There is no better way for a social studies class to study the habits of an ethnic group than to visit a local community. And a group of students interested in aerodynamics could find nothing more meaningful than a visit to a wind tunnel. An agriculture class may benefit tremendously from a visit to an agriculture education agency, an experimental station, or a local farm.

Before you arrange a field trip, first check school policy, because many schools now forbid field trips of any type. But even if you find yourself teaching at such a school, you might try to bring the "field" to the school. For example, a junior-high or middle school earth science teacher might arrange for a few truckloads of several types of soil and rocks to be dumped on the school grounds so that students can take an on-campus geology field trip.

If your school does permit field trips, you might let your students suggest the need for one—assuming that they are mature enough and self-disciplined enough to be trusted. Some groups of students simply present too great a risk, and a teacher would be foolish to pursue a trip with such students. If the idea comes from the students, they may be willing to work harder and organize better.

Next, make sure that the trip is indeed necessary and purposeful. Each student should be assigned, or should assume, definite responsibilities for gathering specific data. Students may also share responsibility for organizing the trip, clearing it with the principal's office, arranging the visits, filling out the necessary insurance forms, and securing the necessary permissions and finances.

After the field trip, a follow-up lesson in which students report their data and discuss implications will accentuate what the trip accomplished. As with all other instructional approaches, evaluation of each trip will improve the quality of future trips. Evaluations are more effective when done immediately after the trip while the teacher and students still remember specifics.

Oral Reports

For several decades, oral reports have been popular in secondary and middle-level schools, but this technique's success depends on its use. When you are considering using oral reports, first decide each report's purpose. Teachers too often give assignments without really thinking through the report's purpose. Oral reports can have several purposes that may be considered important goals.

For example, you might assign a report to an advanced student who is delving into one aspect of a topic. The report would give that student an opportunity to share what he or she has learned while at the same time enable the rest of the class to benefit from the study. Or you might assign a report to a group of students to give them an opportunity to learn to work together cooperatively. Another teacher might assign reports to give students experience in public speaking.

Each of these purposes is legitimate and worthwhile as long as you communicate the main purpose(s) of the reports to the students. However, assigning a report to punish misbehavior or to substitute for effective planning is not wise. Students will quickly connect the report with those purposes and probably assume no significant learning will result. This occurs when reports are used at the end of a grading period to give students an opportunity to improve their grades.

Whatever your reason for assigning oral reports, you must communicate to the reporter(s) the assignment's primary purposes. Tell other class members what you expect of them during the report. Should they take notes? Ask questions? Take issue with the speaker? Should they ask for clarification when they do not understand? Should they interrupt the speaker with comments or wait until the end of the presentation? Will they be held accountable on the next test for the information their peers present orally? By answering these questions before the report is delivered, you can draw other students into their peers' oral presentations and thereby maximize interest and involvement.

As a precaution against students' taking reports too lightly, you might have a policy of always assigning credit for oral reports—and perhaps to the rest of the students for their responses. You can do this without presenting a threat to the students. Consider a positive reward system that would let students earn credit for participation in the discussion without penalizing those whose contributions are minimal.

The timing of oral reports can be critical. Avoid scheduling too many reports in succession. The student who is giving the twelfth consecutive report in class is at a definite disadvantage. To avoid the repetition and the boredom that students experience when too many reports are given, spread the reporting out so that no more than two are given in any week.

Students need ample time to prepare reports. Depending on the subject's level of sophistication, students will need between one and several weeks' lead time. Because many secondary school students and some middle school students hold part-time jobs, and extracurricular activities consume much of their out-of-class time, you might allot some class time for preparing oral presentations. This is needed especially when students are planning group presentations.

Never make assignments without giving students an opportunity to present the results. This would be especially destructive when oral presentations are involved. Of course, a teacher would never intentionally be so callous, but sometimes teachers forget to save enough time in the term for the reports. Avoid this by scheduling the reporting dates when you make the assignments. Then students will not be disappointed, and they will see oral presentations as worthwhile.

Projects

Whatever subject you teach, you will find that assigning projects is valuable. You can choose among many types of projects: long-term projects, which may last for a grading period or even a semester; short-term projects; and individual projects. You have probably considered several types of projects as assignments for oral presentations, but not all projects must end with an oral presentation. Some may conclude with written reports or with presentations of concrete products that have resulted from the assignment. Whatever the product, give students an opportunity to show their creations. For example, a science teacher may want to arrange a local science fair to display students' insect collections, or a music teacher may want to set up a student recital.

Teachers who offer projects as options (i.e., not required of all students) may use a liberal grading system. One great advantage of projects is that they permit students who for one reason or another do not benefit from didactic forms of instruction to become totally involved. Many teachers take advantage of the opportunity to grade these activities in a way that rewards student effort. Many students who appear to be failures on tests can produce excellent projects. Perhaps it is because they want to do the projects, or perhaps they feel more competent doing something with their hands, or it may be a combination. Therefore, many teachers view projects as an opportunity to provide successful experiences for everyone. You might want to experiment by assigning all As and Bs to the projects for one term. Of course, you are free to let it count for as much or as little of the total term grade as you prefer.

HOMEWORK

According to Solomon (1989, p. 63), "The purpose of homework is to prepare the student for his/her next lesson and/or reinforce concepts and skills learned in the previous lesson." Solomon says that homework can play a positive role in student achievement. "A search of the literature proves that homework, assigned by a mentor for practice, participation, preparation, personal development, reinforcement, or as an extension of class study, will increase individual achievement" (Solomon, 1989, p. 63).

During the 1960s and 1970s, homework for the public school student lost much of its prestige, but by the end of the 1970s it had regained a more positive reputation. In fact, half of secondary school students themselves said that the homework was not challenging (Elam, 1979). This is evidence that homework, when properly assigned and used, can be meaningful.

Cooper (1990) researched the effect of homework on achievement across grade levels and reported:

> Homework has a positive effect on achievement, but the effect varies dramatically with grade level. For high school students, homework has substantial positive effects. Junior high school students also benefit from homework, but only about half as much. For elementary school students, the effect of homework on achievement is negligible.
>
> The optimum amount of homework also varies with grade level. For elementary students, no amount of homework—large or small—affects achievement. For junior high school students, achievement continues to improve with more homework until assignments last between one and two hours a night. For high-school students, the more homework, the better the achievement—within reason, of course.
>
> I found no clear pattern indicating that homework is more effective in some subjects than in others. I did conclude however, that homework probably works best when the material is not too complex or completely unfamiliar. Studies comparing alternative feedback strategies revealed no clearly superior approach. (p. 88)

But not all homework results in improved learning. For example, in a review of 24 studies on the effects of homework given in elementary and secondary schools, Friesen (1979) found that of the 24 studies conducted, 12 reported positive effects on achievement and 11 found no difference or negative effects; the remaining study showed that the homework group did better on investigator-designed tests but worse on standardized tests.

One reason students who have homework often score less well is that teachers often do not have a definite purpose for homework assignments. This can lead to busywork. Here are some of the major uses teachers can make of homework assignments (Lee & Pruitt, 1978, p. 31):

1. Practice—designed to reinforce skills and information covered in class
2. Preparation—given to prepare students to profit from subsequent lessons
3. Extension—provided to determine whether a particular student can extend the concept or skill learned in class to a new situation
4. Creative—designed to require students to integrate many skills and concepts in producing some project

This list shows that homework can be used for different proposes and that it can also be used to develop higher-order skills. The purpose of the homework should determine the teacher's instructional behavior. You should always base a decision to use homework (or not to) on a purpose for which it is suited and introduce it accordingly. Far too often homework is used only for practice. Because many states now require all teachers to give homework (many districts specify the number of hours a night), you must become familiar with the variety of uses for which homework is suited. The four uses listed are a good place to begin. The following suggestions will help you design and implement a system for assigning homework that will work well for you.

Homework Guidelines

Clarify the Assignment.   Homework assignments must be clear. If they involve problem solving, you may want to give students an opportunity to work at least one problem of each type in class before you ask them to do problems at home. Simply using verbal instructions and explanations may not be enough. Perhaps you can remember a time when, as a student, you thought you understood how the teacher wanted you to complete an assignment, but when you got home you found that you could not start the problem because you did not know how to begin. If you had been given an opportunity to work just one problem in class, you could have raised questions at that time.

Individualize Homework Assignments.   Students who cannot understand how to do their classwork even with your help will benefit little from a homework assignment of more of the same type of problems. You must consider each student's abilities and needs. Certain homework assignments for slower students will help them catch up with the rest of the class, while the more advanced students can explore areas of special interest in depth. Such an individualistic approach to homework assignments can relieve the ever-present dilemma of teachers—how to challenge the brightest students without losing the slower students.

Make Homework Creative.   Teachers today realize that the old practice of assigning students to "read the next chapter and work the problems at the end of the chapter" is not challenging or stimulating. Homework assignments are more interesting when they contain variety. Students could be asked to respond to something that is on the evening news, in the newspaper, or on an educational television program. Multisensory activities can replace written assignments. Creativity cannot be forced, but you can establish a climate that stimulates and nourishes creativity. Let your students use all their senses and manipulate objects; have them investigate problems that have no fixed answer.

Be Reasonable.   Avoid making too many demands on students' time at home. Many students come from homes that have no books or any place that is well-lit or quiet enough for studying. Disruptions from brothers and sisters make homework difficult for many students. Then, too, many secondary school students and some middle-school students work after school at part-time jobs on which their families depend for some essentials. For such students, homework assignments that require a few hours each evening to complete are impossible. Secondary school teachers must also remember that students have several other courses and may receive homework in all of them.

When you evaluate homework, take into account the conditions under which students must perform. As with classroom or term projects, grade homework leniently enough so that students who are faced with the most adverse environments will not become discouraged.

Follow-up.   Nothing can be more disheartening than spending time and energy on an assignment only to have the teacher forget about it or push it aside for more critical matters. If you schedule a follow-up time at the time of the assignment, you can prevent these annoying situations. Follow-ups also let students know that they are expected to complete each assignment. According to Phelps (1991, p. 242), regular follow-ups result in improved results: "When students are held responsible for assigned work, they are more likely to do the work than when their efforts go unnoticed."

Overview of Steps for Assigning Homework.   The following steps for assigning homework can be used as a summary of this discussion and as a guideline for making homework assignments (Berry, 1977, p. 52).

1. As an alternative, plan for assignments to be completed at some time during the school day in a supervised area.
2. Be sure the purpose of every homework assignment is clear in your mind and that you have made it clear to the students.
3. Try to match assignments with students, making sure each student is treated fairly and equally.
4. Be sure every student knows exactly what is required.
5. Check the assignment when it is due.
6. Don't expect homework to teach a student who is not learning properly in the classroom.
7. Remember that assignments that use a multisensory approach are most effective in teaching.

These seven steps were actually designed for elementary school teachers. Do you think any (or all) of them are adequate guidelines for secondary- and middle-school teachers?

We have now discussed the uses of textbooks, discussions, field trips, oral reports, term projects, and homework. When making any of these assignments, perhaps the most important question a teacher can ask is: What will this homework assignment permit students to do that they cannot do in class? And how can I (we) design the assignment to benefit the student and perhaps the rest of the class?

Parent Involvement

The 1994 Gallup Poll showed that over the last decade the frequency of many forms of parental contact with their schools has practically doubled (Elam, Rose, & Gallup, 1994, p. 54).

Parents' responsibility for helping their children succeed with homework has been recognized for many years; yet, their exact role in this matter has not been clear. Solomon (1989) offers the following suggestions for teachers to help guide parents who wish to help their children achieve in their homework assignments:

> Teachers should encourage parents to: (1) set a definite time for study each day with a beginning and ending time and no interruptions; (2) provide the proper environment; (3) provide the materials needed, (4) require the student to organize school materials including books, notes, assignments, and papers, (5) require a daily list of homework assignments; and (6) provide support and guidance if the child becomes discouraged or frustrated. (p. 63)

The site-based decision-making movement that is sweeping the country offers much hope for garnering family members' support. Most teams will include parents. These teams will make decisions on curriculum, finance, and all other major school matters.

DISCUSSION

This chapter encourages teachers to apply style matching in the classroom. There are indeed a number of advantages to matching teaching and learning styles, but this method is not a solution for all education problems, and teachers should be aware of the limitations and criticisms of this movement. Good and Stipek (1983) identified the four following concerns:

1. There is no single dimension of learners that clearly dictates an instructional prescription. A style the student may find motivating might not be consistent with the student's ability or prior knowledge. Sometimes a mismatch is preferable.
2. Matching styles does not account for the relationship between the student and teacher, the nature of the learning task, and other important variables that affect learning.
3. Such important variables as task clarity, feedback, and opportunities for practice are often ignored, yet these affect learning.
4. Uniform classroom instructional treatments are often superior to differentiated treatment because they are compatible with the teacher's skills.

These criticisms seem fair, and there are others. The general area of grouping itself may present overwhelming problems. Studies show that many teachers, especially inexperienced teachers, find it too much of a challenge to monitor multiple group arrangements in classrooms (Doyle, 1980; Good & Brophy, 1987). Studies show that if the major purpose of style grouping is to accommodate students, a degree of discomfort can be an asset in learning, rather than a detriment to be circumvented (Harvey, Hunt, & Schroder, 1963; Piaget, 1952).

Even the term *learning styles* is not clearly defined in the literature. Hyman and Rosoff (1984) say that a clear definition in terms of student performance would be helpful. They further point out that learning style is not static because learning itself is a highly complex activity. Indeed, learning is such a broad activity that it cannot be contained within the cognitive domain (Stinnett & Henson, 1982).

The study of the effects of matching learning and teaching styles on learning is still in its infancy. The findings hold promise, but students should read these studies and their claims with a critical eye. Having read pros and cons on the matching of teaching and learning styles, consider your own position. Some critics see the entire movement as a unilateral approach in which the teacher assesses the student's learning style and prescribes or selects an acceptable teaching style to match the learner's style. Should the student be involved in this selection? If you agree, identify some ways to make style matching a bilateral process.

As many as one-third of all students face obstacles—at home, in the community, and at school—which makes them at risk of failing and dropping out. Schools and teachers are using many approaches to make school more meaningful for these and other students by attempting to individualize learning. A variety of instructional models are being used. Mastery learning has proven both successful and controversial. Some of its major strengths for learners include unlimited time on each topic, opportunities to remediate without penalty, and the absence of grades. Ironically, each of these strengths can cause major administrative headaches. Flexible time for individual students does not fit the school calendar, and many parents insist on receiving traditional A through F grade reports based on competition.

Another approach to individualizing learning that has also been highly successful with many classes is grade contracts. Such successful approaches to teach at-risk students have some common elements. They spell out the expectations the teacher holds for students, and the teacher carefully monitors student behavior. Maximum success usually requires involving parents, and site-based decision making teams are doing just that.

RECAP OF MAJOR IDEAS

1. Students' instructional needs vary greatly.
2. Ability grouping is one common approach to meet individual students' needs.
3. In-class (intraclass) grouping often results in improved learning, but it does not enhance learning substantially; intraclass grouping usually improves motivation more than it improves learning.
4. Attempts to conceal the levels of ability groups almost always fail.

5. Interclass grouping produces group competition, whereas intraclass grouping produces competition between students.

6. Given adequate motivation, presentation style, and time, most high-school students can master the goals set for them.

7. Instruments are available to determine individuals' preferred learning and teaching styles.

8. Teachers should purposely master and use a variety of teaching styles.

9. Several instructional models such as grade contracts, mastery learning, and information processing can help teachers improve their instruction.

10. Mastery learning offers students flexible timing and opportunities to remediate without penalty, but traditional school schedules and parents who believe competition is essential make it difficult to implement.

11. Grade contracts can be highly successful when teacher and student expectations are clearly specified.

12. Homework assignments should be creative and reasonable and reflect student interests.

13. Teachers should always follow up on assignments.

14. Homework serves two functions. It reinforces concepts learned in the previous lesson, and it prepares students for the coming lesson.

CASES

The five cases here show how matching learning styles and teaching styles can be used. Each case actually occurred in the Wichita, Kansas, area and describes a real-life application of learning-styles theory.

CASE 1: AN INDIVIDUAL TEACHER'S EFFORT

Sometimes teachers must experiment with new educational theories in the isolation of their classrooms with little support from anyone. But teachers who accept the responsibility not only for what they teach but also for what is learned are eager to use any technique they believe will help them in diagnoses, prescription, and treatment of their students.

One such teacher in Wichita, Kansas, attended a district in-service meeting where he learned about learning-styles theory and application. This junior-high teacher decided to experiment with the idea and invited a consultant from the teacher center to come to one of his classes and explain the concept to the students. The teacher and consultant spent a considerable amount of time making sure the students understood the implications of learning-styles theory and the teacher's interest in using it.

The teacher administered a learning-styles preferences questionnaire, and the students scored the survey, developed their profiles, and shared the results within the class. Students were then encouraged to contribute ideas for classroom organization that would take advantage of the variety of preferred learning modalities within the class. They helped set up auditory areas where students could listen to tapes or form discussion groups. They also arranged visual corners, where other students could read or work on written assignments. Student enthusiasm was soon reflected at home, and parents became interested. The teacher decided to carry the program further and arranged a parent meeting. He explained the learning-styles concept and how he was implementing it. He then administered the survey to the parents and helped them interpret the results regarding their own preferences. The teacher then began to use the parents' learning styles when he conducted parent-teacher conferences. The results of this experiment were very positive. In this classroom, responsibilities shared by students and teacher in the planning of learning procedures and outcomes increased. Students' willingness to accept learning differences in others also increased. In addition, the parent-teacher conferences became more effective and mutually appreciated. The enthusiasm for the process in this particular classroom led this teacher to introduce the procedure in his other classes. Other teachers in the school also began experimenting with the concept in their classrooms.

Discussion

When a teacher wants to initiate a new program or other innovation, is it necessary to sell others on the idea? If so, how can the teacher do this? Innovations often require additional facilities, materials, space, and program flexibility, so innovators' success depends on the cooperation received when administrators, teachers, and others understand the importance of the change. A simple approach is first to inform others about the process and then to involve them with the innovation.

CASE 2: A SCHOOL-WIDE INDIVIDUALIZED PROGRAM

Cloud Elementary School in Wichita adopted the IGE (Individually Guided Education) program as its basic instructional process. The IGE approach to schooling provides a framework for individualized instruction and continuous progress. Instead of being organized into the usual self-contained classes in which all students of a single age are grouped together, students and teachers are organized into "learning communities." Each learning community is composed of students of several age-groups and teachers of varying talents and backgrounds.

This elementary school program had several goals, one of which was to determine students' learning styles. After experimenting with several assessment techniques, the teachers in the school decided that the locally developed learning-styles inventory gave them usable and practical information that the faculty could easily manage. They arranged for the local district's computer department to put the student data from the instrument onto a computer program. The computer-based analysis was designed to identify students who fell below a previously defined score.

Style data were shared both with the students in the advisement programs and with the parents during conferences. A profile for each student was developed, and the results were used to determine the best way for each student to reach his or her learning objectives. In addition to developing learning objectives to complement each student's learning preference, the teacher identified students whose styles-preference analysis revealed a possible inability to use a wide range of learning styles successfully. These students were then given help in expanding their styles. Thus, one major learning goal was to increase "style flex" among students.

Results of the experiment were encouraging. There was increased student achievement and parental satisfaction. Teachers were pleased with the effort because they had acquired an additional tool for individualizing instruction. They also believed that student attitudes toward the classroom were enhanced.

Discussion

If a student has a preferred learning style that works well for that student, why introduce that student to other styles?

Students who have only one preferred learning style are in trouble when they are assigned to a teacher whose teaching style varies drastically from the student's style. By introducing students to a variety of styles, students have an opportunity to expand their "style flex."

CASE 3: THE SCHOOL WITHIN A SCHOOL

In response to the career education movement, many high schools throughout the United States established special programs to provide selected students with an opportunity to participate in experience-based learning in the community. This concept provides a less-formal learning environment and more effectively meets certain students' needs.

The Experience Based Career Education Program at Wichita High School East was one such program. It was organized as a school within a school. Soon after the program began in 1976, its director became aware that the learning-styles concept was being used and applied more and more. After appropriate planning, the program staff decided to include a learning-preference assessment—the Student Learning Styles instrument—as one of the diagnostic procedures used as part of each student's admission to the program.

When a student applied for admission to the program, the Student Learning Styles Inventory was administered as one of the standard battery of tests. The results were used to determine the preferred basic learning modalities of the applicants. Faculty served as both teachers and counselors in the program. These teacher-counselors had previously categorized jobs and job skills based on the nine specific characteristics identified in the instrument. The style preferences were strongly considered in the placement procedures and openly shared with prospective employers as an aid to developing learning programs for individual students. (Some employers later requested permission to use and help administer the survey to other employees. They saw it as potentially useful in developing training programs for full-time employees and in hiring procedures.)

The program's positive outcomes, and the student successes, indicated that the assessment of learning modalities helped the program more completely meet students' needs by more closely closer matching work experience and learning-style preferences. Students' confidence in the program's success increased, students' self-concepts were enhanced, and students performed better in other phases of their learning experiences as well.

Discussion Question

1. In what ways can teachers in self-contained classrooms increase students' experience base?

CASE 4: THE ALTERNATIVE SCHOOL

Munger Junior High School (now Alcott Alternative Learning Center) was established in 1978 as an alternative for Wichita youth who had experienced considerable frustration in previous learning environments. Some potential students were drug abusers, some were school dropouts, and others were family dropouts. All had been discipline problems in school. The staff members for the school were selected because of their special interest in "reluctant learners" and their proven ability to work with them. Each teacher functioned as both teacher and counselor.

The principal and staff decided to administer the locally developed student learning-styles survey to determine students' learning preferences and to use the information to develop individual learning programs. Many students reported that this was the first time they felt that their own specific needs were being considered. They were very interested in the concept and its outcomes and began to question the teachers regarding their (the teachers') learning styles. As a result, the program was carried one step further to access the entire staff's learning styles. Survey results were posted publicly, and students and staff became aware of the various learning styles each represented.

One unexpected additional benefit was the increased communication that occurred as a result of greater awareness of cognitive styles. For example, students who were auditory learners made counseling appointments with staff members who had complementary preferences. When teachers had the opportunity to use their own cognitive preferences, they found it easier to work effectively with students. Administration of the learning-styles inventory became a standard procedure for admitting both students and staff members to this alternative junior high school.

Discussion Question

1. What benefit might there be from a situation in which teachers teach students whose learning styles are similar to their own (the teachers') learning styles?

CASE 5: THE DISTRICT-WIDE PROGRAM

Cognitive-style awareness embraces the concept that both students and instructors are accountable for learning. The Remington district, a small, rural district near Wichita, decided to support the concept by experimenting with learning styles through an expanded application of the process on a district-wide basis. The district took steps to administer the student learning-styles survey to every student in the district.

The initial purpose of the district-wide project represented in this case was to confirm the effectiveness of existing classroom management techniques and teaching strategies. To implement the plan, a Project CITE consultant was scheduled for a series of sessions designed to acquaint the entire professional staff with the concept of learning styles, techniques for administering the specific survey, analysis of the results, and possible teacher-student applications for the classroom.

The survey was then administered to every student in the district. Teachers analyzed the scores of their own students and used them to confirm the various learning groups they had previously established in their classes. To expand the use of survey results further, teachers then met as grade-level committees to develop curriculum goals and instructional processes designed to use the styles data available for each student to enhance student learning. Where team teaching existed, the results were also used to assign students to team groups that emphasized certain styles.

District-wide use of the learning-styles data was the goal. To date, satisfaction with the process has been high. School officials reported increased student learning, improved self-concepts, and better communication within the district. The district also anticipates that continued improvement in student learning will be evident as students move through a school system in which their learning styles are taken into consideration each year of their education.

Discussion Question

1. District-wide implementation of an innovation often increases the innovation's success by showing that the district supports the change. How might an individual teacher persuade the district office to try a new approach?

ACTIVITIES

1. Because the success of any method selected to individualize instruction depends greatly on the enthusiasm of the teacher who applies it, you are encouraged to select one of the approaches discussed in this chapter—for example, contingency contracts, mastery learning, matching teacher and learner styles, or a type of ability grouping—and further investigate it. Go to the library, research the method, and determine how you would personalize it to fit your own preferences. An alternative would be to use your library's Educational Resources Information System (ERIC) (or similar reference guide) to discover other approaches to individualizing instruction. Make a list of these approaches and select one to pursue further, then determine how you would adjust the approach to fit your own preferences.

2. Make an appointment to visit a school counselor. Ask the counselor to discuss some students who require special instruction. Do not expect the

counselor to divulge a student's name, but ask for an explanation of how instruction was altered for that student. Make a list of learning activities that the counselor found successful.

3. Visit the reading center or a student assistance center on your campus or at a nearby university or public school. Volunteer your services for as many hours as you can spare. Keep a record of the techniques you observe in use at that center.

4. Because one of the most common problems teachers face is the need to teach students with a wide range of abilities simultaneously, spend a few hours preparing for this task. Visit with several secondary- or middle-school teachers and ask them how they teach a heterogeneous class of varying abilities. Make a list of the techniques they use. Choose one technique and research the literature to learn all you can about it.

5. Use the diagnostic learning styles model shown in Figure 7.4 to analyze your classmates' prepared learning styles. Ask your professor for permission to present the results to the class.

REFERENCES

Aksamit, D. (1990). Mildly handicapped and at-risk students: The greying of the line. *Academic Therapy, 25*(3), 227–289.

Andrews, R. H. (1990, July–September). The development of a learning styles program in a low socioeconomic, underachieving North Carolina elementary school. *Journal of Reading, Writing, and Learning Disabilities International, 6*(3), 307–314.

Andrews, R. H. (1991). Insights into education: An elementary principal's perspective. In Lewis A. Grell (Ed.), *Hands on approaches to learning styles: Practical approaches to successful school* (pp. 50–52). New Wilmington, PA: The Association for the Advancement of International Education.

Arlin, M. (1984, Spring). Time, equality, and mastery of learning. *Review of Educational Research 54,* 71–72.

Banks, R., Kopassi, R., & Wilson, A. M. (1991). Inter-agency networking and linking schools and agencies: A community based approach to at-risk students. In R. C. Morris (Ed.), *At-risk students* (pp. 106–107). Scranton, PA: Technomic.

Beaty, S. A. (1986). The effect of inservice training on the ability of teachers to observe learning styles of students. *Dissertation Abstracts International, 47,* 1998A.

Berry, K. (1977). Homework: Is it for elementary kids? *Instructor, 86,* 52.

Block, J. R., & Henson, K. T. (1986, Spring). Mastery learning and middle school instruction. *American Middle School Education, 9*(2), 21–29.

Blumenthal, C., Holmes, G. V., & Pound, L. (1991). Academic success for students' at-risk. In R. C. Morris (Ed.), *Youth at-risk.* Scranton, PA: Technomic.

Bradley, D. F., & Fisher, J. F. (1995). The inclusion process: Role changes at the middle level. *Middle School Journal, 26*(3), 13–17.

Brophy, J. (1983). Classroom organization and management. *Elementary School Journal, 83,* 265–285.

Burns, R. B. (1979). Mastery learning: Does it work? *Educational Leadership, 37,* 110–113.

Calfee, R., & Brown, R. (1979). Grouping students for instruction. *National Society for the Study of Education,* Yearbook 78, Pt. 2, 144–148.

Carroll, J. B. (1963). A model of school learning. *Teachers College Record, 64,* 723–733.

Centra, J., & Potter, D. (1980). School and teacher effects: An interrelational model. *Review of Educational Research, 50,* 273–291.

Clark-Thayer, S. (1987). The relationship of the knowledge of student-perceived learning style preferences, and study habits and attitudes to achievement of college freshman in a small urban university. *Dissertation Abstracts International, 48,* 872A.

Coleman, J. G. (1991). Risky business: The library's role in dropout prevention. In R. C. Morris (Ed.), *Youth at-risk* (pp. 61–62). Scranton, PA: Technomic.

Cooper, H. (1990). Synthesis of research on homework. *Educational Leadership, 47*(3), 85–91.

Cunningham, Jr., R. D. (1991, September). Modeling mastery teaching through classroom supervision. *NASSP Bulletin, 75*(536), 83–87.

Doyle, W. (1980). *Classroom management.* West Lafayette, IN: Kappa Delta Pi.

Dunn, K. (1981). Madison Prep: Alternative to teenage disaster. *Educational Leadership, 39*(5), 386–387.

Dunn, R., Beasley, M., & Buchanan, K. (1994). What do you believe about how culturally-diverse students learn? *Emergency Librarian, 22*(1), 8–14.

Dunn, R., & Dunn, K. (1978). *Teaching students through their individual learning styles: A practical approach.* Reston, VA: Reston Publishing Division of Prentice-Hall.

Dunn, R., & Dunn, K. (1992). *Teaching elementary students through their individual learning styles.* Boston: Allyn & Bacon.

Dunn, R., & Dunn, K. (1993). *Teaching secondary students through their individual learning styles.* Boston: Allyn and Bacon.

Dunn, R., Dunn, K., & Perrin, J. (1994). *Teaching young children through their individual learning styles.* Boston: Allyn & Bacon.

Dunn, R., Dunn, K., & Price, G.E. (1977). Diagnosing learning styles: Avoiding malpractice suits against school systems. *Phi Delta Kappan, 58*(5), 418–420.

Dunn, R., & Griggs, S.A. (1995). *Multiculturalism and learning style: Teaching and counseling adolescents.* CT: Greenwood Publishers.

Dunn, R., Griggs, S.A., Olson, J., Gorman, B., & Beasley, M. (in press). A meta-analytic validation of the Dunn and Dunn learning styles model. *Journal of Educational Research.*

Edinger, M. (1994). Empowering young writers with technology. *Educational Leadership, 51*(7), 58–60.

Elam, S. M. (1979, June). Gallup finds teenagers generally like their schools. Reports taken in November, 1978. *Phi Delta Kappan, 60,* 700.

Elam, S. M., Rose, L. C., & Gallup, A. M. (1994). The 26th annual Phi Delta Kappa/Gallup poll of the public's attitudes toward the public schools. *Phi Delta Kappan, 76*(1), 41–56.

Elkind, R. (1991). Success in American education. In R. C. Morris (Ed.), *Youth at risk.* Lancaster, PA: Technomic.

Elliot, I. (1991, November-December). The reading place. *Teaching K-8. 21*(3), 30–34.

Friedman, R. S. (1991). Murray high school: A nontraditional approach to meeting the needs of an at-risk population. In R. C. Morris (Ed.), Youth at risk. Lancaster, PA: Technomic.

Frymier, J., & Gansneder, B. (1989, October). The Phi Delta Kappa study of students at risk. *Phi Delta Kappan, 71,* 142–146.

Good, T. L., & Brophy, J. (1987). *Looking in classrooms* (4th ed.). New York: Harper & Row.

Good, T. L., Reys, B. J., Grouws, D. A., & Molyran, C. M. (1990–1991). Using work-groups in mathematics instruction. *Educational Leadership, 47*(4), 56–62.

Good, T. L., & Stipek, D. J. (1983). Individual differences in the classroom: A psychological perspective. In G. D. Fenstermacher (Ed.), *Individual differences and common curriculum.* Eighty-Second Yearbook of the National Society for the Study of Education, Part I. Chicago: University of Chicago Press.

Guskey, T. R., & Gates, S. L. (1986). Synthesis of research on the effects of mastery learning in elementary and secondary classrooms. *Educational Leadership, 43*(8), 73-80.

Harvey, O. J., Hunt, D. E., & Schroder, H. M. (1963). *Conceptual systems and personality organization.* New York: Wiley.

Hyman, J. S., & Cohen, A. (1979). Learning for mastery: Ten conclusions after fifteen years and 3,000 schools. *Educational Leadership, 37,* 104-109.

Hyman, R. T., & Rosoff, B. (1984, Winter). Matching learning and theory styles: The jug and what's in it. In K. T. Henson (Ed.), *Matching learning and teaching styles. Theory into Practice, 23,* 35-43.

Julik, J. A. (1981, April). *The effect of ability grouping on secondary school students.* Paper presented at the American Educational Research Association, Los Angeles.

Karweit, N. (1987). Effective kindergarten programs and practices for students at-risk. Report No. 21. Baltimore: The Johns Hopkins University, Center for Research on Elementary and Middle Schools.

Keefe, J.W. (1982). Assessing students learning styles: An overview of learning styles and cognitive style inquiry. *Student Learning Styles and Brain Behavior.* Reston, VA: National Association of Secondary School Principals.

Kryriacou, M., & Dunn, R. (1994). Synthesis of research: Learning styles of students with learning disabilities. *Special Education Journal, 4*(1), 3-9.

Lee, J., & Pruitt, K. W. (1978). Homework assignments: Classroom games or teaching tools? *The Clearing House, 53,* 31.

Lemmon, P. (1985). A school where learning styles make a difference. *Principal, 64*(4), 26-29.

Levin, H. M. (1987). *New schools for the disadvantaged.* Unpublished manuscript, Stanford, CT.

Lewellen, J. R. (1990, October–November). Systematic and effective teaching. *The High School Journal, 63*(1), 57-63.

Lile, B., Lile, G., & Jefferies, B. (1991). Project rebound: Effective intervention for rural elementary at-risk students. In R. C. Morris (Ed.), *Youth at-risk* (pp. 40-41). Scranton, PA: Technomic.

Lindbald, A. H., Jr. (1994). You can avoid the traps of cooperative learning. *The Clearing House, 67*(5), 291-293.

Marcus, L. (1977). How teachers view learning styles. *NASSP Bulletin, 61*(408), 112-114.

Magney, J. (1990). Game-based teaching. *The Education Digest, 60*(5), 54-57.

Milgram, R. M., Dunn, R., & Price, G. E. (Eds.). (1993). *Teaching and counseling gifted and talented adolescents: An international learning style perspective.* Westport, CT: Praeger.

Morris, R. C. (Ed.). (1991). *Youth at risk.* Lancaster, PA: Technomic.

National Association for Secondary School Principals (1982). *Student learning styles and brain behavior.* Reston, VA: National Association for Secondary School Principals.

Oddliefson, E. (1994). "What do we want our schools to do?" *Phi Delta Kappan, 75*(6), 446-453.

Perrin, J. (1984). An experimental investigation of the relationships among the learning style sociological preferences of gifted and non-gifted primary children, selected instructional strategies, attitudes, and achievement in problem solving and rote memorization. *Dissertation Abstracts International, 46,* 342A.

Perrin, S. (1994). "Education in the arts is an education for life." *Phi Delta Kappan, 75*(6), 452-453.

Phelps, P. H. (1991, March-April). Helping teachers excel as classroom managers. *The Clearing House, 14*(3), 241-242.

Piaget, J. (1952). *The origins of intelligence in children.* New York: International University Press.

Quinn, R. (1993). The New York State compact for learning and learning styles. *Learning Styles Network Newsletter. 15*(1), 1–2.

Research on the Dunn and Dunn learning style model (1994). Jamaica, NY: St. John's University's Center for the Study of Learning and Teaching Styles.

Reyes, D. J. (1990). Models of instruction: Some light on the model muddle. *The Clearing House, 63*(1), 214–216.

Sautter, R. C. (1994). An arts education school reform strategy. *Phi Delta Kappan, 75*(6), 432–437.

Sharon, S. (1980). Cooperative learning in small groups: Recent methods and effects on achievement attitudes and ethnic relations. *Review of Educational Research, 50,* 241–271.

Shavelson, R. J. (1983). Review of research on teachers' pedagogical judgments, plans, and decisions. *Elementary School Journal, 83,* 392–414.

Slavin, R. E. (1980). Cooperative learning. *Review of Educational Research, 50,* 503–527.

Slavin, R. E. (1989, April). On mastery learning and mastery teaching. *Educational Leadership, 46*(7), 77–79.

Solomon, S. (1989). Homework: The great reinforcer. *The Clearing House, 63*(2), 63.

Stinnett, T., & Henson, K. T. (1982). Chapter 16, The Human Equation and School Reform. America's public schools in transition: Future trends and issues. New York: Teachers College Press.

Stone, P. (1992, November). How we turned around a problem school. *The Principal, 71*(2), 34–36.

Thies, A. P. (1979). A brain behavior analysis of learning style. In J. W. Keefe (Ed.), *Student learning styles; Diagnosing and prescribing programs.* Reston, VA: National Association of Secondary School Principals.

Van Gulik, R. C. (1990). Functionalism, information, and content. In W. G. Lylcan (Ed.), *Mind and cognition.* Cambridge, MA: Basil Blackwell.

Walter, L. J. (1994). A synthesis of research findings on teacher planning and decision making. In R. L. Egbert and M. M. Kluender (Eds.). *Using research to improve teacher education.* Lincoln, NE: Clearing House on Teacher Education.

Wellington, P., & Perlin, C. (1991). Palimpsest probability and the writing process: Mega-change for at-risk students. In R. C. Morris (Ed.), *Youth at risk.* Lancaster, PA: Technomic.

SUGGESTED READINGS

Alberg, J., Cook, L., Fiore, T., Friend, M., Sano, S. (1992). *Educational approaches and options for integrating students with disabilities: A decision tool.* Triangle Park, NC: Research Triangle Institute.

Bail, A. L. (1982, November). The secrets of learning style: Your child's and your own. *Redbook, 160,* 73–76.

Brunner, C. E., Majewski, W. S. (1990, October). Mildly handicapped students can succeed with learning styles. *Educational Leadership, 48*(2), 21–23.

Cavanaugh, D. (1981, November). Student learning styles: A diagnostic/prescriptive approach to instruction. *Phi Delta Kappan, 64*(3), 202–203.

Cody, C. (1983). Learning styles, including hemispheric dominance: A comparative study of average, gifted, and highly gifted students in grades five through twelve. *Dissertation Abstracts International, 44,* 1631A.

Copenhaver, R. (1979). *The consistency of student learning as students move from English to mathematics.* Unpublished doctoral dissertation, Indiana University, Bloomington, IN.

Cross, J. A. (1982). Internal locus of control governs talented students (9–12). *Learning Styles Network Newsletter, 3*(3), 3.

Dunn, R., Bruno, J., Sklar, R. I., Zenhausern, R., & Beaudry, J. (1990, May–June). Effects of matching and mismatching minority developmental college students' hemispheric preferences on mathematics scores. *Journal of Educational Research, 83*(5), 283–288.

Dunn, R., & Price, G. E. (1980). The learning style characteristics of gifted children. *Gifted Child Quarterly, 24*(1), 33–36.

Dunn, R., Brennan, P., DeBello, T., & Hodges, H. (1984, Winter). Learning style: State of the science. In K. T. Henson (Ed.), *Theory into Practice, 23,* 10–19.

Friesen, C. D. (1979, January). The results of homework versus no homework research studies. *ERIC 167,* 508.

Gadwa, K., & Griggs, S. A. (1985). The school dropout: Implications for counselors. *The School Counselor, 33,* 9–17.

Geisert, G., & Dunn, R. (1991, March–April). Effective use of computers: Assignments based on individual learning style. *The Clearing House, 64*(4), 219–223.

Griggs, S. A., & Price, G. E. (1980). A comparison between the learning styles of gifted versus average junior high school students. *Phi Delta Kappan, 61,* 361.

Griggs, S. A., & Price, G. E. (1982). A comparison between the learning styles of gifted versus average junior high students. *Creative and Gifted Child Quarterly, 7,* 39–42.

Jarsonbeck, S. (1984). The effects of a right-brain and mathematics curriculum on low achieving, fourth grade students. *Dissertation Abstracts International, 45,* 2791A.

Jones, V. (1971). *The influence of teacher-student introversion achievement, and similarity on teacher-student dyadic classroom interactions.* Unpublished doctoral dissertation, University of Texas at Austin.

Keefe, J. W. (1979). *School applications of the learning style concept: Student learning styles* (pp. 123–132). Reston, VA: National Association of Secondary School Principals.

Klavas, A., Dunn, R., Griggs, S. A., Gemake, J., Geisert, G., & Zenhausern, R. (1994). Factors that facilitated or impeded implementation of the Dunn and Dunn learning style model. *Illinois School Research and Development Journal, 31*(1), 19–23.

Kreitner, K. R. (1981). *Modality strengths and learning styles of musically talented high school students.* Unpublished master's thesis. The Ohio State University, Columbus.

Koshuta, V., & Koshuta, P. (1993, April). Learning styles in a one-room school. *Educational Leadership, 50*(7), 87.

Lenehan, M. C., Dunn, R., Ingham, J., Signer, B., & Murray, J. B. (1994). Learning style: Necessary know-how for academic success in college. *Journal of College Student Development, 35,* 1–6.

Marshall, C. (1991, March–April). Teachers' learning styles: How they affect student learning. *The Clearing House, 64*(4), 225–227.

McDonald, C. (1972). *The influence of pupil liking the teacher, pupil perception of being liked, and pupil socioeconomic states on classroom behavior.* Unpublished doctoral dissertation, University of Texas at Austin.

Mickler, M. L., & Zippert, C. P. (1987). Teaching strategies based on learning styles of adult students. *Community/Junior College Quarterly, 11,* 33–37.

Neely, R. O., & Alm, D. (1992, November–December). *Meeting individual needs: A learning styles success story* (pp. 109–113). Washington, DC: Heldref Publications.

Nelson, B., Dunn, R., Griggs, S. A. Primavera, L., Fitzpatrick, M., Bacillious, Z., & Miller, R. (1993). Effects of learning style intervention on students' retention and achievement. *Journal of College Student Development, 34*(5), 364–369.

Orsak, L. (1990). Learning styles versus the Rip Van Winkle syndrome. *Educational Leadership, 48*(2), 19–20.

Pizzo, J. (1981). *An investigation of the relationships between selected acoustic environments and sound, an element of learning style, as they affect sixth grade students' reading achievement and attitudes.* Unpublished doctoral dissertation, St. John's University, Queens, NY.

Price, G. E., Dunn, K., Dunn, R., & Griggs, S. A. (1981). Studies in students' learning styles. *Roeper Review, 4,* 223–226.

Ricca, J. (1983). Curricular implications of learning style differences between gifted and non-gifted students. Unpublished doctoral dissertation, State University of New York at Buffalo.

Shea, T. C. (1983). *An investigation of the relationship between preferences for the learning style element of design, selected instructional environments, and reading test achievement of ninth-grade students to improve administrative determinations concerning effective educational facilities.* Unpublished doctoral dissertation, St. John's University, Queens, NY.

Smelter, R. W., Rasch, B. W., & Yudewitz, G. J. (1994). Thinking of inclusion for all special needs students? Better think again. *Phi Delta Kappan, 76*(1), 35–38.

Stewart, E. D. (1981). Learning styles among gifted/talented students: Instructional technique preferences. *Exceptional Children, 48,* 113–138.

Thelan, H. (1960). *Education and the human quest.* New York: Harper & Row.

Wasson, F. (1980). A comparative analysis of learning styles and personality characteristics of achieving and underachieving gifted elementary students. Unpublished doctoral dissertation, Florida State University, Tallahassee.

chapter 8

Teaching in Multicultural Settings

In the larger society, tolerances for diversity, a measure of concern for fellow human beings, the responsible exercise of citizenship, and a sense of social responsibility are essential to the functioning of local communities and the nation itself.

*Special Study Panel on Education Indicators for the
National Center for Education Statistics*

OBJECTIVES

Name three qualities of American high schools that inhibit success for minority students.

Give two approaches for helping minority students build a positive self-image.

Write a daily lesson plan that exalts several cultures' unique characteristics.

Explain the significance of the 1975 *Lau v. Nichols* decision by the U.S. Supreme Court.

List 10 things a teacher of a multicultural group should do to adjust to students, then list 10 things the teacher should avoid doing.

Create a one-hour simulation activity that will enable all students in a class to experience different cultural roles.

Name five principles of multicultural education.

Explain the significance of the following quotation in promoting healthy multicultural attitudes: "We must learn to listen and listen to learn."

PRETEST

	Agree	Disagree	Uncertain
1. There is little a teacher can do to meet the needs of students from other cultures unless the teacher has special training.	_____	_____	_____
2. Teachers should not concern themselves with different cultures because all students are Americans and must learn the American way of life.	_____	_____	_____
3. Schools do not have to provide instruction in other languages just because some students speak first languages other than English.	_____	_____	_____
4. Students who belong to other cultures should be grouped with like students throughout the school day.	_____	_____	_____
5. To avoid embarrassment, teachers should not discuss the backgrounds of minority students.	_____	_____	_____
6. It is dangerous to generalize about cultures other than your own.	_____	_____	_____

Demographers predict that American classrooms in the twenty-first century will be populated by a new majority—students of color, low-income students, and students

---

Middle-Level Message

You have often heard of people with a reputation for turning liabilities into assets. Middle-level teachers who teach in multicultural settings have the opportunity to do this. They can view the situation either as a handicap or as a unique opportunity. The results usually parallel the teacher's view.

If you choose to turn your pluralistic classes into an asset, you can do so by identifying the unique contributions each ethnic group has made to U.S. society. Then you should find ways to amplify these contributions. In this chapter you will learn how to make members of each ethnic group more aware of and proud of their heritage. You will also learn how to select textbooks and other materials to facilitate attainment of this goal.

It can be difficult to find appropriate supplementary materials to use in multicultural middle-level classes. Appendix F includes an annotated list of centers and agencies that provide schools with extensive reading lists, many of which are free.

---

of non-English-speaking backgrounds, the same learners currently failing in large numbers in U.S. schools (Gomez & Smith, 1991). Over a third of the entire U.S. population will be nonwhite by the year 2000 (Chimes & Schmidt, 1990). American teaching, however, will remain a white, middle-class occupation, with fewer teachers of color than now exist (Haberman, 1989).

As Alexander (1994, p. 266) notes, demographic changes accentuate the need for teaching students to appreciate cultural diversity: "Developing an appreciation for many cultures is a national educational concern tied to the emerging demographics of our nation and the rapid disappearance of political boundaries that previously isolated many ethnic groups." Hilliard (1991–1992) says that if the curriculum is centered in truth it will be pluralistic because human culture is the product of the struggles of all humanity, not a single racial or ethnic group's possession.

Interest in and commitment to multicultural education peaked in the 1960s and shaped the curricula throughout the 1970s; it was not emphasized during the 1980s but regained its position of major concern in the 1990s (Reed, 1994). Millions of dollars have been spent on programs to raise the academic performance of minority-group children, yet the disappointing results have not been reversed (Stewart, 1975). But as Fantini (1986, p. 12) states, "The school curriculum has to reflect multicultural understandings. Multilingual and multicultural educations are no longer frills but major necessities." The traditional approach to multicultural education has been simply to give students information. Clearly, this approach will not work by itself. Guyton and Fielstein (1991, p. 207) explain: "Although information is necessary, it cannot be expected by itself to modify learned attitudes." Future curricula must provide students with opportunities to express feelings, analyze attitudes, and participate in discussions.

How much, and exactly what, can you do? Teachers may be the only people who can significantly improve the education minorities receive. American schools have several features that make it difficult for multicultural students to succeed (Henson, 1975).

First, U.S. schools are so large that they appear impersonal to immigrants. Second, teachers tend to be overly concerned with tests, grades, and competition. Furthermore, teachers tend to sell minority students short and underestimate their ability to succeed and to contribute.

TAKING A POSITIVE APPROACH

To many students and teachers, the term *multicultural* has negative connotations. "Further, our economy is increasingly based on a global economic model, forcing us to become familiar with ways of life not long ago considered exotic and strange," write Chimes and Schmidt (1990, p. 44). To many, multicultural brings to mind problems, which is unfortunate because this in itself may cause problems. In other words, if teachers interpret multicultural settings as prone to problems, they may approach multicultural classes with skepticism. Students sense this and will not trust the teacher. But if teachers view the multicultural setting as an opportunity to increase their own knowledge and enrich their own values, the classroom experience is more likely to prove rewarding for everyone. According to McCormick (1984, p. 94), "a cornerstone of multiculturalism in education is cultural pluralism, an ideology of cultural diversity, which celebrates the differences among groups of people." The following principles of multiculturalism in education show some reasons for meeting all students' needs (Garcia, 1984, p. 108):

1. In the classroom, as in society at large, cultural diversity should be considered a cause for celebration.
2. Cultural diversity is a valuable asset for society to preserve and enhance.
3. Teachers should strive to provide educational equity for all students.
4. Multicultural education directly counters elitism, sexism, and racism in American public school teaching and learning.
5. Schools should not place too many minority students in classes for the learning disabled or emotionally impaired.
6. Emancipation of minority students from inequitable treatment serves society.

PERSONALIZING TEACHING

The U.S. population has become very mobile. With one family in five moving each year, even many small schools have multicultural student populations. In every situation teachers must recognize and exalt cultural differences to make students feel proud of their cultures and capable of applying their uniqueness to strengthen America. The best way to begin planning for teaching multicultural classes is to learn about your students' cultures (Slavin, 1994).

No matter where you teach, cultural differences will abound. This is true in affluent suburbs, working-class urban areas, and rural areas. Even when students have similar ethnic and economic backgrounds, pronounced differences in religious backgrounds will exist. As long as there is one student whose background is different, you need skills in working with culturally mixed classrooms, even in the smallest communities and schools.

The problems often seem greater in larger schools, where there are so many students that even getting to know them all is difficult. But in this setting the challenge and the need to personalize is even greater, because members of similar cultural backgrounds tend to form cliques. Cultural cliques can be hotbeds of prejudice. This, of course, refers not to organized clubs but to the informal gatherings in parking lots, hallways, and cafeterias with no constructive purpose. Every teacher can contribute to dissolving such groups by getting to know each student on a more personal level and by volunteering to sponsor clubs for students of similar cultural backgrounds. International clubs are excellent for acquainting students with other cultures.

But such techniques are applicable in all classes, multicultural or not. Most students, irrespective of cultural background, would profit if more classes were personalized, if competition among students were reduced, and if realistic demands were made of everyone. All students' self-concepts are enhanced when teachers assign tasks that require students to work together toward common goals (Manning & Lucking, 1991), tasks that are within students' ability and provide encouragement and rewards. However, students from other cultures are different in several specific ways, and you must be aware of these differences when learning how to teach them.

A group of teachers interested in discovering the strengths of various minority and ethnic students surveyed teachers throughout much of southern Florida, identifying 2,000 such strengths (Cheyney, 1976, pp. 41–42). The survey showed that the children were generally:

Highly responsive to affection	Independent
Physically dexterous	Imitative
Protective of siblings	Uninhibited
Academically persevering	Emotionally cool
Musically oriented	Monetarily proficient
Artistic	Rich in humor
Authority minded	Competitive
Resourceful	Forgiving

Although awareness of these qualities can help you design learning experiences for multicultural classes, teachers must resist the temptation to build yet another stereotype for all multicultural children. Each student is an individual, and as such may possess all or none of these traits. This list is included because it provides teachers of multicultural classes with a point at which to begin analyzing their students. And this is how teachers should begin—by analyzing each student's strengths.

Perhaps the greatest obstacle to teaching an appreciation for diversity is teachers' reluctance to teach about cultures that are not their own. Alexander (1994, p. 267) explains: "But the greatest obstacle lurks in the basic human fear of change. Many teachers feel that their own mythology and values, noted in the Renaissance of Western Europe, are being challenged by multicultural texts."

A REASON FOR OPTIMISM

In 1975, in *Lau v. Nichols* (U.S. 563, 18. ct. 786), the Supreme Court mandated that all schools in the United States with 20 or more students who speak a common first language other than English are to provide systematic instruction in that language. This emphasis has had a great impact on many schools, but this or any other federal mandate alone is inadequate. Meeting minority students' needs, will occur through teachers' concerns, skills, and efforts.

Another reason for optimism is professional associations' emphasis on multicultural education. For more than two decades the Association for Supervision and Curriculum Development has given high priority to multicultural education in its publications and meetings. In 1979 the National Council for the Accreditation of Teacher Education (NCATE) added a multicultural standard that colleges of teacher education must meet if they are to attain and retain accreditation. This means that in the future, colleges of teacher education must provide students opportunities to enable them to "understand the unique contributions, needs, similarities, differences and interdependencies of students from varying racial, cultural, linguistic, religious and socio-economic backgrounds" (NCATE, 1985, p. 5). The 1986 revision of NCATE standards continues to stress multicultural education.

Another major reason for optimism is that the public is embracing multiculturalism as part of the curriculum. The 26th Annual Phi Delta Kappa/Gallup Poll of the Public's Attitudes Toward the Public Schools (Elam, Rose, & Gallup, 1994) found that three-fourths of the public think that the schools should promote both a common cultural tradition and the diverse cultural traditions of the different population groups in America.

THE TEACHER'S DECISION

We are fortunate to have multicultural classes. Schooling involves learning about life, and life in the late twentieth century is multicultural. Although all multicultural classes have some unique problems, they also offer students a chance to learn about contemporary life. And to accept themselves and others, students must understand and appreciate cultural diversity (Fantini, 1986). Yet these advantages do not come to our attention as quickly as the problems do. To realize the advantages, teachers must commit themselves to enjoy and capitalize on cultural differences in their classes (Henson & Henry, 1976). It is a matter of teacher attitude. "It is easy for students and faculty to focus only on differences, rather than also paying attention to the issue of common humanity in cultural diversity," write Chimes and Schmidt (1990, p. 46).

In-service education and other information-gathering methods can help improve teacher attitudes toward multicultural education. Although some programs have not done this (Cathey, 1980), other programs have left participants feeling more positive about multicultural education. Over a decade ago, Dandridge (1980) found that the more teachers know about multicultural education, and the more professional preparation they have, the more positive their attitudes will be. Knowledge and preparation can prevent resentful and negative attitudes toward multicultural education.

Glatthorn (1993, p. 38) says that we should be aware that minority students often must cope with an environment outside of school that differs from the school environment. He calls this dilemma "cultural dissonance." These students must learn how to live in the school environment while maintaining their cultural identity (Ross, Bundy, & Kyle, 1993). This cultural dissonance places these students at risk. For many of these students, academic success depends on teachers "who are prepared to understand and meet the needs of students who come to school with varying learning styles, and with differing beliefs about themselves and what school means for them (Darling-Hammond, 1993, p. 775).

All students are members of some culture. We should not think of minority students as being culturally disadvantaged. Every group is rich in heritage. If the Anglo fails to understand the richness of a minority student's background, is not the Anglo culturally disadvantaged? I think so. The teacher who views a multicultural classroom as a positive climate for overall student learning will help erase some of each student's cultural ignorance. People tend to fear and distrust what they do not understand, and you can do much to alleviate this lack of understanding.

Reflection

Assumptions of Cultural Pluralism

After reading the following assumptions (Tesconi, 1984, p. 88), respond to the questions below.

1. An individual's membership in . . . a cultural group life . . . promotes . . . self-esteem, sense of belonging, respect for others, purposefulness, and critical thinking.
2. The development [of] tolerance and openness to different others . . . is dependent upon the opportunity of individuals to encounter and interact with a variety of culturally different others.
3. No one way of life can be said to be better than any other, and to be humane, a society must afford room for many competing and oftentimes conflicting ways of life.
4. It is valuable to have many ways of life in competition. . . . Such competition leads to a balance or equilibrium in the social order.
5. Loyalty to a larger society—a nation—is a function of, and dependent on, socially sanctioned loyalties rooted in a multiplicity of diverse ethnic and cultural groups.

Respond to the following questions.

> **Reflection (*continued*)**
>
> **1.** With which of these assumptions do you agree? Disagree? What are the bases for your disagreement?
> **2.** Do you believe loyalty to a single ethnic group, as opposed to loyalty to a multiplicity of ethnic groups, facilitates or impedes loyalty to the nation? Assumption 3 says that no one way of life is superior to all others; therefore all groups must have some advantages.
> **3.** Name some ethnic groups in the United States, and list at least one advantage of membership in each group. List one contribution each group has made to the United States.

In working with multicultural students, you cannot help but know that there are differences, but the effective teacher will also realize that, basically, children are children (Cheyney, 1976). If you question that time spent preparing to teach minorities is time well spent, remember that lessons and methods that work effectively with these students will also work well with the other students.

THE TEACHER'S ROLE

The history of U.S. treatment of minorities tells us that teachers' actions determine whether multicultural students will receive a quality education. "The courts can grant equal opportunity, but cannot give equal chance" (Payne, 1984, p. 124). As Chimes and Schmidt (1990, p. 46) explain, only teachers can provide all students equal opportunity: "If books and ensuing discussions become magnifiers of guilt, injustice, and shame, no good can come of it. The responsibility to keep discussions informative, challenging, and positive lies solely with the faculty."

As this millennium comes to a close, teachers must consider themselves world citizens. Erasmus (1989) explains:

> Teachers must be able to reach beyond their own world to touch that of their students and assist students to do the same. We can begin by learning to listen. We, as teachers, must confirm and validate the experience and knowledge [of our students] as well as the cultural context in which those experiences live and that knowledge is situated. To do this, we must listen to their stories, and hear who they are. We must learn to listen and listen to learn. (p. 274)

Although this book makes a conscious attempt to avoid long lists, one list is essential at this point. Read and consider each of the following (Dawson, 1974, pp. 53-54). Collectively, these dos and don'ts provide an excellent guide for teachers in multicultural classrooms.

The number of minority teachers is decreasing, yet the number of minority students is rapidly increasing.

Dos for Teachers in Multicultural Classrooms

1. Do use the same scientific approach to gain background information on multicultural groups you would use to tackle a course in science, mathematics, or any subject area in which you might be deficient.

2. Do engage in systematic study of the disciplines that provide insight into the cultural heritage, political struggle, contributions, and present-day problems of minority groups.

3. Do try to develop sincere personal relationships with minorities. You can't teach strangers! Don't give up because one minority person rejects your efforts. All groups have sincere individuals who welcome honest, warm relationships with members of another race. Seek out those who will accept or at least tolerate you.

4. Do recognize that there are often more differences within one group than between two groups. If we recognize diversity among races, we must also recognize diversity within groups.

5. Do remember that there are many ways to gain insight into a group. Visit their churches, homes, communities; read widely and listen to various segments of the group.

6. Do remember that no one approach and no one answer will help you meet the educational needs of all children in a multicultural society.

7. Do select instructional materials that are accurate and free from stereotypes.

8. Do remember that there is a positive relationship between teacher expectation and academic progress.

9. Do provide an opportunity for minority students and students from the mainstream to interact in a positive intellectual setting on a continuous basis.

10. Do use a variety of materials, especially those that utilize positive, real-life experiences.

11. Do provide some structure and direction to children who have unstructured lives, primarily children of the poor.
12. Do expose all students to a wide variety of literature as a part of your cultural sensitivity program.
13. Do remember that even though ethnic groups often share many common problems their needs are diverse.
14. Do utilize the rich resources within your own classroom among various cultural groups.
15. Do remember that human understanding is a lifetime endeavor. You must continue to study and provide meaningful experiences for your students.
16. Do remember to be honest with yourself. If you can't adjust to children from multicultural homes, get out of the classroom.

Don'ts for Teachers in Multicultural Classrooms

1. Don't rely on textbooks, teachers guides, and brief essays to become informed about minorities. Research and resources will be needed.
2. Don't use ignorance as an excuse for not having any insight into the problems and culture of African Americans, Chicano, Native Americans, Puerto Ricans, Asian Americans, and other minorities.
3. Don't rely on the "expert" judgment of one minority person for the answer to all the complicated racial and social problems of his or her people. For example, African Americans, Mexicans, Indians, and Puerto Ricans have various political views on all issues.
4. Don't be fooled by popular slogans and propaganda intended to raise the national consciousness of an oppressed people.
5. Don't get carried away with the "save the world concept." Most minorities have their own savior.
6. Don't be afraid to learn from those who are more familiar with the mores and cultures than you.
7. Don't assume that you have all the answers for solving the other person's problems. It is almost impossible for an outsider to be an expert on the culture of another group.
8. Don't assume that all minority group students are culturally deprived.
9. Don't develop a fatalistic attitude about the progress of minority students.
10. Don't resegregate students through tracking and ability grouping gimmicks.
11. Don't give up when minority students seem to hate school.
12. Don't assume that minorities are the only students who should have multicultural instructional materials. Students in the mainstream can be culturally deprived in their lack of knowledge and understanding of other people and of their own heritage.
13. Don't ask parents and students personal questions in the name of research. Why should they divulge their suffering?

14. Don't get hung up on grade designations when sharing literature that provides insight into the cultural heritage of a people.
15. Don't try to be cool by using the vernacular of a particular racial group.
16. Don't make minority students feel ashamed of their language, dress, or traditions.

Reflection

The following statement was made by a minority ethnic group member who has become a recognized national leader in the study of multicultural education (Garcia, 1984, p. 104). Consider his comments as you respond to the questions below.

Correcting Classroom Discrimination

"I remember well my eighth-grade English teacher who made me write a letter to the school newspaper ten times before submission. The fact that my father was an unemployed coal miner, that my parents had seven years of schooling between them, and that English was spoken minimally in our house did not impede her from making a positive difference in my life. Not only did I learn to write a letter well, but I learned the importance of discipline, perseverance, and mentorship—all very important outcomes of schooling."

1. Some teachers overlook minority group students whose level of success is minimal. Do you think the person who made this statement condones this practice? Can you give one reason teachers should or should not hold high expectations for members of minority groups?
2. As a teacher, what can you do to win minority students' confidence and respect?
3. Assuming that all people have some degree of prejudice toward members of certain minority groups, how can you elevate your appreciation for minorities?

These dos and don'ts are presented as general guidelines for teachers who have members of one or more ethnic minority groups in their classes. Because all teachers have some representatives of other cultures in their classes from time to time, these guidelines should be appropriate for all of us. One additional suggestion, which is so obvious that you may overlook it: Do not give in to the temptation to make quick, automatic generalizations about any culture.

These guidelines are based on volumes of data, but even when you use scientifically derived suggestions, remember that regardless of culture, all students are individuals. Respect their individuality.

SELECTING ETHNIC MATERIALS

Because more than half the states in the nation require multiethnic programs and development of multiethnic materials, special materials for multiethnic groups should not be difficult to find (Klassen & Goilnick, 1977). As Bishop noted (1986, p. 23), "It is promising to realize that efforts to include books that reflect all ethnic backgrounds not only enable minority students to identify more closely with the school while improving their reading ability, but also enable nonminority students to broaden their understanding of other peoples and cultures." In selecting materials for teaching about ethnicity—and in selecting all materials to use in multicultural settings—do not automatically assume that different ethnic groups need elementary or remedial materials. The following classification system was designed to help teachers select multiethnic materials at the appropriate levels of complexity, depending on the units' objectives.

Level I materials are low in complexity and designed to highlight the achievements of all ethnic groups. Such material includes biographies and success stories of ethnic Americans. These materials are usually highly complimentary—so much that they often exaggerate. They are usually attractive and conspicuously displayed in the classroom by teachers. Use them sparingly and selectively.

Level II materials depict "true/real" experiences of ethnic groups. Problems of the group are shown in a way that suggests that members of other groups, such as the majority ethnic group, are responsible for bad experience, but without specifying who the others are. Limit the use of these materials.

Level III materials show the historical experiences of more than one ethnic group. Portrayals are limited to racial groups (blacks, Hispanics, Native Americans) or white groups (Irish Americans, Italian Americans, or Polish Americans), but not both. A common approach is to select a major theme, such as "metropolitan/urban life," and present each group's unique experiences. Such materials purposefully accentuate the differences between minority groups or white ethnic groups and fail to show the experiences and behaviors common to all groups. If misused, this material could widen existing gaps between classmates of differing ethnic groups.

Level IV materials, the most complex materials, are designed around broad content generalizations. They chronicle experiences common to all groups and identify common characteristics. They provide students with a multiethnic perspective on the American experience. Because these materials require critical analysis, use them with students who can conduct sophisticated discussion and critical, objective analysis. The following list of sources shows where to obtain materials at each of the levels (Garcia & Garcia, 1980).

Sources for Materials on Ethnic Groups

Level I.   Materials in Level I can be ordered through major and minor publishing houses and are often packaged as multimedia. Examples of such sources are:

Multicultural Multimedia Services
P.O. Box 669
1603 Hope Street
South Pasadena, CA 91030

Social Studies School Service
P.O. Box 802
1000 Culver Boulevard
Culver City, CA 90230

Level II.   Materials in Level II chronicle the experiences of minority groups. Materials on Chicanos and Chinese Americans can be obtained from:

Handel Film Corporation
8730 Sunset Boulevard
West Hollywood, CA 90060

Level III.   Biethnic materials can be obtained from:

Children's Book and Music Center
5373 West Pico Boulevard
Los Angeles, CA 90019

Level IV.   Multiethnic materials can be obtained from:

Social Studies School Service
P.O. Box 802
1000 Culver Boulevard
Culver City, CA 90230

EMF
P.O. Box 4272
Madison, WI 53711

Case Studies

Multicultural classes offer students an opportunity to learn how to get along with members of various ethnic groups; however, this can happen only in an environment that permits students to interact with their classmates. One method that invites students to interact and share opinions is the case study method (Kowalski, Weaver, & Henson, 1993).

The case study method is fun to use because it encourages the sharing of opinions and insights. Teachers enjoy using this method because is frees them to observe students interacting with each other. Learning how to use the case study is not difficult. One effective way to learn more about case studies is to write your own cases for your students to use (Barnes, Christensen, & Hansen, 1994).

As you approach your first teaching position, you may want to develop a portfolio of materials to use with multicultural groups. But whether you do this or not, you must view multicultural experiences as a challenge and an opportunity, not as an opportunity to "save" minority students from their own ethnic group. All students should learn to appreciate and respect cultures other than their own. A sensible, if not the best, approach to selecting materials for multicultural groups is to achieve some balance of materials from the varying levels of complexity. But the most important criterion for selecting materials is how well a source will help you attain a lesson's objectives.

Because cultural diversity has made America strong, do not try to melt down the cultures into one. On the contrary, schools should help preserve many of the characteristics that make each culture unique. In the past, teachers have made some common mistakes in working with multicultural groups. Often they made such a fuss over the differences between and among groups that they exacerbated the gap in students' minds about groups' differing characteristics. On the opposite end of the continuum, teachers have tried to blend all cultures into one. For 200 years the United States has been considered a melting pot. The concept was first created by a French-born writer, Crevecoeur, in 1782 (Ramirez & Castaneda, 1974).

ACADEMIC ACHIEVEMENT FROM EVERYONE

Too often teachers accept low performance from minority students—"That's just the way they are"—but this is a cop-out. By making an exception for minority students and letting them go along without experiencing maximum success, teachers deny them their right to develop to their maximum potential—a goal that we should hold for all students.

THE TEACHER'S WIDER ROLE

We have been examining the teacher's role in working with multicultural classes with respect to instruction, but the teacher has a much broader role. Because teaching involves more than mere instruction, you should find opportunities to fulfill the goals of multicultural education.

A Teacher Corps/Association of Teacher Educators project resulted in a book titled *In Praise of Diversity: A Resource Book for Multicultural Education* (Grant, Meinich, & Riven, 1977). The book concludes with an article that identifies a number of implications for teachers of multicultural groups that extend beyond the classroom into all areas of the teacher's work.* Two avenues teachers can use to praise diversity are identified. These avenues are process and content. Now we turn to some ways to use process to praise diversity.

---

* Appreciation is extended to Carl A. Grant, Susan L. Melnich, and H. N. Riven, to the Teacher Corps, and to the Association of Teacher Educators for permission to use abstracts from the article "In Praise of Diversity: Some Implications."

USING PROCESS TO PRAISE DIVERSITY

Have you ever considered that as a teacher you will be positioned in a prominent (highly visible) position in the community? This will enable you to affect and shape significantly the community's atmosphere and the general attitudes toward different cultures. Your behavior both inside and outside the classroom is important. According to Grant, Meinich, and Riven (1977), teachers have at least the following functions:

1. Director of learning
2. Counselor and guidance worker
3. Mediator of culture
4. Link with the community
5. Member of the school staff
6. Member of the profession

Director of Learning

Much of this chapter has focused on the teacher's instructional role. Because suggestions were provided to show how teachers should "gear up" their instruction to allow for, praise, and promote cultural differences in the classroom, we need not discuss this dimension again.

Counselor and Guidance Worker

Because this book's philosophy is personalizing education, each chapter emphasizes the need for you to work with each student in a way that extends beyond academics. Only one further comment seems warranted. Each teacher is responsible for vocational guidance. The best vocational guidance programs are interdisciplinary and run throughout the grades. Each teacher should help students become aware of vocational possibilities. Do not assume that members from all cultures feel an equal need for long-range planning; you must introduce some students to this concept and its advantages.

Mediator of Culture

Earlier in this chapter we discussed a need to stress the contributions of all cultures represented in the classroom to "our culture" and to humanity at large. This should not preclude emphasis on the democratic processes and American citizens' rights and responsibilities; rather, it should complement this goal. One way to do this is to teach problem-solving skills for coping with potential conflict areas. Simulations can be used to develop these skills. (See the simulations listed in Appendix E.)

Link with the Community

In the 1970s the LINKS Project was established at Indiana State University. Written by a science educator, Chris Buethe, this project helped nonscience teachers develop science materials for use in their classes. For example, English teachers were able to link the high-interest area of science to their classes by assigning students essays or other projects that would link otherwise seemingly unrelated subjects. This strategy can also be used to link the multicultural class to the community. Cultural diversity should be exalted in the community at large. Since most teachers sooner or later accept leadership roles in the community, they can use these positions toward these ends. Perhaps most important of all, teachers can demonstrate their own commitment by praising diversity and affirming pluralism as they work and live in the community.

Member of the School Staff

Since teachers' roles within the school extend beyond the classroom and involve other teachers, administrators, and auxiliary personnel, they can find many opportunities to influence their colleagues. In most schools an important location for informal influence is the teachers' lounge, but of course not all influence there is positive. In a supervision text, Henry and Beasley (1989) use the phrase *lounge lizards* to caution teachers of the potential damage that can inadvertently result from careless comments in informal settings. But if such settings do affect participants' behavior, the lounge could also be an ideal place for teachers dedicated to multicultural education to demonstrate their concerns, not in negative ways but in positive, constructive behaviors.

Member of the Profession

As members of a profession, teachers must use their influence and skills to improve themselves and the profession. One major responsibility is to communicate education's positive dimensions to all members of society. The previous decade brought criticism and scorn to American schools. Individual teachers can communicate their schools' roles and achievements through conversations, discussions, and the written word. Professional meetings offer excellent opportunities for communication, and professional journals offer similar opportunities. Teachers who are committed to furthering multicultural education will find that many education and teacher associations give top priority to these ends.

RECAP OF MAJOR IDEAS

1. Several qualities of American schools militate against minority group students' efforts to succeed academically and socially.
2. Twenty-first-century classrooms will be populated by a new majority.
3. Having students of several cultural backgrounds strengthens a class and a school.
4. By assigning tasks within students' ability range, by providing encouragement, and by giving rewards, teachers can help minority and other students build their self-concept.
5. Federal law requires schools to teach in the national language of students when 20 or more students share a common first language.
6. Discuss in class the contribution of minority groups to society.
7. Select and use textbooks that portray all cultures in positive and realistic ways.

8. There are more differences within than among cultures.
9. Some professional associations make concentrated efforts to ensure proper education for minority groups and the development of positive attitudes toward multicultural education.
10. Demand continuous academic growth from minority students.
11. Strive to build a positive attitude toward cultural diversity in your classroom.

CASES

CASE 1: A TEACHER BELITTLES A SLOW STUDENT

In terms of performance quality, Jerry Simms was one of the poorest students Shelly had ever had. At first she tried to encourage Jerry to listen, then she tried to force him to do his daily home assignments. Nothing seemed to help. Finally, Shelly made an inexcusable response to his indifferent behavior. She remarked in front of his peers, "Jerry, you don't have one iota of understanding about the subject we are studying, do you?"

Later, when relating the incident to some other teachers, she learned that Jerry had almost no home life. She began to regret what she had said and decided to drive by and see where he lived. The temperature was below freezing, and cracks in the walls let the lights show through. She learned later that the building had once been a storehouse for grain and had dirt floors. A student told her that there were only two chairs and a table inside.

Shelly's experience with Jerry began to haunt her. She began to ask herself, "How can I help him?"

Discussion

1. How can a teacher learn about a student's home life?

   An experience like Shelly's makes the teacher want to see the student's home and family. But this is not always practical and is not necessarily a wise method. It is not practical because there are too many students in similar circumstances. It is not wise because the student may be embarrassed to have his family and home exposed for observation.

   As a beginning teacher, you will be amazed at how much other teachers know about the students in your class—even the teachers who have never taught your students. Do not hesitate to ask other teachers about your students. It is perfectly professional so long as the discussion is directed to understanding the student better and does not degenerate into a gossip session. Your school will keep a cumulative record on each student. This record will contain comments made by students' previous teachers. Here you can learn about a student's general behavior and academic potential.

2. Why might a dedicated teacher lose her temper with a low-performing student like Jerry?

   Most classes have students whose performance is low because they are too lazy to improve. The teacher cannot always know which students are lazy and which are handicapped by a disadvantaged home life. Therefore, instead of becoming irritated with students who are not attentive, try to determine the cause of their apathy.

3. To what ethnic group would you guess Jerry belongs? Shelly?

Shelly and Jerry are both Anglo-Americans.

CASE 2: A POOR SCHOOL HAS A GOOD ATMOSPHERE

When Bob, a supervisor of student teachers, first saw Rio Grande, an inner-city school, his first reaction was disbelief that such a school could exist in the twentieth century—the buildings should have been condemned decades ago because they were firetraps. Placing two beginning teachers in this environment went against Bob's better judgment, but he took a deep breath and went in to meet the principal.

Mr. Lopez was a delightful middle-aged man, gregarious and energetic. He introduced Bob to his secretaries and to several members of his large faculty, which was 95 percent Latin American. Each teacher had the same spark of enthusiasm and pleasantness.

Bob was still suspicious because he had been inside many dilapidated inner-city schools. He was keenly aware that in schools like this the students were often discourteous, rude, disrespectful, and difficult to control. Nevertheless, his responsibility was to assign two student teachers to this staff for the next term, so he promised himself he would visit frequently and provide encouragement and reassurance to make the experience tolerable for them.

When Bob visited, both student teachers assured him they were getting along well. There were apparently no major discipline problems in their classes. Both worked hard and enjoyed teaching in this school. From talking with the principal, some of the faculty members, and these two student teachers, Bob found three elements that seemed to be working together to produce the wholesome, optimistic atmosphere in a physical environment that had initially seemed so depressing. First, the principal stressed the importance of total involvement by all, including faculty and students, on both academic and extracurricular matters. These student teachers were immediately involved in evening and weekend school activities. The principal considered them important members of the faculty.

Second, the principal's enthusiasm was reflected in every faculty member and classroom. Most of the students were very poor readers, which severely limited the rate of learning, but the teachers were patient and continually encouraged their students.

Bob discovered the third element contributing to this school's wholesome atmosphere when he expressed his concern at the slow rate at which material was being covered. A faculty member responded that because many of the students were academically slow and had poor home lives that destroyed their concern and respect for others, one of the most important objectives was to teach the students to cooperate with others. The faculty members at Rio Grande certainly set good examples for their students.

Discussion Questions

1. Teaching respect for others should be an important objective in any deprived community, but exactly what can the teacher do to teach students to respect others?
2. Some student teachers never intend to teach in rundown buildings located in inner-city ghettos, so why do they need the experience of teaching in such schools?
3. Could the fact that this faculty was almost entirely composed of Latin Americans explain the unexpected open climate in this school?

ACTIVITIES

At one time or another, all of us will teach classes that represent different cultures, so we will need strategies for working with cultural differences. In fact, even in a class whose ethnic composition is similar, there is often a diversity of cultural backgrounds. The following activities will help you work with multicultural groups.

1. Most of us are biased toward our own ethnic group. Make a list of your own biases.
2. All ethnic groups have some cultural qualities that can make a contribution to American society. Name some ethnic groups, and identify one such quality of each.
3. Describe a strategy that would be appropriate in your subject and grade level for breaking down cultural prejudices. Consider including techniques for showing the attributes of different classes and groups.

REFERENCES

Alexander, J. (1994). Multicultural literature: Overcoming the hurdles to successful study. *The Clearing House, 67*(5), 266-268.

Barnes, L. B., Christensen, C. R., & Hansen, A. J. (1994). *Teaching and the case study method* (3rd ed.). Boston: Harvard Business School Press.

Bishop, G. R. (1986). The identification of multicultural materials for the middle school library: Annotations and sources. *American Middle School Education, 9,* 23-27.

Cathey, F. M. (1980). *Teacher perceptions of multicultural education in comparison with their previous multicultural education preparation.* Unpublished doctoral dissertation, George Peabody College for Teachers. Nashville, TN.

Cheyney, A. B. (1976). *Teaching children of different cultures in the classroom* (2nd ed.). Columbus, OH: Merrill.

Chimes, M., & Schmidt, P. (1990, September–October). What I read over my summer vacation: Readings on cultural diversity. *The Clearing House, 64*(1), 44-46.

Dandridge, J. A. (1980). *The attitudes, knowledge of subject matter and classroom behaviors of teachers using multicultural/multiethnic programs.* Unpublished doctoral dissertation, University of Southern California, Los Angeles.

Darling-Hammond, L. (1993). Reforming the school reform agenda. *Phi Delta Kappan, 74*(10), 756–761.

Dawson, M. E. (Ed.) (1974). *Are there unwelcome guests in your classroom?* Washington, DC: Association for Childhood Education International.

Elam, S. M., Rose, L. C., & Gallup, G. (1994). The 26th Annual Phi Delta Kappa/Gallup Poll of the Public's Attitudes Toward the Public Schools. *Phi Delta Kappan, 76* (1), 41–56.

Erasmus, C. C. (1989). Ways with stories: Listening to the stories aboriginal people tell. *Language Arts, 66*(3), 267–275.

Fantini, M. D. (1986). *Regaining excellence in education.* Columbus, OH: Merrill.

Garcia, J., & Garcia, R. (1980). Selecting ethnic materials. *Social Studies, 44,* 232–234.

Garcia, R. L. (1984). Countering classroom discrimination. *Theory into Practice, 23,* 104–108.

Glatthorn, A. A. (1993). *Learning twice.* New York: HarperCollins.

Gomez, M. L., & Smith, R. J. (1991, January–February). Building interactive reading and writing curricula with diverse learners. *The Clearing House, 64*(3), 147–151.

Grant, C. A., Meinich, S. L., & Riven, H. N. (1977). *In praise of diversity: A resource book for multicultural education.* Washington, DC: Association of Teacher Educators.

Guyton, J. M., & Fielstein, L. L. (1991, January–February). A classroom activity to increase student awareness of racial prejudice. *The Clearing House, 64*(3), 207–209.

Haberman, M. (1989). More minority teachers. *Phi Delta Kappan, 70*(10), 771–776.

Henry, M. A., & Beasley, W. W. (1989). *Supervising student teachers: The professional way* (4th ed.). Terre Haute, IN: Sycamore Press, Inc.

Henson, K. T. (1975). American schools vs. cultural pluralism. *Educational Leadership, 32,* 405–408.

Henson, K. T., & Henry, M. A. (1976). *Becoming involved in teaching* (chap. 9). Terre Haute, IN: Sycamore.

Hilliard, J. (1991/92). Why must we pluralize the curriculum? *Educational Leadership, 49*(4), 12–13.

Klassen, F., & Goilnick, D. (1977). *Pluralism and the American teacher.* Washington, DC: American Association of Colleges for Teacher Education.

Kowalski, T. J., Weaver, R. A., & Henson, K. T. (1993). *Case studies on beginning teachers.* White Plains, NY: Longman.

Manning, M. L., & Lucking, R. (1991, January–February). The what, why, and how of cooperative learning. *The Clearing House, 64*(3), 152–156.

McCormick, T. E. (1984). Multiculturalism: Some principles and issues, *Theory into Practice, 23,* 93–97.

National Council for the Accreditation of Teacher Education (1985). *Standards for the accreditation of basic and advanced preparation programs for professional school personnel* (p. 5). Washington, DC: NCATE.

Payne, C. (1984). Multicultural education and racism in American schools. *Theory into Practice, 23,* 124.

Ramirez, M., & Castaneda, A. (1974). *Cultural democracy.* New York: Academic Press.

Reed, D. F. (1994). Multicultural education for preservice students. *Action in Teacher Education, 15*(3), 27–34.

Ross, D. D., Bundy, E., & Kyle, D. W. (1993). *Reflective teaching for student empowerment.* New York: Macmillan.

Slavin, R. E. (1994). *Educational psychology: Theory and practice* (4th ed.). Needham Heights, MA: Allyn & Bacon.

Stewart, I. S. (1975). Cultural differences between Anglos and Chicanos. *Integration, 8,* 21–23.

Tesconi, C. A. (1984). Multicultural education: A valued but problematic ideal. *Theory into Practice, 23,* 88.

SUGGESTED READINGS

Johnson, D. W., & Johnson, R. (1989–1990). Social skills for successful group work. *Educational Leadership, 47*(4), 29–33.

Smith, F. R., & Cox, C. B. (1976). *Secondary schools in a changing society.* New York: Holt, Rinehart, & Winston.

Special Study Panel on Education Indicators for the National Center for Education Statistics (1991, September). *Education counts* (p. 67). Washington, DC: U.S. Department of Education,

chapter **9**

Teaching Students
with Special Needs

*Children who are treated as if they are uneducable almost invariably become
uneducable.*

Kenneth B. Clark

OBJECTIVES

Name the main five categories of handicapped students.

Name the three factors you should always consider when working with handicapped students.

List three minimum requirements of all individualized educational programs as set forth by Public Law (PL) 94-142.

Give two definitions of "gifted students."

Explain why the length of time a specific handicap has existed is important.

List three characteristics of mildly retarded students.

Name several rights that PL 94-142 gives to handicapped students and their parents.

Develop an individualized educational program for a hypothetical handicapped student.

Describe the results from grouping gifted students together.

Design a lesson to promote creativity.

PRETEST

	Agree	Disagree	Uncertain
1. Most needs of handicapped students can best be met when the student is placed with other students with similar handicaps.	___	___	___
2. Federal law requires that individualized programs be offered to each handicapped student.	___	___	___
3. The length of time a student has had a handicap is irrelevant; the handicap itself is the issue.	___	___	___
4. People who are not handicapped tend to overestimate physically handicapped students' mental abilities.	___	___	___
5. Except for certain physical or mental limitations, handicapped students behave no differently than nonhandicapped students.	___	___	___
6. Emotionally disturbed students tend to be either hostile or apathetic.	___	___	___

7. Some traumatic experiences are actually good for emotionally disturbed students. _____ _____ _____

8. The teacher of sensory-handicapped students should help them learn to ignore their handicaps. _____ _____ _____

9. Students with learning disabilities usually have below-average mental ability. _____ _____ _____

10. Mainstreaming is nothing more than moving handicapped students from special classes back into the regular classroom. _____ _____ _____

11. The mainstreaming movement will probably remove the need for special-education teachers. _____ _____ _____

Middle-Level Message

Handicaps among students vary. To cope with a students' handicap, you must first recognize the severity of that handicap. An equally important factor is your ability to recognize and identify developing stages of handicaps. Some handicaps, such as social adjustment problems and emotional problems, develop over a period of years.

Most children are amazingly resilient. They are often able to suppress their pain so well that even their peers do not recognize it. Unfortunately, such damage can be cumulative and continue to build until something snaps. More often than not this occurs near puberty. For that reason, this age-group has the highest rate of suicide and other serious crimes of any age-group.

You should learn all you can from this chapter and from other sources about identifying troubled students, but your responsibility does not stop there. You must learn how to deal with students who have mild adjustment problems, and you must learn how to refer more severely troubled students to specialists for the help you cannot provide.

Secondary and middle schools should enable all students to develop to their maximum potential. Without a positive attitude toward self, teachers, peers, and school itself, the student cannot reach that potential. Some students, however, have special needs that require additional teacher support to help them realize and develop their potential.

This chapter covers several categories of "special" students, ranging from several types of handicapped learners to the gifted and talented. As you read, remember that it is good practice to involve all students in planning their programs. Too often educators believe that their role is to do something to the students or for the students rather than to do something with them. As Ungerleider (1986, p. 465) says, "Their parents brought them in for fixin', but they didn't want to be fixed. . . . [But] if we join with them, teach them what they want to know, and give them reasons for learning what they need to know, they will truly learn [what we want them to learn]."

WHAT IS SPECIAL EDUCATION?

Special education is that part of the education process that attempts to meet the needs of youngsters who require modification of regularly accepted school practices to develop to their maximum potential. The problem is not so much that the student is different, but that the educational process must be different. "But," you may say, "isn't this the job of specialists who have been trained to work with these students?" The answer is yes, there are specialists whose training enables them to work with these students, but the classroom teacher is the one who helps them move into the mainstream. Many contemporary educators believe that the mainstreaming approach to working with handicapped children is the best approach because:

1. Every child has a right to an equal education opportunity, even at the expense of having different education experiences.
2. Most exceptional children need integration, not segregation.
3. Labeling is an administrative crutch that says nothing about a student's assets and desires to be accepted as a normal person.

For many years American society has recognized that a free or public education is all citizens' right. Although each state determines the methods of providing such education, federal legislation guarantees the right. On average, special education costs nearly twice as much as regular education (Robert Wood Johnson Foundation, 1990). Because some states have been too casual about providing education for handicapped youngsters, federal legislation now specifies exactly what services must be provided and supplies the funds needed to run these programs. You must become familiar with some of the more important laws that guarantee quality education for your handicapped students. Professional journals can alert you to new legislation.

PUBLIC LAW 94-142

The greatest single legislative action on behalf of handicapped students is PL 94-142 (the Education for All Handicapped Children Act, enacted in 1977). This law requires that each state provide special education services for its handicapped students at public expense and under public supervision and direction. These special services must meet state education agency standards; include an appropriate preschool, elementary, and secondary school education; and conform with the individualized education program. The law required that by Sept. 1, 1978, all students aged 3 to 19 (later extended to 21) were to be served, which includes receiving adequate classroom instruction. The impact of this law on schools continues to grow.

PL 94-142 is a complicated law. Nowhere in its many pages does it mention "mainstreaming." Instead it uses the words "least restrictive environment," which does allow for special students to be removed from special classes if those students are restricted when placed in special classrooms. The thrust of the law seems to be to keep handicapped students in the classroom with nonhandicapped students, as opposed to grouping handicapped students together for instruction. Although the term *mainstreaming* is not used, PL 94-142 requires the practice.

The findings that led to enactment of PL 94-142 may help us understand the need for this legislation:

1. There are more than 8 million handicapped children in the United States today.
2. Handicapped children's educational needs are not being fully met.
3. More than half the handicapped children do not receive appropriate educational services.
4. One million handicapped children are excluded entirely from the public school system.
5. There are many students in regular programs whose handicaps are undetected.
6. Because public school systems lack adequate services, families must find other services at their own expense.
7. With appropriate funding, state and local educational agencies have the knowledge and the methods to provide effective special education and related services.
8. State and local educational agencies have this responsibility, but they have inadequate financial resources.
9. It is in the national interest to help state and local educational agencies provide programs to meet handicapped children's educational needs to ensure equal protection under the law.

One major provision of this law is that before placement or denial of placement in educational programs, students and their parents must be offered (1) notice of the proposed action, (2) the right to a hearing before final action, (3) the right to counsel at that hearing, (4) the right to present evidence, (5) the right to full access to relevant school records, (6) the right to confront and cross-examine officials or employees who might have evidence of the basis for the proposed action, (7) the right to an independent evaluation, (8) the right to have the hearing open or closed to the public at the parent's option, and (9) the right to an impartial hearing officer. The hearings must be held at a place and time convenient for the parents. In other words, students and their parents have a right to question the appropriateness of individual educational plans or programs.

As a teacher, you will probably be directly involved in complying with the guidelines set forth in PL 94-142 and its successor, PL 101-476. This will include developing a program plan each year to show how your school is meeting the requirements. If your school fails to meet these requirements, it will lose its federal funding. One of your responsibilities as a teacher is to help handicapped students get the support to which they are entitled.

MEETING SPECIAL NEEDS IN THE REGULAR CLASSROOM

Regular classroom teachers have voiced strong concerns about having handicapped students in their classes. One reason for these concerns is the additional responsibilities this law places on classroom teachers. (These responsibilities are discussed later in this chapter.) But basic to the worries and frustrations that PL 94-142 and the resultant mainstreaming have caused is teachers' lack of knowledge about their new role and responsibilities. Put simply, most teachers do not think they are adequately prepared to meet this challenge. Indeed, many insist that their preparatory programs contained little or no information about teaching handicapped students.

Morbeck (1980) investigated this problem and reported that teachers do need in-service education to prepare them for mainstreaming. Studies of the effects of in-service programs designed to inform teachers of their responsibilities have reported positive results—in-service programs are an effective means of preparing teachers for their responsibilities with handicapped students (Hurtado-Portillo, 1980; Koci, 1980; Althoff, 1981). However, some in-service programs have failed to improve teacher attitudes toward mainstreaming (Baines & Baines, 1994). Sometimes additional contact with mainstreamed students improves teachers' attitudes toward handicapped students (Marston & Leslie, 1983), but in other instances additional contact with handicapped students failed to improve teachers' attitudes (Baines & Baines, 1994). Another factor affecting teachers' attitudes toward mainstreaming is the level of support services available to them.

The most important thing for pre-service teachers to know is that the more information about mainstreaming teachers accumulate before actually becoming involved in the process, the more positive their attitude about mainstreaming will be (Pietroski, 1979). Accordingly, pre-service teachers should seek out opportunities to learn more about handicapped students and about the roles of regular teachers who have one or more handicapped students in their classrooms. The remainder of this chapter is a good beginning point. The "Activities" section at the end of the chapter will facilitate your continuing this pursuit.

Inclusion

A similar concept to mainstreaming is inclusion, which has several definitions. One definition is: inclusion involves keeping special education students in regular classrooms and bringing support services to the child, rather than bringing the child to the support services (Smelter, Rasch, & Yudewitz, 1994). Another definition of inclusion is offered by Bradley and Fisher (1995, p. 13), "Inclusive education is the formal name given to an educational arrangement in which all students are given the opportunity to participate in general education with their typical age peers to the greatest extent possible." A major distinguishing quality between mainstreaming and inclusion is the time students with disabilities spend in the regular classroom; mainstreamed students spend part of the day in regular classrooms whereas students in inclusion curricula spend the entire day with all students.

A Special Curriculum

One approach to meeting the needs of special students is through modifying the curriculum. In traditional curricula, students with disabilities were perceived as problems for the teacher, but today the curriculum is considered the problem. In other words, if we accept the premise that *all children can learn,* then teachers and schools are responsible for ensuring this premise (Bradley and Fisher, 1995). Having determined that the existing curriculum is inappropriate for these students, the next step is to identify special elements that need modification (Hoover, 1990, pp. 410–411). The following checklist can be used:

1. Content: Does student possess sufficient reading level?
   a. Has student demonstrated mastery of prerequisite skills?
   b. Does student possess sufficient language abilities?
   c. Does student possess appropriate prior experience?
2. Instructional strategy: Is student motivated to learn through strategy?
   a. Does strategy facilitate active participation?
   b. Is strategy effectiveness relative to content to be learned?
   c. In what conditions is strategy effective/ineffective?
3. Instructional setting: Does setting facilitate active participation?
   a. Is student able to complete tasks in selected setting?
   b. Is student able to learn in selected setting?
   c. Is setting appropriate for learning selected?
4. Student behavior: What types of behaviors are exhibited by the learner?
   a. Time on task?
   b. Attention to task?
   c. Self-control abilities?
   d. Time-management skills?
   e. What are the most appropriate behaviors exhibited in selecting a strategy?

When changing the curriculum, pay careful attention to the materials you use, especially textbooks and other written materials. Cheney (1989) suggests a nine-step process for adapting strategies to teach written materials to special learners:

1. Change the nature of the learning task from one that requires reading and written responses to one that requires listening with oral responses (e.g., use a cassette tape or peer tutor).
2. Allow the student to demonstrate understanding through group projects or oral reports.
3. Allow the student to complete smaller amounts of material in a given time.

4. Have the student circle or underline the correct responses rather than write them.
5. Fasten the student's materials to the desk to help with coordination problems.
6. Provide extra drill-and-practice for those students who understand the material but need more time to master it.
7. Present information using graphs, illustrations, or diagrams.
8. Incorporate rhyming, rhythm, music, or movement into lessons.
9. Lessen distractions from other sources within the learning environment.

Special education teachers, however, encounter additional organizational problems peculiar to an individualized learning environment. "Factors such as student expectations, instructional goals, record keeping strategies, and behavior or social patterns pose a unique managerial dilemma for the teacher of special needs students" (Guernsey, 1989, p. 55).

CATEGORIZING STUDENTS WITH DISABILITIES

We can categorize all students with disabilities by type of impairment—physical, mental, emotional, sensory, and neurological—but we cannot assign a group of students to these subgroups without noticing much overlap. It is better to view the individual differences as lying on a continuum grouped around a norm. Furthermore, keep in mind the degree of involvement (mild, moderate, or severe), the length of time the student has had the condition, and the stability of the condition.

The following sections discuss categories of disabilities. As you read about each, remember to consider all the above criteria (degree of involvement, length of time the student has had the condition, and stability of the condition) when deciding how to serve these students best.

The Physically Impaired

Orthopedically handicapped persons have crippling impairments that interfere with normal bone, joint, or muscle function, including impairment of internal organs and systemic malfunctions. These impairments range from congenital conditions and deformities—such as dwarfism, limb absence, heart defects, hemophilia, cerebral palsy, epilepsy, and spina bifida—to traumatic conditions, such as amputations or burns.

Students with physical impairments may have limited mobility and use of certain materials or equipment and may lack motor control. As is true of most categories, the degree of impairment among orthopedically handicapped students varies greatly. If the cause was congenital (a birth defect), as with cerebral palsy, the student may not have had experiences needed for intellectual growth and may now suffer from secondary handicaps, such as mental retardation. Visual and speech defects are common; poor facial muscle control may cause drooling, giving the false impression of mental retardation. Thus, view and treat each handicapped student as an individual.

Be careful to avoid the common tendency of nonhandicapped people to underestimate orthopedically handicapped students' abilities, because these students are often able to succeed with extremely complicated tasks. Their ability to conceptualize, or "know how" to do things, yet not be able to do them because of physical handicaps, may frustrate them. Kirk (1972) lists behaviors that indicate frustration in orthopedically handicapped students:

1. Verbal aggressiveness
2. Blaming other people
3. Repressing desires
4. Withdrawing into fantasy
5. Degrading the original goals
6. Acting less mature
7. Compensating by shifting to different interests

All students display these behaviors at times but probably to a lesser degree because their successes minimize their frustrations. You can reduce frustration in orthopedically handicapped students by providing a climate of success and by accepting and including them in the schools' social activities. Teacher pity, overprotection, and ignoring may perpetuate their condition. These students must become involved if they are to learn to function and become independent. Above all else, remember that physical impairment does not automatically mean lowered mental functioning.

The Mentally Retarded

Mentally retarded students have learning rates and potentials that are considerably lower than the average for other students. Depending on the degree of retardation, there are four classifications of mental retardation, based on intelligence test scores. (Score ranges may vary slightly among states.)

Mild	55–59
Moderate	40–54
Severe	25–39
Profound	24 and below

Mildly retarded students may appear similar to normal classmates in height and weight, but closer observation reveals that they lack strength, speed, and coordination. They also tend to have more general health problems.

Students who are mentally retarded may experience frustration, especially when they have been expected to function at their chronological age with materials and methods geared above their ability. They often have short attention spans and are unable to concentrate. Antisocial or impersonal behavior can also be attributed to expectations of teachers and others that they perform beyond their abilities.

The Trainable Retarded

Trainable retarded students respond slowly to education and training because their intellectual development is only 25 to 50 percent of normal, yet many can be trained for jobs that require single skills under adequate supervision.

Retarded mental development may include slow maturation of intellectual functions needed for schoolwork. Because the retarded may be significantly low in memory skills, ability to generalize, language skills, conceptual and perceptual abilities, and creative abilities, give them tasks that are simple, brief, relevant, sequential, and designed for success.

The Emotionally Disturbed

Emotionally disturbed children are most simply perceived as those who are confused or bewildered. They do not understand their own social stresses, and they feel unaccepted in their efforts to resolve them (Love, 1974). "Aha," you say, "so that is the category used to describe the troublemakers." Often this is true. The emotionally disturbed do tend to be either hostile or apathetic. Seriously emotionally disturbed students require psychological services. Less seriously or socially maladjusted students do not.

Most students who exhibit apathy and hostility should not be classified as emotionally disturbed. The key element is how frequently they display such behavior. For example, the student who occasionally disrupts or hits a classmate is probably not disturbed, but the one who disrupts a lesson or bothers others several times during the hour may be emotionally disturbed. At the middle and secondary levels, emotionally disturbed students often show oversensitivity to criticism and unusual anxiety because of a weak self-concept. Some may show extreme depression. Again, the behavior's frequency, duration, and intensity indicate the condition's seriousness.

In dealing with emotionally disturbed students, you must arrange opportunities for them to succeed. You must also use a considerable amount of reinforcement and avoid creating a highly threatening climate in the classroom, such as overemphasizing the importance of examinations. Do not force students who appear unusually aggressive or timid to speak in front of classmates. Ensure that the classroom is free of threat, ridicule, and other abuses from peers.

The Sensory Deprived

Students who have visual and hearing impairments are among the sensory deprived. The visually handicapped category includes the partially sighted and the blind, while the hearing impairment category includes the deaf and the hard of hearing.

Visually handicapped students vary tremendously in the degrees to which they are handicapped; only about 10 percent of the legally blind are actually totally blind. Therefore, the first thing to consider when working with visually handicapped students is the degree of the handicap. Another thing to consider is the length of time the student has had the handicap. Those whose problems have been lifelong will need help developing concepts of space and form, whereas those whose blindness is recent will need help adjusting to their handicap.

Students who have hearing problems range from those who can hear and understand speech with difficulty, using such supports as hearing aids, to the deaf, who at most are able to distinguish only amplified sounds. In considering the extent of the hearing handicap, try to determine how much and how clearly the student can hear. Again, determine how long the student has had the handicap, because whether it occurred before or after speech and language comprehension developed makes a difference. The major problem of students who have been deaf since birth is not that they are deaf but that they are unable to develop speech and language comprehension through hearing.

When working with visually and hearing handicapped students, begin by providing psychological support. You can do this by accepting the students in their condition and believing in their ability to adjust to their handicap and to become productive individuals. Indeed, students with sensory handicaps can learn to do extremely complicated tasks. Your expression of confidence in students leads to increased self-confidence.

You must create this climate of acceptance among the student's peers. Because both blind students and deaf students are unable to pick up on all the stimuli that provide cues on how and when people respond, their timing may be off or they may not respond at all. Peers who are sensitive to these limitations may interpret their response (or absence of response) as unfriendly or antisocial. Handicapped students' limited vocabulary may further limit their response. Above all else, do not show pity. On the contrary, provide a positive climate that focuses on these students' abilities and potentials rather than on their limitations.

The Learning Disabled

Students who are learning disabled have normal intelligence but are unable to process information. In other words, their problem involves a dysfunction or emotional disturbance, as opposed to mental retardation or sensory deprivation. Such students may be awkward, hyperkinetic, and impulsive; a few may appear slow. Because most school programs are not designed to accommodate this type of behavior, these students are frequently viewed as having behavior problems. Some students with learning disabilities tend to be aggressive, irritable, and highly emotional; others may be even-tempered and cooperative. They may have quick changes of behavior from high-tempered to remorseful. They may even feel panic in what others see as only mildly stressful situations.

The basis of the problem with learning-disabled students can lie in the psychomotor, visual, or auditory domain. Students who have psychomotor disabilities are likely to be in poor physical condition or may frequently bump into things, for example. Their written assignments can also give clues—handwriting may be unusually large or small and crammed into one corner of the paper.

If the student's problem is visual, you may notice that the student cannot follow visual directions, may tend to forget things seen, and may be easily distracted by surrounding activities. Furthermore, students may tend to move their eyes excessively or inappropriately. Teachers can recognize auditory disabilities when students fail to follow oral directions, forget directions, are easily distracted by noise, and confuse similar sounds.

One method of getting information on students with learning disabilities is to use learning styles inventories. Once you determine learning styles, you can then choose and use instructional treatments that match those styles. When applying this process to learning disabled mathematics classes, Dunn et al. (1994–1995, p. 3) learned that the teachers were able to improve students' achievement and attitudes." Teachers who have disabled students should also make special efforts to combine technology and small group instruction (Bradley & Fisher, 1995).

THE INDIVIDUALIZED EDUCATIONAL PROGRAM

The current mode of working with handicapped students is to move them from groups consisting of only handicapped students and to put them back into the regular classroom, but this alone does not mean that their special needs will be met. To make certain that each student's needs are met—and the special needs of each differ from those of others who may share a general problem—PL 94-142 requires that a specific individualized program be provided for each handicapped student from age 3 to age 21. This approach, called Individualized Educational Programming (IEP), calls for a written statement for each handicapped child that identifies that child's particular needs and describes how those needs are being met.

There must be a special meeting to develop the program for each handicapped student. The representative of the local education authority who will be assigned to supervise the student's program, the student's teacher(s), and parents will attend. When appropriate, the student will attend the meeting too. In effect, you will be held responsible for seeing that the services planned are actually rendered. Furthermore, you are required to see that the program of each handicapped student in your class is constantly evaluated. Federal law requires at least one progress review each year, and the state may require more. If a parent does not request the review, you should.

The teacher of a handicapped middle or secondary student should try to establish good communications and a good working relationship with the student and parents. Because many handicapped students of this age can participate in developing their own program, you should try to create a team spirit. By uniting your efforts, you, the student, and the parents can provide a program that is superior to one you plan alone. During conferences with parents, avoid using educational jargon. As McNamara (1986, p. 309) explains, "Being clear, precise, and up-front with parents will pay high dividends in [your] ability to assist in carrying out the educational plan."

Each IEP must contain, as a minimum, these statements and projections:

1. The child's present level of educational performance.
2. Annual goals and short-term instructional goals.
3. The specific educational services to be provided—by whom, when, and for how long.

4. To what extent the child will be able to participate in regular educational programs.
5. Appropriate, objective criteria for evaluation, and a schedule for determining (at least annually) whether instructional objectives are being achieved.
6. The program's beginning and ending dates.
7. A statement of the parents' roles in relation to the plan.
8. Changes needed in the school situation (staffing, in-service education, etc.).

Any member of the planning team, including the student, can make the initial draft of the IEP. The rest of the team can accept the plan, revise it, or develop another plan they consider more useful for teachers and other school personnel.

Figure 9.1 is an example of an individualized educational plan. Although each program must include the preceding eight features, no two programs must or should be exactly alike. Therefore, view this not as a model of an ideal program but as what one particular program might look like. The sample forms below were developed by the staff of the Wasioja Area Special Education Cooperative in Minnesota. They include forms for requesting an individual educational assessment, for reporting assessment findings, and for recording an IEP.

If you find meeting the requirements and filling out all the forms difficult or strange, remember that these requirements are equally strange to most experienced teachers, who have seldom if ever been required to keep any type of individualized instruction plan for any students. Second, remember that the plan's purpose is to ensure help for the student; therefore, there is a place for decisions based on common sense.

Since each IEP is a cooperative effort involving the parents, you should keep the parents informed at every stage and solicit the parents' ideas, suggestions, and reactions. Assure the parents that if part of the plan proves inoperative or ineffective you will recommend changes to serve their child better. Ask the parents to let you know how the plan is working at home. A "we" approach will help you minimize any parental resistance and maximize parental cooperation. Parental cooperation is especially important because this is a team project in which you will need parental suggestions.

To further enhance your relationship with the parents, remind them that they have complete access to their child's records. Give them copies of each report, and explain exactly how assessments are made. Whenever possible, make the parents team members in the diagnosis, treatment, and education processes. Have a positive attitude. Be sure the parents understand their child's abilities and assets. Emphasize the things their child can do rather than those he or she cannot do. Help the parents learn how they can influence their child to think positively about himself or herself. Parents can also help others who might be working with the child to focus on the child's strengths and assets.

For years educators have been aware of the value of involving parents of students at all stages, but recently we have discovered the advantages of allowing students to help plan their own educational experiences. Now we have the opportunity (and responsibility) to involve both parties in planning, administering, and evaluating these

FIGURE 9.1 Sample individualized educational program

SOURCE: Sample IEP Maynard C. Reynolds and Jack W. Birch in *Teaching Exceptional Children in All America's Schools* (Reston, Va.: Council for Exceptional Children, 1977), pp. 164–171.

REQUEST FOR INDIVIDUAL EDUCATIONAL
ASSESSMENT/REASSESSMENT FORM

Student's Name: Sebastian Wynott   Age: 10-7   Grade: 5
School Building: Sleepy Hollow Elementary
Date of Conference: 3/15/96   Teacher/Referrer: Ms. Portia Streight
Parent/s Name: Olga & Ole Wynott   Address: $114\frac{1}{2}$ Plumb Ave.

Phone: CU2-0000

Rationale for Assessment: Sebbie has significant difficulty with academics and cannot attend to a task for any length of time. He cannot read any of the classroom material. What can be expected of him and should he be in a special program?

Preassessment/Reassessment Staffing Team Members (parents, etc.): Mr. & Mrs. Ole Wynott (parents), Mr. Dilly Dillingham (principal), Ms. Portia Streight (5th grade teacher), Ms. Aggie Knolage (SLBP teacher).

Objectives to be addressed (code to assessment team members):

1. To determine his capability to learn and the most appropriate styles and modalities to be used in learning processes for him.
2. To determine his levels of reading in all components: comprehension, attack skills, etc.
3. To determine his levels of academic success in areas other than reading: math, science, spelling, etc.
4. To determine his levels of functioning in all areas of perceptual development.

Assessment Team Members (code responsibility/objectives, when, where to be accomplished): Ms. Wilma Reedit, Remedial Reading Teacher (2,3)—Dr. Yen, Optometrist (4).

Mr. Herkimer Humperdinck, Psychologist (1,4)

Ms. Portia Streight, 5th Grade Teacher (1,2,3)

Ms. Aggie Knolage, SLBP Teacher (1,2,3,4)

Additional Data on Attached Sheet

Assessment: Summarization/Verification Date: 3/30/87

I (we) consent to the individual educational assessment described above, in order to determine the educational needs of my (our) child.

Signature _____   Date _3/15/96_

I (we) do not consent to the individual educational assessment described above, in order to determine the educational needs of my (our) child.

Signature _____   Date _____

If the Parent/s-Student Reject the Assessment, State the Reasons and an Acceptable Alternative:

The following RIGHTS and procedures MUST be reviewed prior to the conducting of the individual educational assessment:

Parent's-Student's rights to obtain an independent educational assessment records, information, and results.

Parent's-Student's rights to obtain an independent educational assessment at their own expense.

That Parent's-Student's may request assistance in locating the names, addresses, etc., and fee structures of resources that they may go to for an independent educational assessment.

That the student's educational status will not change unless the parent/s have signed the individual educational plan.

That a "conciliation conference" may be requested if the parent/s-student refuse to permit the assessment.

That an "impartial hearing" may be requested if mutual agreement is not reached after the conciliation conference.

Any Objection Should Be Sent to: _____

Any Objection Must Be Received by:

Address Objection Is to be Sent to:

(continued)

FIGURE 9.1 (continued)

Date Received:
Report Completed by: Miss Aggie Knolage, Case Facilitator
Copy of Report to Parent/Student: 3/15/96   Parent/Student: O.W.
Case Management Log Updated: 3/15/96   Update By: Aggie Knolage

INDIVIDUAL EDUCATION ASSESSMENT REPORT

Student's Name: Sebastian Wynott
Assessment By: Miss Aggie Knolage   SLBP Teacher
(name)(position)
School: Sleepy Hollow Elementary   Phone: CU4-0002
Date/s Assessment Conducted: 3/16, 18, 20/96
Specific Objectives Addressed by Specialist:
All (1 thru 4): 1—capability to learn and styles/modalities of learning; 2—reading levels; 3—other academic success; 4—perceptual development.
RESULTS:

    a. Indicate Assessment Setting and Materials Used: Setting: Sleepy Hollow Elem. School—SLBP room and classroom. Instruments used: Informal observations and tests in classroom and resource room; Detroit Test of Learning Aptitude; Peabody Individual Achievement Test; Key Math Diagnostic Arithmetic Test; Durrell Analysis of Reading Difficulty.

    b. Specific Results (indicate by number from "Specific Objectives To Be Addressed")

        1. Sebbie will need considerable help throughout all learning, emphasis on a tactile kinesthetic approach should be used both in the regular classroom and the resource room. Based on informal assessment Sebbie appears to be a very bright child who certainly has the capability to learn.

        2. Based on the PIAT, the Durrell, and informal assessment, Sebbie is functioning approximately one year below grade placement. Major areas of difficulty were in listening comprehension, work recognition and analysis, hearing sounds in words, and phonic spelling of words.

        3. Based on the PIAT, Key Math, and informal assessment, Sebbie is functioning approximately one year below grade placement in spelling, and approximately five months below in math. No attempt was made to measure other areas of academic achievement.

        4. Based on the Detroit and informal assessment, Sebbie is noted to be having significant difficulty in areas of auditory discrimination and closure.

    c. Additional Comments and/or Recommendations For Additional Assessment(s)/Specialist(s) (specify objectives to be addressed). Sebbie is very interested in athletics and finds a great deal of success in it, even though he is small. He should be encouraged to participate in any extra-curricular activities of this nature as well as at recess. Additional assessment may be needed as to physiological and neurological factors.

    d. Statement of Constraints On Performance Or On Special Learning Conditions. Sebbie has difficulty listening and needs to have concrete visual clues presented to him at the same time. He needs concrete, specific directions and repetition of instructions within short time frames. Sebbie works best through direct involvement with tactile/kinesthetic approach.

    e. Recommended Application Of Results In Performance Statements. Sebbie should receive approximately one-third of his educational program from the resource programs. Provisions need to be made between the regular classroom and the resource rooms so that when Sebbie needs a break from the classroom he can go to the resource rooms to do his work. (This should not become a daily ongoing activity.) Sebbie should receive a special reading program provided by the remedial reading teacher dealing with specific skills in phonics and other word attack skills; listening skills, etc. He should be provided services by the SLBP program dealing with math, auditory skills, and attention. Within the classroom expectations should be matched with supplementary services provided by the resource programs. Emphasis should be placed on a tactile/kinesthetic approach to learning. Verbal instructions should be short, to the point and reinforced with visual clues. Parents should be incorporated into the educational plan to help reinforce newly learned skills. This should not be a laborious task.

Additional Data on Attached Sheet.
Signature: Aggie Knolage   Date: 3/22/96
Copy of Report to Parent/Student: 3/30/96   Parent/Student O.W.
Case Management Log Updated: 3/30/96   Update By: Aggie Knolage

INDIVIDUAL EDUCATIONAL ASSESSMENT/VERIFICATION
STAFFING SUMMARY REPORT

Student's Name: Sebastian Wynott
Assessment Team Members (name, position, phone, address):
Ms. Wilma Reedit—Remedial Reading Teacher, CU4-0002, Sleepy Hollow Elem.
Ms. Aggie Knolage—SLBP Teacher, CU4-0002, Sleepy Hollow Elem.
Mr. Herkimer Humperdinck—Psychologist, CU2-4000, Sleepy Hollow Admin. Office
Ms. Portia Streight—5th Grade Teacher, CU4-0002, Sleepy Hollow Elem.
Dr. Yen—Optometrist—CU2-4002, Medical Center of Sleepy Hollow
Date of Meeting: 3/30/96
Results—Specific Objectives (INDIVIDUAL ASSESSMENT REPORTS MUST BE ATTACHED)

1. Sebbie is above average in intellectual functioning and will be functioning academically at grade level within two years as measured by group standardized achievement tests. Learning modalities that are not of a tactile/kinesthetic nature are extremely difficult for him. Visual clues should be used to reinforce any verbal directions.

2. Sebbie will make a minimum of at least three months growth by the end of the school year (June 10) in reading. Growth shall be measured based on pre-post assessment conducted by the remedial reading teacher. A special summer program in reading shall be developed and implemented for him, at the end of which he will have made an additional three months' gain based on pre-post assessment conducted by the remedial reading teacher. At the conclusion of the summer program he will no longer be in need of special instruction in phonics and other word attack skills, as measured by sampling his oral reading and other appropriate assessment.

3. By the end of the year Sebbie will be completing his spelling tests each week, correctly spelling at least 14 of 20 words. Special help will be provided by his fifth-grade teacher and reinforced by exercises at home with his parents. Through an individualized math program, Sebbie will be able to demonstrate three months' growth in math by the end of the school year, which will be measured by the SLBP teacher with the Key Math Test. The parents will be given supplementary math materials to work with Sebbie during the summer to ensure maintenance of the skills that he has gained prior to summer break. (Practice time will not interfere with his summer recreational activities.)

4. Sebbie will be able to demonstrate four months' growth on the ITPA in auditory skill development by the end of the school year, after receiving individualized instruction from the SLBP teacher.

5. By the end of the school year, Sebbie will not be leaving his seat without prior permission. After that time he will be held accountable for a plan that has been agreed to by him and his teacher's.
Additional Summarization Data On Attached Sheet:

Report Completed by: Aggie Knolage, Case Facilitator
Copy of Report to Parent/Student: 3/30/96   Parent/Student: O.W.
Case Management Log Updated: 3/30/96   Update by: Aggie Knolage
Additional Comments: The parents are very concerned that no matter what plan is developed that it will be carried out and not forgotten about. They have requested that the providers of the program meet with them on at least a monthly basis to review progress and to readdress what they can do to help. Concentration of academics shall be on reading, math, and spelling.

INDIVIDUAL EDUCATION PLAN

Student's Name: Sebastian Wynott   Date Completed: 3/30/96
Assessment Team Members (name, position, phone, address):
Ms. Wilma Reedit—Remedial Reading Teacher, CU4-0002, Sleepy Hollow Elem.
Ms. Aggie Knolage—SLBP Teacher, CU4-0002, Sleepy Hollow Elem.
Mr. Herkimer Humperdinck—Psychologist, CU2-4000, Sleepy Hollow Admin. Office

(continued)

FIGURE 9.1 (continued)

Ms. Portia Streight—5th Grade Teacher, CU4-0002, Sleepy Hollow Elem.

Dr. Yen—Optometrist. CU2-4002, Medical Center of Sleepy Hollow

Description of Needs: Sebbie has a prolonged history of poor academic achievement: difficulty with auditory discrimination and closure, reading and spelling levels, year below grade placement, doesn't complete assignments, and can't seem to sit still in classroom. Learning Style/Modality: Sebbie learns best with concrete materials and a tactile/kinesthetic approach. Verbal instructions should be in short time frames and reinforced with visual clues; it may be necessary to repeat several times.

Measurable Physical Constraints: Auditory discrimination and closure appears to be the basis of the majority of Sebbie's problems.

Statement of Specific Type of Service Needed: Sebbie will need special supplementary instruction in reading which shall be supplied by the remedial reading teacher (a summer program shall be supplied). He will receive special help from his regular teacher in the area of spelling and completion of appropriate assignments. The SLBP teacher will supply special help to Sebbie in the areas of math and auditory discrimination and closure. A joint program will be worked out by his classroom teacher, the remedial reading teacher and the SLBP teacher dealing with his staying in his seat, etc.

Annual Goals: Sebbie will be able to demonstrate the following gains within 12 months.

1. No problem with being out of his seat without prior permission.
2. In reading a 12-month gain in functional level.
3. In math to be functioning within 2 months of grade level.
4. In spelling to be within 4 months of grade level.
5. In auditory development to be within 4 months of his age level.

Short Term Objectives with Criteria for Attainment (first 3 months):

1. By June 10, Sebbie will not leave his seat more than twice per day without prior permission of the teacher. The teacher will keep appropriate charts of his behavior.
2. By June 10, after receiving a remedial reading instruction, Sebbie will demonstrate at least a 3-month growth in reading level based on pre-post assessment as measured by the remedial reading teacher.
3. By June 10, Sebbie will be able to demonstrate at least a 3-month growth in math skills as measured by pre-post assessment on the Key Math Test. The SLBP teacher will be responsible for carrying out the supplementary services in math.
4. By June 10, Sebbie will consistently complete his spelling tests and spell correctly at least 14 of 20 words on each weekly test. His regular classroom teacher shall be responsible for supplying supplementary instruction in the area of spelling.
5. By June 10, Sebbie will demonstrate a minimum of 4 months' growth based on pre-post assessment on the ITPA, after having received special help from the SLBP teacher.

Long-Term Objectives With Criteria For Attainment (beyond 3 months for school year):

1. Objectives 1, 4, and 5 will be further addressed in the new educational plan that will be developed in Sept.
2. By Sept. 1, after receiving special reading instruction throughout the summer, Sebbie will demonstrate a 6-month gain (from this date 3/30/87), in reading as measured by pre-post assessment administered by the remedial reading teacher.
3. By Sept. 1, Sebbie will demonstrate that he has maintained the 3 months' growth that he had achieved by June 1, through a maintenance program carried out by his parents during the summer. This level of achievement shall be demonstrated by pre-post assessment on the Key Math Test.

Special Instructional Materials/Supplies/Equipment: None

Other Specific Modifications: Approximately one-third of his individual educational plan shall be carried out in the resource rooms. A special program in reading will be carried out during the summer. The parents will be given special materials to use during the summer to ensure that Sebbie maintains his math skills.

Specify Means Of Coordination with Other Programs (regular classroom, etc.): SLBP remedial reading and regular classroom teachers will meet at least weekly to review progress on the instructional objectives and to further coordinate activities. Each specialist will spend at least 20 minutes per week in the regular classroom providing assistance in Sebbie's program. Monthly meetings will be held with the parents.

Personnel Responsible For Providing Service—Include Telephone Numbers, Addresses, etc. (regular classroom teacher, etc.):

    Ms. Aggie Knolage—SLBP Teacher, CU4-0002, Sleepy Hollow Elem.

    Ms. Wilma Reedit—Remedial Reading Teacher, CU4-0002, Sleepy Hollow Elem.

    Ms. Portia Streight—5th Grade Teacher, CU4-0002, Sleepy Hollow Elem.

Location of Program to Carry Out Plan: Sleepy Hollow Elem. School—regular classroom and resource rooms.

Describe Transportation Plan If Needed: None

Program Will Begin: 4/1/96 Number Of Days Per Week/Month/Year: 5 days/week; 20 days/month; for the remainder of the year—48 days.

Daily Duration of Plan: 2 hrs. 20 minutes per day

Method and Frequency of Initial and Periodic Reviews (dates, etc.):

Assessment Team Members—Initial Review—6/9/96

Ongoing monitoring of program with parents and teachers—at least monthly.

Description of Integrated Educational Activities (must be included when the student's primary placement is in special education): Not pertinent

I (we) do consent to the individual educational plan described above.

Signature: Mr. and Mrs. Ole Wynott   Date: 3/30/96

I (we) do not consent to the individual educational plan described above.

Signature: _____ Date: _____

If the Parent/s-Student Reject the Individual Educational Plan, State the Reason and an Acceptable Alternative:

Report Completed by: Aggie Knolage, Case Facilitator

Copy of Report to Parent/Student: 3/30/96   Parent/Student: O.W.

Case Management Log Updated: 3/30/96   Updated by: Aggie Knolage

special programs. Although the paperwork may be a hassle, there is no doubt that we will learn a great deal about individualizing instruction as we participate in IEPs. Most teachers will want to do whatever is necessary to help handicapped students profit from their instruction.

TEACHER REACTIONS TO PUBLIC LAW 94-142

Although several years have passed since PL 94-142 was introduced, many teachers are uncomfortable with this additional responsibility. A major concern is teachers' lack of faith in their ability to help handicapped students. Stephens and Braun (1981) attribute teachers' reluctance to integrate special students into regular classes to their lack of knowledge of special students. At Michigan State University a three-credit-hour course on mainstreaming was used to measure the effect that increased knowledge about handicapped students has on teacher confidence about putting these students into regular classes (Pernell, McInytre, & Bader, 1985). The 28 participants in the course had an average of six years' teaching experience. Initially, the attitudes toward mainstreaming were in the negative to neutral ranges, but at the last session the attitudes were all in the high-positive range. The conclusions were that "the results of the findings support the importance of increased experience, knowledge attainment, and skill acquisition as a catalyst in the formation of positive attitudes towards main-streaming students" (Pernell, McIntyre, & Bader, 1985, p. 136).

As a beginning teacher, you will have help from experienced personnel when you do your first IEPs. This book gives you a good introduction, but you must learn as much as you can about PL 94-142 during your clinical experiences and once you begin teaching. You must continue learning about this law and similar laws as they emerge and change.

Public Law 101-476

PL 94-142 (The Education for All Handicapped Act) was amended on Oct. 30, 1990, becoming PL 101-476. The title of the new law is "Individuals with Disabilities Education Act (IDEA)." This new law refers to handicapped children as "children with disabilities." The law's definition of children with disabilities has expanded to include autistic children and children with traumatic brain injury. The act also adds "rehabilitation counseling" and "social work services."

PL 101-476 provides help for students in moving beyond high school. A category titled "Transition Services" provides for movement to college education, vocational training, integrated employment, continuing and adult education, adult services, independent living, or community participation.

New IEP Requirements

PL 101-476 requires an IEP for all students with disabilities. Each IEP must include a statement of transition services needed. These services must begin no later than age 16 and must be reevaluated annually thereafter.

Hearing impairments often require sign language.

Summary of Major Changes in Parts A through H

Part A contains the general provisions of the act. Part B addresses the assistance for education of all handicapped individuals. Part C describes the centers and the services the public schools must provide to meet the needs of students with disabilities. For example, extended school-year demonstrations for infants, toddlers, and youths with severe disabilities are provided. Also, money is available to state education agencies and state vocational rehabilitation agencies to fund state grant proposals to increase the availability, access, and quality of transition services (NASDSE, pa. 12). Such services include:

- Increasing the availability, access, and quality of transition assistance through the development/improvement of policies, procedures, systems, and other mechanisms for youth and their families
- Improve the ability of professionals, parents, and advocates to work with such youth to make the transition from student to adult
- Improve working relationships among educators, relevant state agencies, the private sector, employment agencies, PICS, families, and advocates to identify and achieve consensus on the general nature and application of transition services to meet the needs of youth with disabilities

Part C also provides for children and youth with serious emotional disturbance (NASDSE, p. 13). For example, money is provided for local education agencies in collaboration with mental health entities to:

- Increase the availability, access, and quality of community services
- Improve working relations among education, community mental health and other personnel, families, and their advocates
- Target resources to school settings (e.g., providing access to school and/or community mental health and other resources to students who are in community school settings)
- Address the needs of minority children

Part D provides training to educate students with disabilities. For example, grant proposals may be written for funds to recruit and train members of minority groups and groups with disabilities.

Part E supports research to advance and improve the knowledge base and practice of professionals, parents, and others who provide intervention, special education, and related services to improve learning and instruction (NASDSE, p. 15). These activities may include:

- Organization, synthesis, and interpretation of current knowledge and identification of knowledge gaps
- Identification of knowledge and skill competencies needed by personnel

- Improvement of knowledge regarding the development and learning characteristics of children in order to improve the design and effectiveness of interventions and instruction
- Evaluation of approaches and interventions
- Development of instructional strategies, techniques, and activities
- Improvement of curricula and instructional tools
- Development of assessment techniques, instruments, and strategies for the identification, location, and evaluation of eligible students and for measurement of their progress
- Testing of research findings in practice settings
- Improvement of knowledge regarding families, minorities, LEP, and disabling conditions
- Identification of environmental, organizational, resource, and other conditions necessary for effective professional practice

Activities to advance the use of knowledge by personnel providing services may include (NASDSE, p. 16):

- Improvement of knowledge regarding how such individuals learn new knowledge and skills, and strategies for effectively facilitating such learning
- Organization, integration, and presentation of knowledge so it can be incorporated into training programs
- Expansion and improvement of networks that exchange knowledge and practice information

Part G supports the use of technology in the education of infants, children, and youth with disabilities (NASDSE, p. 17):

- Funds may be used to increase access to and use of assistance technology devices and assistance technology services in the education of infants, toddlers, children, and youth with disabilities and other activities authorized under the Technology Related Assistance for Individuals with Disabilities Act (PL 100-407) as such Act relates to the education of students with disabilities
- Funds may be used to examine how program purposes can address the problem of illiteracy among individuals with disabilities
- With respect to new technology, media, and materials utilized with funds under this section, the Secretary is directed to make efforts to ensure that such instructional materials are closed captioned
- No funds may be awarded under Sec. 661(a)(1)-(4) unless the applicant agrees that activities carried out with the assistance will be coordinated, as appropriate, with the state entity receiving funds under the Title I State Grant Program of PL 100-407

Part H provides guidelines for parents of infants and toddlers in need of early intervention services (NASDSE, p. 18):

- Under the Public Awareness component of the statewide system, the lead agency must prepare and disseminate to all primary referral sources information materials for parents on the availability of early intervention services, and procedures for determining the extent to which primary referral sources disseminate information on the availability of early intervention services to parents
- Under the CSPD component, the system must include training of primary referral sources regarding the basic components of early intervention services available in the state

THE GIFTED AND TALENTED

Some of the most neglected students in American schools today are students whose abilities are unusually high—gifted and talented students. According to the U.S. Commissioner of Education, "Gifted children are frequently overlooked in our schools. A review of current educational practices shows that the majority of public schools need to do more to meet the needs of this special group of children." The average classroom of 35 students has two gifted students (Alvins & Gourley, 1977), but very little money is spent to provide programs for them. "During the 1970s, some $6.5 million was allotted to gifted students annually, compared with the $600 million allotted to the handicapped and the staggering $2 billion allotted to the economically disadvantaged" (Stevens, 1977). The gifted have been ignored in recent years, and their unique needs have not been attended to by any of the many new programs that have emerged to provide for other groups of needy students.

Although educators would like to believe that ignoring the gifted has not been intentional, there is evidence that the neglect was purposeful. Working against programs for the gifted are the following attitudes (L'Abate & Curtis, 1975):

1. The programs are undemocratic.
2. They are unpopular with parents of children who are not identified as being gifted and who always compose the majority of the school population.
3. There is fear that special provision for the gifted will hamper improvement of general education for all.
4. The gifted already have many advantages, and this will enable them to outdistance the average child further and to obtain a number of exclusive opportunities.
5. Some feel that any extra effort and money should be used to benefit handicapped students.
6. The gifted are able to take care of themselves without any extra assistance.

There are still more reasons for opposition to programs for the gifted (Kaplan, 1974, pp. 7-8):

1. Programs for the gifted and talented reinforce the segregation of students.
2. The utilization of individualized instruction abolishes the need for separate programs for the gifted and talented.
3. Overemphasizing the gifted and talented through a special program creates an elitist population.
4. What is good for the gifted and talented is good for all children.
5. If classroom teachers were doing their job, there would be no need to offer a special program for the gifted.
6. What is offered to the gifted should be commensurate with what is offered to the students in other special education programs.

Some teachers and administrators believe it is undemocratic to give bright students special attention; other teachers, resenting the superior student's competency, enforce egalitarianism as a sort of equalizer (Cutts & Moseley, 1952).

Teachers of gifted and talented students have more positive attitudes toward these students than do regular teachers, and schools that have gifted programs have less-positive attitudes toward gifted students (Ferrante, 1983). The prevailing negative attitudes in schools with gifted programs can be attributed to the disruption of classes when these students are pulled out periodically to attend the special programs. Nicely (1980) found that teachers are more willing to have this occur when they know more about gifted children. But some educators are questioning purposeful neglect of this group of special students and point out that there is historical precedent in Thomas Jefferson's advocacy of special education provisions and settings for students of more able learning capacity (Durr, 1964). During the nineteenth century, private schools for the intellectually elite proliferated in New England and in the South. The first systematic provision of special programs for the gifted in the public school setting was in the St. Louis school system in 1868 (Witty, 1951). The first federal legislation for the gifted student was the 1958 National Defense Education Act, which provided loans for the gifted to pursue higher education (Johnson, 1976). Only two years later the U.S. Office of Education began operating "Project Talent" programs to stimulate discovery and development of national human resources. In 1969, PL 91-230 mandated a report to Congress from the U.S. Office of Education on the education of the gifted and talented. During the mid-1980s many states created combinations of loans and grants to attract gifted students into math and science teacher-education programs.

WHO ARE THE GIFTED?

In the past there was a tendency to use intelligence quotient (IQ) scores to identify the gifted, but recent studies suggest that this method overlooks some gifted students who do not have the aspiration or motivation needed to score highly on these tests. Unfortunately there are few other measuring devices, so most schools and researchers continue to use standardized intelligence tests.

Some authors insist that the term *gifted* be reserved for students who are highly motivated as well as capable. Another author provides the following definition: "The gifted student is likely to have above-average language development, persistence in at-tacking difficult mental tasks, the ability to generalize and see relationships, unusual curiosity, and a wide variety of deep interests" (Durr, 1964). Other authors who ac-cept a broad definition of gifted still consider only the high performers on intelligence tests in their programs for the gifted (DeHann & Havinghurst, 1961). Whatever the cur-rent status of the definition, the best method for identifying the gifted is, at least at this time, the individual intelligence test (Gallagher, 1975).

Teaching Gifted Students

In attempting to meet gifted students' needs, schools have made many adjustments in school curricula. One of the most common adjustments has been grouping these stu-dents for either part or all of the school day. This enables the teachers to present chal-lenges to them. According to Feldhusen (1989), a grouping can enable teachers to en-rich the curriculum, providing additional motivation, which he says gifted students need:

> Gifted and talented children complain a great deal about the boredom of their classroom experiences; they are forced to spend a lot of time being taught things they already know, doing repetitive drill sheets and activities, and re-ceiving instructions on new material at too slow a pace. These experiences probably cause gifted youth to lose motivation to learn, to get by with min-imum effort, or to reject school as a worthwhile experience. Grouping gifted and talented youth for all or part of the school day or week also serves as a stimulus or motivator. Interaction with other students who are enthusiastic about astronomy, robotics, Shakespeare, or algebra motivates gifted and tal-ented students. (p. 9)

Once gifted students are grouped, a special curriculum is needed. VanTassel-Baska (1989) describes some components she says are needed in this new curriculum:

> An appropriate curriculum for gifted students has three equally important di-mensions: (1) a content-based mastery dimension that allows gifted learners to move more rapidly through the curriculum; (2) a process/product/re-search dimension that encourages in-depth and independent learning, and (3) an epistemological concept dimension that allows for the exploration of issues, themes, and ideas across curriculum areas

VanTassel-Baska et al. (1989) note the following:

> Effective differentiation takes into account both the written and the deliv-ered curriculum. Manipulation of the written curriculum alone will not bring about curriculum appropriateness for the gifted; but if it is accompanied by a shift in instructional techniques and a procedure for reviewing and adopt-ing text materials, the results should be positive. (p. 9)

Over the years the gifted have been victimized by such false stereotypes as "social misfits," "weird," or "mad scientists." Like all other people, the gifted feel a need to use their talents. When a teacher does not challenge students or provide opportunities for them to use their abilities, like all other students they are apt to become frustrated.

As a teacher, you will want to find different materials and assign different tasks to challenge these students. Education programs for the gifted "must deal with their subject matter profoundly" (Bull, 1986, p. 42). The traditional practices of giving the gifted the same assignments—and, perhaps even worse, assigning more of the same problems—must be replaced by activities that will hold their interest and challenge their minds. Many school systems have specially trained professionals to work in programs for the gifted. Find out if your school or school system has such a person, and inquire about testing programs for identifying gifted students. The first responsibility you have to these students is to identify them. Then you must either try to provide adequate challenges or see that someone else does.

Creative Projects

Another way that teachers can enrich the curriculum for gifted students is by providing more creative projects. Burns (1990), who says that gifted students need more opportunities to use their creative abilities, tested 515 subjects to determine whether students who had prior experience with a creative project would be likely to choose to become involved in future creative projects. She reported:

> This study indicates that there is value in teaching students how to manage, focus, and plan a project or investigation. . . . Along with the development of lessons to teach strategies for creative productivity, gifted education teachers might also become more aware of the importance of self-efface in increasing the likelihood that students will begin curative investigations. (pp. 35-36)

Gifted students often feel isolated from their classmates. Although previous studies of gifted students' personality traits and emotional adjustment have generally concluded that the gifted are, at best, as well adjusted emotionally as the average student, a recent study by Dauber and Benbow (1990) concluded that extremely precocious adolescents, especially the verbally precocious, may be at greater risk for developing problems in peer relations than modestly gifted youth.

Teachers should be sensitive to any feelings of isolation extremely gifted students may have and should realize that these students may need help in gaining peer acceptance. Many students face peer pressure to limit their level of academic performance. This is particularly true of high achievers. Brown and Steinberg (1990) explain why so many students try to limit their peers' achievements:

> First, high achievers seem to be swimming against the development tide of adolescence. A second reason is that by doing well in school, high achievers

Art can be planned into any lesson for any students.

help raise teachers' expectations, which forces other students to work harder just to get by. Third, even with extra effort, some students simply can't make the grades, and they blame high achievers for setting the standards that make them look bad. (p. 57)

Research has shown that a focus on weaknesses at the expense of developing gifts can result in poor self-esteem, a lack of motivation, depression, and stress. What is needed in addition to remediation is attention focused on the development of strengths, interests, and superior intellectual capacities in their own right. (p. 55)

Feldhusen (1989) presents a good summary for this section in the following highlights of research on gifted youth:

Highlights of Research on Gifted Youth
The voluminous research on gifted and talented students provides educators with guidelines for serving this special population.

Identification. Schools are often ineffective in identifying gifted students, especially in finding talent among children from poverty and minority backgrounds, among very young children, and among underachievers. Identification is most often based on intelligence tests; use of creativity tests or achievement tests is rare. Multiple data sources should be used to identify alternate types of giftedness and to specify appropriate program services.

Acceleration. Acceleration motivates gifted students by providing them with instruction that challenges them to realize their potential. Accelerated students show superior achievement in school and beyond. Despite the fears of some educators, acceleration does not damage the social-emotional adjustment of gifted youth.

Grouping. Grouping gifted and talented youth for all or part of the school day or week serves as a motivator. In special classes or cluster groups for the gifted, mutual reinforcement of enthusiasm for academic interests prevails. Removing gifted students from regular classrooms does not deprive other students of role models; instead, it allows them to be leaders and top performers.

Overall. to provide for the gifted, we must upgrade the level and pace of instruction to fit their abilities, achievement levels, and interests. The only suitable enrichment is instruction on special enriching topics at a high level and a fast pace. We must also provide them with highly competent teachers and with opportunities to work with other gifted and talented youth. (p. 10)

The Learning Styles of Gifted Students

Students identified as gifted because of their high IQ scores and academic achievement consistently report learning style characteristics significantly different from those of students not so identified. For example, they invariably were persistent, highly motivated, and perceptually strong. In addition, the gifted strongly preferred to learn alone rather than with others (Cross, 1982). They also consistently preferred learning in a formal, rather than an informal, relaxed instructional environment when concentrating on new or difficult material.

Many gifted students reported that they required absolute quiet (Cody, 1983) and bright light (Griggs & Price, 1980) when concentrating on demanding tasks. Moreover, they seemed to prefer learning in the early morning in contrast with average and low achievers. Furthermore, gifted youngsters, as a group, strongly resisted learning directly with their teachers, preferring more autonomy in the learning process (Perrin, 1984).

Preference for low rather than high structure was another element of learning style that consistently discriminated between the gifted and nongifted. Dunn and Price (1980) found that gifted children preferred minimum external structure and extensive flexibility while learning; they much preferred doing things their way rather than following other people's directions.

Findings concerning perceptual modalities revealed that gifted students often learned new and difficult material in a variety of ways, including auditorially (by listening), visually (by seeing or reading), tactually (by taking notes or manipulating materials), and kinesthetically (by active involvement and experiencing) (Dunn & Price, 1980; Ricca, 1983). The ability of gifted students to learn through two or more modalities contrasted with the singular modality preferences of average and underachieving students.

Different diagnostic instruments and extensive interviews also documented that high achievers actually disliked drill, recitation, lectures, and class discussions. Ricca

(1983) and Wasson (1980) reported that they preferred learning through games, projects, independent studies, and programmed learning sequences. Peer teaching ranked fourth in Ricca's (1983) findings and was only desired among gifted first- and second-graders when they were permitted to learn with equally gifted classmates (Perrin, 1984).

This information about gifted students demonstrated clearly that their learning style patterns differed significantly from those of their nongifted counterparts. And, although gifted students could be either analytic or global processors, the higher their IQ the more global they tended to be (Cody, 1983). Furthermore, extremely global students were categorized as either extremely gifted (Cody, 1983) or as underachievers (Dunn, Bruno, Sklar, & Beaudry, 1990; Jarsonbeck, 1984). The learning style elements that differentiated most between global gifted students who performed well in school and global underachievers were motivation, responsibility (conformity versus nonconformity), and perceptual strengths.

TEACHING THE UNDERACHIEVER

Underachievers are students with high intellectual or academic potential whose performance falls in the middle third in scholastic achievement—or worse, in the lowest third (Gowan, 1957). Few educators realize how serious this problem is. First, the percentage of gifted students who are achieving far below their abilities is staggering. One study found that more than half the highly gifted students work well below their abilities (Milner, 1957). The tremendous waste in potential is enough to prompt serious concern.

A second reason for concern is that these gifted students who are achieving below their abilities academically are also contributing socially below their abilities (Newland, 1976). Thus, there is a further waste of human resources. Still another reason for concern about underachievers is that once gifted students begin to perform below their ability, the trend is difficult to reverse. It quickly becomes accepted as a way of life (Heinemann, 1977).

Identifying the Underachiever

Underachievers, like all special students, must first be identified by the teacher before they can get help. You may find it more difficult to recognize underachievers because they are frequently mistaken for low-ability students. One teacher in-service program lists the following characteristics of underachievers (Heinemann, 1977, p. 4):

1. Belligerent toward classmates and others.
2. Extremely defensive (given to rationalizing, ad-libbing, excusing failures, lying).
3. Fearful of failure and of attempting new tasks because of the likelihood of failure.
4. Resentful of criticism, yet likely to be highly critical of others.

5. Prone to habitual procrastination, dawdling, daydreaming, sulking, brooding.
6. Frequently absent.
7. Inattentive—wriggling, doodling, whispering.
8. Suspicious, distrustful of overtures of affection.
9. Rebellious.
10. Negative about own abilities.

No student would display all these characteristics simultaneously, but one who shows several at once should be investigated.

Some of the likely causes of underachievers are physical limitations (such as poor vision or hearing), learning disabilities, dysfunctional families, and even social maladjustments. Often low performance is a result of low expectations at home and school, which eventually lead to low expectations by the student. Students afflicted with learned helplessness are often unwilling to try because they expect to fail (Tyrrell, 1990). But to be sure that a particular student is indeed performing well below ability, you must check previous performance records or report cards and standardized tests. For example, a student who is making Cs but has stanine scores of 8s and 9s is clearly performing far below ability.

Learning Styles of Underachievers

Seven learning style traits significantly discriminate between high-risk or dropout students and students who perform well in school. Many—but not all—dropouts and underachievers need (1) frequent opportunities for mobility, (2) choices, (3) a *variety* of instructional resources, environments, and sociological groupings rather than routines and patterns, (4) to learn during late morning, afternoon, or evening hours—not in the early morning, (5) informal seating—not wooden, steel, or plastic chairs and desks, (6) soft lighting to concentrate; bright lights contribute to hyperactivity, and (7) to be introduced to a new topic with either tactual-visual instructional resources reinforced by kinesthetic-visual resources or kinesthetic-visual instructional resources reinforced by tactual-visual resources. Underachievers find it extremely difficult to remember what they have been taught through lectures. They tend to have poor auditory memory, although short verbal explanations can be used to reinforce learning after new material has been introduced through manipulatives or activities. When underachievers have visual preferences, they often learn through pictures, drawings, graphs, symbols, and cartoons rather than printed text. They also learn well with highly structured multisensory instructional resources. Although underachievers often *are* motivated, they cannot remember many facts taught through lectures, discussions, or readings.

Helping the Underachiever

Once you have identified the underachievers in your classes, you may have many approaches to help them improve their performance, academically and socially. You may want to consider using some of the following:

1. Special guidance to develop positive self-concept
2. Extensive use of films and captioned filmstrips instead of textbooks; use of taped lessons to improve listening, thinking, reading skills
3. Firsthand experiences to stimulate and motivate, especially for students from disadvantaged backgrounds (remember, middle-class Anglo students, as well as the poor and some minority students, may come from such backgrounds)
4. Assignments and teaching methods adjusted to students' individual interests and abilities and relating to hoped-for or established goals, whether personal or academic
5. Teacher-student sessions for planning work to be covered
6. Tutoring by willing and able senior citizens who can provide the warmth and understanding, kind encouragement, and praise often missing at home
7. A special opportunity class for underachievers of mixed ages with similar problems working out of the regular class, even out of the regular school where possible, for at least part of the day
8. Group therapy with a warm, understanding counselor or teacher to discuss freely any fears, frustrations, angers
9. A team approach to working with underachievers who are gifted and talented, including the teacher(s), parent(s), a counselor, and perhaps the student
10. Use of grades and tests only as measures of progress and thus as indicators of areas needing additional work
11. Instruction in how to learn—how to concentrate, remember, understand and follow directions, use key words, etc.
12. Instruction in problem-solving techniques and the inquiry method

Many contemporary programs for the gifted and talented students include nontraditional content and skill. Research shows that basic research skills can be taught to gifted children of middle school level and even younger (Kent & Esgar, 1983). Scientific research methodology has been taught successfully in science classes. There are numerous reports of junior high students being employed by school districts to conduct workshops for teachers on the use of computers (Torrence, 1986). Other common trends include teaching gifted students inventing (Hoffman, 1982), debating (Lengel, 1983), logical reasoning (Weinstein & Laughman, 1980), creative writing (Stoddard & Renzulli, 1983), thinking (Cinquino, 1980), and forecasting (Crabbe, 1982). Whatever method(s) you choose, remember that no one type of program will meet all the needs of all gifted and talented students (Stewart, 1982).

RECAP OF MAJOR IDEAS

1. There is a strong trend toward keeping handicapped students in classes with nonhandicapped peers whenever possible.
2. Nonhandicapped people tend to underestimate physically handicapped students' mental ability.

3. Federal law requires teachers to design a special learning program for each handicapped student.
4. In working with handicapped students, always consider how severe the handicap is, how long the student has had it, and how stable the condition is.
5. Emotionally disturbed students also need to experience success and should not be subjected to threats or ridicule.
6. Parents of handicapped children have a right to help plan the program for their children and a right to evaluate it and even insist on changes to improve it.
7. The percentage of gifted students whose performance is substandard is very high.
8. There are ways to identify underachievers and help them.
9. PL 94-142 was amended in 1990 to become PL 101-476, Individuals with Learning Disabilities Act.

CASES

CASE 1: AN EXPLOSIVE EXPERIENCE

Shirley Norton was excited about her new teaching assignment. She had edged out 40 other applicants for the one vacancy in the physical education department at Sherwood High. Her first day started off with a rush. By noon she was so tired she hardly tasted the cafeteria food she was consuming all too rapidly. But according to the many complaints from the more established teachers, she wasn't missing much. Shirley quickly swallowed the last bite, bused her tray to the long conveyor belt, and walked back toward the gym.

When Shirley entered the gym she found one of her seniors, Debbie, breaking out the windows. Debbie was running, screaming, and crying hysterically as she punched out the panes with a broom handle. Shirley knew that Debbie had been in her class playing volleyball just before lunch and had become very upset. Approaching Debbie, Shirley asked her to hand over the broom. This was a mistake. Debbie whirled around and began hitting Shirley, swearing each time. Just as Shirley was about to collapse, Debbie dropped the broom and collapsed on the floor, sobbing.

As perplexed as she was shocked, Shirley was relieved to see one of the senior physical education teachers enter the room and take over the situation as if it were just another part of the job.

Discussion

1. How should a teacher approach a student who is behaving frantically and irrationally?

Very carefully. When people are in such a state, their behavior is unpredictable. This was evidenced by Debbie's attacking a new teacher, whom she hardly knew.

2. What should Shirley do about this incident?

Debbie clearly needs help. She might begin by checking Debbie's record for previous similar incidents. The school (or school system) psychologist should be apprised of the incident. If no psychologist is available, the school counselor should be informed. If the school has neither a psychologist nor a counselor, the principal should be alerted. Otherwise, Debbie will be a threat to herself and to her classmates and teachers.

CASE 2: AN INTRODUCTION TO MAINSTREAMING

After teaching social studies for three years, Dave no longer thought of himself as a novice teacher, and he had experienced some unusual and challenging encounters with parents. At the beginning of Dave's fourth year, a student named Arnold Swartz transferred to Edison High and was assigned to one of Dave's classes. Arnold was classified as mildly retarded, and from the very beginning it was obvious that he could not meet the demands Dave made of all his students. Dave asked that Arnold be removed from the class, but the principal refused to transfer Arnold. Dave decided to ignore Arnold—after all, the education of the other 28 students should not be sacrificed. Arnold seemed content, and everything was working well until the first report cards were sent home.

That evening Arnold's mother, very upset, telephoned Dave. Arnold had received a D− in social studies and there was no explanation of why he had done so poorly. Dave wanted to tell her that Arnold was not capable of doing any better, but he knew that Mrs. Swartz was already aware of her son's limitations. Before the conversation ended, Dave and Mrs. Swartz agreed to meet with the principal, at which time Dave would then explain exactly what he was doing (or not doing) to help Arnold. As he went to bed, Dave was wondering how the principal would react and what he could do to help a boy like Arnold.

Discussion Questions

1. Was Dave wrong in wanting to give his time and energy to the students who could benefit most?

2. What alternative does Dave have if Mrs. Swartz insists on meeting with him periodically to discuss the progress of her son?

3. What if Mrs. Swartz demands special attention for her son? Will Dave have to make exceptions for Arnold just because he is different?

ACTIVITIES

All teachers should seek to learn more about students who differ significantly from most of their classmates. Some may be brighter, some may be slower. Some may be physically handicapped, others emotionally handicapped. All teachers now deal with students in each of these categories. Instead of ignoring them or separating them from their "normal" peers, teachers will alter the classroom to accommodate these individuals.

The following activities will help you begin to answer this question: How will you provide for the special students in your classes?

1. Because most classes have students whose IQs range from considerably below average to well above average, how will you attempt to meet the needs of the students on both ends of this continuum? Include a few strategies for simplifying content and making it more accurate. Also include techniques for challenging the bright students.
2. Suppose you recognize a handicapped student in your class. Describe the steps you will use to gather information about this student.

REFERENCES

Althoff, R. H. (1981). *The effects of an inservice training procedure on the attitudes of regular education teachers toward mainstreaming of handicapped students.* Unpublished doctoral dissertation, Wayne State University.

Alvins, J. J., & Gourly, T. J. (1977). The challenge of our gifted children. *Teacher, 96,* 45.

Baines, L., & Baines, C. (1994). Mainstreaming: One school's reality. *Phi Delta Kappan, 76*(1), 39-40, 57-64.

Bradley, D. F., & Fisher, J. F. (1995). The inclusion process: Role changes at the middle level. *Middle School Journal, 26*(3), 13-19.

Brown, D. B., & Steinberg, L. (1990). Academic achievement and social acceptance. *Education Digest, 40*(7), 57-60.

Bull, B. L. (1986). Education for gifts and talents: A change in emphasis. *Education Digest, 51*(5), 40.

Burns, D. E. (1990). The effects of group training activities on students' initiation of creative investigations. *Gifted Child Quarterly, 34*(1), 31-36.

Cheney, C. D. (1989). The systematic adaptation or instructional materials and techniques for problem learners. *Academic Theory, 25*(1), 25-30.

Cinquino, D. (1980). An evaluation of a philosophy program with fifth and sixth grade academically talented students. *Thinking, 2,*(3&4), 79-83.

Clark-Thayer, S. (1987). The relationship of the knowledge of student-perceived learning style preferences, and study habits and attitudes to achievement of college freshman in a small urban university. *Dissertation Abstracts International, 48,* 872A.

Cody, C. (1983). Learning styles, including hemispheric dominance: A comparative study of average, gifted, and highly gifted students in grades five through twelve. *Dissertation Abstracts International, 44,* 1631A.

Crabbe, A. B. (1982). Creating a brighter future: An update on the future problem solving problem. *Journal for the Education of the Gifted, 5*(1), 2-11.

Cross, J. A. (1982). Internal locus of control governs talented students (9-12). *Learning Styles Network Newsletter, 3*(3), 3.

Cutts, N., & Moseley, N. (1952). *Teaching the bright and gifted.* Englewood Cliffs, NJ: Prentice-Hall.

Dauber, S. L., & Benbow, C. P. (1990). Aspects of personality and peer relations of extremely talented adolescents. *Gifted Child Quarterly, 34*(1), 10-14.

DeHann, R., & Havinghurst, R. (1961). *Educating gifted children.* Chicago: University of Chicago Press.

Dunn, R., Bauer, E., Gemake, J., Gegory, J., Primavera, L., & Singer, B. (1994-1995). Matching and mismatching junior high school urban learning-disabled and emotionally-handicapped students' perceptual preferences on mathematics scores. *National Forum of Teacher Education Journal, 5*(1), 3-13.

Dunn, R., Bruno, J., Sklar, R.I., Zenhausern, R., & Beaudry, J. (1990, May–June). Effects of matching and mismatching minority developmental college students' hemispheric preferences on mathematics scores. *Journal of Educational Research, 83*(5), 283-288.

Dunn, R., & Price, G.E. (1980). The learning style characteristics of gifted children. *Gifted Child Quarterly, 24*(1), 33-36.

Durr, W. K. (1964). *The gifted student.* New York: Oxford University Press.

Feldhusen, J. F. (1989). Synthesis of research on gifted youth. *Educational Leadership, 46*(6), 6-11.

Ferrante, R. A. (1983). *Survey of attitudes of regular teachers, teachers of the gifted and talented, and administrators toward gifted education.* Unpublished doctoral dissertation, University of South Carolina.

Gallagher, J. J. (1975). *Teaching the gifted child.* Boston: Allyn & Bacon.

Gowan, J. C. (1957). Dynamics of the underachievement of gifted children. *Exceptional Children, 24,* 98-101.

Guernsey, M. A. (1989). Classroom organization: A key to successful management. *Academic Therapy, 25*(1), 55-58.

Heinemann, A. (1977). *Module 6: Underachievers among the gifted/talented—Star power: Providing for the gifted* (p. 4). Austin, TX: Educational Service Center, Region XIII.

Hoffman, J. G. (1982). Inventions. *G/C/T (Gifted Child Today), 24,* 54-55.

Hurtado-Portillo, J. L. (1980). *Effects of an inservice program on the attitudes of regular classroom teachers toward mainstreaming mildly handicapped students.* Unpublished doctoral dissertation, University of North Carolina at Chapel Hill.

Jarsonbeck, S. (1984). The effects of a right-brain and mathematics curriculum on low achieving, fourth grade students. *Dissertation Abstracts International, 45,* 2791A.

Johnson, B. (Ed.) (1976). *Federal legislative history on gifted and talented.* Bulletin 2. Washington DC: U.S. Government Printing Office.

Kaplan, S. (1974). *Providing programs for the gifted and talented: A handbook* (pp. 93-123). Ventura, CA: Office of Ventura Co. Superintendent of Schools.

Kent, S., & Esgar, L. V. (1983, May–June). Research techniques for gifted primary students. *G/C/T(28),* 28-29.

Kirk, S. A. (1972). *Educating exceptional children.* Boston: Houghton Mifflin.

Koci, J. I. L. (1980). *A study of the needs of regular classroom teachers in implementing Public Law 94-142.* Unpublished doctoral dissertation, University of Houston.

L'Abate, L., & Curtis, L. T. (1975). *Teaching the exceptional child.* Philadelphia: Saunders.

Lengel, A. L. (1983). Classroom debating in the elementary school. *G/C/T, 28,* 57-60.

Love, H. D. (1974). *Educating exceptional children in a changing society.* Springfield, IL: Thomas.

Marston, R., & Leslie, D. (1983). Teacher perceptions from mainstreamed versus nonmainstreamed teaching environments. *Physical Educator, 40,* 8-15.

McNamara, B. E. (1986). Parents as partners in the I.E.P. process. *Academic Therapy, 21.*

Milner, J. B. (1957). *Intelligence in the United States.* New York: Springer.

Morbeck, J. U. (1980). *In-service education needs of senior high school regular classroom teachers relative to mainstreaming learning disabled students.* Unpublished doctoral dissertation, University of Idaho,

Nelson, B., Dunn, R., Griggs, S. A. Primavera, L., Fitzpatrick, M., Bacillious, Z., Miller, R. (1993).

Effects of learning style intervention on students' retention and achievement. *Journal of College Student Development, 34*(5), 364–369.

Newland, T. E. (1976). *The gifted in socio-educational perspective.* Englewood Cliffs, NJ: Prentice-Hall.

Nicely, R. F., Jr. (1980). Teachers' attitudes toward gifted children and programs: Implication for instructional leadership. *Education, 101,* 12–15.

Pernell, E., McIntyre, L., & Bader, L. A. (1985, Winter). Mainstreaming: A continuing concern for teachers. *Education, 106,* 131–137.

Perrin, J. (1984). An experimental investigation of the relationships among the learning style sociological preferences of gifted and non-gifted primary children, selected instructional strategies, attitudes, and achievement in problem solving and rote memorization. *Dissertation Abstracts International, 46,* 342A.

Pietroski, M. S. (1979). *An analysis of background variables associated with classroom teachers' attitudes toward mainstreaming.* Unpublished doctoral dissertation, Boston University.

Ricca, J. (1983). *Curricular implications of learning style differences between gifted and non-gifted students.* Unpublished doctoral dissertation, State University of New York at Buffalo.

Smelter, R. W., Rasch, B. W., & Yudewitz, G. J. (1994). Thinking of inclusion for all special needs students? Better think again. *Phi Delta Kappan, 76*(1), 35–38.

Stephens, T. M., & Braun, B. L. (1981). Measure of regular classroom teachers' attitudes toward handicapped children. *Exceptional Children, 46,* 4.

Stevens, B. J. (1977). What about that other special education? *Pennsylvania School Journal, 126,* 32.

Stoddard, E. P., & Renzulli, J. S. (1983). Improving the writing skills of talent pool students. *Gifted Child Quarterly, 27,* 21–27.

Torrence, E. P. (1986). Teaching creative and gifted learners. In M. C. Whittrock (Ed.), *Handbook of research on teaching* (3rd ed.). New York: Macmillan.

Tyrrell, R. (1990). What teachers say about cooperative learning. *Middle School Journal, 21*(3), 16–19.

Ungerleider, D. E. (1986). The organic curriculum. *Academic Therapy, 21,* 465–466.

VanTassel-Baska, J. (1989). Appropriate curriculum for gifted learners. *Educational Leadership, 46,* 13–15.

VanTassel-Baska, J., Feldhusen, J., Seeley, K., Wheatley, G., Silverman, L., & Foster, W. (1988). *Comprehensive curriculum for gifted learners.* Boston: Allyn & Bacon.

Wasson, F. (1980). *A comparative analysis of learning styles and personality characteristics of achieving and underachieving gifted elementary students.* Unpublished doctoral dissertation, Florida State University, Tallahassee.

Weinstein, J., & Laughman, L. (1980). Teaching logical reasoning to gifted students. *Gifted Child Quarterly, 24,* 186–190.

Witty, P. (Ed.) (1951). *The gifted child.* Boston: D. C. Heath.

SUGGESTED READINGS

Aksamit, D. (1990). Mildly handicapped and at-risk students: The greying of the line. *Academic Therapy, 25*(3), 227–289.

Alberg, J., Cook, L., Fiore, T., Friend, M., & Sano, S., (1992). *Educational approaches and options for integrating students with disabilities: A decision tool.* Triangle Park, NC: Research Triangle Institute.

Andrews, R. H. (1990, July–September). The development of a learning styles program in a low socioeconomic, underachieving North Carolina elementary school. *Journal of Reading, Writing, and Learning Disabilities International, 6*(3), 307-314.

Andrews, R. H. (1991). Insights into education: An elementary principal's perspective. In Lewis A. Grell (Ed.), *Hands on approaches to learning styles: Practical approaches to successful school* (pp. 50-52). New Wilmington, PA: The Association for the Advancement of International Education.

Barbe, W. B., & Renzulli, J. S. (Eds.) (1981). *Psychology and education of the gifted.* New York: Irvington.

Baum, S. (1990). The gifted/learning disabled: A paradox for teachers. *Education Digest,* LV(8), 54-56.

Beaty, S. A. (1986). The effect of inservice training on the ability of teachers to observe learning styles of students. *Dissertation Abstracts International, 47,* 1998A.

Bender, W. N., & Evans, N. (1989, December). Mainstream and special class strategies for managing behavioral disordered students in secondary classes. *The High School Journal,* 89-96.

Brunner, C.E., & Majewski, W.S. (1990, October). Mildly handicapped students can succeed with learning styles. *Educational Leadership, 48*(2), 21-23.

Carri, L. (1985). Inservice teachers' assessed needs in behavioral disorders, mental retardation, and learning disabilities: Are they similar? *Exceptional Children, 51,* 411-416.

Cavanaugh, D. (1981, November). Student learning styles: A diagnostic/prescriptive approach to instruction. *Phi Delta Kappan, 64*(3), 202-203.

Clark, K. B. (1978). In Edward F. Murphy (Ed.), Children who are treated as if they are uneducable almost invariably become uneducable. *Webster's treasury of relevant quotations.* New York: Greenwich House.

DeLisle, J. R. (1984). *Gifted children speak out.* New York: Walker.

Doubrave-Harris, M. J. (1982). *The relationship of inservice training to the attitudes toward, and knowledge of, mainstreaming of three groups of educators.* Unpublished doctoral dissertation, Bowling Green State University,

Dunn, R., Beasley, M., & Buchanan, K. (1994). What do you believe about how culturally-diverse students learn? *Emergency Librarian, 22*(1), 8-14.

Dunn, R., & Dunn, K. (1992). *Teaching elementary students through their individual learning styles.* Boston: Allyn & Bacon.

Dunn, R., Dunn, K., & Perrin, J. (1994). *Teaching young children through their individual learning styles.* Boston: Allyn & Bacon.

Dunn, R., Dunn, K., & Price, G. E. (1977). Diagnosing learning styles: Avoiding malpractice suits against school systems. *Phi Delta Kappan, 58*(5), 418-420.

Dunn, R., & Griggs, S. A. (1995). *Multiculturalism and learning style: Teaching and counseling adolescents.* Westport, CT: Greenwood Publishers.

Dunn, R., Griggs, S. A., Olson, J., Gorman, B., & Beasley, M. (in press). A meta-analytic validation of the Dunn and Dunn learning styles model. *Journal of Educational Research.*

Elkind, R. (1991). Success in American education. In R. C. Morris (Ed.), *Youth at risk.* Lancaster, PA: Technomic.

Elliot, I. (1991, November–December). The reading place. *Teaching K-8. 21*(3), 30-34.

Enoch, M. M. (1979). *Relationship of teacher attitudes toward mainstreaming with respect to previous special education training, teaching level, and experience with exceptional children.* Unpublished doctoral dissertation, George Peabody College for Teachers.

Friedman, R. S. (1991). Murray high school: A nontraditional approach to meeting the needs of an at-risk population. In R. C. Morris (Ed.), *Youth at risk.* Lancaster, PA: Technomic.

Gadwa, K., & Griggs, S. A. (1985). The school dropout: Implications for counselors. *The School Counselor, 33,* 9-17.

Griggs, S. A., & Price, G.E. (1980). A comparison between the learning styles of gifted versus average junior high school students. *Phi Delta Kappan, 61*(8), 361.

Griggs, S. A., & Price, G. E. (1982). A comparison between the learning styles of gifted versus average junior high students. *Creative and Gifted Child Quarterly, 7,* 39-42.

Guskin, S. L., Okolo, C., Zimmerman, E., & Ping, C. Y. J. (1986). Being labelled gifted and talented: Meanings and effects perceived by students in special programs. *Gifted Child Quarterly, 30,* 61-65.

Hanline, J. G., & Murray, C. (1984). Integrating severely handicapped children into regular public schools. *Phi Delta Kappan, 66*(4), 273-276.

Hoover, J. J. (1990, March). Curriculum adaptation: A five step process for classroom implementation. *Academic Therapy, 25*(4), 407-416.

Keefe, J. W. (1982). Assessing students learning styles: An overview of learning styles and cognitive style inquiry. In J. W. Keefe (Ed.), *Student Learning Styles and Brain Behavior.* Reston, VA: National Association of Secondary School Principals.

Klausmeier, K., Mishra, S. P., & Maker, C. J. (1987). Identification of gifted learners: A national survey of assessment practices and training needs of school psychologists. *Gifted Child Quarterly, 31*(3), 135-137.

Klavas, A., Dunn, R., Griggs, S. A., Gemake, J., Geisert, G., & Zenhausern, R. (1994). Factors that facilitated or impeded implementation of the Dunn and Dunn learning style model. *Illinois School Research and Development Journal, 31*(1), 19-23.

Lemmon, P. (1985). A school where learning styles make a difference. *Principal, 64*(4), 26-29.

Koshuta, V., & Koshuta, P. (1993, April). Learning styles in a one-room school. *Educational Leadership, 50*(7), 87.

Kreitner, K. R. (1981). *Modality strengths and learning styles of musically talented high school students.* Unpublished master's dissertation, The Ohio State University, Columbus.

Kryiacou, M., & Dunn, R. (1994). Synthesis of research: Learning styles of students with learning disabilities. *Special Education Journal, 4*(1), 3-9.

Lenehan, M.C., Dunn, R., Ingham, J., Signer, B., & Murray, J. B. (1994). Learning style: Necessary know-how for academic success in college. *Journal of College Student Development, 35,* 1-6.

Levin. H. M. (1987). *New schools for the disadvantaged.* Unpublished manuscript, Stanford University, Stanford, CT: Mid-Continent Regional Educational Laboratory.

Marcus, L. (1977). How teachers view learning styles. *NASSP Bulletin, 61*(408), 112-114.

Marolgis, H., & Schwartz, E. (1989). Facilitating mainstreaming through cooperative learning. *The High School Journal, 72,* 83-88.

McIntyre, T. C., & Brulle, A. R. (1989). The effectiveness of various types of teacher directions with students labeled behavior disordered. *Academic Therapy, 25*(2), 123-131.

McRainey, G. (1981). *Teacher-pupil contact as a factor in the development of positive attitudes toward handicapped students.* Unpublished doctoral dissertation, George Peabody College for Teachers,

Mickler, M. L., & Zippert, C. P. (1987). Teaching strategies based on learning styles of adult students. *Community/Junior College Quarterly, 11*(1), 33-37.

Milgram, R. M., Dunn, R., & Price, G. E. (Eds.) (1993). *Teaching and Counseling Gifted and Talented Adolescents: An International Learning Style Perspective.* Norwalk, CT: Praeger.

Morris, R. C. (Ed.) (1991). *Youth at risk.* Lancaster, PA: Technomic.

National Association of State Directors of Special Education. Education of the Handicapped Act amendments of 1990 (P.L. 101-476: Summary of major changes in Parts A through H of the act). (1990, October). Washington, DC: NASDSE.

Neely, R. O., & Alm, D. (1992, November–December). Meeting individual needs: A learning styles success story. Washington, DC: Heldref Publications, (2), 109–113.

Neely, R. O., & Alm, D. (1993). Empowering students with styles. *Principal, 72*(4), 32–35.

Orsak, L. (1990). Learning styles versus the Rip Van Winkle syndrome. *Educational Leadership, 48*(2), 19–20.

Price, G. E., Dunn, K., Dunn, R., & Griggs, S. A. (1981). Studies in students' learning styles. *Roeper Review, 4,* 223–226.

Quinn, R. (1993). The New York State compact for learning and learning styles. *Learning Styles Network Newsletter. 15*(1), 1–2.

Dunn, R. (1995). *Research on the Dunn and Dunn learning style model* (1994). Jamacia, NY: St. John's University Center for the Study of Learning and Teaching styles.

Reynolds, M. C., & Birch, J. W. (1977). *Teaching exceptional children in all America's schools* (chap. 4). Reston, VA: Council for Exceptional Children.

Riner, P. S. (1983). Establishing scientific methodology with elementary gifted children through field biology. *G/C/T, 28,* 46–49.

Robert Wood Johnson Foundation (1990). Serving handicapped children. Education Digest, LV(6), 33–36.

Stewart, E. (1982). Myth: One program, indivisible for all. *Gifted Child Quarterly, 26,* 27–29.

Stewart, E. D. (1981). Learning styles among gifted/talented students: Instructional technique preferences. *Exceptional Children, 48,* 113–138.

Stone, P. (1992, November). How we turned around a problem school. *The Principal, 71*(2), 34–36.

Thies, A.P. (1979). A brain behavior analysis of learning style. In J. W. Keefe (Ed.), *Student learning styles: Diagnosing and prescribing programs.* Reston, VA: National Association of Secondary School Principals.

Wellington, P., & Perlin, C. (1991). Palimpsest probability and the writing process: Mega-change for at-risk students. In R. C. Morris (Ed.), *Youth at risk.* Lancaster, PA: Technomic.

part FOUR

Applying Technology to Teaching

Today's teachers have at their fingertips a variety of technologies with potential as broad as the teacher's background and perspective. Chapter 10 will make you aware of the wide range of commercially produced media and prepare you to make your own materials. Chapter 11 explains the microcomputer's status in the schools and discusses ways to use it to elevate students' levels of thinking. As you read these two chapters, think about the subjects and the grade levels you plan to teach. Think also about your own strengths and preferences, and as you learn about new technological developments, think of ways you can adjust the old and new developments to increase their effectiveness in your future classes.

chapter 10

Using Media

The medium is the message.
Marshall McLuhan

OBJECTIVES

Name two widely used forms of media in middle and secondary schools.

Give two guidelines for using the bulletin board.

Give one guideline for introducing any audio or visual presentation and two guidelines for concluding a presentation.

Name two types of teacher- or pupil-made media.

Name two newer types of media and explain an advantage of each over its predecessors.

Name and explain a common misuse of media.

Name two areas in which teachers today perceive a need for more instruction.

Provide a theoretical rationale supporting the use of media in instruction.

Interpret the following statement in the context of the role of media in the classroom: "There has never been an outstanding teacher, only outstanding facilitators of learning" (Stefanich, 1990, p. 50).

Explain the advantages and limitations of interactive and noninteractive discs for use in distance learning.

PRETEST

	Agree	Disagree	Uncertain
1. Use films only when they have instructional value.	____	____	____
2. Audiovisual equipment is most effective when kept separate. Therefore, use only one machine for each lesson.	____	____	____
3. The need for hands-on activities in secondary and middle school classrooms is diminishing.	____	____	____
4. Films that contain a professional introduction need no further introduction from you.	____	____	____
5. Generally, the best bulletin boards are those designed by students.	____	____	____
6. By consulting research data, you can determine what medium is best for each purpose.	____	____	____

7. Middle and secondary school students spend more time watching television than they spend in the classroom.

_____   _____   _____

8. Symbolism, such as that provided through media, is an essential part of the learning process.

_____   _____   _____

Middle-Level Message

Transescence is an age of activity and excitement. Instead of fighting these natural behaviors, middle-level teachers should learn to channel these students' abundant energy and enthusiasm into productive activities. Media are especially important to this age-group—their world is one of radios, tape recorders, and televisions. These students' love for media frequently conflicts with teachers' academic expectations for this age-group, but this need not be a problem if you use media constructively in your lessons. Students can attain even higher levels of success if you involve them in developing media-based presentations. How much your students will benefit from media depends on your skills in clarifying the relationships between the media you use and each lesson's academic objectives. Remember that in one national survey, half the middle-level teachers reported that they have inadequate knowledge of media and how to apply it in their classrooms (Henson, Chissom, & Buttery, 1986).

USE OF MEDIA DEVELOPMENT EXCEEDS PLANNING

For several decades, the rate of technological development in the United States has greatly exceeded educators' ability to determine the impact the various media have on American youth. It has also exceeded schools' ability to integrate media into the classroom. In the United States, however, the effort to introduce systematic study and use of media in the curriculum has been sporadic at best (Sneed, Wolfemeyer, Riffe, & Ommeren, 1990). As a result, most teachers do not have the knowledge and skills they need to use media effectively. In one study, 49 percent of a random national sample of middle school teachers reported that their background in instructional media was insufficient to prepare them for their instructional responsibilities (Henson, Chissom, & Buttery, 1986). Yet improving teaching strategies requires knowledge of and comfort with technology (Rock & Cummings, 1994).

As Lessinger (1994–1995, p. 16) has said, "Technology brings to classroom teaching the notion of learning as a deliberate or planned means-end activity." If this is true, then why do so many of teacher education programs fail to prepare teachers to use media and other technology effectively? The answer may be no more than conjecture, but this is an important question. Perhaps few educators understand the role that media and the symbols they produce play in learning.

Sneed, Wolfemeyer, Riffe, and Ommeren (1990, p. 36) explain the role that visual messages play in learning: "Students need to be able to interpret and analyze a variety of video messages in this highly visual world. . . . They especially need critical viewing so they can cut through the visual undergrowth and become critical video consumers who are literate in 'reading' visual messages."

MEDIA: AN ALTERNATIVE WHEN DIRECT INVOLVEMENT IS IMPOSSIBLE

Maximum learning occurs when students are involved with activities, but sometimes it is difficult to involve students with hands-on activities. Media offer a viable alternative. Stefanich (1990) explains:

> Teaching must occur in an arena of active manipulation of concrete hands-on experiences. When a concrete experience is impossible, semi-concrete opportunities (i.e., films, simulations, games, illustrations) must be utilized. . . . There has never been an outstanding teacher. Learning requires active participation on the part of the learner, therefore, there have only been outstanding facilitators of learning. (p. 50)

HISTORY OF MEDIA USE IN INSTRUCTIONAL PLANNING

Much of our contemporary understanding of the learning process has its roots in the work of John Locke. During the last half of the seventeenth century, Locke postulated that the mind is like a blank slate (tabula rasa) that remains empty until something is placed on it. He believed that the only way to fill this slate was through experience. Most current educators recognize that much of what we know comes through indirect or vicarious experience, and the history and practice of education in the United States supports Locke's emphasis on experience.

During the last quarter of the nineteenth century, John Dewey and Colonel Francis Parker introduced child-centered education into American schools. Lecture and recitation were replaced with student activities. This child-centered education, called the Progressive Movement, dominated the curricula from the early 1920s to the early 1940s, and Harvard University was commissioned to study its effectiveness. The study ran from 1933 to 1941 and was named the Eight-Year Study. It found that students who graduated from the child-centered schools equaled their counterparts in traditional schools in learning subject matter, and they outperformed them in attaining academic honors and grades. Furthermore, graduates of the progressive curricula were significantly superior in intellectual curiosity, creativity, drive, leadership, and intraclass activities. They were also more objective and more aware of world events. Heinich, Molenda, and Russell (1985) remind us of Bruner's (1966) advice that instruction should proceed from direct experience through iconic representations of experience—that is, through symbolic representation, such as pictures, films, and other media.

The exact roles that media play in learning are complex and not fully understood at this time. Some studies suggest that different types of images produce varying influences on memory (Kosslyn, 1981). Other research suggests that images are coded into abstractions, stored in memory, and later reconstructed as they are recalled (Gagne, 1970). The following conclusions by Clark and Salomon (1986, p. 474) summarize the latest understandings of how media should be used in instruction. First, "it appears that media do not affect learning in and of themselves," and second, "past research on media has shown quite clearly that no medium enhances learning more than any other medium regardless of learning tasks, learner traits, symbolic elements, curriculum content, or setting."

This does not suggest minimizing the use of media in instructional planning. Rather, it reflects the complexity involved in learning and the premature stage of educational research on media instruction. It does suggest that, in planning to use media in curricula, teachers should not attempt to locate research that shows what particular medium is best for each lesson. Clark and Salomon (1986, p. 474) hasten to add that "newer media also afford convenient and often novel ways to shape instructional presentations."

THE POWER TO MOTIVATE

Conroy and Hedley (1990) emphasize the power that media and other forms of technology have to motivate students:

> Because of the special appeal that technology education holds for most students—the excitement of manipulating tools and machines, the satisfaction associated with solving problems of a technical nature—it is a particularly vital environment in which to integrate and perfect communication skills. (p. 231)

This chapter introduces a wide variety of media available in most schools and gives suggestions for using each medium. Become familiar with these media so you will be prepared to use a variety of media during student teaching and other clinical experience opportunities. The "Activities" section at the end of this chapter suggests other ways you can prepare to make full use of media to enrich your future teaching.

THE MEDIA IN YOUR OWN SCHOOL

Most teachers have access to many teaching aids—for example, projectors, films, posters, and records. Most larger schools have a media center; other schools provide media through the school library. Some school districts keep all their media in one location and make it available to each teacher on one or two days' notice. Teachers who avoid using media may shortchange their students by omitting an additional learning experience that might reach some students better than any other strategy. As you examine some of the media available, decide what will be worthwhile for you and your future students.

The Overhead Projector

Aside from the chalkboard, the most commonly used audio or visual medium in the classroom is the overhead projector. It offers two distinct advantages over most other types of audiovisual equipment. First, it is available and versatile. You can make transparencies easily with a few sheets of inexpensive clear acetate and a grease pencil, or you can use colored felt-tip pens made for writing on the acetate. The color will add interest to the lesson. A second advantage of the overhead projector is that it allows you to face the class at all times, seeing hands as they are raised, watching facial expressions, and retaining good control. The chalkboard does not provide these opportunities. Success with the overhead projector depends on whether there are appropriate quality materials and whether you use the machine correctly.

Securing Materials. The quality of overhead projectors in the United States is high. Most machines have a standard-size surface and produce a clear image. Their 500-watt intensity can produce a clear image without your having to darken the room or even turn off the lights. These machines are durable and, unless abused, seldom require maintenance. A major concern, then, is how to get good transparencies to use on the projector.

There are two ways to acquire good transparencies: Teachers can persuade the school to purchase them, or teachers can produce their own materials. The most commonly purchased material for the overhead projector is the simple transparency. Commercial publishers offer a wide range of transparencies in most subjects for use at different grade levels. Most of the transparencies sold today are multicolored and designed to capture students' attention. Many communicate major concepts simply and clearly.

Check with your department head and your school's learning or media center for available supplies and catalogs. When ordering transparencies, check the age-group (or range of ages) for which the transparencies are designed. Following is a list of sources for transparencies:

Audio Visual Communications, Inc., 159 Verdi Street, Farmingdale, NY 01135

AeVac Educational Publishers, 1604 Park Avenue, South Plainfield, NJ 07018

Encyclopedia Britannica Film, Inc., 425 Michigan Avenue, Chicago, IL 60611

ESSCO Educational Supply Co., Inc., 2825 East Gage Avenue, Huntington Park, CA 90255

Johnson Plastic, Inc., 526 Pine Street, Elizabeth, NJ 07206

Miliken Publishing Company, 611 Olive Street, St. Louis, MO 63101

Scott Reprographs Division, Holyoke, MA 01040

Lansford Publishing Company, 2516 Lansford Avenue, San Jose, CA 95125

Valiant Industries, 172 Walker Lane, Englewood, NJ 07631

Producing Materials.   Because of cost, convenience, and suitability for lesson plans, many teachers make their own overhead transparencies. There are several processes for doing this, but because some are quite elaborate and require machinery not available to most teachers, only the easiest and fastest methods will be discussed.

If your school has a thermal copying machine (most schools do), you can place a sheet of special transparency film over the sheet you want to copy and run it through the machine. This method, which takes about 10 seconds, can be used to copy pictures or print with a carbon base. Because most printed materials do use carbon, they can be reproduced quickly. Even pencil drawings, theme papers, problems, and the like usually work well. Copyright laws forbid reproducing copyrighted material for profit. In the past, teachers were permitted to copy materials for use in their classes, but because of abuse and because copyright laws are changing, check with your administrators to see that your projects do not violate the law.

A second method of producing transparencies is equally inexpensive, easy, and fast. Just run a sheet of frosted acetate through the spirit duplicator as you would a piece of paper. The image will be printed on the sheet. For further details on producing transparencies, see this chapter's "References," especially the entries for Kemp (1975) and for Haney and Ullmer (1975).

Using the Overhead Projector.   As mentioned earlier, effective results with the overhead projector depend on good materials and good use. The following list provides guidelines for using the overhead projector.

1. Use a good transparency pencil or pen (not an ordinary felt-tip pen).
2. Select the best classroom position for projection so that all students can see the projection clearly.
3. Face students when speaking to them—you do not have to turn around every time, as you would when using a chalkboard.
4. You can vividly project any transparent models or objects, such as plastic rulers, protractors, ripple tanks, and test tubes.
5. Trace charts or drawings on construction paper or on chalkboards by simply projecting the original transparency.
6. When you do not want to show the entire transparency, cover up the portion of the contents with paper (masking technique).
7. When you want to add or correlate the contents simultaneously, simply add on another transparency (overlay technique).

Once you have the materials, concentrate on the next important step—positioning and focusing the machine. Before attempting to focus it, determine how far from the screen the machine will be. This is easy: Direct the light onto the screen and move the projector away from the screen until the light fits just immediately within the boundaries of the screen. Then bring the image into focus simply by changing the distance between the lens and the machine's surface. Most machines have a knob that can be turned to achieve focus.

There is one more matter to consider when you use the overhead projector. You may prepare the transparency in advance, or you may write, sketch, or draw on a clear sheet of acetate during the lesson. Bringing the transparency to class already prepared offers an advantage over using the chalkboard; you do not have to take time from the lesson and attention from the students to write the paragraphs, make the lists, or draw the diagrams. But there is an advantage to developing the visual material during the lesson: You can stop and involve students at strategic points. Perhaps the best method is to prepare transparencies in advance, leaving some empty spaces for the students and you to complete during the lesson.

Overlays. Transparencies are clear, so they can be stacked on top of each other to add dimensions or details to the image. Because such superimposure requires accuracy in placing each transparency exactly over the one underneath, you will find it helpful to make a cardboard frame for the first transparency, then tape one side of the second transparency to the left side of the frame. If yet another superimposure is desired, tape the top of the next transparency to the top of the frame. Continuing to tape one side of each transparency at a 90-degree angle to the previous one, you can stack up as many transparencies as you want.

During education courses that provide opportunities to teach peer lessons, and during your student-teaching internship, you will have opportunities to experiment with making your own transparencies, with using prepared materials, and with preparing materials during the lesson. Experiment with all these approaches.

Cognitive Mapping

Cognitive mapping is the process of identifying a lesson's major concepts and making a drawing of these concepts. Slavin (1994, p. 243) explains, "In networking and mapping, students identify main ideas and then diagram connections between them." An effective use of mapping is to let groups of students make cognitive maps to show how they perceive relationships among related concepts and use the overhead projector to show and control these maps.

The Opaque Projector

Before the thermal copy machine and the overhead projector were available, the opaque projector was frequently used in classroom instruction, and it does have some advantages. It can project an image on a screen directly from the book, saving the time and expense of making a permanent copy of the material. Also, there is no question of copyright infringement.

Its greatest problem is its bulky size, blocking the image from many students' view and becoming a major barrier between the teacher and some students. A second problem is the image's weakness. A good image often requires total darkness in the room, leaving students unable to take notes or work problems but free to engage in other less academic pursuits of their own choosing. It is noisy, and its opening, although adjustable, prevents the use of very thick books. In addition, if a book is left too long on the projector, the intense heat will damage the page.

With so many disadvantages, you may choose never to use this machine for teaching a lesson, yet you may find it useful for projecting very large images on the wall for the purpose of tracing.

The Slide Projector

Like the overhead projector, the slide projector projects an image so intense that it can be seen in most lighted classrooms. One advantage of slides is that they can capture real scenery, people, and events that are relevant to the subject under study. Just think how much more interesting Spanish class can be if the teacher shows a collection of slides taken on a vacation to Mexico. Or the social studies teacher can intensify interest by showing slides of people at work in different countries. The biology teacher can produce a similar effect with slides of plants and animals taken on a visit to the desert, mountains, plains, and seashore.

The 35-mm camera, which has become increasingly affordable in recent years, is excellent for taking slides. By increasing the shutter speed, you can reduce the blur that movement causes. Or to accentuate the sense of movement, you can decrease the shutter speed. Or you can increase the blurring by moving closer to the object. When taking pictures for slides, take more than one of each promising subject to increase the likelihood of getting quality results. If you are photographing people at close range, be sure to get their permission. Encourage students to take slides to share with the class. Field trips should always have follow-up discussions, and good slides will enhance the discussion.

Table 10.1 has some suggestions for using traditional forms of media in the classroom.

The Record Player

Even though you may associate the record player with music and dancing, do not limit its use to these alone. A story or poem read by Orson Welles, or a ballad sung by Burl Ives, can communicate in special ways. As with other media, clarify the purpose from the beginning and reemphasize it at the end. Assign students tasks to involve them with the content the media portrays. The record player can be useful in language arts, most specifically in helping students develop listening skills. Ask students relevant questions after the record ends to reinforce those students who listened attentively.

Television

The impact that television has had on our youth has been a concern for some time. A previous edition of this book (Henson, 1988) said:

> The effect of television on today's youth is reflected in statistics that show that Americans spend between 23 hours a week (for children under five) and 44 hours a week (for adults) watching television (Miller, 1977). American students spend more time watching television than they spend in school

TABLE 10.1   Some suggestions for using some traditional forms of media in the classroom

Medium	Effective Purposes	Benefits	Suggestions for Using
16mm Projector	To introduce units or topics	Comprehensive	Communicate the purposes for its use *before* showing a film
	To increase enthusiasm for a topic	Motivating	Identify a *few* major concepts for students to watch for
	To review units or topics		
Filmstrip/Film Loop	Learn sequences in multistop processes	Provides for student questions	Before showing the filmstrip/film loop alert students to a few important concepts to look for
	In-depth learning on a limited number of concepts	Provides opportunities for discussion	Freeze and discuss during the viewing
Overhead Projector	Emphasize major concepts in each lesson	Availability	Use of transparency for each major concept in the lesson
	Teacher can introduce the lesson in steps, allowing students to see it unfold	Simple and easy to use	Use color transparencies to increase level of motivation
	Students can use to present class projects	Versatility	Give assignments providing opportunities for student use
		Economic—can use teacher transparencies	
		Allows teacher to free the class	
Slide Projector	Students can use to present projects	Highly motivational	Invite student input into selection of student projects

(Morrisett, 1984). In the classroom, televisions have become a common medium for instruction. Today, more than half of all teachers in the United States use television material in their classes (Riccobono, 1984).

In the future, television will play an important role in educating students. You can help by holding discussions about quality programs in your classroom. Teachers' professional associations and unions can lobby for more quality programs designed for adolescents at each age level. And of course you can support the educational networks and encourage others to do likewise.

Alan November (1992, March), a technology consultant for Glenbrook High School, (Northbrook, IL), says:

Today, television has replaced print as the information medium. . . . The more I learn about the impact of visual technologies on the human spirit and how people think, the more concerned I become. . . . How do we learn to think critically about its structure and content? How do we learn to detect its biases and learn if we are being manipulated either by design or accident?

As you read November's statement, you probably thought he was referring to commercials, which we know are designed to be persuasive or biased in a product's favor. But November explains that most other television material is by its nature seductive; it is designed to cause viewers to accept what they see and hear as facts. Even the news tends to lure viewers to think shallowly or not at all.

The Bulletin Board

Good media are not always purchased—you or your students can make them. The bulletin board (or cork board or felt board) can be an excellent way to stimulate thinking. Never allow the board to become dated, and make sure its contents revolve around a central theme.

A bulletin board can help make subjects come alive. Posters and pictures depicting one aspect of a unit under study give all students a similar opportunity to learn, regardless of their home situation or background. Consider, for example, a teacher who is starting a unit on Africa. On the bulletin board that teacher places a map of Africa with a photograph of the leader of each country pasted in the respective country. During discussions of leaders, countries, and events, each student can identify the leaders and locate the events. Without this visual aid, students who do not watch the news regularly and who have never visited Africa would be at a disadvantage. Although a picture cannot replace personal experience, it does narrow the gap between the students who have some awareness of the country and those who do not.

Bulletin boards have other uses. Placing a "Problem of the Week" in one corner of the board and encouraging students to attempt solutions any time their other work is completed can be motivating. In a week's time, all students will have had the opportunity to solve it and will be eager to compare their answers with the teacher's.

Today's students use many types of media.

One teacher uses the bulletin board to make a time line for social studies. Each day a few students are responsible for "bringing it up to date," based on the material covered that day.

Many teachers are concerned less with how a bulletin board looks than with what it says or does. They let the students be solely responsible for it, so that everything on it represents their efforts. Throughout the year, the board is constantly changing, because the world is always changing. Some teachers believe that an attractive, neat bulletin board is the mark of a good teacher. They will spend hours cutting out letters and making an eye-catching display, especially before an open house or parent-teacher meeting and definitely during American Education Week. As long as it looks good and visitors will be impressed, they think, it doesn't matter that the bulletin board lacks function—that students actually learn nothing from it. Unfortunately, some principals, wanting to see such neatness, encourage teachers in this direction.

The Chalkboard

The chalkboard has value beyond its most common use. Students' attention should focus on it automatically, without a request from the teacher. Some teachers achieve this by placing a "thought for the day" at the top of the chalkboard and leaving it there all day. Graffiti can also get students' attention. For example, imagine students entering a room to see the message

HELP! I'M TRAPPED BACK HERE!

Colored chalk can be stimulating, but check with the custodian before you use it. Some colored chalk is difficult to remove from certain surfaces, even with soap and water. Chalkboards have been permanently damaged by nonstandard white or colored chalk.

SOME NEWER TYPES OF MEDIA

In recent years, audiovisual equipment has become more attractive and effective. The dimension of sound has been added to filmstrip and slide projectors. Some schools even have facilities for teachers to make their own sound slides. This could be an interesting project for you and your classes, regardless of subject content. Check out your school's audiovisual facilities and possibilities.

The videocassette recorder (VCR) has great potential for use in secondary and middle school classrooms. It is unique in that it makes possible for students to view television programs aired at times other than class time.

Before copying a program, always get permission from the network showing the program. This should not be a problem if you make the request on the school's letterhead stationery and ask an administrator to cosign it. Wait for permission to be granted. One network filed a lawsuit against a university that used its newscasts regularly without network permission.

The VCR can also be useful for capturing students' behavior as they perform psychomotor skills (e.g., a student bowling or a drama class acting), permitting students to study their technique. This allows them to see their mistakes either in isolation (by freezing the picture) or as a part of the total process.

Videodiscs

The videodiscs that are now entering the schools are the same chrome-plated discs dominating the music stores. Videodiscs can retain large amounts of data and audio and video material in digital form (Lockard, Abrams, & Many, 1990).

Although videodiscs look like long-playing records, they differ in two major ways. Obviously, they have the video component. Not so obvious is their tremendously large storage capacity.

There are basically two types of videodiscs: interactive and noninteractive. Noninteractive discs are becoming inexpensive enough that most schools can afford them. Noninteractive discs send audio and video signals one way. The advantage is that schools can access them by having only a down-link (receiver). Therefore, they do not permit students to ask questions or offer comments to the teacher. In contrast, interactive discs require schools to have the means to transmit a signal (up-link capability), but they enable students to converse with their distant teacher. Interactive discs are highly motivational, and they can stimulate students' creativity as well as their interest. Currently, interactive discs are so expensive that some schools cannot afford them. But the cost will probably drop as companies compete in this market.

Consider the potential that the interactive videodiscs offers to students who take speech classes and drama classes and participate in debates and mock trials. Through using this technology, students can choose role models to emulate and can compare their own performances with those of master artists.

Table 10.2 has some suggestions for using newer media in the classroom.

Distance Education

Recent economic limitations have prompted school districts to look for less expensive ways to reach students in rural areas. One answer that both universities and public schools are finding effective is distance education. Distance education is audio and visual instruction transmitted from one location to a distant location electronically, usually involving satellites. For over three decades some states have used distance education to teach subjects when teachers are scarce. For example, distance learning programs frequently teach chemistry, physics, and foreign language.

The advent of interactive and satellite discs has introduced an interactive dimension to distance education. Satellite programs require an up-link capability to get the program from the studio to the satellite. To receive these programs schools must have their own down-link systems to retrieve the signal from the satellite. Typically, such

TABLE 10.2   Some suggestions for using some newer media in the classroom

Medium	Effective Purposes	Benefits	Suggestions for Using
Videodiscs	Stimulate student interest	Highly motivational	Invite students to use in class projects
	Enable students to develop creativity	Invite creativity	
Distance education	Stimulate student interest	Reach across great distances	Link your students with other students in other locations
		Motivational	Academic competitions
			Share similar projects (e.g., science projects) and show progress over time

classroom facilities include student stations. Each station has a television monitor to provide one-way video from the station to the student, a cordless phone, and key pads that students use to provide feedback to the station. Some stations are also equipped with a video recorder. A common type of storage disk used in distance education is the compact disc–read only memory (CD-ROM), as opposed to the floppy disk and the hard drive.

MEDIA COMBINATIONS

Media combinations can enhance almost any lesson. For example, before showing a film, filmstrip, or videotape, you can outline the lesson's objectives on the chalkboard or overhead projector. You can use these lesson objectives for review at the end of the period. Or, as a tape or record plays a new dance, you can outline the steps on the overhead projector. Some teachers become very sophisticated with the way they develop and use audiovisual equipment. Others use media only in simple ways, which still can be quite effective.

This chapter has discussed several media. Correctly used, each can improve teaching effectiveness. The microcomputer was not among the media discussed in this chapter because of its impact on education. Chapter 11 discusses using computers to improve instruction.

RECAP OF MAJOR IDEAS

1. Base media decisions on how much a particular medium facilitates and enhances a particular lesson's effectiveness.
2. Preview films, tapes, and records before using them in the classroom.
3. Preface the use of tapes, films, filmstrips, and records by an introduction that instructs students to look for particular objectives; follow with a review of these objectives.

4. Use media to their maximum advantage.
5. Transparencies for the overhead projector are versatile and easily prepared by the teacher.
6. Whenever feasible, involve middle and secondary students in preparing and using media for instructional purposes.
7. Such media as bulletin boards, photography, slides, and videotapes offer excellent opportunities for students to use their creative abilities.
8. While neatness is always desirable, bulletin boards' value depends more on their function than their beauty.
9. The advent of interactive videodiscs and satellites has made effective distance education possible.
10. Most school districts can afford noninteractive videodiscs.

CASES

The following cases show several mistakes that teachers make when using media. For each misuse, make your own mental corrections to reverse the effects of these media on students.

CASE 1: TOO MUCH RESEARCH IS CONDUCTED IN THE TEACHERS' LOUNGE

Mark found his first two weeks of teaching to be a variety of everything but teaching. He called rolls, made seating charts, made entries in a state attendance record book, and distributed textbooks—although he wasn't sure why because there seemed to be no time to use them. By the beginning of his third week he overheard some colleagues expressing his exact sentiments in the teachers' lounge.

MR. MILLER: Mary, I don't know how you do it. You seem to have your classes running so smoothly, yet you are acting chairperson of the Social Studies Department and sponsor of the Teachers of Social Studies Club. What is your secret?

MRS. JENKINS: Tom, you're flattering, but I'm sure your classes are well organized too.

MR. MILLER: No, I'm dead serious. I seem to work harder and get further behind. You know the old adage "The harder I work etc., etc." I just barely have time to put one foot in front of the other. I mean, having to lecture for five hours daily with only one planning period is more than a full-time job. Then we have all the paperwork and the ballgames. I really mean it. I'd like to know how you manage everything.

MRS. JENKINS: Well, I may not know what I do, but I know one thing I don't do, and that's lecture all day. I order a number of good films during the summer and have them coming in all during the year.

With this news in mind, Mark went to the resource center. Within the next 20 minutes he found dozens of films that seemed appropriate for his classes. He chose only those that ran for one or two full periods and that he could use in both his history and government classes. With this accomplished, he felt he could relax a little.

Indeed, the coming weeks saw a new Mark with a fresh, new style. With films on Tuesdays and Thursdays, he could relax and plan for the other days. This was much less demanding than the old style of planning new lessons for each day. The students welcomed it too. The first few films provided great entertainment. Mark's classes soon earned the reputation and title "Mark's Cinema." He enjoyed the joke and laughed when a colleague kiddingly accused him of serving popcorn and soft drinks.

But all good things must come to an end, and this magic system was no different. As strange as it sounds, the students were the first to tire of the films. When the class turned into chaos, Mark was astounded and perplexed. How could such a neat system turn so sour?

Discussion

1. Was Mark wrong to select films several months in advance?

No. This is a good practice, because it ensures that the popular films will be available, and it enables the teacher to coordinate the films with the lessons. Good films can complement even the most interesting lessons. A good film is often an excellent way to introduce a new study unit because of the vast amount of material a film can cover in a short time.

2. Why did Mark's students come to dislike the new system?

Because of the way Mark used the films, all they offered his students was a change from the old routine. Soon the films became an old routine, equally as boring as the lectures.

3. What was wrong with Mark's system?

First, Mark chose films that took up the whole period, leaving no time to introduce or summarize each film's main concepts. Second, Mark tried to substitute the films for lessons instead of using them to enrich each lesson. Finally, Mark used each film in both his history classes and his government classes, but it is unlikely that one film was appropriate for both subjects. Mark apparently did not even bother to preview any of the films, which is an essential step before you show any film.

CASE 2: A BULLETIN BOARD IS MISUSED

During her second full week of student teaching in ninth-grade English, Carla Cromwell was assigned to take over composition writing. Carla was aware that students who do good work must be positively reinforced, so she included in her plans a way to give those students a feeling of success. On Friday, after giving a special writing assignment, she posted the six best papers from the group of 23. The caption at the top of the bulletin board in large, colorful letters read "We Have Some Good Writers." In the same class, six other students had papers with A grades, and only three had made below a C.

Discussion

1. Should a teacher post student papers on bulletin boards?

The answer to this question depends on the circumstances. In general, putting the "good" papers on the board will positively reinforce the owners of those papers, but the teacher must also consider the effects on other students. Perhaps other papers should have been posted, especially the six with grades of A. By ignoring these, the teacher implies that they are less than good. Usually the student whose paper is displayed because of its quality is the student who already has high self-esteem. The students who seldom do good work also need positive reinforcement but are not likely to see their papers posted.

There are also nonacademic talents and behaviors that are worth promoting. The teacher who looks for promptness, cooperation, creativity, decision-making ability, communication skills, or other desirable traits will be able to recognize every student for being good at something. This is the time to make it known to all by placing the actual work, or a note describing it, on the bulletin board. The following list is only a sample of what could be displayed.

Paula was the first to complete the term project.

Did you see the paintings that Carol and Susan entered in the school exhibit?

John and Dave really make a smooth team in tennis doubles.

The point is that when only good work in a single subject is posted, some students will become discouraged. They will think they have no chance to be recognized. On the other hand, never giving reinforcement this way can be detrimental to higher-achieving students' motivation. Therefore, it is a good idea to mix up the routine, making sure that each student is positively recognized from time to time.

2. How could Carla have been more humane in dealing with the compositions?

Although there are many alternatives, some stand out. First, why post them at all? Instead, write words such as "Good work" or "Way to go!" Carla could talk individually with the few who did poorly and encourage them to improve their work. Another approach would be to establish standards for each student. For instance, Jack, a poor speller, has fewer spelling errors on a new paper than on a previous paper. That should be considered progress—indeed, even success—regardless of the number of errors on the latest paper. Carla can enter into a contract with him to get a score commensurate with his abilities. She could do the same for each of Jack's classmates. All students who fulfill the contract would get their names entered on the board under the heading "Writers of the Week."

CASE 3: A TEACHER HAS PROBLEMS WITH A FILM

Sharon Croft was in her first month of teaching a twelfth-grade Spanish class. In the film catalog she located a 12-minute color film that was appropriate for her class. She ordered it from the school system's central media library, but instead of receiving it on the day she requested, she received it the day she planned to show it.

Having taken a course in college dealing with the use of multimedia, Sharon felt confident about using the projector. Getting ready to show the film proved to be no problem, but during the actual presentation Sharon noticed something was wrong. The takeup reel was spilling film onto the floor, and by the time she realized it, much of the film lay in disarray next to the projector stand. Although she was alarmed, Sharon decided to finish the film rather than turn off the machine.

Discussion Questions

1. Was Sharon's decision a wise one?
2. Is film harmed when it spills onto the floor?

CASE 4: DATED MATERIAL DECORATES THE ROOM

Ms. Jefferson's room in Public School No. 128 had a bulletin board running the entire length of the wall from the front of the room to the back, ending at the doorway. Having taught in this room for more years than she cared to admit, Ms. Jefferson was constantly faced with finding a use for the bulletin board. Out of frustration she had decided to caption it "What's Happening Now" and began gathering newspaper and magazine articles about developments in the Spanish-speaking countries of the world. When completed, it was a colorful collage, a mixed bag of names, places, faces, and events. All visitors to the room noticed it immediately, but on closer inspection they realized the material all was at least a year old.

Discussion Questions

1. How might displaying old news affect students?
2. How can you avoid the problem of bulletin board obsolescence?

ACTIVITIES

Because you have grown up in a world of multimedia, you probably know a lot about media and have many additional ideas about applying it to instruction. The following activities will allow you to relate the material in this chapter and your previous knowledge about media to improve the teaching of your own subjects.

1. Make a list of anecdotes to communicate to your students. Explain the media you will use for each. For example, will you post them on the bulletin board, write them on the chalkboard or overhead transparency, or distribute them on mimeograph handouts?
2. Select an important theme or concept in your field of study and devise several ways to introduce it using a different medium with each.
3. Devise one good multimedia presentation to introduce a topic in your major

field. If you have skills in photography, art, music, or drama, consider using these in your presentation.

4. Visit your university's media center. Ask about new or recent media developments. Select one of these new developments and research the literature to determine its potential for classroom use.

REFERENCES

Bruner, J. C. (1966). *Toward a theory of instruction.* Cambridge: Harvard University Press.

Clark, R. E., & Salomon, G. (1986). Media in teaching. In M. C. Wittrock (Ed.), *Handbook of research on teaching* (3rd ed.). New York: Macmillan.

Conroy, M. T., & Hedley, C. (1990). Communication skills: The technology-education student and whole language strategies. *The Clearing House, 63*(5), 231-234.

Gagne, R. N. (1970). *The conditions of learning.* New York: Holt, Rinehart & Winston.

Haney, J. B., & Ullmer, E. J. (1975). *Educational communications and technology.* Dubuque, IA: Brown.

Heinich, R., Molenda, M., & Russell, J. D. (1985). *Instructional media and the new technologies of instruction* (2nd ed.). New York: Macmillan.

Henson, K. T., Chissom, B., & Buttery, T. J. (1986). Improving instruction in middle schools by attending to teachers' needs. *American Middle School Education, 2,* 2-7.

Kemp, G. E. (1975). *Planning and producing audio-visual materials* (2nd ed.). New York: Crowell.

Kosslyn, S. M. (1981). The medium and the message in mental imagery: A theory. *Psychological Review, 88,* 44-66.

Lessinger, L. M. (1994-1995). Improving the classroom learning process. *National Forum of Teacher Education Journal, 5*(1), 14-17.

Lockard, J., Abrams, P. D., & Many, W. A. (1990). *Micro computers for educators.* Glenville, IL: Scott-Foresman/Little, Brown Higher Education.

Miller, M. S. (1977, June). The Farrah factor. *Ladies Home Journal,* p. 34.

November, A. (1992, March). Brave new world revisited. *Electronic Learning, 11*(6), 50.

Riccobono, J. A. (1984). *Availability, use, and support of instructional media, 1982-1983.* Washington, DC: National Center for Educational Statistics.

Rock, H. M., & Cummings, A. (1994). Can videodiscs improve student outcomes? *Educational Leadership, 51*(7), 46-50.

Slavin, R. E. (1994). *Educational psychology: Theory and practice* (4th ed.). Needham, Ma.: Aallyn and Bacon.

Sneed, D., Wolfemeyer, K. T., Riffe, D., & Ommeren, R. V. (1990, September-October). Promoting media literacy in the high school social science curriculum. *The Clearing House, 64*(1), 36-38.

Stefanich, G. P. (1990, November). Cycles of cognition. *Middle School Journal, 22*(2), 47-52.

SUGGESTED READINGS

Armstrong, D. G., Henson, K. T., & Savage, T. V. (1993). *Education: An introduction* (4th ed.) (chap. 4). New York: Macmillan.

Eller, B. F., & Henson, K. T. (in press). *Educational psychology for effective teaching.* Atlanta, GA: West Publishing Company.

King, A. (1990, November–December). Reciprocal peer questioning: A strategy for teaching students how to learn from lectures. *The Clearing House, 64*(2), 131–135.

London, B., & Upton, J. (1992). *Photography.* New York: HarperCollins.

McLuhan, M. (1964). *Understanding media: The extension of man.* New York: McGraw-Hill.

Morrisett, L. (1984). Foreword to J. Murray and G. Salomon (Eds.), *The future of children's television.* Boys Town, NE: Boys Town Center.

chapter **11**

Using Microcomputers in Education

One machine can do the work of fifty ordinary men. No machine can do the work of one extraordinary man.

Elbert Hubbard

Probably the most dynamic force impacting education today is the implementation of technological advancements.

Robert Anderson

But to really take advantage of the Information Age tools in education, the challenge is not to use them to do the old job better but to do something new.

David Thornburg

OBJECTIVES

Name and discuss axioms that teachers can use as guidelines for selecting computer knowledge and skills to improve their teaching.

List pre-service and in-service teachers' common misconceptions about microcomputers.

Make a list of attitudes that facilitate mastery of computer skills and a corresponding list of impeding attitudes.

Define computer literacy and contrast it with computer awareness.

Differentiate between computer managed instruction (CMI) and computer assisted instruction (CAI).

Name at least three levels at which computers can be applied to teaching.

Explain how the computer can be used to help teach both slow students and advanced students.

Design a system for evaluating computer software for classroom use.

Differentiate between technological literacy and technological competency and relate these terms to contemporary student needs.

PRETEST

	Agree	Disagree	Uncertain
1. All teachers must develop some proficiency with computers.	_____	_____	_____
2. People who are not quantitatively inclined usually have difficulty understanding and mastering the computer.	_____	_____	_____
3. In selecting a computer, individuals or schools should begin by asking, "What can I afford?" and "Which brand is best?"	_____	_____	_____
4. Like many people who purchase computers for personal use, many school systems have rushed into buying computers without understanding the computer's unique capabilities and limitations.	_____	_____	_____
5. Select a computer according to how you intend to use it.	_____	_____	_____
6. The major instructional advantage that computers offer is their ability to improve drill-and-practice type of instruction.	_____	_____	_____

7. Anyone who is able to meet all other teaching certification requirements should be able to master the computer at the level needed to improve teaching responsibilities.   _____   _____   _____

8. Some of the newest microcomputers have creative abilities.

9. Eventually, all teachers must become experts at designing new programs.   _____   _____   _____

10. Teachers beginning to develop their computer skills need a high level of confidence.   _____   _____   _____

Middle-Level Message

The rapid expansion of microcomputers into the schools has had an important impact on middle-level teachers in two ways. First, it made them realize that they must learn to use this tool if they are to be effective teachers in today's society. Second, the speed with which computers appeared in schools made many teachers fearful. When the telephone and the automobile were invented, people felt similar fear. As a result, many Americans avoided these new inventions and never learned to use them. As with the telephone and the automobile, the best way to become competent and comfortable with the computer is to have direct contact with it.

    As you read this chapter, note the many advantages that the computer offers for your classes. If you have not taken courses in computer education, locate a microcomputer on your campus and spend some time learning everything you can about it. If your college or department of education has a computer lab, ask to see a demonstration of software that is appropriate for middle-level classrooms.

THE ARRIVAL OF COMPUTERS

The arrival of computers at schools is long overdue. Some say that the pace at which schools have adopted computers and other technology has been too slow. James A. Mecklenburger (1990, p. 106), who directs the National School Boards Association Institute for the Transfer of Technology to Education, has commented that "schools today reflect their nineteenth century technological roots more than do most other institutions."

    Although teachers have been blamed for the slow pace at which computers have entered the schools, other factors have contributed to this delay. Armstrong, Henson, and Savage (1993) explain: "The relatively slow pace of school adoption of electronic innovations is not a matter of ill will on the part of school authorities. For many years, educators have been asked to embrace changes that have been promoted as 'cures' for persistent problems."

Lewis (1994, p. 356) has warned, "This gap between the schools and the rest of society will only widen as the technology available to students outside of schools continues to increase their access to information." But computers have entered the schools much more rapidly during the past decade.

In the early 1980s computers were in approximately 10 percent of U.S. schools; by the beginning of the 1990s computers were in over 90 percent of U.S. schools (Rothstein, 1990). A separate study (Becker, 1986) found that computers were in 85 percent of U.S. elementary schools, 95 percent of U.S. junior high schools, and 97 percent of U.S. senior high schools. Furthermore, these schools reported having at least one computer for instruction.

Initially, most school systems purchased microcomputers for their central offices. Because of their vast management capacity, microcomputers save important administrative time. For example, they significantly reduce the time needed to issue payrolls and grade reports. As they became less expensive, they became more affordable for instructional use. This use is commonly known as computer managed instruction (CMI). Price (1991) reminds readers that the microcomputer can assist teachers in a wide range of responsibilities including managing student records, diagnosing and prescribing material, monitoring progress, and constructing tests.

USING COMPUTERS IN TEACHING

The popularity of microcomputers in education has had an irreversible impact on schools. Today's teachers must be prepared to use computers in the classroom to avoid creating a gap between their students and themselves. Lewis (1994, p. 356) expresses this concern, "This gap between the schools and the rest of society will only widen as the technology available to students outside of schools continues to increase their access to information." Computers are changing our lives, and because schools prepare future citizens, school programs would be grossly inadequate if they failed to prepare graduates to function productively in society at large. Fortunately, this scenario is unlikely to occur if teachers respond wisely to the challenges they face. Robert Anderson (Dagenais, 1994, p. 52) explains, "Probably the most dynamic force impacting education today is the implementation of technological advancements." If teachers respond to this challenge by learning all they can about new technology, the increased technology in U.S. society can be more reason to celebrate than fear. Rock and Cummings (1994, p. 50) have said, "Teachers need to feel comfortable with technology. Until using the technology becomes second nature, they cannot effectively change their teaching strategies."

But teachers and schools have another equally important need for computers, a need related to the computer's increasing potential. Computers have become less expensive and more versatile. The range of computer use in all fields, including education, is limited only by the mind's creative limitations. Teachers can use computers to manage instruction, or they can use computers as tutors. The computer can be used for drill and practice, simulation, problem solving, and creating. In other words, the computer can be used to expand the types of instruction students receive, and it can be used to improve a teacher's current mode of instruction. A less-recognized advantage is the computer's ability to free the teacher to give more personal attention to students. But are teachers ready for this role? Do they have the expertise required to provide quality individualized counseling? Too often the answer is no.

This chapter will help you develop positive attitudes toward the use of computers in schools and will cover ways you can use computers to manage, improve, and test instruction. Suggestions for evaluating programs will be provided. But schools will realize the computer's positive potential only if teachers prepare themselves and their students to use the computer in new and creative ways.

> To me, technology is not the driving force for education. If we allow technology to be the engine, we're going to end up being quite disappointed. We make a mistake if we just bring a bunch of technology into a room and then think that an excellent educational program is going to materialize.

Thornburg (see Bitts, 1994, p. 22) is not alone in believing that real education progress through technology will be achieved through preparing students to use it in creative ways.

> We know that students learn by constructing their own knowledge through using new information in meaningful ways. This new knowledge must build directly on what each student already knows, and the students must see the connection between the new ideas and their world. Further, students need to be actually involved in their own learning and the decisions about their learning. (p. 30)

COMPUTER MANAGED INSTRUCTION (CMI)

Resulting largely from external accountability programs (often at the state level), many schools have adopted massive programs to improve the quality of instruction and ultimately increase the standardized test scores of large numbers of students. The mastery learning program and interclass grouping mentioned in Chapter 7 are examples. Such programs require extensive record keeping. Some of the programs are districtwide and involve thousands of students; they are so large that they could not be managed at all without computers. Using computers, schools and school systems can provide individualized education programs (IEPs) for thousands of students.

The managing of student records, diagnosing and prescribing material, monitoring progress, and testing are collectively called CMI. By definition, CMI does just as the name implies and no more—it manages records. It does not provide instruction, although it may contain instructional programs. Do not underestimate the value of CMI, however. Some CMI programs are packages or systems that include course objectives and corresponding test items.

Because CMI programs are usually quite expensive, select them carefully. If your future school(s) offer the opportunity, try to provide input into this selection process.

Preview CMI programs to see whether they are easy to operate—"user-friendly." Determine whether a program can keep the types of information you would want for your classes. If at this time you are not sure what kind of information you will need the computer to manage for you, examine the lesson plans and learning units in Chapters 2 and 3. Another factor to consider when selecting CMI programs is the degree to which the program involves students.

Some of the most effective CMI programs have been developed for particular school districts or states. Personnel in local school district offices will often design a program to match the district's objectives, curricula, and schedules. In many instances, outside entrepreneurs have learned about state-wide instructional management accountability requirements and developed programs for individual schools or districts.

Ideally, your school should have a committee to select CMI programs. Express your desire to be a member of that committee. When the committee selects a few programs, ask the vendor for names of other schools that have used the programs and contact them for their input.

COMPUTER ASSISTED INSTRUCTION (CAI)

Unlike CMI, which in its purest form is limited to testing and record keeping, CAI links the student directly to the material to be learned through the computer. Bitter (1989) defines CAI as the use of computers to enhance students' education. The student is actively involved in the learning process. The involvement itself is motivating. Various levels of involvement exist, depending on the CAI program used. The elements of effective CAI include presenting information, guiding the learner, practice, and assessing student learning (Alessi & Trollip, 1991).

Drill and Practice

At the lowest level, the computer behaves much like the early teacher, who lectured and then had students recite the material in the same form. Typically, drill and practice helps students to remember and use subject matter they have been taught previously (Lockard, Abrams, & Many, 1990). In all secondary and middle-level subjects at all grade levels some information is basic to the mastery of each discipline. For example, at the entry middle school level, students must know the multiplication tables to succeed in their math classes. In beginning chemistry, high school students are often required to memorize the Periodic Table of Elements. Drill and practice is an effective approach for learning at this level of knowledge. The computer can give questions, score the answers, and give immediate feedback.

Tutorial

The drill-and-practice application describes the computer in the role of the teacher, tutoring the student, but not all tutorial application of computers is limited to this simple recall or knowledge level. In fact, one of the first applications of computers to education was a tutorial program that used simulations. Project PLATO, founded by the National Science Foundation, began in the 1950s at the University of Illinois. This program has several thousand students at elementary through college levels. Other PLATO projects have sprung up throughout the United States. Preceding the development of BASIC language, PLATO uses a higher-level language. Some CAI programs that use BASIC include a project at the Minnesota Educational Computing Consortium in Minnesota and the Chicago City Schools Project, which provides several thousand fourth- through eighth-grade students with tutorial lessons in mathematics and reading.

How effective are CAI programs when compared with traditional instruction? Chambers and Sprecher (1980) reviewed the literature to determine what research studies have found about CAI's effectiveness. They cited eight separate studies that found that CAI either improved learning or showed no difference when compared with traditional instruction, seven studies that found that CAI reduced learning time compared with the regular classroom, and six studies that found that CAI improved student attitudes about using computers for instruction. These studies included a variety of CAI programs (e.g., drill and practice, tutorial, and simulations). Do not judge CAI's success compared with teacher instruction, however, because most of these studies (as in most studies in general) had teachers present who participated in the instruction.

Simulation

As you have already seen, CAI usually combines different types of instruction. This makes it impossible to put programs into completely separate categories. For instance, tutorial programs can include drill and practice or simulations, and simulation programs can include tutorials and drill and practice. Although simulations can be used simply to provide examples to reinforce memorization, most simulations involve the learner in problem solving. Students can live out roles and find solutions to complex problems.

Simulations offer many advantages. Magney (1990, p. 55) says, "On three dimensions—the cognitive, motivational, and attitudinal—game players are believed to reap benefits." Following is a list of advantages computer simulation offers:

1. There is no risk involved in simulation. Simulation software teaches people to operate equipment that is potentially dangerous to a novice. Students can bring nuclear reactors to "critical mass" in a safe classroom environment.
2. There is less expense involved in simulation. Students can study and learn the results of their decision making by experimentally investing millions of dollars in the stock market, and the only cost to the school is the simulation software and hardware involved.
3. Simulated experiences are more realistic and convenient for students than real experiences. A student can sit in the cockpit of an airplane with simulated flight controls.
4. Simulation overcomes the limitations of time. Students do not have to wait for several generations to observe the effects of ocean pollution, and simula-

tion software can give students a realistic picture of the environmental impact of a volcano eruption that occurred 100 or 10,000 years ago.

5. Simulation software makes it possible to focus on specific aspects of a topic or event. By slowing down or replaying cell division, students can highlight and detail the critical parts of the reproductive process.

6. The user can repeat simulated experiences many times. If a student is absent, he or she can do the simulation on another day with little teacher supervision. Also, students can often pursue "what if" questions and try different combinations of variable conditions (Eller & Henson, in press).

Appendix D is a directory of simulation sources.

SOME MISCONCEPTIONS

The most obvious and common misconception since the development of the early "teaching machines" of the 1940s is that the machine will replace the person. So it has been in education—many still fear that computers will replace teachers. But this can never happen. Although the popular microcomputers dazzle the mind with their speed and ability to store large quantities of information that can be recalled and assembled in millionths of a second, the microcomputer, like all other computers, has no imagination. It is not creative. It does not have the ability to appreciate or love. Therefore, it cannot attend to students' many human needs.

In essence, by itself, the computer cannot teach at all. Students cannot be made to learn, but sometimes they can be encouraged, enticed, and led to learn. The computer cannot provide the role model that students need to encourage them to learn, keep them on a steady track, and occasionally put them back on track when they go astray. Ironically, the nonhuman qualities that give the computer its advantages (vast speed, capacity, and the ability to work endlessly without getting tired or making errors) are also the qualities that make the computer depend on the teacher. More helpless than the students themselves, the computer cannot do anything but follow commands.

A second misconception that impedes computer application in instruction is teachers' tendency to think of the computer as a simple drill-and-practice machine. Strive to use the computer in a variety of ways. Give special attention to using computers to promote higher levels of thinking and even creativity. Teach students to use the computer to solve problems. Correctly used, the computer can expand students' creative abilities. You should search for ways to require students to develop problems they must then solve. More advanced students can learn to write programs to solve these problems.

Future classrooms must look at the computer's effect on society. Encourage students at all levels to look at ways computers threaten to diminish the quality of human life in modern societies. As Geisert and Dunn (1991) suggest, it is critical to use computers effectively in this information age, too critical to let a lack of technological training get in the way. Generally, CAI's emphasis has shifted from drill and practice to tutorial to simulation. The age levels using computers for instruction have spread from university to high school to elementary school.

Another common myth is that technology is a impersonal approach to learning that leaves the student detached from other students. As Taggert (1994, p. 35) explains, this idea is false: "Technology encourages cooperative learning, as well. As my students discover their own capabilities and expertise, I see a greater cooperative effort and exchange of knowledge."

Henson (1984) found that teacher education programs in major American universities are lagging behind other American institutions in using microcomputers and that as late as the mid-1980s universities were not giving adequate attention to preparing future teachers to select computer hardware and software. The findings of this study reinforced a study by Berg (1983), which showed that teachers have concerns about using computers in the classroom and that most teachers are inadequately prepared to use computers.

Fortunately, in many states the education reform movement has provided significant support for educational technology. For example, in 1992 Kentucky legislators appropriated $500 million to upgrade technology in public schools.

TEACHERS' FEAR OF COMPUTERS

Some of teachers' misconceptions about computers account for the fear of computers. By counteracting these false beliefs, teachers can lower their anxiety level. In retrospect, some of the more recent dominating fears now seem totally irrational, and others seem inane. For example, when teaching machines were introduced, many teachers were afraid that they would be replaced by a machine. For years many teachers refused to use television in the classroom for fear television would replace them. The same fear resurfaced when teachers began using microcomputers. Recognizing that many teachers are still afraid of using computers, Geisert and Dunn (1991, p. 223) report, "Some teachers acknowledge still having computer phobia and remain apprehensive about using computers as either an instructional or management tool." Ironically, when students develop computer competency, the same computers that initially frightened them can increase their sense of efficacy or self-confidence. The same phenomenon is true for teachers (Edinger, 1994).

Many teachers find the computer threatening because of the many things it can do so well, but they fail to realize that without an operator the computer can do nothing. There is a direct correlation between the microcomputer's ability to contribute to teaching and the degree to which the developers of software and the users understand the learning process. Put simply, teachers will never become subservient to computers.

Without teacher involvement, microcomputers can do little to facilitate learning in the classroom. For example, although the computer can be programmed to help students memorize facts, the teacher must become involved with problem solving, weighing values, and making complex decisions based on logical reasoning. The teacher must first identify these higher-level goals and objectives and then be able to select appropriate software to achieve them. The teacher's mental powers are always needed in the use of computers.

Do not interpret the common fear of microcomputers among many teachers as dislike or disapproval of the use of computers in the classroom. On the contrary, Floyd (1983) found that even teachers in rural schools who have limited knowledge about microcomputers have positive attitudes toward their use. Fear of computers does not appear to be associated with teachers' sex or age. The extent to which teachers have had positive experiences with computers, however, does affect their attitudes toward computers (Placke, 1983). Positive experiences can come from meaningful interactions with computers in professional methods courses, especially when students learn concepts concurrently with applying those concepts—that is, with "hands-on" experience. Muller (1978) found that teachers acquired more positive attitudes when they learned concepts and their applications concurrently, instead of first learning the concepts and then learning how to apply them.

EDUCATIONAL SOFTWARE AND CURRICULUM PLANNING

The development of educational software began slowly. Much of the early software was designed to be glamorous but lacked a sound theoretical base—in other words, it was not instructionally sound. Since 1950 there has been considerable progress in the United States toward teacher-developed curricula, following a period of having curricula developed by federal, state, and local agencies. This was a positive shift, but the current trend toward using more prepackaged computer programs threatens to reverse the trend toward teacher-developed curricula.

Armstrong, Henson, and Savage (1993, p. 333) give an account of the transition that educational computer software has experienced:

Much early school-related software was directed at teaching learners computer programming skills. Today, this is a minor emphasis. Instructional software increasingly is oriented to teaching academic content associated with the individual school subjects. For example, software is available that focuses on developing learners' writing skills, on increasing their sophisticated analytical thinking processes through exposure to data associated with simulation activities, and on helping them develop their mechanical drawing proficiency. The best of the new instructional programs require students to confront content and to work actively with it to develop a "product" (a chart, a written response, a formal presentation, or something else that will evidence that higher-level thinking processes have been engaged).

Another promising trend that should improve software quality and availability are the software clearinghouses that evaluate educational software's quality and suitability. For example, California's State Department of Education funds the California Instructional Video Clearinghouse and the California Software Clearinghouse, which review instructional software (Bakker & Piper, 1994).

Emphasis on the Student

As early as the late nineteenth century, student participation in the development of curricula was being encouraged. This was continued in the Progressive Education Era, from World War I to World War II, when student involvement was determined to have more advantages than disadvantages. Students who were involved learned more, were more motivated, developed more self-reliance, and were more creative than their traditional counterparts. Will tomorrow's students be encouraged to improve their curricula? Will they be taught to evaluate their CAI programs and modify them to produce better curricula? Not necessarily.

The 1960s and 1970s brought increased interest in humanizing the curriculum and in values clarification. Many educators considered these to be positive directions. But will developers of educational software continue to produce programs of second-wave mentality—programs that lack imagination and variety? According to Siegel and Davis (1986), there is reason to believe so, as reflected in the great number of computer books written to teach amateurs to program and the very few books that tell how to select educationally sound software.

In the past, curriculum guides tied daily instruction to overall aims. Do we have any assurance that computer programs will do this, or that, even if they do, students and teachers will see the relationships between the two? These are a few of my concerns about the direction and effects of the computer movement on education. The following is a list that includes these and other concerns.

Some Problems and Limitations of Computers in Education

A tendency to overuse drill and practice at the expense of higher levels of application, such as simulation and problem solving

A belief that computers can replace teachers

Dehumanizing effects of CAI

Limited availability of good educational software

Lack of student involvement in program design

Lack of teacher involvement in curriculum development

Use of programs unrelated to educational aims

Emphasis on narrow facts rather than on broad generalizations

Limited opportunities for students to express their ideas orally and in writing

Lack of necessary counseling skills

Lack of opportunities to apply new knowledge

An instructional process so complex that attempts to compare CAI with traditional teaching methods are almost impossible

Uncertainty about the teacher's role

You can probably double the number of entries on this list, yet you should consider CAI as a tool that can become more important as new and better ways to apply it are discovered. Instead of dwelling on computer's limitations and problems in education, take a few minutes to list some advantages computers can bring to education. For each advantage, list ways to increase the likelihood of realizing its potential.

SOURCES OF SOFTWARE

The development of educational software is gaining momentum. Following are the addresses of several sources.

Educational Activities
1937 Grand Avenue
Baldwin, NY 11510

Grolier Electronic Publishing
Sherman Turnpike
Danbury, CT 06816

Learning Arts
P.O. Box 179
Wichita, KS 67201

MicroEd
P.O. Box 24750
Edina, MN 55424

Milliken
1100 Research Boulevard
St. Louis, MO 63132

Scholastic Incorporated
P.O. Box 7502
Jefferson City, MO 65102

SVE
1345 Diversey Parkway
Chicago, IL 60614

Tom Snyder Productions
90 Sherman Street
Cambridge, MA 02140

Unicorn Software
2950 E. Flamingo Road
Las Vegas, NV 89121

Aquarius
P.O. Box 128
Indian Rocks, FL 33535

Broderbund Software
345 Fourth Street
San Francisco, CA 94107

WHAT IS COMPUTER LITERACY?

The term *computer awareness* means knowing about computers. In contrast, computer literacy is often thought to mean knowing enough about computers to function competently in society today. Tomorrow it will mean even more—perhaps including being able to use the computer to counteract its negative effects in U.S. classrooms and in society at large. Even with its current definition, computer literacy means different things to different people. To the professional programmer it means being able to design programs, but to the secondary and middle-level teacher its meaning is not so specific.

Armstrong, Henson, and Savage (1993) contrast technological literacy with technological competency:

Today, technological literacy is no longer enough. Our society is increasingly insisting that employees be "technologically competent." This refers to a level

Today's teachers recognize the need to help students become proficient with computers.

of understanding that goes well beyond technological "literacy." "Competence" suggests the presence of a confident ability to use and extend present technologies and to adapt quickly to new technologies as they emerge. (p. 326)

As a minimum, all teachers share several specific technological needs. Following is a list you can use to measure your own computer proficiency.

- Knowledge of current software in your field
- The ability to evaluate computer software
- Basic programming skills
- Data base skills
- Spread sheet skills
- Word processing skills

Beyond these very basic skills, teachers can benefit from the ability to use computer graphics programs to design transparencies and handouts.

By now, most teachers recognize the need to know more about computers. Current concerns have two major dimensions. First, teachers want to know more about computers so they can use them in their teaching and improve learning in the classroom. Second, teachers want to help students acquire the understandings and skills they need to perform effectively in their future chosen occupations, where computer knowledge will undoubtedly be needed. In other words, today's teachers want to be computer literate themselves, and they want to be able to help their students become computer literate too.

Because these two goals are different—one is practical and teacher oriented, the other is student and future oriented—the exact computer knowledge and skills one teacher or student needs may differ from what others need. For this reason we cannot identify a specific set of computer knowledge and skills that can meet all teachers' needs. But teachers do share certain basic needs. Through its elementary and secondary schools committee, the Association for Computing Machinery recommends that all teachers be able to understand computing (Schall, Leake, & Whitaker, 1986, p. v) and lists the following essential competencies: All teachers should:

1. Be able to read and write simple programs that work correctly and understand how programs and subprograms fit together into systems
2. Have experience using educational application software and documentation
3. Have a working knowledge of computer terminology, particularly as it relates to hardware
4. Know by example, particularly in using computers in education, types of problems that are and some general types of problems that are not currently amenable to computer solution
5. Be able to identify and use alternate sources of current information on computing as it relates to education
6. Be able to discuss at the level of an intelligent layperson some of the history of computing, particularly as it relates to education
7. Be able to discuss moral or human-impact issues of computing as they relate to societal use of computers, generally, and educational use, particularly

---

Reflection

Identifying Your Own Computer Needs

As you begin to sort out the facts, principles, and skills you will need to work with computers, remember to take an inventory of your needs at this time. Begin with yourself, because your needs may be quite different from those of your classmates. Think about your own attitudes toward the computer and the subject(s) you will be teaching and respond to the following questions.

1. How enthusiastic are you about the microcomputer itself?
2. How threatened do you feel by the task of operating machines and equipment such as telephones, televisions, recorders, and typewriters?
3. What special opportunities does your subject offer for students to be creative?
4. Are there certain aspects of your subject that are especially boring?

5. Do you enjoy simulations and games? If so, what about them do you find satisfying?

6. In what type of school system do you plan to seek employment (e.g., Urban, rural, affluent, impoverished, conservative, progressive)?

BASIC AXIOMS OF COMPUTER USE FOR TEACHERS

Many prospective teachers, like many existing teachers, have uncertainties and fears about computers. The following basic content generalizations, in the form of axioms about applying computers to education, will help you sort out your emotional reactions to or doubts about computers as you begin to fill this broad gap in your knowledge and skills. They also give you an opportunity to begin preparing yourself in this area. Computers will be an important part of your future teaching responsibilities.

Application Axioms

The following axioms address the body of computer knowledge you will need to carry out your teaching responsibilities.

Axiom No. 1: There is a definite body of computer knowledge that is indispensable for all teachers. Although computer needs vary among teachers, all teachers need certain basic information. Included is a minimum vocabulary, set out in the Glossary. Teachers also should know the broader generalizations in the field. You can acquire this information by studying the following axioms.

Axiom No. 2: Teachers' computer needs vary from teacher to teacher and location to location. Some individuals have a natural affinity for computer knowledge, to the point that they become engulfed with, even obsessed by, computers. You will notice among your own future students that this natural liking for computers is not limited to adults. Teachers and students who experience this level of excitement about computers should be encouraged to pursue the area of study as much as they desire. For some teachers, computers will never have this level of fascination. Teachers who are not inclined in this direction should not be required to make a lifetime study of computers.

The level to which a particular school system is involved in computers also influences the degree to which teachers must pursue study of computers. Teachers who have computers in their classrooms have greater immediate need for knowledge about computers and their application than do teachers whose school has no computers.

Axiom No. 3: Teachers should first learn to operate the brand(s) of computers that are in their schools. As teachers begin preparing for their future computer responsibilities, one of the first questions is "How many computers should I learn to operate?" Another common remark is, "Once you learn to operate one microcomputer, it is no problem to transfer this knowledge to another brand." The latter statement is not without its limitations. It may be true that someone who has mastered a certain brand of computer and who thoroughly understands how it operates may have little difficulty using other computers. However, although many teachers have become quite adept at writing their own programs, most teachers will not attempt to reach a high level of computer mastery. As teachers become involved with computers, they would be wise to limit the number of brands they work with. An attempt to learn to operate several types of computers at once may lead to confusion, frustration, and discouragement. As we shall see, a positive, confident attitude is important to success here.

Axiom No. 4: Examine your philosophy before selecting a particular brand of computer. An important criterion for selecting a computer is how you intend to use the computer. The answer to this question depends on you. By itself, the computer can do nothing. Your enthusiasm, interest, and priorities will determine the degree to which computers can improve your effectiveness.

Ask two questions as you begin selecting a computer: What can I do with this computer that I could not do without it? And what noninstructional responsibilities that take away from my teaching time can a computer perform for me? In addition, consider the quality of software each brand offers because it may restrict the computer's ability to deliver these goals.

Most teachers would like to have exciting and challenging lessons, but teachers—even the most effective ones—are limited. We are limited by our own abilities to be creative and to develop creative assignments, and we are limited by the many non-teaching chores that befall all teachers. Analyze your goals and limitations before selecting a computer brand.

Axiom No. 5: Teachers should use computers to attain higher-order goals. Those whose familiarity with computers is limited often also have a limited view of the computer's capabilities. They are apt to associate computers with the old teaching machines, whose primary objectives were aimed at facilitating rote memorization. Today's teachers must realize that microcomputer can do much more than drill-and-practice functions. Teachers should use the computer to attain higher instructional goals. For example, many commercial programs require problem solving, and in doing so they help students develop problem-solving skills. Some teachers write their own programs to add new challenges for their students. Indeed, many students are writing their own programs and are learning ways to use the computer to solve a multitude of real, practical problems. Software for instructional goals falls into four general categories: drill and practice, tutorial, simulation, and administrative.

Attitudinal Axioms

Your attitudes and feelings will influence how proficient with the computer you will become. As you examine the next set of axioms, carefully analyze your own attitudes and feelings. Realize that almost everyone has some suspicions and reservations about the computer's abilities to improve learning and that most of us have fears about our own ability to become proficient with the computer.

Axiom No. 6: A confident posture is essential for teacher success with computers. The immediate appearance and rapid distribution of microcomputers, intensified by the thrusting of new computer requirements on teachers (many of whom have had no former contact with computers), has caused a great amount of fear in many teachers throughout the United States. The ultimate question is "What if I can't master the computer?" This is unfortunate and tragic, because confidence is a prerequisite to optimal success with the computer.

Axiom No. 7: All teachers can learn to use computers effectively to improve learning in their classrooms. All teachers and prospective teachers who can meet all other certification requirements can learn to use the computer effectively in their teaching roles. Take a determined stance and view the computer as the tool it is—a tool you can use to help students attain your course objectives.

Axiom No. 8: A proactive posture is essential for teacher success with computers. Although confidence is probably 90 percent of the task of learning to use conventional software, without action you will fall short of your goal. Begin your efforts now, while you are still taking this course. Once you start learning to program, your logical-thinking skills will improve. When this happens, your initial fears will most likely be replaced by enthusiasm and eagerness in your lessons and in other aspects of your teaching role.

Reflection

Analyzing Your Own Attitudes

Read the following paragraph and respond to the questions below.

Most of us have reservations about the computer's potential to make substantial improvements in our classrooms. We also have reservations about our own abilities to learn to master the computer. Because these reservations severely limit your future ability to use the computer effectively, you must search out your own feelings and begin to develop the confident and assertive posture that will help you attain the proficiency you will need.

1. How responsible do you feel for promoting problem-solving skills in your students?
2. Do you believe the microcomputer offers much potential for promoting creative thinking?
3. How would you feel if you were asked to attend a computer in-service program or workshop?
4. What evidence is there that the computer will become a permanent fixture in most American schools?
5. How do you feel about teachers having so many nonteaching responsibilities, which include such clerical tasks as issuing textbooks, maintaining daily attendance records, and collecting money for various projects? Would you be able to use this time more constructively if these tasks could be performed by computers?
6. How do you feel about test-item banks? Do you think it is always better to start from scratch each time you begin developing a test, or do you believe there is an advantage in using questions again and again, perfecting them as needed?

COCURRICULAR AND EXTRACURRICULAR COMPUTER APPLICATIONS

The microcomputer's potential unlimited use to improve instruction in the classroom is perhaps the greatest area of promise it offers teachers, but it is not the only important area of contribution. What follows are two real-life examples of different yet important noninstructional computer applications. Although neither brought about a direct change in instruction, each greatly increased students' ability to learn.

Improving a Local School Program

Improving technology programs in schools is neither easy nor quick if you want permanent improvements. Royal Van Horn (1994) who writes a technology column in the *Phi Delta Kappan,* estimates that converting a conventional school into a high-tech school takes a minimum of four years.

A school district in suburban Indianapolis developed a successful computer application to improve lower-achieving students' academic performance. Some teachers had become concerned that many students were not being challenged to improve their academic performance. The mediocre and poor students received little recognition, no matter how hard they worked. What these students needed was a motivator, an incentive, some kind of recognition. Thus the idea for the "Roaring 500 Club" was born.

Membership in this club was reserved for the 500 students throughout the whole district who had the greatest improvement in each six-week grading period. The computer facilities in the school system were such that a computer program was quickly written to select those 500 students at the end of each grading period. The names of the 500 students who had improved the most during each grading period were incorporated into a large attractive display in a glassed-in case located right inside the main entrance of each school. The display was titled in bold lettering "The Roaring 500 Club." It is the first thing everyone who enters sees.

The advantages are obvious. First, students who had little or no chance of attaining academic recognition under the previous system could now earn recognition. Second, in this program the low achievers had a greater opportunity to succeed than did the straight-A students, who had little margin for improvement.

Improving District and State-wide School Programs

When we think of using the microcomputer to improve instruction, our first thoughts may be limited to unique ways of applying the microcomputer in the classroom. Some fantastic programs are being, and will continue to be, developed at this level, but do not overlook the broader possibilities that the computer offers school systems.

The computer can improve educational programs at state and district levels. State accountability programs continue to grow. By the early 1980s, more than 75 percent of the states had already developed their own accountability programs. For example, one state developed a state-wide accountability program known as AIM (Accountability in Instructional Management) (see Henson [1995], pp. 30–31). This program requires each of the state's 150 school districts to develop a unified curriculum from grade 1 through grade 12. Each program must have objectives, teacher and student activities, and resources for each lesson throughout the year. Furthermore, each objective must have some test items. These curricula must be developed by the teachers working together in their own areas to develop systematic, sequenced lessons. Because each teacher must write objectives and then select activities to teach these objectives, this program's ultimate benefit is that each teacher will be more aware of course objectives and how to attain them. Furthermore, the testing program will measure and reinforce the objectives.

But imagine the logistical chore of having to keep up with hundreds of objectives and thousands of test items. The answer to this complicated problem for many school systems will be the microcomputer. Programs that require a computer to store all the test items and objectives are already available, and on the command of any teacher the computer will randomly select test items and make up a test to match the objectives of a grading period. In fact, because each objective is keyed according to its level in its respective taxonomy domain, the teacher can request a tailor-made test of items designed to fit each group of students. Without the computer, these improvements would be too time-consuming to implement.

Goodspeed (1988) provides a useful checklist for school districts to use. As you examine this checklist, think of ways that you might influence your future school district to provide more technological support.

- Classroom management software should be made available to all teachers throughout the school district.
- School districts and teacher associations should investigate options for teachers to have access to computers in their homes.
- The NEA should help to create interlinked, nationwide interactive networks for teachers.
- Education planners must make strong efforts to ensure that all teachers and students have equitable access to technologies. (p. 16)

RECAP OF MAJOR IDEAS

1. The development of an advanced microprocessor unit in the mid-1970s revolutionized the computer industry, making computers smaller, faster, and cheaper.
2. Other U.S. institutions and professions have been quick to take advantage of the microcomputer to improve their operations.
3. The rapid speed at which school systems are purchasing computers may result in their procuring millions of dollars worth of machines that will not be used effectively.
4. At this time, computer literacy is an ill-defined term. What one teacher

needs to become computer literate may be quite different from what another needs.

5. Although some may believe that the computer movement has more disadvantages than advantages, the microcomputer will have dramatic effects on education in U.S. schools.
6. Base computer selection on intended use and local school setting.
7. Many current and prospective teachers doubt their ability to master the computer at a level necessary to improve their teaching. Yet most if not all can attain these skills and understanding.
8. You must learn to use the computer to teach problem solving and to develop creative thinking, not just for drill and practice.
9. Use computers to take over many nonteaching responsibilities, thus freeing you for several hours each week. Use this time to plan lessons, design programs, examine software, or otherwise improve instruction.
10. When you first begin learning to operate microcomputers, simplify this process by learning to operate only one or two brands.
11. Work with your local administrators and with professional associations to improve classroom technology.

CASES

The success of computer use in any school depends largely on teachers' enthusiasm and determination. As you read the following cases, consider how you would handle each predicament if you were involved.

CASE 1: A FACULTY RESISTS MICROCOMPUTERS

The members of the Parent-Teacher Association at Eastside Middle School decided that their major project for the year would be to purchase three microcomputers—one for the school's administrator and two for students and faculty. A first-year teacher, Larry Worley, was excited when he learned he might have the opportunity to apply his knowledge of computers, but he was shocked to learn later that the majority of the faculty opposed the purchase. In the teacher's lounge he heard two senior faculty members discuss plans to express their concern at the next faculty meeting. They wanted to ask their colleagues to support them in openly opposing the computer purchase. The reasons they gave for their opposition were:

1. Microcomputer use in schools is a fad that will soon pass, leaving thousands of dollars of hardware and software to gather dust in storage.
2. Eastside Middle School serves the town's lower socioeconomic residents. Student performance on standardized tests is consistently below that of other schools in town. Concern for improving the general level of basic skills should take precedence over beginning a new project.

3. Few, if any, teachers at Eastside have any computer expertise.
   Larry wants to stifle these plans to abort the purchase of microcomputers, but he realizes that as a first-year teacher he may not have any influence with the faculty.

Discussion

1. What could a faculty do to ensure computer programs' longevity?

   The most obvious method might be for each teacher to learn more about microcomputers, but this is not likely to occur on an individual basis. Frequently, a group of teachers take the initiative to seek help from outside consultants. Local universities, community colleges, and business and technical colleges are usually eager to develop a special course to teach computer awareness and computer literacy when enough teachers are interested. Should such an approach be chosen, these teachers should involve the school's administrator(s), since the teachers will ultimately need financial support and perhaps time off for the courses.

2. How could one respond to the claim that schools should first do a good job with basic skills before buying computers?

   First, there is a tendency to associate computers with gifted students. Although it may be true that more gifted students than slower students take advantage of computers, this need not happen. Microcomputers offer tremendous potential for students to attain basic skills. Drill-and-practice computer programs can be more motivating than teacher-directed drill and practice.

   As a future teacher, you should try to find ways to use the computer to benefit all students, regardless of their academic ability and interests. In this respect, teaching with the microcomputer is as difficult as traditional teaching. Finding ways to challenge all students has always been difficult, but it has been and continues to be an important responsibility of all teachers.

CASE 2: A PROBLEM OF MORALE

Microcomputers are no novelty at Brookwood High, which for the past five years has served as a testing ground for a privately funded project. By graduation, most Brookwood students have written their own programs, which range from farm management projects that 4-H club members have designed to perform mundane chores, to more sophisticated but less practical individual programs, such as chess and other games designed for amusement.

At the beginning of the school year, each junior and senior student is assigned a microcomputer. Centrally located, these microcomputers are available to students throughout the day. It has been five years since microcomputers were introduced at Brookwood. Student enthusiasm has not diminished, and every day some students continue to forfeit part of their lunch periods for increased time on the computer.

Unfortunately, the computers have failed to bring equal stimulation to the

Brookwood faculty. On the contrary, the experiment initially aroused fears in some faculty members that computers might someday reduce the number of teachers needed. A good publicity program that praises the success of the project keeps this concern alive. Although the teachers seldom discuss the effects of the program, their concerns are manifested in their general behavior toward the students and even toward one another. Sarcasm has become commonplace in Brookwood classrooms, and teachers seldom congregate socially.

Discussion Questions

1. Was the Brookwood teachers' fear of replacement rational?
2. How can you avoid computer-based fear?

ACTIVITIES

1. Consider the direction that the definition of computer literacy has taken. Now try to extend this definition into the future. (Hint: Look at the major trends in U.S. society today, such as increased population, the faster pace of life, and transportation, then consider the effects these will have on numerous lifestyles. Now redefine computer literacy.)
2. Make a list of the advantages the microcomputer offers to secondary and middle schools. Make a corresponding list of disadvantages. Now see if you can find ways to convert any of the disadvantages to advantages. (Hint: Consider the effects on the levels of student involvement and on levels of thinking.)
3. Suppose you have accepted a teaching position in a school that has never used microcomputers. The administration has agreed to purchase a computer for each department, but your department opposes the purchase. Devise a rationale to convince your colleagues that the department needs a microcomputer.

FINAL NOTE

The manuscript for this book was printed out by a microcomputer. The computer operator was a high school English teacher who mastered the microcomputer on her own without any formal instruction.

REFERENCES

Alessi, S. M., & Trollip, S. R. (1991). *Computer-based instruction, methods and development.* Englewood Cliffs, NJ: Prentice Hall.

Armstrong, D. G., Henson, K. T., & Savage, T. V. (1993). *Education: An introduction* (4th ed.) (chap. 13). New York: Macmillan.

Bakker, H. E., & Piper, J. B. (1994). California provides technology evaluations to teachers. *Educational Leadership, 51*(7), 67–68.

Berg, R. (1983). Resisting changes: What the literature says about computers in the social studies classroom. *Social Education, 47,* 314–316.

Betts, F. (1994). On the best of the communication age: A conversation with David Thornburg. *Educational Leadership, 51*(7), 20–23.

Bitter, G. G. (1989). *Microcomputers in education today.* Watsonville, CA: Mitchell.

Chambers, J. A., & Sprecher, J. W. (1980). Computer assisted instruction: Current trends and critical issues. In *Communications of the ACM.* New York: Association for Computing Machinery.

Dagenais, R. J. (1994). Professional development of teachers and administrators: Yesterday, today, and tomorrow, the views of Robert Anderson. *Kappa Delta Pi Record, 30*(2), 50–54.

Edinger, M. (1994). Empowering young writers with technology. *Educational Leadership, 51*(7), 58–60.

Eller, B. F., & Henson, K. T. (in press). *Educational psychology for effective teaching.* Atlanta: West Publishers.

Floyd, M. A. (1983). *An investigation of public school teachers: Knowledge about, attitude toward and willingness to use microcomputers as instructional tools.* Unpublished doctoral dissertation, Pennsylvania State University.

Garrison, D. R. (1989). *Understanding distance education.* London: Routledge.

Geisert, G., & Dunn, R. (1991, March–April). Effective use of computers: Assignments based on individual learning style. *The Clearing House, 64*(4), 219–223.

Goodspeed, J. (1988). Two million microcomputers now used in U.S. schools. *Electronic Learning, 7*(8), 16.

Henson, K. T. (1984). *The status of microcomputers in colleges of education in major American universities.* Unpublished manuscript.

Henson, K. T. (1995). *Curriculum development for education reform.* New York: Harper Collins.

Lewis, A. (1994). Reinventing local school governance. *Phi Delta Kappan, 75*(5), 356–357.

Lockard, J., Abrams, P. D., & Many, W. A. (1990). *Microcomputers for educators.* Glenville, IL: Scott/Foresman/Little, Brown Higher Education.

Magney, J. (1990). Game-based teaching. *Education Digest, 60*(5), 54–57.

Mecklenburger, J. A. (1990, October). Educational technology is not enough. *Phi Delta Kappan, 72*(2), 105–108.

Muller, G. E. (1978). *The effects on teacher knowledge, attitude, and classroom behavior of simulated practice versus application of behavior management techniques during in-service instruction.* Unpublished doctoral dissertation, University of Texas at Austin.

Placke, J. E. (1983). *A study of the relationship between teacher attitude toward computers and leadership styles.* Unpublished doctoral dissertation, University of Tulsa, Tulsa, OK.

Price, R. V. (1991). *Computer aided instruction: A guide for authors.* Belmont, CA: Brooks/Cole.

Rock, H. M., & Cummings, A. (1994). Can videodiscs improve student outcomes? *Educational Leadership, 51*(7), 46–50.

Rothstein, P. R. (1990). *Educational psychology.* New York: McGraw Hill.

Schall, W. E., Leake, L., Jr., & Whitaker, D. R. (1986). *Computer education: Literacy and beyond.* Monterey, CA: Brooks/Cole.

Siegel, M. A., & Davis, D. M. (1986). *Understanding computer-based education.* New York: Random House.

Taggert, L. (1994). Student autobiographies with a twist of technology. *Educational Leadership, 51*(7), 34–35.

Van Horn, R. (1994). Power tools: Building high-tech schools. *Phi Delta Kappan, 76* (1), 90–91.

SUGGESTED READINGS

Baker, C. C. (Ed.), & Ogle L. T. (Assoc. Ed.) (1989). *The condition of education, 1989* (Vol. 1). *Elementary and secondary education.* Washington, DC: National Center for Education Statistics.

Becker, H. J. (1986). *Instructional uses of school computer: Report from the 1985 National Survey.* Baltimore, MD: Johns Hopkins University, Center for Social Organization of Schools.

Evans, B. (1968). *Dictionary of quotations.* New York: Delacorte Press.

Grunwald, P. (1990, October). The new generation of information systems. *Phi Delta Kappan, 72*(2), 113–114.

Hancock, V., & Betts, F. (1994). From the lagging to the leading edge. *Educational Leadership, 51*(7), 24–27.

International Society for the Study of Technology in Education (1990). *Vision test: Three Rs for education.* Eugene, OR: ISTE.

Lepper, M. R., & Gurtner, J. L. (1989). Children and computers: Approaching the twenty-first century. *American Psychologist, 44,* 170–179.

Levinson, E. (1990, October). Will technology transform education or will the schools-co-opt technology? *Phi Delta Kappan,* 121–126.

Pawloski, B. (1994). How I found out about Internet. *Educational Leadership, 51*(7), 69–73.

Phillips, J. (1989, June). CD-ROM: A new research and study skills tool for the classroom. *Electronic Learning,* pp. 40–41.

Seal-Warner, C. (1988). Interactive video systems: Their promise and educational potential. In R. O. McClintock (Ed.), *Computing and education: The second frontier* (pp. 22–23). New York: Teachers College.

Washor, E., & Couture, D. (1990, December). A distance learning system that pays all its own costs. *T.H.E. Journal, 7*(8), 62–64.

Watson, B. (1990, October). The wired classroom: American education goes on-line. *Phi Delta Kappan,* 109–112.

part FIVE

Classroom Management

By this time you are probably wondering when we are going to get to the heart of the matter and discuss the teacher's role in the classroom. After all, such topics as discipline, classroom management, and motivation are the survival skills—without them, everything else you might learn about teaching becomes insignificant. Without good discipline, management, and motivation skills, today's teacher will have a short career. These skills are not merely desirable or important—they are indispensable.

As you read, think beyond the survival point. Effective instruction demands interaction with students. The higher levels of thinking are best achieved through dialectic teaching, where the teacher and students share ideas. You must establish a climate where student-student and teacher-student interaction occur freely.

chapter 12

Motivation

No man can reveal to you aught but that which already lies half asleep in the dawning of your knowledge.

Kahlil Gibran

OBJECTIVES

List 10 techniques for stimulating student interest.

Explain how competition motivates students.

Name two ways a teacher can solicit parents' cooperation.

Explain Piaget's concept of "equilibrium."

Role-play a teacher being confronted by an angry parent.

State the relationship between self-concept and motivation.

Describe the teacher's main responsibility in developing students' self-concepts.

Explain the teacher's role in using humor in the classroom.

Give three guidelines for using grade contracts.

List five guidelines for using reinforcement in the classroom.

Explain this statement: "Motivation is learning."

PRETEST

	Agree	Disagree	Uncertain
1. The more reinforcement the better.	____	____	____
2. The U.S. family has become more closely knit in recent years.	____	____	____
3. Teacher enthusiasm cannot be planned.	____	____	____
4. Effective motivation requires a variety of strategies.	____	____	____
5. Teachers must tell students how to apply highly theoretical knowledge.	____	____	____
6. The family is becoming less important in children's education.	____	____	____
7. All teachers should allow their students to succeed every day.	____	____	____
8. Humor in the classroom succeeds best when it is systematically planned to fit the lesson.	____	____	____
9. Behavior modification is an example of internal motivation.	____	____	____

Today's world has many qualities that militate against students' progress in school. Earlier generations of teachers could always call Johnny's parents if his interests took a downward turn. But efforts to ensure student success today do not have such sup-

---

Middle-Level Message

William Alexander, the father of the middle school, advised that the middle school should serve not just the intellect but the whole child. This chapter will show you how to relate better to the whole child. This is essential for motivating the transescent. For example, you will learn to use humor and enthusiasm to stimulate student interest. You will also learn how to protect students' self-concepts and nurture them toward positive growth.

As you read this chapter, think about the relationship between the emotional self and cognitive development and how you can apply the understanding shared through Piaget's work to your own teaching career. Remember that although you cannot make your students succeed, you must create a climate that encourages and facilitates their achievement. This means that you must motivate your students.

---

port. Even worse, the world is becoming an increasingly difficult place for young people. Miller (1994, p. 207) expresses this concern: "The numbers of adolescents facing significant life difficulties are growing."

Hootstein (1994) reported on a teacher who asked students what motivational strategies they would use if they could become the teacher. Their responses in rank order of popularity were:

acting

watch videos and films

play games for review

give more sense of control

Although teachers recognize the need to motivate all students, obstacles often prevent them from doing so. Hootstein (1994) found that the main obstacles to motivation are lack of time and lack of funding.

The family, as it was once thought of, no longer exists for most students. In 1989, when the Massachusetts Mutual Life Insurance Company asked 1,200 randomly selected adults to describe the word "family," only 22 percent picked the traditional definition of a group of people related by blood, marriage, or adoption; about 75 percent selected "a group of people who love and care for each other" (Seligmann, 1989).

Stefanich (1990) says that students' levels of motivation are often proportional to the degree to which they see relationships between their curricula and their outside lives:

Soon after beginning school, many students that come from cultures which do not reflect the European traditions, make a decision that there is no relationship between what they learn at school and the world which exists outside the school. . . . It is not surprising that these students become passive in educational settings. (p. 48)

Although Stefanich cites members of cultural minority groups as being estranged from their curricula, mainstream ethnic group members may be estranged as well.

Do not assume that students who are not interested in the lesson are not motivated. Borich (1988) defines motivation as what energizes or directs a learner's attention, emotions, and activities. According to this definition, all students are motivated by something. The teacher must find ways to redirect the attention of those students who are not interested in the lesson.

Teachers daily face uninterested students who, skeptical of the teacher's wares, feel that their time and energy could be spent more wisely elsewhere. You are largely responsible for changing these attitudes. Effective teachers exert much control over learning.

The prudent teacher is very aware that the classroom environment and the attitude of teachers, peers, and parents all affect the student's motivation to interact socially and succeed academically (Bandura, 1986). Peer pressure's negative effects on achievement are well known. The 1994 Gallup Poll (Elam, Rose, & Gallup, p. 52) reported that 88 percent of the public consider negative attitudes of peers important and 63 percent consider the effects very important. Brophy and Good (1986) say that measures of teacher control typically relate either positively or curvilinearly to achievement. Effective teachers use praise frequently, ask more questions, and move their classes at a brisk pace.

Having just spent four or five years studying a particular subject, you may assume, like other enthusiastic young teachers, that others share at least some of this interest. This assumption is dangerous. Instead, you would be wiser to analyze students and identify any existing interests about the subject. Once you identify any, you may kindle a spark of interest into a more serious commitment.

But can a teacher really make all students like a particular subject and every lesson? This is an excellent question, the answer to which is no. Motivation is a prerequisite to learning. In fact, it is more; motivation *is* learning (Campbell, 1990). You can no more interest students against their will than you can force students to learn. Your best strategy is to entice students, but before you can do this successfully your students must have an appropriate mind-set toward the subject, toward themselves, and toward you, the teacher. "It is only when several strategies are carefully and systematically integrated that substantial improvements in learning become possible" (Guskey, 1990, p. 12).

The 26th Annual Phi Delta Kappa/Gallup Poll of the public's attitudes toward the public schools (Elam, Rose, & Gallup, 1994) found that three-fourths of the public think that the schools should promote both a common cultural tradition and the diverse cultural traditions of America's different population groups.

Farris (1990, p. 22), notes that "recognizing the needs of students and focusing on meeting those needs in the classroom are ways to generate solutions to motivation problems."

STUDENT ATTITUDES TOWARD THE SUBJECT

Although many students dislike studying, others are interested in learning. If members from both groups described the subjects they were taking in school, they would choose very different adjectives. This is true for every subject—some students actually love it, others hate it. Most who hate it find it boring, difficult, or both. The wellspring for motivation is the search for understanding, or attempting to comprehend why events happen (Weiner, 1979). Let us first look at the students who find your subject boring and learn what you can do about it.

Students are concerned with relevance. They are confronted with so much knowledge that they must be highly selective, choosing what they can use. Therefore teachers must show students how to apply what they are learning to practical problems, preferably in their own lives. For example, math ratios may bore some students until they learn to use them to determine their automobile's power and economy. One fullsize station wagon retained the same size engine and relatively the same carburetor from one year to the next, but the manufacturer changed the ratio in the transmission, resulting in a gas-mileage loss of more than 33 percent. Other students may find ratios useless until they realize that they use them daily in cooking.

The wise teacher prepares a response to the age-old question "Why do we have to study this stuff?" After all, it does seem unfair to force students to listen to something they perceive as useless. A textbook cannot provide this answer. It must come from you. You might begin by analyzing your own reasons for enjoying the subject. Take a moment now and list a few reasons why you majored in your subject. Now look at your list of reasons and determine how each can convince an uninterested student that this subject is worth studying. If your explanations seem ineffective, consider other ways you might convince students of your subject's worth. Try to recall your teachers' successful efforts. Perhaps they used demonstrations, anecdotes, or personal examples to awaken your interest. Can you think of a few techniques to stimulate your students? Imagine you are introducing a new unit of study. How might you use each of the following approaches to gain everyone's attention?

Demonstration	Questioning session
Problem	Debate
Personal experience	Joke
Group assignment	Discussion

Remember that students always see things in terms of their experiences, not yours. Can you alter each of your ideas to fit your class's age-group?

Learning flourishes when students are involved vigorously. Involvement is a prerequisite for maximum learning. Wiske (1994, p. 19) says that "understanding is . . . a capacity developed through the free exchange of ideas." Students need an opportunity to develop their own theories, which is unlikely to occur in classrooms where students are passive. When students are not permitted to discuss their theories they may harbor many misunderstandings. Heckman, Confer, and Hakim (1994) insist that students' theories are quite different than their teachers think they are. This is not to imply that the teacher's theories are always correct. All concepts are tentative (Gardner & Boix-Mansilla, 1994). For example, you could have students help with the demonstration. Remember, though, that involvement is a better motivator when it is meaningful. Also allow students to participate in the demonstration itself. With the problems approach, you might introduce a puzzle for everyone to work. When you use personal experiences, you could ask for volunteers to share their own experiences.

Were you able to think of ways to increase student involvement in the other areas? If not, give it another try. Once you begin to think of classrooms as places where students are always active, it becomes easier to plan meaningful experiences.

Reflection

Abraham Maslow Speaks about Intrinsic Learning

Read the following paragraph and respond to the questions below.

> To understand the breadth of the role of the teacher, a differentiation has to be made between extrinsic learning and intrinsic learning. Extrinsic learning is based on the goals of the teacher, not on the values of the learner. Intrinsic learning, on the other hand, is learning to be and to become a human being, and a particular human being. It is the learning that accompanies the profound personal experiences in our lives. . . . As I go back in my own life, I find my greatest education experiences, the ones I value most in retrospect, were highly personal, highly subjective, very poignant combinations of the emotional and the cognitive. Some insight was accompanied by all sorts of autonomic nervous system fireworks that felt very good at the time and which left as a residue the insight that has remained with me forever. (Maslow, 1973, p. 159)

Such personal relationships with students affect the learning that occurs in classrooms. Brophy and Evertson (1976) found that more achievement occurs in classrooms where teachers take a teacher-student approach. This reinforces the need for teachers to involve students in planning and executing lessons. Solicit student suggestions about content selection and classroom activities, and use reasonable student-generated suggestions.

1. What does Maslow mean by intrinsic learning?
2. What is the teacher's role in promoting intrinsic learning?
3. How would you explain intrinsic learning in terms of the domains of the educational taxonomies? More exactly, which two of the domains does Maslow address? What does he say about the relationship between these two domains?

STUDENT ATTITUDES TOWARD THEMSELVES

Motivation depends on self-perception. Each student comes to your room with a definite self-image as a person and as a student. A negative image is a strong barrier against learning. Your job is to recognize these attitudes so that you can help the student change a negative self-concept. The task may seem monumental, but one of the greatest rewards of teaching is knowing that you will help some students find themselves and discover their own potential. Unfortunately, not all students have this experience—some drop out of school before making that discovery. Others just seem to putter along, somehow managing to get through high school or complete a high school equivalency program. Some of those who go to college come to realize that they can do more than even they ever believed.

You may hear a teacher say, "It's not my fault if they bring these attitudes to my class." This may be true. The fault may belong to previous teachers, parents, friends, or the student. But that is not the point. Teachers must know that they can become powerful negative motivators simply by the way they relate to students. Therefore, avoid making negative comments to the student or about the student, such as "You know him—he's a hopeless case" or "Her entire family is that way—dumb." Another common remark of teachers is "You can't make a sculpture out of mud." But remember that, at first, all clay looks a great deal like mud!

Teachers can and should help all students feel good about themselves. Schomoker (1990) explains the responsibility that effective teachers assume for ensuring that students earn the recognition that is so important in classroom motivation:

> [Self-esteem] has become less a quality to be slowly earned than one quickly and easily given—not something wrought but spontaneously realized. The emphasis is more on creating good feelings than on connecting self-respect to effort and attainment. . . . There is something sadly comical about whole auditoriums full of students being told, indiscriminately, to feel good about themselves, even to stand up (I've seen this) and give testimonials on how much they like themselves. (p. 55)

Jenkins (1994, p. 270) also warns against using unearned compliments to improve self-esteem: "Don't make kids reinforcement junkies. . . . Real self-esteem comes not from hollow praise or little prizes given for effortless tasks, but from accomplishing something difficult."

Not everyone is an Einstein, and we cannot always mold people into the patterns we design, but that is not your role. Your role is to provide a climate in which students can see their own strengths, believe in themselves, and become what they want to become (Combs, 1962). They must perceive the possibility of success before they attempt something. Once they experience success repeatedly, they have a good chance of succeeding in any field of endeavor, school or otherwise. It is worth repeating: Students who perceive themselves as good students will work hard to protect that image, just as athletes with good reputations are willing to give it their very best.

The old cliche "success breeds success" is very true, but it does not explain how the teacher can help students who are not usually successful to succeed. Actually, no teacher can make anyone succeed. All you can do is create a climate conducive to learning, experimenting, or even failing. Some failure is inevitable and must be expected. What is important is how your students perceive and respond to failure, not the failure itself. If they see failure as defeat it can be devastating, but if you teach them to see failure as stumbling blocks for growth, they can learn and grow from their mistakes.

ARTS EDUCATION AFFECTS STUDENTS' ATTITUDES TOWARD THEMSELVES

A recent study at Florida State University has shown that arts education, when integrated throughout the curriculum, can promote learning in various subjects. Although the research does not show firm cause-effect relationships, there is reason to believe that arts-integrated instruction can stimulate learning. Sautter (1994) explains:

> Years of experience among arts educators and classroom teachers who use the arts to motivate and instruct students, thousands of successful artists-in-residence programs over the last 25 years, and a growing body of research in arts education all strongly suggest that education in and through the arts can play a significant role in changing the agenda, environment, methods, and effectiveness of ordinary elementary and secondary schools. (p. 433)

The arts-integrated curriculum can help students enrich their expression, enrich their knowledge in other subjects, give them another way of perceiving, and improve their performance in all their subjects. The College of Education Examination Board found that students who took more than four years of music and art scored 34 points higher on the verbal sections of the Scholastic Aptitude Test (SAT) and 18 points higher on the math sections than students who took less than a year of these subjects (Sautter, 1994).

STUDENT ATTITUDES TOWARD THE TEACHER

What teacher qualities are important to you? Close your eyes for a moment and think of the best teacher you ever had. Can you remember and list the five most important qualities that made you like that teacher?

Now compare your list with the results of a survey taken to determine what teacher characteristics students prefer most. Did you include a statement that tells how the teacher felt about you? The students in the survey did. In fact, the most frequently mentioned quality was that the "favorite" teacher was concerned about the student—and in a very special way. The ideal teacher was determined to see that the student achieved in the subject and took whatever time necessary, in class or out, to explain the subject. An expert in the subject, this teacher knew how to get things across and was even willing to help students in areas other than academics.

The teacher's expertise in the subject also affects students' attitudes toward the teacher; however, the day has long since passed when students valued their teachers' knowledge more than their attitudes toward their students, if indeed this were ever true. As Fielding and Pearson noted (1994, p. 66), "Recently, the process of allowing students to build, express, and defend their own interpretations has become a revalued goal of text discussion." Such practice reflects the nature of constructivism.

The profile of a good teacher is beginning to emerge, and this profile extends beyond knowledge and teaching skills—it includes how the teacher actually feels about the subject and the students. Few students will get excited about a subject if it appears to bore the teacher (Figure 12.1). A teacher who shows excitement or a serious love for the subject entices students to seek the reason for that excitement. Students develop positive attitudes toward teachers who are enthusiastic and task-oriented and present the material clearly (McConnell, 1977).

Another teacher quality that rated high in the survey was humor. Educators are just beginning to learn about the role humor plays in motivation. Described as a social lubricant (Lemke, 1982), humor can relax the class in tense moments. For the prospective teacher, many questions quickly emerge: "How can I use humor when I can't even tell a joke? How much humor should I allow? And by encouraging humor, am I inviting discipline problems?"

One of the strongest messages is relayed to students by the teacher's willingness to take time to listen to students and hear their concerns. In a survey of personal qualities of excellent teachers, two-thirds of the students rated these instructors as those who "are willing to listen" (Buckner & Bickel, 1991, p. 26). In another survey of personal qualities of excellent teachers, two-thirds of the students rated these instructors as "those who are respectful toward students, accept students, are easy to talk with, demonstrate warmth and kindness, and are friendly" (Buckner & Bickel, 1991, p. 26). The personal teacher qualities that students rated highest are shown in Table 12.1. The top quality on this list—willingness to listen to their students—can be understood by considering the following passage by Gardner and Boix-Mansilla (1994, p. 18):

"The most important answers are those that individuals ultimately craft for themselves, based on their disciplinary understandings, their personal experiences, and their own feelings and values."

A special study for the National Center for Education Statistics (Special Study Panel on Education Indicators for the National Center for Education Statistics, 1991) recognized the importance of personalization in effective schools:

FIGURE 12.1 An epitaph for student victims

TABLE 12.1   Rank order of "very important" middle school teacher personal characteristics N = 394

Excellent Teachers . . .	†f	%
1. Are willing to listen	325	82.5
2. Are respectful toward students	302	76.7
3. Accept students	291	73.9
4. Are easy to talk with	288	73.1
5. Demonstrate warmth and kindness	274	69.5
6. Are friendly	260	66.2
7. Are enthusiastic	232	58.9
8. Are optimistic	201	51.0
9. Are flexible	173	44.9
10. Are humorous	160	40.6
11. Are spontaneous	152	38.6
12. Look like they feel good about themselves	120	30.5

† Frequency of responses

SOURCE: Buckner, J. H., & Bickel, F. (1991, January) If you want to know about effective teaching, why not ask your middle school kids? *Middle School Journal, 22*(3), 27. Used with permission.

Personal accounts of school dropouts describe schools as places that are often large, bureaucratic, and impersonal. In contrast, good schools are described as having a human scale in which concern for the students and cooperation are highly valued. Even if large, the ethic that "every student matters" is made real in the day-to-day life and interactions within the school. Teachers try to know and engage each student. Students believe that teachers are interested in them and care about their progress. Cooperation characterizes the relationships among adults as well. (p. 77)

THE ROLE OF HUMOR

Baughman's Handbook of Humor in Education (Baughman, 1974) says that effective classroom humor is not always planned: humor is better described as an attitude or philosophy. In other words, the teacher's role is to accept humor. The students will provide the creativity and the delivery skills if you provide a climate for humor to develop. As Weber and Roff (1983, p. 38) note, "[Humor] can be used to remove tension." It should be gentle because "sarcasm endangers student-teacher relationships and student feelings of self worth" (Weber & Roff, 1985, p. 39). The current literature will help you learn new ways to use humor in your classes.

The concern about discipline is justified. You do not want your classroom to turn into a circus. Achievement is higher where serious misbehavior is minimal (Evertson, Emmer, & Brophy, 1980). You can control the humor by establishing an understanding that it must be kept clean in content and vocabulary and that rudeness is not permitted. Sarcasm and ridicule endanger both the teacher-student relationship and students' feelings of self-worth (Charles, 1981; Gnagey, 1981). Short interruptions in a serious lesson might provide needed relaxation, because humor is psychologically relaxing. But you must keep such interruptions short.

It is easy to return to the lesson if the lesson is interesting and well structured. For this reason, a good lesson plan with clear objectives and adequate student involvement is indispensable to classroom motivation. The pace should be crisp, and students should remain challenged. For students to learn in an informal setting, however, you must have a well-structured lesson planned. A balance must be achieved. Do not become so enslaved to a lesson plan that you lose the students along the way.

How informal should a class be? A good rule of thumb is to make each class as informal as possible, retaining only enough structure to move through the lesson systematically, according to the plan. When the students become especially interested in a part of the lesson, allow time for discussing that part, but always return to the lesson plan.

Reflection

Reread John Steinbeck's speech in the beginning of Chapter 1. After you have reread this brief passage, respond to the following questions.

1. What techniques did Steinbeck's teacher use to motivate her students?
2. Steinbeck suggests that, in addition to her techniques for motivating students, this teacher had a special quality. Can you remember that quality? Can it be learned?
3. Defend or challenge Steinbeck's assertion that teaching is an art (as opposed to a science).
4. Identify the best teacher you have ever had. List four or five of this teacher's most important qualities.
5. Examine your list of teacher qualities in the preceding response. Does your favorite teacher meet Steinbeck's criteria for a "real" teacher?

ENTHUSIASM

You can talk at length about the importance of learning a particular subject or about certain information being essential to future learning, but unless you yourself appear to be interested in a lesson, your words will probably go unheard. On the other hand, if each day you are excited about the lesson, students will wonder what you find so interesting.

To behave enthusiastically does not mean becoming overly emotional, yet you cannot afford to be nonchalant or just mildly interested. You need not compete with the entertainment world, because what you have to offer—useful knowledge and leadership—is better than entertainment. When you explain why the lesson is being pursued and how it can be applied, you want to be taken seriously.

How can you appear both serious and excited? Think for a moment about the college courses you are taking now, and select a class you really enjoy. How would you describe the teacher? Does the teacher speak in a monotone? Does the teacher read a lecture to the class each day? Is the teacher afraid to let the class laugh a little when a humorous incident occurs? Does the teacher always sit behind a desk and require you to sit at your desk? Probably not. Most teachers we enjoy are neither foolishly funny nor extremely straightlaced, but they probably are intensely interested in the subject. For most teachers this is not a problem as long as their lesson has been well planned. Through mastering their subjects, teachers develop intellectual authority. Ironically, teachers must learn that their ownership of knowledge is always provisional. As Wiske (1994, p. 20) explains, "Intellectual authority is provisional because truth is debatable." As noted by Fielding and Pearson (1994, p. 66), "Recently the process of allowing students to build, express, and defend their own interpretations has become a revalued goal of text discussions."

KEEPING STUDENTS CHALLENGED

The most important type of behavior is internal. It often follows success. According to Jean Piaget, each individual strives to achieve and maintain a state of equilibrium (Evans, 1973). In other words, when students see inconsistency in information, they are internally motivated to remove that inconsistency. Figure 12.2 shows how a student's learning progresses in steps or plateaus. The distance from A_1 to $A_2\{$ represents a quest for learning as it is being satisfied. When satisfaction is reached at $A_2\{$, the stu-

FIGURE 12.2 The learning pattern

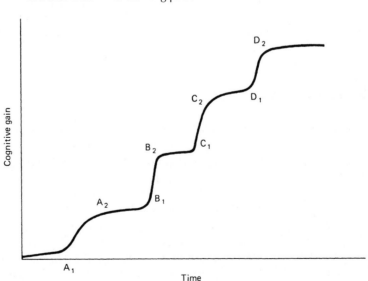

dent is in a state of equilibrium and remains there until another contradiction arises at B$_1$ (Evans, 1973). Each time students satisfy the reason for an apparent inconsistency in information, they gain a higher plateau and reach a state of equilibrium in their thinking.

Do not allow students to become idle when they level off. Always be prepared to present students with further contradictions to their knowledge.

Does this suggest that your role is to introduce problems or contradictions purposely to puzzle students instead of helping students find answers? Piaget would answer yes.

In simple terms, a contradiction occurs when students discover that understandings they hold contradict or appear to contradict each other. The teacher guides students to realize that they lack certain knowledge and then provides one or more learning experiences to help them gain necessary understanding. There is no force-feeding. Students must internally want to erase this contradiction. Once learning has occurred, those students are at peace, resting on a plateau. The teacher must then make them aware of another contradiction, and the whole process repeats itself. This is motivation by keeping the student challenged—my interpretation of Piaget's theory of equilibrium.

Presenting too many contradictions at one time can have a nonmotivating effect. When faced with what seems to be an impossible task, students will tend to give up, feeling that they cannot succeed.

You can increase student interest dramatically simply by increasing the academic demands in the classroom: Today's students want to be challenged more. Most teachers do not realize it, but many students are bored because teachers do not adequately challenge them (Frymier, 1979). A 1985 Gallup Poll supported this claim. Approximately half the teenagers contacted throughout the nation said that students do not have to work hard enough in school or on homework (Gallup, 1985). Even the learning materials in most schools are not interesting. According to Frymier (1979), 70 to 90 percent of the curricula are low in their ability to motivate, to stimulate creativity, and to challenge students' intellect. Therefore, the teacher must initiate the challenge by introducing more rigorous, yet relevant, knowledge and activities.

CLARIFYING GOALS AND PROCEDURES

As we saw in Chapters 2, 3, and 4, students will work more intensely when they know where they are headed and how to get there. Unfortunately, teachers and students do not talk much about content's meaning and purpose. In fact, teachers seldom give feedback, even when students make mistakes (Anderson, 1983). When students lose sight of the goals, they often lose interest. When they do not understand how to do assigned tasks, they become frustrated and discouraged. In both cases poor work is usually the result.

Each task should begin with a clarification of the expected outcome. In other words, show your students how to recognize the answer, or concept or principle, when they find it. To be sure that students understand the proper procedures, you might begin each assignment by working a simple problem and then having the students work another problem collectively. Encourage questions and have students help one another with the sample problem.

Once you give the assignment, however, your job is far from over. Some students will still have questions about goals and procedures. Now you can help by circulating among the students and answering individual questions as they arise. Your availability and concern will motivate students who need help to ask questions.

Another way teachers can communicate their concern for students is by following up on each assignment. Such follow-ups increase the probability that students will complete the assignments (Phelps, 1991).

USING STUDENTS' OPINIONS

Make a special effort to seek students' opinions, letting them know that you value their suggestions, their likes and their dislikes, and above all their judgment. Giving them an opportunity to voice their ideas can help identify misconceptions. Until people have had an opportunity to express their opinions, they are not apt to consider others' opinions. In addition, just knowing that their questions and opinions are valued is great motivation. Consider one or more teachers you had who appeared to be intolerant of your questions or concerns. You probably soon lost the desire to ask about anything, and you probably also lost some respect for yourself and for those teachers.

STUDENT CONTRACTS AS MOTIVATORS

Contracts were introduced in Chapter 7. Now let us examine their power to motivate. There are basically two kinds of student contracts: behavior contracts and grade contracts. Both are contingency contracts, and both affect behavior.

Behavior Contracts

A behavior contract is an agreement between the student and the teacher that if a student behaves in a specified manner the teacher will reward that behavior in a certain way. The reward for good behavior might range from a piece of candy for young children to free time for older students. Several authors have reported successful contingency contracting (Redmon & Farris, 1985; Salend, 1987).

Grade Contracts

Competition among students can have serious side-effects—such as making the less capable feel inept, alienating students from their peers, and encouraging snobbishness in high achievers, but competition can be a strong motivator too. Americans are a competitive people, and the competitive attitude has been largely responsible for this nation's rapid development.

FIGURE 12.3   Student contract for art history

Grade Requirements

A	Meet the requirements for the grade of B and visit a local art gallery. Sketch an example of a gothic painting. Visit a carpenter-gothic-style house and sketch the house. Show at least three similarities in the two products.
B	Meet the requirements for the grade of C and name and draw an example of each of the major classes of columns used in buildings.
C	Meet the requirements for the grade of D and submit a notebook record of the major developments in art since 1900, naming at least six major painting styles and two authors of each style.
D	Attend class regularly and participate in all classroom activities.
I	_____ agree to work for the grade of _____ as described in this contract.

One way to retain the motivation and avoid the undesirable side-effects is to encourage students to compete with themselves. Many of the best athletes do this. In fact, once golfers or bowlers become too interested in others' performance, their own performance often fails. Like bowling and golf, learning is in certain respects an individual activity in which learners compete with themselves. They are always challenged, yet they find that success is possible.

You can use student contracts to encourage students to compete with themselves. Unlike most teacher-made tests, which are norm-referenced and force students to compete with their classmates, student contracts are criterion-referenced and set the student only against the tasks at hand. Most contracts run for the duration of a grading period. Figure 12.3 is an example of a contract for a unit on art history.

To encourage students to be realistic in their expectations, you may stipulate that students can lower their expectations at any time, but the contract may contain a built-in penalty for any alterations. Most contracts do not permit students to raise their grade expectation, but in designing your contracts, try to fit them to your particular students' needs. The major disadvantage of using contracts is that you will need additional time to design, complete, and keep up with a large number of contracts.

GRADES, TESTS, PROJECTS

Many teachers believe that unannounced tests and threats of assigning low grades can be effective motivators, but research does not support this. When tests and threats are used in the traditional manner, the downgraded students continue to fail. Low test scores can also be discouraging, especially if the teacher does nothing to help the student acquire the missed knowledge and skills. Unfortunately, teachers and students spend very little effort on reviewing and building skills that have not been learned (Chansky, 1962). Another study found that anxiety produced by grades actually lowered middle-ability students' grades (Phillips, 1962). So it appears that, although tests themselves can be sources of learning when time is spent going over the material covered, the use of tests or grades (or threats of either) to motivate is a serious misuse of tests that will not significantly increase students' motivational level.

But, when used correctly, tests can spark students' interest in content. Markle, Johnston, Geer, & Meichtry (1990) explain:

> The power of tests and other evaluation procedures to shape students' perceptions of their teachers' expectations cannot be overestimated. Teachers can motivate students to strive for understanding by using evaluation procedures that determine how well new information can be related to other knowledge and how well students can use the newly taught information to solve novel problems. (p. 56)

Term Projects

Individual or group term projects can be a highly motivating device in secondary and middle schools when correctly used. First, they must be truly term projects—lasting the entire term. This gives students time to select and research their chosen area of study. You can provide a list of topics to suggest ideas and boundaries, but you should let students choose their own particular project.

To increase motivation, find ways to display the projects. A science fair, art exhibit, or similar event is an excellent means of exposure. Parents and relatives can spur on the investigators and whet their enthusiasm.

Role playing can be motivating.

Assignments for Extra Credit

Assignments for extra credit are common in many classrooms, yet they have limited power to stimulate interest. In fact, they often have the opposite effect. If extra credit assignments are to motivate positively, the task must be meaningful and must be selected far in advance of the end of the term, preferably at the beginning of the term or study unit. Giving a student an opportunity to copy a 10,000-word report from an encyclopedia at the end of a semester is likely to produce a negative attitude toward learning rather than increase the student's motivation.

Extra Assignments for Corrective Measures

A major mistake that many teachers continue to make is assigning extra classwork or homework in an attempt to correct misbehavior (e.g., assigning extra math problems or a written report to a student who becomes too loud or too active in class). Wasicsko (1994, p. 25) says, "One of the worst sins a teacher can commit is to use school work as punishment."

OTHER STRATEGIES

Reward and Reinforcement

Rewards can be an important motivator or stimulator of student interest. Substantial use of corrective feedback in the academic areas, praise for correct or proper behavior, and making use of students' ideas to let them know that their contributions are valued all have a positive relationship to achievement and attitudes (Gage & Berliner, 1984). Some students work to please their teachers; others watch their teachers closely for feedback to assure them they are achieving at an acceptable rate. Your use of rewards can reinforce both types of students. Clark and Starr (1976, p. 55) offer the following suggestions for teachers who want to improve their skills using rewards:

Techniques for Improving the Use of Rewards
1. Reward new [good] behavior every time it occurs.
2. Once a student becomes established, gradually reduce the frequency of reinforcement until the reinforcement comes at occasional and haphazard intervals.
3. At first, reward the behavior as soon as it occurs. Then, as students become more confident, delay the reward somewhat.
4. Select rewards that are suitable for the individual pupils.
5. With recalcitrant or resistive pupils, begin by giving small rewards.
6. Use contingency contracts.

Students need reinforcement on a regular basis. Phelps (1991, p. 241) offers an example of daily use of a motivational strategy: "Teachers who 'shine the spotlight' on at least one student each day are more likely to see positive student behavior than teachers who merely recognize negative behaviors."

Behavior Modification

In education, behavior modification, like contingency contracts, is an agreement. Instead of earning grades, however, the student earns certain stated rewards for displaying specified types of behavior or for completing certain tasks. Behavior modification is more popular in middle schools; it is much more difficult to find adequate reinforcers for high school students (Warshaw, 1975). One reinforcer that has proved effective for secondary school classes is free time the student earns through certain specified performance. For example, in one English grammar class a 75 percent level of bad behavior was reduced to 15 percent by a contract that rewarded proper behavior by giving free time (Sapp, 1973).

In one program for a predominantly inner-city class of underachievers that provided the opportunity to earn free time, listen to records, read comic books, play games, receive candy bars and bubble gum, and participate in planning class activities, the average student grades rose from D to B and class attendance rose from 50 to 80 percent (Sapp, 1973). You should not expect such dramatic effects in every case, but these results are encouraging.

SUMMARY

Because any one technique for motivation is apt to produce different results with each application and each group of students, you will probably profit more if you concentrate less on specific techniques and more on general strategies for motivating students. Here is a summary of these strategies:

1. Be honest with students. Don't pretend to know everything. It is far more important to be a teacher who is approachable than a teacher who is impeccable.
2. Use the subject to motivate. Emphasize the areas of knowledge that have special appeal to each class's particular age-group.
3. Be pragmatic. Show students how they can use the knowledge in their daily lives.
4. Use a variety of approaches. For each topic of study, select the approach(es) you believe will best stimulate student interest.
5. Involve all students. Actively involve all students in each lesson. Remember that in a sense all individuals are motivated. The teacher's challenge is to provide meaningful activities for students to pursue—activities that lead to the discovery of knowledge and relationships pertinent to the lesson.
6. Be positive. Students work harder and achieve more when they feel competent in what they are doing. Serious use of reinforcement can improve students' self-confidence.

7. Be personal. Don't be afraid to relate to students on a personal basis. Teachers who remain formal at all times build barriers between themselves and their students.
8. Use humor. Don't be afraid to enjoy your students. There's no time when student attention is more completely captured than when humor is occurring. Relax occasionally and let it happen.
9. Be enthusiastic. Plan into the lesson events that you will enjoy. Enthusiasm is highly contagious.
10. Challenge your students. Nothing is more boring than a lesson that fails to challenge the learners. Keep the pace brisk yet within students' reach.
11. Use self-competition to motivate. Self-competition is challenging because all students can realistically compete with themselves. Grade contracts make expectations clear.
12. Use rewards to reinforce positive behavior. Start rewarding all good behavior, then gradually decrease the frequency of the rewards.

Savage (1991) gives three general suggestions for applying motivation in the classroom. These guidelines provide a nice conclusion for this chapter:

> Three factors of motivation can be helpful as teachers seek to apply motivation theory in the classroom: the needs and interest of the individual, the perception of the difficulty of the task, and the probability of success. If the teacher can relate school tasks to the interests and the needs of youngsters, reduce the perception of effort required to an acceptable level, and increase the probability of success, the resultant increased attention to school tasks and decrease of discipline problems will help make teaching a very rewarding career. (p. 53)

The opportunities that teachers have to motivate their students are growing, and the future is exciting. For example, new microcomputer software offers exciting ways to motivate students. Magney (1990, p. 56) explains: "Under the research microscope, the computer gaming curriculum comes off as clearly superior to conventional teaching on the affective dimension, both fostering higher levels of student interest and in promoting positive attitudes toward subject matter."

RECAP OF MAJOR IDEAS

1. You must convince students that the topics they study are worthwhile to them. This requires basing motivational efforts on students' perspectives, which may differ from yours.
2. Do not try to compete with the entertainment world. Teachers offer leadership, a quality that middle and high school students need in their often unstructured lives.
3. You cannot force students to become interested in a lesson. At best, you can only spark student interest.

4. Application is an important avenue to motivation. Strive to show students how they can apply the material you teach to their daily lives.
5. Involving all students in lessons is a great motivation technique, yet teachers and students seldom discuss a lesson's purpose.
6. Positive student self-concepts are strong motivators, whereas negative concepts undermine your efforts to motivate.
7. Humor holds much potential for motivation. Successful use of humor does not require you to entertain students constantly. By relaxing the classroom atmosphere, you can allow natural humor to develop among the students.
8. Thorough planning and a well-structured lesson will enable you to be less formal. A controlled degree of informality can contribute to students' motivational level.
9. Teacher enthusiasm is an indispensable element in motivation. You can ensure your own excitement by planning into each lesson activities that both the students and you will enjoy.
10. Class tempo affects students' motivational level. Students tend to be more highly motivated when the lesson is fast enough to challenge them but not so fast that it confuses them.
11. Clarify goals. Students are more interested when they know what they are doing.
12. Give rewards and reinforcement only when students succeed. Therefore, assign tasks students can perform well.
13. Space reinforcement at varying intervals.
14. Personal teacher-student relationships increase students' level of interest.
15. Use several strategies to achieve an effectively motivated classroom.

CASES

You must include motivation strategies in each daily lesson plan. As you read the following cases, begin making a list of strategies that you will use each day and throughout the year to elevate your own enthusiasm level as well as your students'.

CASE 1: A STUDENT IS LABELED A FAILURE

Mike Creswell was a quiet boy, although a bit mischievous at times. He often blushed and bowed his head whenever Jane, his teacher, spoke his name in the classroom. Jane's heart went out to Mike because he reminded her of an animal that had been kicked around so much it never knew when more punishment was coming. Mike appeared to distrust everyone, which probably explains why he had no close friends.

Jane met Mike's parents at a social affair and noticed that his father avoided mentioning that Mike was in her class. When she became convinced that he was not going to bring it up, Jane simply stated that she was pleased to have Mike in her class. Mr. Creswell immediately apologized for his son's inadequacies and then quickly changed the subject to another son, who was more academically inclined. Jane could see that Mr. Creswell was ashamed of Mike and that he did not really like the boy.

Through talking with other teachers, Jane learned that Mike's father constantly yelled at him at home, and some past incidents showed that Mike was actually beaten when he failed to live up to his father's expectations. Jane guessed that Mike preferred the beatings to the verbal downgrading, because the pain of physical punishment is temporary but the pain of being told you are unable to measure up never ends.

Some students never get over the damage their parents and teachers do by measuring them against a brother or sister who performed better in school. Most youths do not have the insight to see that what they can and do achieve is important, regardless of how much more or less someone else achieves. Unfortunately, many adults measure students against their parents.

Jane began encouraging Mike and verbally rewarding him for each task he performed successfully. By the end of the year, the quality of Mike's work had improved, and he had begun to relate better to her and to some of his classmates.

Discussion

1. If a parent of one of your students seems ashamed of the child, how should you react?

    The parent who is ashamed of a son or daughter will probably try to avoid discussing the child. Many teachers feel obligated to talk about the student at every opportunity without being obvious about it. The parent who reacts to an apparent weakness by ignoring the child is not behaving in an acceptable way. You can encourage discussion of the child's weakness with the parent if the weakness does exist. You can always offer to help the parent help the child correct it. You may be able to think of other approaches that suit your personality more.

2. How could the teacher make Mr. Creswell proud of his son?

    The teacher could initiate discussions about the areas in which Mike is most capable, which may or may not be academic. By checking Mike's cumulative records, standardized examination scores, and previous grades and by talking with other teachers, the teacher could identify Mike's strong areas. This would provide topics for discussion with Mr. Creswell.

3. How can you encourage other students to associate with a lonely child?

    By assigning the student tasks that the student can do, you allow the student to experience some success, and peers will begin to take notice. You can also assign group projects, making sure that the student can contribute to the group's assignment.

4. How can the teacher convince a parent not to compare one sibling with another?

    Emphasize that individuals excel in different areas. Furthermore, remind the parent that a child's failure to achieve does not always indicate lack of ability, but could indicate that the teacher or parents have failed to motivate the student.

A Final Note: Although state laws vary, Jane is responsible to report to the law any evidence that suggests a student is being physically abused. The school administrators and especially the counselor should become involved.

CASE 2: A STUDENT TEACHER USES THREATS TO MOTIVATE

Bob Wright was eager to begin student teaching. On the first day that Ms. Lee, his supervisor, visited, Bob was presenting a well-organized lesson. He had a beautiful outline on the board and was discussing some interesting topics. However, the students were complacent and appeared to be unconcerned. The supervisor did not mention this to Bob, leaving him unaware of the students' response, or lack of it. During later observations, it was obvious that Bob had noticed something was wrong and was becoming upset with the students because they seemed so uninterested. Throughout the period he would remark, "You had better pay attention because this will be on our next test." Some of the few who initially were interested began to lose interest.

Ms. Lee suggested to Bob that instead of threatening to give a test he try actually giving the test, that each time he caught himself on the verge of saying "You had better . . . or else" he should go ahead and administer the "or else." By the end of the semester Bob's class was having healthy discussions. The students began listening to Bob and interacting with him.

Discussion

1. Is the teacher justified in giving a pop quiz when students fail to complete homework assignments?

    Probably not, unless the teacher believes that the failure is the result of laziness and the quiz will motivate. The teacher's energy would be better spent improving lessons. Using pop quizzes can even lead to punishing students for what is really the teacher's inadequacy. An announced quiz set at a specific time each week would probably be a stronger motivator than an unannounced quiz. How do you feel about the use of pop quizzes to motivate? Can you defend your position?

2. How did Bob use the idea of a test?

    Bob used tests as a force to coerce students to study. His students' success probably occurred because he involved them in discussions and not because he gave unannounced tests. Students can be led to understand the worthwhile uses of test results. By using a test as a weapon against student misbehavior, the idea of testing becomes negative. Threatening students in any way is poor teaching practice.

CASE 3: A TEACHER RUNS OUT OF MATERIAL

The day had finally arrived for Mrs. King to begin teaching her own classes. It was exciting just to hear her describe the experience in the teacher's lounge later that morning. All had not gone well, however, and some teachers recalled similar experiences early in their own careers.

Mrs. King's first class started well. She had a well-structured lesson that immediately captured the class's attention. When after a few moments she realized that the students were more interested in the lesson than in her, she felt relieved, and the first half of the hour went well. Time passed quickly and so did the lesson, and suddenly it was all over. The material was covered, but there were a good 15 minutes left in the period. What could she do?

Mrs. King did not have much experience, but she did not lack creativity. She immediately decided to review the lesson, but when this was accomplished in five minutes she was again at the point of panic. Then one student asked a question. From Mrs. King's report, the question was apparently answered thoroughly, since all 10 remaining minutes were used in answering that one question. It was not an experience Mrs. King wanted to repeat. She began thinking of ways to avoid the task of stalling and ad-libbing to kill time.

Discussion Questions

1. What can a teacher do to prevent running out of planned lesson material?
2. If there are no questions, how can a teacher fill the remainder of a class period?

ACTIVITIES

The following activities will help you plan for a more stimulating climate in the classroom.

1. Examine your own personal traits. For each adjective you use to describe yourself, describe at least one way you can use this trait to make your class environment more interesting.
2. A degree of informality seems essential for maximum motivation in the classroom. Student teachers often ask, "How informal can I or should I be with my students without having them take advantage of my friendship?" Make a list of ways you can show your concern for your students. For each of these, explain how you can prepare to prevent their taking unfair advantage. It may be helpful if you decide at this time exactly where you will draw the line.

REFERENCES

Anderson, L. (1983, April). *Achievement-related differences in students' responses to seatwork.* Paper presented at the annual conference of the American Educational Research Association, Montreal.

Bandura, A. (1986). *Social foundations of thought and action.* Englewood Cliffs, NJ: Prentice-Hall.

Baughman, M. D. (1974). *Baughman's handbook of humor in education.* New York: Parker.

Borich, G. D. (1988). *Effective teaching methods.* Columbus, OH: Merrill.

Brophy, J., & Good, T. L. (1986). Teacher behavior and student achievement. In Merlin C. Whittrock (Ed.), *Handbook of research on teaching* (3rd ed.) (p. 337). New York: Macmillan,

Buckner, J. H., & Bickel, F. (1991, January). If you want to know about effective teaching, why not ask your middle school kids? *Middle School Journal, 22*(3), 26-29.

Campbell, L. P. (1990, September–October). Philosophy = methodology = motivation = learning. *The Clearing House, 64*(1), 21-22.

Chansky, N. M. (1962). The X-ray of the school mark. *Educational Forum, 12,* 347-352.

Charles, C. (1981). *Building classroom discipline: From models to practice.* New York: Longman.

Clark, L. H., & Starr, I. S. (1976). *Secondary school teaching methods.* New York: Macmillan.

Combs, A. (Ed.) (1962 Yearbook of the Association for Supervision and Curriculum Development). *Perceiving, behaving, becoming.* Washington, DC: Association for Supervision and Curriculum Development.

Elam, S. M., Rose, L. C., & Gallup, A. M. (1994). The 26th annual Phi Delta Kappa Gallup poll of the public's attitudes toward the public schools. *Phi Delta Kappan, 76*(1), 41-56.

Evans, R. I. (1973). *Jean Piaget: The man and his ideas* (3rd ed.) (p. 141). New York: Dutton.

Evertson, C., Emmer, E., & Brophy, J. (1980). Predictors of effective teaching in junior high mathematics classrooms. *Journal for Research in Mathematics Education, 11,* 167-168.

Farris, R. A. (1990, November). Meeting their needs: Motivating middle level learners. *Middle School Journal, 22,* 22-26.

Fielding, L. G., & Pearson, P. D. (1994). Reading comprehension: What works. *Educational Leadership, 51*(5), 62-67.

Frymier, J. (1979, February). Keynote speech at Southwest Educational Research Association. Houston, TX.

Gage, N. L., & Berliner, D. C. (1984). *Educational psychology* (3rd ed.). Boston: Houghton Mifflin.

Gallup, A. M. (1985). The seventeenth annual Gallup poll of the public's attitude toward the public schools. *Phi Delta Kappan, 67,* 35-47.

Gardner, H., & Boix-Mansilla, V. (1994). Teaching for understanding within and across the disciplines. *Educational Leadership, 51*(5), 14-18.

Gnagney, W. J. (1981). *Motivating classroom discipline.* New York: Longman.

Guskey, T. R. (1990, February). Integrating innovations. *Educational Leadership, 47,* 11-15.

Heckman, P. E., Confer, C. B., & Hakim, D. C. (1994). Planting seeds: Understanding through investigation. *Educational Leadership, 51*(5), 36-39.

Hootstein, E. W. (1994). Motivating students to learn. *The Clearing House, 67*(4), 213-216.

Jenkins, D. R. (1994). An eight step plan for teaching responsibility. *The Clearing House, 67*(5), 269-270.

Lemke, J. L. (1982, April). *Classroom communication of science.* Final report to National Science Foundation/Rising to Individual Scholastic Excellence.

Magney, J. (1990). Game-based teaching. *Education Digest, 60*(5), 54-57.

Markle, G., Johnston, J. H., Geer, C., & Meichtry, Y. (1990, November). Teaching for understanding. *Middle School Journal, 22*(2), 53-57.

Maslow, A. (1973). What is a taoistic teacher? In L. J. Rubin (Ed.), *Facts and feelings in the classroom.* New York: Walker.

McConnell, J. (1977). *Relationships between selected teacher behaviors and attitudes/achievements of algebra classes.* Paper presented at the annual meeting of the American Educational Research Association.

Miller, D. (1994). Using literature to build self-esteem in adolescents with learning and behavior problems. *The Clearing House, 67*(4), 207-211.

Phelps, P. H. (1991, March–April). Helping teachers excel as classroom teachers. *The Clearing House, 64*(4), 241-242.

Phillips, B. (1962). Sex, social class, and anxiety as sources of variation in school activity. *Journal of Educational Psychology, 53,* 361-362.

Redmon, W. K., & Farris, H. E. (1985, January). Improving the academic productivity of high school students through behavior contracting: A model project. *Journal of Instructional Psychology, 12,* 46-58.

Salend, S. J. (1987). Contingency management systems. *Academic Therapy, 22,* 245-253.

Sapp, G. L. (1973). Classroom management and student involvement. *High School Journal, 56,* 276-283.

Sautter, R. C. (1994). An arts education school reform strategy. *Phi Delta Kappan, 75*(6), 432-437.

Savage, T. V. (1991). *Discipline for self-control.* Englewood Cliffs, NJ: Prentice-Hall.

Schomoker, M. (1990). Sentimentalizing self-esteem. *The Education Digest, 60*(7), 55-56.

Seligmann, J. (1989, Winter/Spring). Variations on a theme. *Newsweek, 22*(2), 38-46.

Special Study Panel on Education Indicators for the National Center for Education Statistics (1991, September). *Education Counts.* Washington, DC: U.S. Department of Education.

Stefanich, G. P. (1990, November). Cycles of cognition. *Middle School Journal, 22*(2), 47-52.

Warshaw, M. (1975, August). Behavior modification in secondary schools. *Educational Technology, 15*(8), 25-52.

Weber, W. A., & Roff, L. A. (1983). A review of the teacher education literature on classroom management. In W. A. Weber, L. A. Roff, J. Crawford, & C. Robinson (Eds.), *Classroom management: Reviews of the teacher education and research literature.* Princeton: Educational Testing Service.

Weiner, B. (1979). A theory of motivation for some classroom experiences. *Journal of Educational Psychology, 71,* 2-25.

Wiske, M. S. (1994). How teaching for understanding changes the rules in the classroom. *Educational Leadership, 51*(5), 19-21.

SUGGESTED READINGS

Augustine, D. K., Gruber, K. D., & Hanson, L. R. (1989-1990). Cooperation works! *Educational Leadership, 47*(4), 8-11.

Barth, R. S. (1990). A personal vision of a good school. *Phi Delta Kappan, 71,* 512-516.

Brophy, J., & Evertson, C. (1976). Learning from teaching: A developmental perspective. Boston: Allyn & Bacon.

Cornbleth, C., & Korth, W. (1983, April). *Doing the work: Teacher prospectus and meanings of responsibility.* Paper presented at the annual meeting of the American Educational Research Association, Montreal.

Diamond, S. C. (1991, March–April). Working with disturbed adolescents. *The Clearing House, 64,* 232-234.

Gibran, K. (1987). In Robert I. Fitzhenry (Ed.), *Barnes & Noble book of quotations.* New York: Harper & Row.

Johnson, D. W., & Johnson, R. (1989-1990). Social skills for successful group work. *Educational Leadership, 47*(4), 29-33.

Kagan, S. (1989-1990). On cooperative learning: A conversation with Spencer Kagan. *Educational Leadership, 47*(4), 8-11.

Manning, M. L., & Lucking, R. (1991, January–February). The what, why, and how of cooperative learning. *The Clearing House, 64*(3), 152–156.

Pinsker, M., Porter, S., Seaton, C., Beasley, R., Legg, P., & Tester, C. (1985, September). Project success: A contingency model for ninth grade. *National Association of Secondary School Principals Bulletin, 69,* 127–129.

Scott, P. (1993). *Case studies in teacher education: Reflection on diversity.* Unpublished manuscript. Tallahassee, Fl.: Florida State University.

Wasicsko, M. M., & Ross, S. M. (1994). How to create discipline problems. *The Clearing House, 67*(5), 248–251.

chapter 13

From Discipline
to Self-Discipline

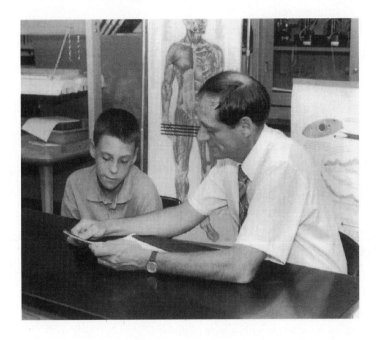

Good discipline is a by-product of interesting, exciting, and engaging instruction.
C. M. Evertson

OBJECTIVES

Give two reasons why teachers must not rely on power and punishment for discipline.

Contrast two different approaches to classroom discipline.

Describe the public's attitude toward discipline in today's secondary and middle schools.

Define discipline in terms of order and control.

Explain the relationship between quietness and discipline.

List three guidelines for conducting a private talk with a student who has misbehaved.

Tell what is wrong with the adage "Be tough at first and relax the rules as time passes."

Describe at least one way that the teacher's role in discipline has changed.

Explain the role of teacher efficacy in classroom discipline.

PRETEST

	Agree	Disagree	Uncertain
1. Truly effective discipline and classroom management are inseparable terms.	____	____	____
2. The American public perceives discipline as the greatest problem in U.S. schools today.	____	____	____
3. Discipline is the same as restraint.	____	____	____
4. Physical punishment is sometimes the best approach to resolve a discipline problem.	____	____	____
5. A quiet class is usually a well-disciplined one, and a noisy class is usually undisciplined.	____	____	____
6. At the beginning of the year, the teacher should be strict, since it is easier to loosen the rules than to strengthen them.	____	____	____
7. Discipline models should be consistent with accepted learning theories and with management theories in other fields.	____	____	____
8. The ultimate goal should be to get students to discipline themselves.	____	____	____

9. Teachers can become good disciplinarians without understanding psychology.   _____   _____   _____

10. The pros of corporal punishment outweigh its cons.   _____   _____   _____

Middle-Level Message

Discipline presents a special challenge for the middle-level teacher. A recent survey shows that most middle-level teachers feel a strong need for more classroom management skills. The best approach is a preventive one. Use this chapter to learn how to prevent discipline problems. Avoid relying on your position of authority or, worse, corporal punishment to achieve discipline in your classes.

Your position as teacher should get you through the first five minutes of your career. From then on, you will need the knowledge and skills offered in this chapter. To survive, you must master them. As the teacher, you must learn how to earn your students' respect and cooperation. Only then can you lead them to a state of self-discipline. Do not settle for anything less.

A PREVIEW OF DISCIPLINE

Following a brief period of secondary and middle school classroom observations for a seminar, a group of pre-service college students gave the following reports.

Report 1

The eighth-grade English class was a farce. Chaos prevailed. At any one time it was impossible to tell who had the floor. Despite the teacher's efforts to gain control and focus the students' attention on the lesson, the discussion resembled a racquetball, forever bouncing in undetermined directions. The teacher's repeated reprimands and threats to the reluctant learners were evidence that the teacher did want to gain control of the situation, but each lesson was like all others—the teacher simply had no control. Each day students made little if any cognitive gain.

Report 2

The junior biology class was all business. When the teacher looked over his pair of narrow bifocals a deadly silence fell over the room. Everyone knew who had control. When each daily lecture began, students sat upright and took notes. When seats were assigned, there were no disruptions, no discussion, and no questions. No one even thought about getting off task in this class. When the bell rang at the beginning of the period, it signaled the end of all social interaction. Even such nonverbal communications as smiles and nods of approval were seldom seen.

Report 3

Sixth grade was time for enjoying learning. Each day the students arrived alive with curiosity. Students brought with them truths captured as insects, rocks, leaves, and other treasures they often carried in their hands and pockets. When the class began, they always knew the daily objectives and how each activity led to one or more of those objectives. Almost every student felt capable of mastering the class's goals. But the classroom's organization and structure did not get in the way of learning or of enjoying each lesson. They also did not cause unnecessary quiet. In fact, this sixth-grade class was usually quite noisy. Somehow even private conversations seemed to focus at least to some degree on the topics being studied. Although a constant chattering and buzzing characterized the class, the teacher seemed able to get the students' attention.

A 1991 Gallup Poll (Elam, Rose, & Gallup, 1991) cited discipline and drugs as the public's two major concerns about U.S. schools. In fact, discipline and drugs have been the major concerns every year for the 23 years that this poll has been conducted. The public perceives the discipline problem in the U.S. schools to be so great that Elam, Rose, and Gallup (1991, p. 56) drew the following conclusions:

Views on Discipline

The public is thoroughly consistent in its perceptions that (1) students in the public schools of the U.S. lack discipline and (2) improved discipline is the answer to many of the schools' problems.

In the 1991 poll the general public ranked discipline second among the biggest problems with which public schools in their communities must deal, gave a disciplined environment (free of drugs and violence) the number-one ranking among the six national goals, ranked maintenance of student discipline second among factors important to parents in choosing a public school for their child, and rated firmer discipline first among suggestions for helping low-income and racial or ethnic minority students succeed in school.

These perceptions clash with the opinions of teachers, who usually perceive discipline problems to be much less serious than parents' lack of interest and support, lack of proper financial support, and pupils' lack of interest and truancy as major problems. Either the public has been misled, or the teachers are mistaken. Wherever the truth lies, this discrepancy in perceptions is a cause for serious concern.

The rapid deterioration of youth's behavior is reflected in the 1994 Gallup Poll, which reported that "for the first time ever 'fighting', 'violence' and 'gangs' shared the number one position with lack of discipline" (Elam, Rose, & Gallup, 1994, p. 42). Yet some of the concern results from the increased media attention this topic receives.

This poll also reported that only a small percentage of teachers and students felt that violence has increased in the past year.

DISCIPLINE: A DEFINITION

Discipline is defined in many ways. In the past, the term was associated with such concepts as punishment, restraint, and forced behavior, but many educators now reject such negative interpretations. A more contemporary view of discipline involves such concepts as order and control. Because order implies direction, discipline might be defined as a climate that is controlled to provide order. Even the manner in which teachers introduce control varies. The manner in which teachers give directives can affect whether students obey or ignore those directives. Hanny (1994, p. 252) gives some practical advice: "Avoid making statements intended to change behavior by using the interrogatives." For example, instead of saying, "Will you sit down?", it is better to say, "Please sit down," giving them no choice.

Reflection

Some, possibly most, contemporary educators reject the use of excessive force and constraint in the name of discipline. Yet some insist that force and even punishment are essential for disciplining certain students who, they maintain, do not understand anything else. These educators say that the teacher is justified, even obligated, to use whatever measures are necessary to discipline their students. What is your position on this issue? Do you agree with either of these extremes?

DESIRABLE TEACHER ATTITUDES TOWARD DISCIPLINE

Discipline Is a Must

Discipline, defined as order and control, is essential. Because each teacher must ensure that maximum learning occurs in the classroom, each teacher is responsible for maintaining the discipline necessary to meet this goal. Following is one author's explanation of why all teachers must learn to manage their classes. Phelps (1991) says:

> One of the most difficult challenges beginning teachers face is classroom management. If teachers do not succeed in this aspect of teaching, then their instructional efforts may fail as well. Many otherwise good teachers have left the profession because of their inability to manage the classroom effectively. (p. 241)

Hanny (1994, p. 252) reinforces Phelp's assertion that all teachers must maintain an organized and controlled classroom climate: "You must have rules and the consequences of breaking them must be clear." McDaniel (1994, p. 247) echoes the importance of having effective discipline and management skills: "The principles and practices of effective discipline and classroom management are among the most important professional concerns that practicing educators must deal with daily."

Discipline and Instruction

Deciding how to manage the classroom to prevent and control behavioral problems depends to a large degree on the type of instruction. For example, during a lecture—even a very short lecture—students must listen to the teacher or to classmates who are asking or answering questions. But during a problem-solving lesson such as an inquiry lesson, a simulation game, or a case study, talking and sometimes moving around are not only tolerated but may even be required if the lesson is to succeed. Constructivist teachers recognize that students often require more activity to develop understanding, activity that disrupt a lecture.

Attaining affective and psychomotor objectives may require even more interaction among students. Teachers who use an eclectic approach, choosing to lecture for part of a period and then using a student-centered approach such as giving small discussions for the rest of the period, should be more tolerant of productive noise and movement during the latter part of the period. To avoid sending a confusing message to students, explain why more noise and movement are permitted at one time but not another.

Some constants are vital during all types of lessons (e.g., a high level of respect for everyone and continuous focus on the lesson objectives). Student-centered lessons should not alter either of these goals; noise and movement should be productive, which can happen only in a climate of respect and focus. Focus is likely to be maintained only if the teacher begins the lesson, and indeed each part of the lesson, by reminding students of the objectives set for each teacher activity and each student activity.

Too often, students either listen passively or even participate in excellent activities without being aware of the lesson's major concepts. Near the end of each lesson, you should lead the students in reflecting on the major concepts addressed. After the lesson, at your first opportunity, reflect on the activities and whether they worked or not; vow to improve the lesson before teaching it again.

Use of Nonverbal Communications

Through their actions, teachers can communicate their attitudes and their expectations. Grubaugh (1989, p. 34) explains the importance of using nonverbal communications in classroom management and offers an example of how teachers can use this tool: The instructional setting and the teacher's nonverbal (body) language give students extremely strong impressions about a teacher's management and disciplinary intentions, tolerances, strengths, and weaknesses. In nearly all instances, the sound of people speaking rises and falls in patterns or waves. Time your remarks at the trough of a wave of sound in the classroom so that you can begin speaking in a softer voice to set a more quiet tone (Grubaugh, 1989, p. 38).

Some teachers already have a tremendous influence on their students' behavior, and all teachers can attain this influence. Thompson (1994, p. 264) suggests the use of a nonintrusive approach to problem management: "There is no purpose in making a major crises out of every disciplinary situation." Teachers must realize they have this capacity. A desirable attitude is: As the teacher, I must and will establish and maintain in my classroom the climate necessary for maximum learning. Such an attitude makes students feel secure and is apt to earn more respect for a teacher than an attitude of doubt and insecurity.

Because discipline and instruction are inseparable, all good teachers are concerned with discipline: MacNaughton and Johns (1991) explain:

> Good school and classroom discipline is not necessarily something that is attained once and for all. Schools, student body characteristics, and teacher backgrounds and personalities are all subject to change. This requires that you keep working at management and discipline much the same way as you would curriculum development. (p. 56)

Teachers must prepare to manage their classrooms. As Ban (1994, p. 257) says: "Teaching school poses no more formidable challenge than managing student behavior."

TEACHER EFFICACY

Teacher efficacy or teachers' belief in their ability to ensure their students' success influences classroom behavior more than most people realized until recently. Many teachers believe that they cannot control their students, which they want to be able to do. In 1991, the National Center for Education Statistics reported the results of a 1988 study that found that about one-third of all high school teachers felt that they had little or no disciplinary control over their students (Figure 13.1).

The types of behaviors now considered serious show the extent of discipline problems in the schools (Table 13.1).

But there is more at stake than the teacher's survival that makes discipline a must for all teachers, and as Savage (1991, p. 204) explains, teachers not only have the right to discipline students, they do not have the right not to. Savage says, "Teachers should not think that they have no rights, nor should misbehaving students interfere with their right to teach and the right of others to learn." Hanny (1994, p. 252) shares this belief: "Those who want to learn have a right not to be disrupted by others."

FIGURE 13.1 Teacher disciplinary control over classrooms

SOURCE: National Center for Education Statistics. (1991). *Education counts.* Washington, D.C.: U.S. Department of Education, p. 20.

TABLE 13.1   The top problems perceived in schools in 1940 and 1982.

1940	1982
1. Talking	1. Rape
2. Chewing gum	2. Robbery
3. Making noise	3. Assault
4. Running in the halls	4. Burglary
5. Getting out of turn in line	5. Arson
6. Wearing improper clothing	6. Bombings
7. Not putting paper in wastebaskets	7. Murder
	8. Suicide
	9. Absenteeism
	10. Vandalism
	11. Extortion
	12. Drug abuse
	13. Alcohol abuse
	14. Gang warfare
	15. Pregnancy
	16. Abortion
	17. Venereal disease

SOURCE: Reprinted from *Harper's Magazine,* March 1985, and the Presidential Biblical Scoreboard with permission from the Biblical News Service, Costa Mesa, California. Taken from Johnston, W. J. (1985), *Education on Trial* (p. 20). San Francisco: ICS Press.

Teachers must know and accept their responsibility to establish and maintain discipline, because that is a prerequisite to achieving good behavior in most classrooms. Good discipline does not just happen; it begins with certain teacher attitudes. Teachers must accept responsibility for classroom discipline, and "each teacher must find the discipline techniques most congruent with his or her educational philosophy and individual student needs" (Bell & Stefanich, 1984, p. 134).

Furthermore, instruction in classroom management can diminish behavior problems and improve learning. Evertson (1989, p. 90) studied these effects and reported that "this study supports the position that giving teachers opportunities to plan and develop academic and administrative routines that keep students productively engaged and keep inappropriate behavior to a minimum results in preserving instructional time."

A predictable pattern of how teachers view discipline occurs as teachers mature. Compare the difference in the way student teachers have been reported to view discipline with the assumptions that two experts use to describe discipline in their book. Pre-service teachers tend to see problem behavior not as a result of the environment but rather as an intentional and controllable act by the student (Cunningham, 1989). In their book *Comprehensive Classroom Management,* Jones and Jones (1986, p. 333) present five key assumptions relative to effective classroom management:

1. Classroom management should be based on a solid understanding of students' personal, psychological and learning needs.

2. Classroom management involves establishing positive teacher-student and peer relationships that help meet students' basic psychological needs.
3. Classroom management involves employing classroom organization and group management methods that maximize on-task student behavior.
4. Classroom management involves using instructional methods that facilitate optimal learning by responding to the academic needs of individual students and the classroom group.
5. Classroom management includes the ability to employ a wide range of counseling and behavioral methods that involve students in examining and correcting their inappropriate behavior.

These qualities (clear objectives, high expectations, regular homework, and careful monitoring) do not make the environment in effective schools rigid. Rather, these demands on students are balanced by a climate that reflects concern for all students. As Gathercoal (1990, p. 23) explains: "Effective schools try to adapt to the child, not adapt the child to the school."

Educators' perception of the teacher's role in managing student behavior has changed over the years. Initially, the use of negative responses to misbehavior was stressed. Jones (1989) explains:

Historically teachers often depended on a loud voice, a paddle or some other form of intimidation to maintain control. Until very recently many teachers were presented with such oversimplified generalizations as don't smile until Christmas and don't grin until Thanksgiving. However, during the past two decades researchers have conducted both correlational and experimental studies the results of which suggest a variety of teacher behaviors that are associated with positive student behavior and student achievement gains. (p. 330)

But the latter half of this century saw a shift from teachers' negative response to bad behavior to teachers' positive, preventive behavior. As Jones (1988) has said:

A new emphasis on classroom management was developed during the 1970s. This new direction emphasized not what teachers did in response to student misconduct, but rather how teachers prevented or contributed to students' misbehavior. This research, later labeled Teacher Effectiveness, has focused attention on three sets of teacher behaviors that influence students' behavior and learning: (1) Student-teacher relationships, (2) teachers' skill in organizing and managing classroom activities, and (3) teachers' instructional skills. (p. 331)

Too often teachers get a very narrow view of the causes of behavior problems. Others have noted this problem. Jones (1989, p. 333) said: "Researchers, writers and trainers have presented various aspects of classroom management as isolated, often relatively simple solutions to a complex problem." McDaniel (1994, p. 255) reminds educators that problems in the classroom often develop outside the classroom and are transported to the classroom: "The school is indeed a microcosm of the world outside." Oana (1993, p. 5) says this more emphatically: "The problem is, today's schools, no matter how much they change, cannot cope with all the social ills its clients bring to their doors each day."

A Focus on Learning

There have been some major shifts in the ways discipline has been defined over the years. Paramount among these is a recent tendency to substitute the term *classroom management* for discipline. The major difference is that classroom management is generally more positive. It connotes skills and leadership, but more important it implies a specific purpose—which is to develop and maintain a classroom climate that maximizes learning. This placing of learning as the basis for decision making is another important teacher attitude. Teacher remedies for discipline problems today can be grouped into two categories: reactive and proactive. Proactive discipline is predicated on the necessity for forethought, anticipation, preparation, and consistency with regard to teacher behavior and the consequences occasioned by student behavior (Ban, 1994, p. 257).

Teaching and Discipline Are Inseparable

Whether a teacher uses the term *discipline* or *classroom management* does not matter, as long as the teacher realizes that these cannot be separated from the act of teaching. Nothing works better for establishing and maintaining discipline in a classroom than planning and executing a good lesson.

As explained by Evertson (1989, p. 84): "Of course, good discipline is a by product of interesting, exciting, and engaging instruction." This idea was developed in Chapter 3 on planning daily lessons.

The Cooperative Approach

Thus far, we have described discipline as the teacher's sole responsibility. Teacher efficacy can contribute to establishing a desirable classroom climate. But teachers should not be alone in their concern for maintaining a well-disciplined class. After all, if chaos prevails, the students suffer most. Therefore, many teachers choose to involve their students in maintaining discipline in their classrooms. This makes the job easier, and it also promotes a very important student attitude toward discipline. That attitude is self-discipline.

Data show that teachers can plan effective strategies for controlling classroom behavior. For example, Ban (1994, p. 258) says "teachers should ask students to identify common behavior problems in school" and "students should formulate a behavior statement of rule that deals with these identified misbehaviors." Students should be involved in setting some of the job classroom behavior rules. Ban (1994, p. 258) explains: "In classrooms where students have had a part in shaping the rules of behavior, the power of peer pressure will work to ensure students' compliance with these rules."

Imposed Discipline   Self-Discipline

FIGURE 13.2   Discipline continuum

DISCIPLINE: A CONTINUUM OF VIEWS

The wide range of views about discipline can be seen by placing them on a continuum (Figure 13.2). Clearly, some teachers remain at the far left side of the continuum.
Other teachers (such as the sixth-grade teacher at the beginning of the chapter) have
moved to the opposite extreme. Teachers at the right side of the continuum often appear to have few or no discipline problems. In fact, they often seem to ignore the topic
altogether, whereas teachers on the left side of the continuum may seem obsessed with
the idea.

Reflection

Review the range of views of discipline shown in Figure 13.2 and make a list of
objectives or statements to describe teachers who fall on the left side of the discipline continuum. Then make a list to describe teachers who belong on the right
side. Perhaps you have already surmised that your next task will be to determine
where you belong on this continuum. This may not be easy, but it is important
because you must know where you stand concerning discipline so you can act
accordingly.

MANAGEMENT THEORIES AND EDUCATION

Teachers are not alone in their tendency to span the spectrum with their perceptions
of discipline. Management practices should be consistent with our knowledge and theories of learning, and even these vary greatly. The following is a review of some major
learning theories. As you recognize each of these from your earlier courses in educational psychology, see if you can accurately place each theory on the discipline continuum.

Faculty Psychology

Before the twentieth century there was little effort to understand the process of learning. The first collective beliefs that were actually written down and accepted by a significant number of psychologists (perhaps the vast majority) became known as faculty psychology. Perceiving the brain as a muscle that had special capacities (faculties),
these theorists believed that further development of the brain hinged on certain conditions. They believed that, like any muscle, the brain needed exercise to grow. This

exercise should be difficult and boring, not enjoyable, and therefore lectures and recitation should be the major teaching methods.

Although faculty psychology seems absurd to many contemporary educators, this theory still plays a role in modern education. A visit to almost any school will reveal that faculty psychology continues to shape the climate in many classrooms. Some recent reports on education have given renewed life to these theories. Private schools designed and established according to the faculty psychology theory are growing in popularity and number.

Stimulus-Response Psychology

By the turn of the century, a new school of thought had become influential in shaping American education. The stimulus-response (S → R) psychologists perceived all behavior as responses to stimuli. To effect learning, the teacher merely needed to change the classroom stimuli. This school of thought has some validity, because student behavior is indeed shaped to some degree by the total stimuli in the classroom environment. By removing undesirable stimuli, the teacher can remove much of the undesirable behavior. By adding other stimuli (rewards), new behavior could be added. But recognizing that the degree to which a stimulus shapes behavior is determined somewhat by the individual (organism) who is responding, the S → R symbol that represented the stimulus-response theory was changed to S → O → R.

Behavioral Psychology

Some psychologists disagree with the stimulus-response psychologists, maintaining that only a small portion of human behaviors are responses to stimuli. Behavioral psychologists believe that most human behavior is overt—that is, purposive and self-initiated. They recognize that repetition, rewards, and reinforcements play important roles in shaping behavior. Some of the major education programs that emerged from this school of thought are programmed instruction, behavior modification, and computer assisted instruction (CAI).

Phenomenology

By the middle of the twentieth century, some psychologists began paying more attention to the individual. Rogerian psychologists listened carefully to their clients and considered the individual's own perceptions. From this concern grew a new psychological theory called phenomenology. Unlike earlier psychologists, who focused their energy on finding more effective ways of forcing or persuading students to change their behavior, phenomenologists studied ways of getting students to change their own behavior.

From this school of thought came the idea of the self-concept. These psychologists realized that students will work diligently to protect their self-image. By helping their students develop a positive image of themselves as competent students, a teacher could indirectly cause students to channel their own behavior in more positive directions.

Reflection

Now see where you would place each of the above learning theories on the discipline continuum. Clearly, they belong somewhere left of center because each uses external stimuli. In effect, each perceives the teacher's role as combining repetition, rewards, reinforcements, and punishments to alter student behavior.

Reality Therapy

Reality therapy is an approach to behavior management that has been modified for classroom use by Dr. William Glasser, who contends that misbehavior results from a lack of involvement in the school process. Failure and lack of a sense of students' responsibility for the outcomes of their behavior causes misbehavior. Conversely, success begets success. According to this theory, teachers should (1) display strong positive emotional characters, (2) state rules clearly so they are understood, (3) spend some time each day with each student, (4) focus on present behavior and not refer to past behavior, and (5) require students to evaluate their own behavior. In addition, teacher and student(s) should (6) develop together a corrective plan that is simple, short, and success oriented. It should have only a few rules, but they must be obeyed. Finally (7), the teacher should obtain a verbal or written commitment from the student(s) (Curwin & Mendler, 1984).

The philosophical basis for Glasser's theory is that society as a whole has shifted from socially sanctioned goals to personal goals—know yourself and know what you want. The result has been the emergence of an "identity society." For this reason, schools should shift from an external locus of control—do what the teacher says—to an internal locus of control, whereby students are involved in planning and directing the school activities.

According to Glasser, the major cause of classroom misbehavior is teachers' failure to involve students. Control theory is based on the belief that individuals are motivated internally, not externally, as Glasser contends many teachers think. More specifically, this internal motivation results from five basic needs: survival, love, power, fun, and freedom.

Control theory can best be thought of as self-control, since it refers to the student's being in control of his or her life. Unfortunately, according to this theory, the individual's genes know nothing about delayed gratification. A baby's needs are usually addressed immediately. By the time a child is old enough to enter school, the family usually has taught the child that the good feeling that good behavior brings is not immediate. In other words, the message is "work hard, succeed, and continue working hard; the reward will come later." Unfortunately, children without a supportive family find it hard to behave without immediate rewards.

Glasser warns that too many teachers believe that many students are getting support at home when actually they are not. The misconception occurs because most teachers come from supportive families. Another problem is that teachers mistake what they assume will bring good feelings to students. As explained in Chapter 12, by definition reinforcers must mean something to the student. Teachers have very few rewards at their disposal that most students find desirable.

In school as in the adult world, high achievers have an internal locus of control; they feel that they can control their behavior and, to a large extent, their life. In contrast, low achievers usually have an external locus of control; they perceive their life's circumstances as beyond their own control. For example, "Others are more successful because they have better luck than I have," or "I couldn't get to class on time because throughout the semester my alarm clock failed to ring." Reality therapy focuses on developing an internal locus of control.

Teachers who effectively use reality therapy demonstrate certain common behaviors. From the first day of school they work hard to create a warm, friendly, and totally noncoercive climate. They accept a certain amount of noise. They encourage students, yet remain realistic. For example, "Algebra will require hard work, but you can do it." They explain that grades themselves are meaningless and insignificant, yet because grades reflect behaviors that will empower students to fulfill real needs, grades are important.

Group Management Theory

In contrast to Glasser, who perceives discipline as a one-on-one cooperative endeavor between the teacher and each student, Fritz Redl and William W. Wattenberg (1959) believe that discipline problems are a product of group behavior and should be approached accordingly. As early as 300 BC, Plato warned about the negative influence urbanization can have on a culture. In his *Republic,* he predicted that as cities grow, inhabitants' behavior changes, often for the worse. Group management theory recognizes that groups behave differently than individuals. Furthermore, as groups become larger they also develop definite characteristics.

Teachers must recognize groups' effects on the total classroom or on smaller groups within the classroom. The teacher can exert influence either directly or indirectly in two major directions. First, the teacher gives support to the group—for example, provides encouragement while standing ready to help the group achieve its goals. This requires guiding the class carefully toward the goals. Suppose one of the class's behavioral goals is for each student to remain at his or her desk. The teacher's role is to monitor the group and, when signs of restlessness appear, to alter the situation to provide for more movement. Or suppose near the end of the period students get off-target and wander—mentally if not physically. Recognizing the situation, the teacher introduces an assignment, summarizes the day's lesson, or uses a similar technique to pull the students back to the lesson.

Group management techniques are not concerned with blaming either the group or the individual for misbehaving. The perspective is more one of being alert at all times, managing the environment to reduce the number of problems and problem-causing elements, and helping the group and individuals overcome hurdles and reach their goals.

Group management is based on the philosophy that neither individuals nor groups want to misbehave and that misbehavior is the result of barriers. When individuals or groups fail to make progress toward their goals, the goals are unclear or too demanding or environmental elements prevent their attainment—not because the individual or group wants to be difficult.

Redl and Wattenberg (1959) endorsed the use of punishment, but only under certain conditions. Punishment should never be the teacher's first attempted solution to a problem, and when used it should be administered objectively. The individual or groups being punished must clearly understand the reason, and the teacher must remain calm. Wasicsko and Ross (1994, p. 249) recommend that teachers select punishments that are natural consequences of the misbehavior being addressed: "Research indicates that punishments are most effective when they are natural consequences of the behavior." Consider how much more appropriate it is to punish a student for breaking a window by having that student clean up the broken glass than to require the student to write "I will not break any more windows" a thousand times. "By warning and rewarding students, teachers actually cultivate misbehavior" (Wasicsko & Ross, p. 250). You may learn that it is helpful to keep a written record of student misbehavior, "a necessary element in any effective classroom discipline system" (p. 259). The essential elements in records of misbehavior include the student, data, time, location, incident, description, corrective action, and follow-up (see Figure 13.2). It is important to recognize that punishment can easily become a trap for teachers if they make it too harsh, get others to administer it, overuse it, or use it to make impossible demands of students. The ultimate goal of group management is, by helping students to analyze their own behavior, to lead them to a state of self-control—that is, self-discipline. Wasicsko and Ross (1994, p. 249) provide further cautions and suggestions to guide the use of punishment in the classroom: "A major factor in creating classroom discipline problems is the overuse of punishments as an answer to misbehavior." They list several negative side-effects that often accompany the use of punishment: bringing attention to those who misbehave, causing aggression, depression, anxiety, or embarrassment, bringing only a temporary halt to bad behavior, and disrupting the continuity of lessons.

Assertive Discipline

A popular management model that many educators do not support is assertive discipline. MacNaughton and Johns (1991, p. 53) provide a summary discussion of this model:

> A popular example of behavior management on one end of the continuum representing the degree of teacher power over students is assertive discipline. This strategy emphasizes systematic reinforcement and is more punishment-oriented than some of the other behavior management procedures.

The basic theme of assertive discipline is that the assertive teacher clearly and firmly communicates requirements to the students and backs up words with appropriate actions that maximize compliance without violating students' best interests. Assertive discipline requires teachers to take the following steps:

1. Make clear that they will not tolerate anyone preventing them from teaching, stopping learning, or doing anything else that is not in the best interest of the class, the individual, or the teacher.
2. Instruct students clearly and in specific terms about what behaviors are desired and what behaviors are not tolerated.
3. Plan positive and negative consequences for predetermined acceptable or unacceptable behaviors.
4. Plan positive reinforcement for compliance. Reinforcement includes verbal acknowledgement, notes, free time for talking, and, of course, tokens that can be exchanged for appropriate rewards.
5. Plan a sequence of steps to punish noncompliance. These range from writing a youngster's name on the board to sending the student to the principal's office. (p. 53)

Corporal Punishment

Corporal punishment is technically defined as the infliction of physical pain upon the occurrence of a misbehavior (Vockell, 1991, p. 278).

Although most educators oppose the use of corporal punishment in schools, some support its use. Johns and MacNaughton (1990) provide lists of arguments for and against the use of corporal punishment:

Pros and Cons of Corporal Punishment.   Clearly, there are arguments for and against corporal punishment (Johns & MacNaughton, 1990, pp. 390–391). Arguments in favor of retaining corporal punishment include the following:

1. Corporal punishment is one procedure among many. As a consequence of rule infraction, it works with some students in some circumstances.
2. Many parents support the practice. In such cases, use of corporal punishment is consistent support of home procedure.
3. Corporal punishment is a considerably less severe form of punishment than many other kinds. Administered judiciously and without rancor, it is far less harmful than suspension.
4. Denying teachers the right to exercise judgment about the proper use of corporal punishment is to maintain that they are not fully capable of making professional decisions in the area of punishment.
5. Use of corporal punishment in some aggravated situations and with some

students reinforces the concept that a just society can deliver punishment where deemed appropriate.

6. Corporal punishment is immediate, concrete, clears the air, and terminates the event. Aside from proper guidelines in its use, corporal punishment is simple and easily understood. Unlike many of the more complex models for promoting classroom management and discipline, corporal punishment does not require training and lengthy, time-consuming efforts to bring about changes in pupil's behavior.

Arguments against corporal punishment include:

1. There are many examples of the nonjudicious use of corporal punishment. Stories about the use of the paddle for minor offenses abound. Once paddling is institutionalized, it may well be used for every offense.
2. The practice is discriminatory. It is used more on minorities and children of lower socioeconomic background, inner-city children, and nonconformists.
3. It is ineffectual. To be at all effective, paddling of disruptive students would have to be repeated continuously and probably become more severe as the student got older and more accustomed to it.
4. It is a dehumanizing practice, long outlawed in the U.S. military and in prisons in most Western nations. Schools are the only institution where striking another person is permitted. Corporal punishment is an aggressive, violent means of discipline that is antithetical to the purpose of American education. It makes the teacher a poor model by promoting force as a means to settling arguments and establishing rights.
5. The practice of corporal punishment causes psychological as well as physical harm. It can be the cause of posttraumatic stress disorders and school avoidance. It is harmful to the self-esteem a school may be trying to encourage students to develop.
6. Corporal punishment may be considered child abuse and even sexual abuse if its use is viewed as a violation of the body. In such a charged atmosphere, the use of corporal punishment is highly subject to lawsuits.

Recognizing the limitations and harmful effects of corporal punishment, most countries forbid its use in their public schools. Jambor (1988, p. 220) identifies the few countries that permit its use: "Presently only a few developed countries still condone corporal punishment in their public schools: Australia, New Zealand, South Africa, and the United States."

Maslow's Hierarchy of Needs

Abraham Maslow (1954) developed a theory based on clinical observation and logic. According to Maslow, all human beings have some common needs, which fall into five clusters that can be arranged in the following hierarchy:

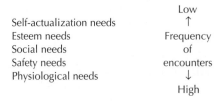

We experience the needs at the lower levels of the hierarchy more frequently. Furthermore, we must satisfy each level of needs before moving to the higher levels. Maslow's Hierarchy of Needs has been used extensively by management in business and industry for several decades.

McGregor's Theories X and Y

Douglas McGregor noticed that in a large national chain of department stores some of the stores were highly successful while some were financial failures. On closer inspection he noted that the successful stores and the unsuccessful stores were managed under very different types of management. He named the successful management style Theory Y and the unsuccessful management style Theory X. The unsuccessful Theory X managers were the traditional type of managers. They all shared the following perceptions:

Most people are inherently lazy.

People must be closely supervised.

People tend to shun responsibility.

People like to be directed.

Getting people to attain objectives requires
the use of coercion, control, and threats of punishment.

In contrast, the highly successful Theory Y managers espoused the following beliefs:

The expenditure of mental and physical effort is natural.

If the conditions are right, people will not only accept
responsibility but also seek it.

If people become committed to objectives, they will
exercise self-direction and self-control.

Most people have a high degree of imagination, ingenuity,
and creativity.

This more positive approach to management has become identified as modern management theory. However, some contemporary management theorists reject this theory as too idealistic. In all fairness, its accuracy depends on the particular environment.

Reflection

Consider Maslow's Hierarchy of Needs, McGregor's Theory X, and McGregor's Theory Y. Where would you place each of these on the discipline continuum? Can you see a relationship between Maslow's Hierarchy of Needs and student behavior in the classroom? For example, can you name some physiological needs that must be met before students improve their self-esteem? Can you name any social needs that must be met before students can improve their self-image as competent students? Have you known teachers whom you would label Theory X managers? Theory Y managers? What traits did each exhibit?

CLASSROOM MANAGEMENT (DISCIPLINE) MODELS

Being aware of learning theories and management theories from disciplines outside education will help us relate education discipline and management theories to the discipline continuum in Figure 13.2. Following are a few of the many discipline and management theories in use in education today. Weber, Roff, Crawford, and Robinson (1983) reviewed the literature on classroom management and grouped the strategies into the following eight categories: authoritarian, behavior modification, group process, instructional, intimidation, permissive, sociomotional climate, and cookbook. Because these groups are both numerous and self-descriptive, only selective examples will be given.

Authoritarian Strategies

The authoritarian approach to classroom management places the teacher in control from the very beginning. Using nonpunitive measures, the teacher establishes and enforces rules, issues commands, and uses mild desists (explains privately why the student is being asked to discontinue the behavior), proximity control (stays near the misbehaving student), and isolation. Jacob Kounin (1977) introduced the mild-desists strategy because he found that teachers seldom tell students why they consider certain behaviors bad. He further noticed that when teachers use strong reprimands they often do so publicly, making other students feel anxious.

Group Process Strategies

Group process strategies are based on a belief that classroom behavior occurs in a social or group context. The teacher's role is to set reasonable expectations, stay alert to the classroom group interactions (exhibit "with-it-ness"), foster group cohesiveness, involve students in decision making, and resolve conflicts through discussion, role playing, and negotiation.

Many education reform programs stress the use of small groups.

Instructional Strategies

The instructional approach to classroom management uses the belief that the teacher's time is better spent preventing problems than solving them. Chapter 12 discusses this approach in detail.

Intimidation Strategies

Intimidation strategies put the teacher in charge. The teacher uses harsh reprimands, threats, physical restraint, and corporal punishment. These teachers do not tolerate any foolishness. Classes managed by this style may or may not be characterized by a high degree of learning.

MODELS DEVELOPED SPECIFICALLY FOR EDUCATION

The learning and management theories presented thus far in this chapter are adopted from other disciplines, and their relevance to the secondary and middle school classroom varies. This has prompted development of models designed specifically for classroom use. Following are descriptions of several popular ones. As you read about each model, see if you can place it on the discipline continuum (Figure 13.2).

Do not use the techniques presented thus far in this chapter in isolation; incorporate them into an overall consistent pattern. Several models showing examples of such structured approaches to discipline are available. In her book *Classroom Discipline*, Laurel Tanner (1978, p. 6) introduces the following models.

1. Training model
2. Behavior modification model
3. Psychodynamic model
4. Group dynamics model
5. Personal-social growth model

Training Model

Discipline is always concerned with regulating or changing behavior. This may be achieved either externally or internally—that is, change can be effected by external stimuli, or it can be the result of the subject's own purposive behavior. The training model is concerned totally with the former category, since any training program for classroom behavior is almost certain to result from the teacher's effort rather than the students'.

Although the training model's effectiveness has been demonstrated by police officers, soldiers, and firefighters (to name only a few professions), who must learn to respond immediately and automatically to certain stimuli, most educators believe that this model is less desirable than the others for use with middle school and high school students. Their attitude is understandable, because school should prepare students to think for themselves rather than always to respond to others' desires or demands.

Even in the high school classroom, though, some degree of training is helpful. For example, students can learn to stop talking when the class is being addressed, to remain seated when they complete an assignment, or to raise their hands when they want to speak. Most of these patterns, though, are holdovers from the earlier grades. High school discipline programs should not overemphasize or overuse the training model.

Behavior Modification Model

Like the training model, behavior modification depends on external stimuli to effect the desired changes in behavior. But unlike the training model—which does not require its subjects to think, just respond automatically—behavior modification does require students to change their behavior to receive definite rewards.

Neither the training model nor the behavior modification model requires students to think through their behavior at a very high level; instead, students are conditioned to behave the way the teacher wants them to. Still, behavior modification strategies do work at the high school level. Behavior modification programs can reduce the amount of inappropriate behavior in secondary school classrooms by as much as 75 percent (Sapp, Clough, Pittman, & Toben, 1973). This method is used extensively with mentally and emotionally handicapped students.

Psychodynamic Model

Unlike the training model and the behavior modification model, the psychodynamic model requires that the teacher know and understand each student. As an outgrowth of Freudian psychology, the model is based on the belief that knowing and understanding a student's behavior will lead to improvement in that behavior. This model is more advanced than the previous models in that it involves a search for the cause of misbehavior. Some educators criticize this model, however, because it does not offer suggestions to correct the behavior.

Group Dynamics Model

The group dynamics model recognizes that social interaction and social pressure affect students. Instead of focusing on an individual student, it looks at the individual in relation to the total group's behavior. The focus is on the teacher, and the goal is to design good working conditions for the total group.

This model differs further from the models previously discussed in that it ties discipline to instruction. To avoid (or in response to) a behavior problem, the teacher would design a learning activity to divert students' attention from the problem to learning the lesson at hand. Use of this model requires an awareness of student behavior so that problems can be nipped in the bud as soon as they develop.

Like the psychodynamic model, this model recognizes that learning is a group activity, but it goes one important step further. Whereas the psychodynamic model depends solely on the teacher's understanding the students, this model requires the teacher to take action. In this sense it is far more practical.

Personal-Social Growth Model

Contemporary educators recognize that merely being able to regulate student behavior and suppress undesirable behavior is not enough. The title of this chapter reflects this concern. To become good citizens in a democratic society, students must ultimately learn to discipline themselves, to manage their own behavior. This requires experience—which means that you, the teacher, must be willing to share your power and responsibility for discipline with your students. Indeed, students must feel that they are in control. They must also understand the purpose(s) behind desired behavioral patterns. Ideally, they should see the class's desired goals and choose the ways to behave to attain these goals. This model is consistent with the school's responsibility for helping students become responsible citizens. As Chamberlin and Chambers (1994, p. 204) attest, "Teaching students to be responsible should be viewed as an important and vital part of the total curriculum."

TRENDS IN DISCIPLINE TODAY

The order of strategies and models just discussed reflects the chronological pattern of metamorphosis of discipline in American education. At one time the school assumed total authority to define good discipline. Explains one educator, "With evangelic fervor . . . teachers have taught, indoctrinated, and compelled students to whom and what they were to comply with and become the ideal model that the school mystically judged as being desirable" (Hansen, 1974, p. 173).

Today, good discipline is not considered synonymous with total, blind conformity. Students are involved with deciding what type of discipline is best for doing the job in their particular setting. Educational psychologist Theodore Chandler (1990) says that the current trend of involving students in setting discipline strategies is an essential move:

> Most discipline strategies are developed without student input and employ an external agent to identify, monitor, and remediate classroom disturbances. . . . Such an approach violates the tenets of at least four different cognitive-based theories and fails to address some psychological principles involved in the dynamics of change. (p. 124)

The principles that Chandler says most discipline strategies violate are:

1. When people perceive that their freedom to act is hampered, they will act the opposite way.
2. Students (should be) at the center and (should have) nearly complete responsibility for their own fate.
3. Perceived inefficacy in coping with negative wants produces fearful expectations and avoidance behavior.
4. The way students perceive causes of their behavioral and academic performance determines whether they will take charge of a change or assume that change is external to them and out of their control. (p. 124)

Plymouth Junior High School's program for discipline reflects many current programs. It strives to put the responsibility on the student whenever possible, be consistent but flexible in enforcing the basic rules, and find alternatives for classroom activities, rewards, and consequences so that students do not force themselves into corners (Shook, 1975).

A school in Houston, Texas, developed a disciplinary system that reduced the frequency of corporal punishment to 7 percent and suspensions to 20 percent (Sanders & Yarbrough, 1976). The program's strategies were to provide a personal atmosphere, to help students clarify their values, to provide a crisis-intervention center for students with serious problems, and to provide an ever-changing set of objectives relating to students' real-life needs.

One reason that schools are turning to less-authoritative means for disciplining is that teachers today realize that power does not bring student cooperation—on the contrary, it stimulates more resistance. A second and equally important reason is that it would be inconsistent to use force. The aim is to produce students who approach life's challenges courageously because they are able to relate to others, solve problems, and be responsible (Dinkmeyer & Dinkmeyer, 1976). Thompson (1994) addresses this current trend:

> The ultimate goal of any disciplinary approach should be not merely to maintain an efficient learning environment but rather to develop within individ-

ual pupils a kind of self-discipline, the kind of self-discipline that arises out of risk-taking and coping with consequences. (p. 265)

THE CASCADE MODEL FOR CLASSROOM DISCIPLINE

Another modern classroom discipline model is the cascade model. This model presents a systematic plan for maintaining classroom discipline. Like a waterfall, it involves stages arranged in a particular sequence. By following the sequence, the teacher can approach classroom management logically. The early stages are preventive.

Preventive Discipline

Basic to the cascade model is a set of premises that includes certain attitudes. One premise holds that a good, positive climate will prevent discipline problems. This climate includes both the physical environment and a positive attitude toward students. Expectations are made clear to students. Wasicsko and Ross (1994, p. 248) tie these last two suggestions together (i.e. positive climate and clear expectations) in one brief statement: "The first step in reducing discipline problems is to demonstrate positive expectations toward students."

The teacher is encouraged to involve students in developing rules at the beginning of each year. Even the rules are stated in positive terms: "If you need to say something, raise your hand" or "Have your homework completely finished, neat, and in on time." Consequences for violating the rules are also developed with student input. These consequences come in a certain order—for example (1) warning, (2) detention, (3) time out, (4) in-school suspension, and (5) immediate removal from the classroom. If because of the nature of a particular student's history this sequence must be altered, explain the reason for the inconsistency to the student.

Plan early in the year. Evertson (1989, p. 90) explains: "Thus, solving managerial and organizational problems at the beginning of the year is essential in laying the groundwork for quality learning opportunities for students." Dagley and Orso (1991, p. 52) reinforce the need teachers have to communicate their expectations to their students early in the year: "Research on effective teachers strongly verifies the emphasis on getting the year off to a good start."

Good preventive discipline can occur only when students are relatively free. Another way of saying this is that good discipline cannot exist in classrooms where all students feel they are restricted unnecessarily. Thompson (1994) explains:

Preventive discipline is nothing other than the establishment of a positive learning environment that at once affords the pupils as much freedom of behavior as they can handle without infringing on the rights of others and minimizes the instances of challenge between teacher and pupils. (p. 264)

Teachers who stop the class each time an infraction occurs actually promote problems.

	LEARNING THEORIES		
Faculty Psychology	Stimulus-Response Psychology	Behavioral Psychology	Phenomenology

	NONEDUCATION MANAGEMENT THEORIES	
McGregor X Theory	Maslow's Needs Theory	McGregor Y Theory

		CLASSROOM MANAGEMENT THEORIES		
Training Model	Behavior Modification Model	Psychodynamic Model	Group Dynamics Model	Personal-Social Growth Model
			Group Management Theory	Reality Therapy

(Left margin: Externally Imposed Discipline; Right margin: Self-Controlled Discipline)

FIGURE 13.3 Discipline continuum showing general locations of major learning theories, management theories, and discipline theories

Supportive Discipline

Another premise involves supportive discipline, or reinforcing desired behaviors. These reinforcers may be verbal or nonverbal and written or nonwritten. Students are praised in specific terms and told why. Parents are often told about students' accomplishments and are encouraged to give praise at home for achievements at school.

Corrective Discipline

The next tier of steps in the cascade model is labeled corrective discipline. At this level the teacher approaches the students with the problem using the "I" approach—for example, "I can't start the class until the room is quieter. We waste several minutes at the beginning of each hour. Have you any suggestions how we might solve this problem?" Each suggestion is discussed, the students vote, and their choice is tried.

Reflection

Now add to your discipline continuum these additional classroom management models. Examine your final map. Where would your own philosophy of discipline be located on this continuum? When you have finished this task, compare your chart with the sample in Figure 13.3. The exact position of any of these theories on the continuum would be somewhat subjective and therefore could vary. Figure 13.3 shows the general locations of these theories as I perceive them. Study this chart and see if you agree or disagree. Be prepared to defend your perception.

Adaptive Discipline

The fourth and final tier of the cascade model, adaptive discipline, is used when all else fails. Here, a private conference takes place. The teacher tries to remain positive to avoid damaging the student's self-image. Teacher and student identify a satisfactory or acceptable behavior and sign a contract. If the plan fails, they rework it until it succeeds. (For further references, see Rutter, Maughan, Mortimore, & Duston, 1979.)

AVOIDING DISCIPLINE PROBLEMS

Control: Getting Off to a Good Start

Rudeness begets rudeness, and sarcasm can spawn a climate of mistrust, dislike, and disrespect. Teachers can develop a climate of mutual respect by showing respect to all students at all times and by requiring that students treat their classmates and teachers with respect. Maximum learning requires a climate of respect and control.

Control is best achieved by cooperation between teacher and students, but it is your responsibility as teacher to have control from the first minute—before discussing a cooperative arrangement. Begin each year by setting rules that students understand. Make the rules specific, clear, and firm (McDaniel, 1994, p. 255), being especially alert to "Teachers must use action not anger to control misbehavior." Continue the year being especially alert to students' needs and desires. In this context, "needs" refers not so much to present whims but to serious present and future needs. Some of these may be the adolescent's needs for approval, success, and independence and social needs. As students show that they can handle freedom, you can gradually remove restrictions. Each time you feel that the class has progressed beyond the need for a rule, suggest that it be removed. This lets students know that the class has earned the prerogative of canceling the rule if they so wish and that you are not just being inconsistent.

The firm teacher can become less strict more easily than the lenient teacher can become more strict, but there is danger in beginning the year with too many rules. Establish only essential rules and restrictions. In the 1950s a principal ruled that all boys must wear belts. This was in reaction to jeans worn so low on the hips that the navel showed through the often unbuttoned shirt. But the boys noticed that the principal did not define "belt." The rule was obeyed—the boys wore short ropes through belt loops, they wore ropes eight feet long (dragging on the floor), they wore string belts, they wore leather belts, but belts they did wear. The principal was also a learner, and he rescinded the rule promptly. One common mistake teachers make is to establish unnecessary and unenforceable rules.

Using Enthusiasm

The best single diversion from behavior problems is a well-planned and well-executed lesson that involves all students, especially if you are enthusiastic about the subject. Clear objectives and frequent feedback will contribute to a lesson's success. In addition to being clear, involving students, and giving frequent feedback, teachers can become more enthusiastic by including material and activities that both they and students will enjoy.

Using Names

The teacher who knows a student's name has more influence over that student, if that teacher uses the name appropriately. For example, suppose you are teaching a lesson on the first day of school and a boy sitting in the back row begins to distract other students while you are talking. It would be awkward to have to stop, look at the seating chart, and count seats to direct your reprimand to the right person. To say "You in the red-and-black-striped shirt" would get him the entire class's attention and encourage him to repeat the disruption to regain that attention. But to reprimand without designating the student might alienate other class members. Simply walking near the disruptive student is often all you must do to alleviate the problem. This technique is known as proximity control.

If you knew the boy's name, you could drop his name in the middle of a sentence as you presented the lesson, without even looking at him and without breaking the pace of the lesson. Such an action tells him and the rest of the class that you are very much aware of his attempts to disrupt the class but that the lesson is too important to be impeded by anyone's selfish attempt to gain attention.

Helping Students Learn Self-Respect

Students who perceive themselves as troublemakers make trouble. Those who perceive themselves as good students or good guys must live up to this image. Avoid saying and doing things that tend to downgrade students, and take any opportunity to say and do things to improve a student's self-image.

Avoiding Threats

Some teachers threaten groups of students and individuals, not realizing that the threatened person is challenged to misbehave. It is not uncommon for a teacher to remark "All right, class, I am not going to tell you again to be quiet," implying "I can make you wish you had behaved." Such a statement usually promotes misbehavior and diminishes learning. As Hart (1983) explains, the brain tends to "downshift" under threat. Avoid threats you never intend to carry out—better yet, avoid threats completely.

Avoid Public Reprimand

Deal with any serious problem you have with a particular student privately. Reprimanding a student in the presence of peers will damage peer relationships, which are important to people of all ages, and it forces the student to rebut or concede. A rebuttal damages the student's relationship with you; a concession causes the student to lose face with peers. Public reprimand also threatens the rest of the class. Believing that they could receive the same treatment, students may lose confidence and trust in you. Your own behavior can set a tone for students to follow. McDaniel (1994, pp. 255–256) explains: "Teachers should employ the "soft reprimand" when a student's in-class behavior needs correcting" (p. 255) and "only after students have accepted their teachers as leaders can teachers begin refining and humanizing their techniques for discipline."

Avoiding Ridicule

When students misbehave, try to change their future behavior patterns. That is all. Never ridicule a student, whether in public or in private. Ridicule is directed at a person, not at correcting behavior. Chamberlin and Chambers (1994, p. 206) have recommended, "Praise in public, punish in private helps to create a trusting atmosphere."

DEALING WITH PROBLEMS

Be Prepared to Handle Problems When They Do Develop

The best way to avoid problems in the classroom is to be well prepared each day and to have interesting experiences for each class. However, even the most effective teachers have discipline problems, so it is good to be prepared and to think ahead to when a discipline problem might develop. What will you do?

Beginning teachers often ask for the best way to handle discipline problems. Any teacher's major goal should be to discover an approach to dealing with problems that leads students to discipline themselves. Savage (1991), who supports such an approach, explains how to achieve this goal:

> An important step for teachers who expect to work toward self-control in the classroom is the development of a hierarchy of consequences. The hierarchy should begin with relatively simply and unobtrusive responses and move progressively to more intrusive and serious ones. The development of this hierarchy can provide teachers with a plan of action and a sense of security when facing serious discipline problems. (p. 204)

Always Ask Yourself Why

As Thompson (1994, p. 261) said, "All behavior is caused or purposive." Yet each teacher must determine his or her threshold of tolerance. Any classroom limitations or rules should exist to enhance student learning. "Preventive discipline is nothing other than the establishment of a positive learning environment that at once affords the pupils as much freedom of behavior as they can handle without infringing on the rights of others and minimizes the instances of challenge between teacher and pupils" (p. 264).

No students want to misbehave, so why do they? There is a cause for all behavior. Classic psychologists say that all behavior is a reaction to a stimulus—that is, everything we do is in reaction to other people or other things. Phenomenologists believe that every misbehavior is an expression of a need and that therefore each time a student misbehaves we should ask ourselves "What need is that student trying to satisfy?"

The need may be for more attention or perhaps for peer approval if a student does not get adequate reinforcement from family and teachers. Hostile misbehavior may be an attempt to alleviate frustration because of some perceived injustice. Sometimes you cannot determine the need or the cause of the behavior. To ask misbehaving students what the need is would not help, because they probably do not know.

The creative teacher is often able to provide acceptable avenues for students to express themselves. When a student causes serious disruptions, study that student's cumulative record and discuss the problem with the school counselor. Learning more about the student may give you ideas about how to work more effectively with that student. Become more tolerant when you see that the student is attempting to improve previous unsatisfactory behavior.

Avoiding Confrontations

Because misbehavior is often an attempt to get attention or to express discontent, the person who misbehaves may seek to create a scene to confront the person who could draw the most attention to the disruption—the teacher.

Sometimes you may be tempted to engage in emotionally charged disputes with students. Remember, though, that an emotional person does not seek reasonable or rational answers but instead seeks to justify the behavior. Any argument will only make the student more defensive. You may be able to help students realize that their misbehavior is disruptive and provide opportunities for them to express their opinions, but you can do so only after they have calmed down.

The Private Talk

Avoiding a serious confrontation does not necessarily mean ignoring the student. If you do not ask a student to refrain from the undesirable behavior, that student and other class members may assume that you do not really care if rules are broken. The difference between noting a disruption and engaging in a confrontation is in the manner in which you take action. Be as quiet and uneventful as possible. If the student responds negatively, ignore the student, but if the disruption continues, ask the student to leave the room and wait outside until the end of the period, when you are free to arrange for a private talk. Private conferences can be effective if they place part of the responsibility for correcting the student's behavior on both the student and you and if you look for the cause of the misbehavior.

If you ask a student to leave the classroom, you must have a private talk with the student before allowing him or her to reenter. Keep your emotions under cover during the private talk. You can express disappointment with the student's behavior, but make certain that the student does not interpret this as personal dislike. In an extreme case, where the student continues to misbehave after the private talk, call for the principal's assistance. Your mission, after all, is to provide a classroom environment conducive to learning; you cannot afford to allow one student to continue disrupting it.

Using Firmness and Consistency

All teachers should assert themselves. Apply whatever tactics you use to maintain discipline consistently with all students every day. Firmness does not imply harshness and constant sternness. If you are firm but calm, your students will appreciate it and your health will be better.

This chapter has provided several concrete suggestions to help you maintain a healthy, productive climate in your classroom. It has also attempted to shape your attitudes about discipline and cause you to think of this important part of your role as the complex phenomenon that it is. This chapter also attempts to help you base your own classroom management strategies on accepted models and on sound, accepted principles of adolescent psychology and learning theories. Avoid oversimplistic approaches that lack the support of research. Jones (1989) gives this advice:

> Rather than providing teachers with a clear understanding of the breadth of research and practice in classroom management and encouraging teachers to be informal decision makers, many school districts and some universities present teachers with limited methods such as Assertive Discipline, ITIP, and Discipline With Love and Logic. (p. 332)

As you continue in this class and throughout your teaching career, take every opportunity to learn all you can about students' highly complex behavior. As a teacher, you must maintain a classroom climate that encourages maximum learning, yet your relationship with your students will improve if you remember that every misbehavior has a cause. All students must discover behaviors that are acceptable to their peers and to their teachers.

RECAP OF MAJOR IDEAS

1. All teachers experience discipline problems.
2. Good classroom discipline is essential for maximum learning. Because you are in charge of instruction, discipline is your responsibility.
3. Good discipline implies order and control. Quiet is important to facilitate order and control and for effective communication.
4. Begin each year by being firm yet friendly. Classroom humor is desirable, but it must not cause excessive disruption.
5. Too many rules can cause added problems. Tell students why each rule is necessary. Whenever feasible, involve students in setting classroom rules.
6. Be consistent and fair when establishing and maintaining good discipline.
7. The best deterrent to discipline problems is a well-planned and well-exe-

cuted lesson, with clear goals, that involves all students. Your enthusiasm for the lesson helps motivate students.

8. Concentrate on preventing problems rather than trying to learn how to manage disasters. Although the latter skill may be helpful, few teachers feel they are experts in that area.

9. Avoid making threats and using sarcasm and public reprimands because these tend to lower students' self-esteem and self-respect. Instead, look for opportunities to compliment students, thus helping them build a positive self-image.

10. When planned and executed correctly, private conferences can be an effective means of handling disruptive students. When private conferences fail, arrange a joint conference with the principal, counselor, and parents or guardians.

CASES

Discipline is a problem in our schools. You must maintain discipline in the classroom. The following cases will help you develop the ability to discipline your future students. They show some of the real dilemmas in which teachers often find themselves. As you read each case, imagine yourself in the situation and decide how you would handle it.

CASE 1: A PRINCIPAL HAS TOO MANY DISCIPLINE PROBLEMS

Middletown School was divided into a junior and senior high with the lower grades in one building, the upper grades in another, and the principal's office in a breezeway connecting the two buildings. The windows in Jan's classroom faced the breezeway. Jan had taught for only a few weeks at Middletown. Each time a discipline problem developed, she immediately referred the offender to the principal's office.

One day Jan was amused to see another teacher leading a student to the principal's office. Later that day she saw a replay of the event. After that, Jan began counting the number of times teachers marched offenders to the principal's office. The record for one day was nine trips; the record for one teacher in one day was three trips.

Jan began to realize that this principal was spending a large amount of time disciplining the students of teachers who could not or would not assume the responsibility. She resolved to handle all future discipline problems herself, except in an emergency.

Discussion

1. How are the student's impressions of a teacher affected when the teacher takes discipline problems to the principal?

   The first time this occurs it may go unnoticed by the students, but if it is repeated again and again, the students will soon realize that the teacher is weak and unable to handle problems. Troubles in this teacher's class will increase.

2. Does the number of discipline problems reflect the quality of that teacher's teaching?

Yes. The teacher who has planned an interesting lesson that involves the students will have fewer discipline problems than the teacher who is dull, boring, and poorly prepared.

CASE 2: A FIRST TELEPHONE CALL FROM A PARENT

Don Harrader was a quiet member of the ninth-grade science class that John taught. In fact, it was difficult for John to think of Don as a member of the class because Don was so withdrawn. Don was making above-average grades until a unit on simple machines began. He received an F at the end of the unit when an examination was administered. When John talked to Don about the grade, he replied that he just did not care for that part of the course.

The next day John was having lunch when the message arrived that Mr. Harrader had called and asked that he call back. John recalled Don's recent decline in grades and suspected this was why his father had called. John left the lunchroom and went directly to the telephone. Mr. Harrader immediately asked why Don had an F in John's class. Trying to be objective and honest, John answered that Don claimed to have no interest in simple machines. Don's father replied, "I understand, but I want to know if Don has been misbehaving in class." John assured him the answer was no, and the conversation ended.

In the days following, John did a lot of thinking about Don, Don's relationship with his father, and Don's lack of real friends among his peers. One weekend John parked by the tennis courts and was watching a match when Don walked by and saw him. He asked if John played tennis and would play a set with him. John agreed. He found that Don was certainly not the same boy he saw each day in science class. There was never a happier person. From that day on, John had no trouble stimulating Don's interest in class. When Don learned that his teacher was interested in rocks, he brought his rock collection to share with the rest of the class.

A simple telephone call had stimulated John's interest in Don. An unplanned tennis match had removed Don's apathy. Together these two events had resulted indirectly in motivating a shy student.

Discussion

1. If an angry parent telephones, how should you respond?

First, refrain from showing your emotions, so the parent can see that you are being objective regarding the student. This is the best way to show the irate parent that the parent is the one who is being unreasonable. Second, be honest with the parent. If the student is failing to do satisfactory work, say so. Frankness and honesty must prevail before the parent and you can begin working together to motivate the student, and you must initiate the honesty.

2. Parental neglect is the cause of many discipline problems at school. How can you provide attention for the neglected child?

You can probably think of many ways to show interest in a student who is neglected at home. Most students have an area in which they have a strong interest, although they may never reveal it in the classroom. The teacher can often identify a student's interests by observing the student's activities outside the classroom. A teacher who shows an interest in a student's nonacademic activities may find that the student pays more attention to the teacher in class and to school assignments.

CASE 3: A STUDENT CONQUERS HER PARENTS

School had been in session for only two weeks when we had the first PTA meeting of the year. Mrs. Snyder came by and told me, "Our daughter Sandy is in your class. Do what you can with her. Just because we have little control over her doesn't mean we approve of her behavior. Do what you can to discipline her. If it means beating her, that's okay too." I shuddered, because I knew this parent actually meant it. The only Sandy I could recall was a neat and attractive girl—I remembered seeing her the first day and thinking she might become a top student.

One of the greatest values of PTA meetings is that they stimulate teachers to become personally interested in their students. This happened here, for Mrs. Snyder's words led me to learn more about Sandy. I found out that Sandy was indeed the neat, attractive, pleasant girl in my eighth-grade class, but it soon became obvious that she was not living up to my hopes for her. She was dating juniors and seniors, staying out past midnight during the week, and never completing homework assignments, if she even tried.

I still do not know how Sandy conquered her parents and took away all their control, but by admitting to her that they could no longer control her, they made it impossible for her teachers to motivate her to learn. A person's behavioral patterns do not change much when he or she walks into a classroom. It is not realistic to expect the teacher to make dramatic progress with a student at school when the parents cannot make any progress at home. Fortunately, there is always a chance that together parents and teachers can stimulate the student to change behavior patterns and direct energy toward academic achievement, but only if the parents and teacher openly discuss the student's problem. Although Mrs. Snyder had made the mistake of giving up, she was closer to helping Sandy than she knew, because she had admitted that Sandy needed help.

I began to watch Sandy every day. When she began to goof off, I was there to offer help. Sandy soon learned that, unlike her parents, I expected quality work from her—in fact, that I insisted on it. Sandy became more responsible. By the end of the year she was enjoying the class and doing the assignments. Her parents soon learned that punishment, which would not help anyway, was not necessary.

Discussion

1. Should you defend a student against her parents if they are clearly mistreating her?

    Respecting the close ties between the parent and the student, you must not do anything that will destroy whatever positive feelings apparently unconcerned parents have for their child. Instead, try to improve the situation by helping parents and child learn to respect each other. Avoid downgrading either the student or the parent(s) in the other's presence. If the conditions are really serious, consult the school counselor for advice and assistance.

2. What precautions can you take against losing control of an unrestrained student like Sandy?

    How much control you will have over students like Sandy is determined during the first few class periods. Begin by showing a keen interest and a determination to help all students, even those who appear hopelessly unmanageable. Above all, let them know you expect the highest quality work that each student can provide and improvement each day.

CASE 4: POOR MANAGEMENT RESULTS IN A NEAR CATASTROPHE

Of the students in my five sections of eighth-grade science, Tim Walker was the most easygoing, quiet, and pleasant. Tim was a model student—that is why I was surprised when the accident occurred.

I had stepped outside the room to help patrol the hallway traffic between periods. Tim and another boy were the first students to enter the classroom. Because they were alone for a minute before the rest of the class arrived, they began horsing around. Tim tripped. As he fell, he grabbed for a desk, and one of his fingers caught in the corner of the metal desk frame. The finger was almost entirely cut off. Tim was rushed to a hospital, where the finger was sewn back in place. The doctors advised him that the finger had been saved and could be rehabilitated.

This was a close call for Tim and me. I was excused because I had been responsible for hall duty at the time of the accident, but for weeks I shuddered when I thought of the many times I had left my room for brief intervals. Since this accident occurred, I have not permitted roughhousing in my classroom.

Discussion

1. Should you ever leave a student in charge of a class?

    Even if you have placed a student in charge, you are responsible and legally liable for the welfare of every student in your classroom. When you go out, do not leave a student in charge unless you are willing to accept the legal blame and pay the penalty for whatever may happen during your absence.

2. If a parent comes to your room to talk to you while your class is in session, what should you do?

    Do not leave the room to go elsewhere and talk to the parent. Tell the parent that you are sorry you cannot talk now, and make an appointment to see the parent during your next planning period.

3. What are your legal responsibilities for being in the classroom at specified times?

As the teacher, you are responsible for the safety of students in your classroom at the times you are scheduled to be there. An exception can be made when an emergency requires you to leave your room—for example, if the principal calls for you or if you must take a student to the principal's office for discipline.

CASE 5: A REAL PRO GOES INTO ACTION

Randy Graham, a bright and witty student, was especially troublesome in Mr. Hall's junior history class. One day, to show the spirit of a certain age, Mr. Hall read a few verses of poetry while the students followed along in their books. At the end of the first verse, Randy applauded Mr. Hall. Because Mr. Hall was large, solemn, and stern-looking, the other class members were shocked. Looking directly at Randy, Mr. Hall said solemnly, "Thank you, Mr. Graham," and continued reading. Randy never again misbehaved in that class.

Discussion Questions

1. Should a teacher ever attempt to control misbehavior by applying humor to the event, as Mr. Hall did?
2. If Randy had caused trouble later during the hour, should Mr. Hall again have used humor?

CASE 6: AN EXPERIMENT WITH ORAL REPRIMAND

In my first teaching position my homeroom consisted of 47 seventh-graders who were also my first-period math class. There were so many rows that they seemed to merge at the back of the room. From my desk I could see only about two-thirds of the faces at any time. Disruptions were common in the hidden areas of the back rows.

I talked with the class about it, but each day was a little worse than the day before. I did not want to use derogatory comments, but I finally ran out of options. When two boys in the back row kept jabbing each other, I asked them to come with me out into the hall. The other class members were silent. They could hear the reprimands I directed to each boy in the hall. The boys were embarrassed, and there were no more disturbances for the rest of the week.

The following week, when things again appeared to be getting out of hand, I repeated the verbal reprimands. As we left the room this time, the class was not silent, and several giggles could be heard. During my second month I was reprimanding one student or another almost every day. It was difficult to believe that such corrective measures were having so little effect in curbing the problems. On the contrary, my reprimands seemed to be promoting more problems. I was baffled.

I vowed to stop using reprimands. Each time a problem developed, I stopped the lesson, walked over near the troubled area, and silently and unsmilingly stared for a moment, then continued with the lesson. The effect was tremendous. I kept verbal reprimands to a minimum because the few positive results were surely outweighed by the trouble that they caused me.

Discussion Questions

1. When reprimand or verbal attack is used, what effect does it have on the rest of the class?
2. Why was verbal reprimand more effective at first than later on?
3. Can the teacher make verbal reprimand more effective by being increasingly stern?

ACTIVITIES

The following activities will help you deal with all these discipline concerns.

1. You have undoubtedly heard or read statements about school discipline that you do not agree with. Explain one way in which your idea of how students should behave differs from others' ideas.
2. Describe a problem that the schools in your community face. Explain how you would work to eliminate that problem if you were teaching in a local school.
3. Develop a discipline strategy building on one of your personal strengths.
4. What would you do if a student became enraged and refused to be quiet? The other students are waiting to see your reaction. How will you handle the situation?

REFERENCES

Ban, J. R. (1994). A lesson plan approach for dealing with school discipline. *The Clearing House, 67*(5), 257-260.

Bell, L. C., & Stefanich, G. P. (1984). Building effective discipline using the Cascade Model, *The Clearing House, 58,* 134-137.

Chamberlin, L. J., & Chambers, N. S. (1994). Developing responsibility in today's students. *The Clearing House, 67*(4), 204-206.

Chandler, T. A. (1990, November-December). Why discipline strategies are bound to fail. *The Clearing House,* 124-126.

Cunningham, B. (1988). Preservice teachers' perceptions of children's problem behaviors. *Journal of Educational Research, 82*(1), 34-39.

Curwin, R. L., & Mendler, A. N. (1984, May). High standards for effective discipline. *Educational Leadership, 41,* 75-76.

Curwin, R. L., & Mendler, A. N. (1980). *The discipline book.* Reston, VA: Reston.

Dagley, D. L., & Orso, S. K. (1991). Integrating summative and formative modes of evaluation. *NASSP Bulletin, 75,* 72-82.

Dinkmeyer, D., & Dinkmeyer, D., Jr. (1976). Logical consequences: A key to the reduction of disciplinary problems. *Phi Delta Kappan, 57,* 664-666.

Elam, S. M., Rose, L. C., & Gallup, A. M. (1991, September). The 23rd Annual Gallup Poll of the Public's Attitude Toward the Public Schools. *Phi Delta Kappan, 73*(1), 41-56.

Elam, S. M., Rose, L. C., & Gallup, A. M. (1994). The 26th Annual Phi Delta Kappan/Gallup Poll of the Public's Attitude Toward the Public Schools. *Phi Delta Kappan, 76*(d1), 41-56.

Evertson, C. M. (1989). Improving elementary classroom management: A school based training program for beginning the year. *Journal of Educational Research, 83,* 82-90.

Gathercoal, F. (1990, February). Judicious discipline. *Education Digest,* 20-24.

Grubaugh, S. (1989, October). Nonverbal language techniques for better classroom management and discipline. *High School Journal, 73,* 34-40.

Hanny, R. J. (1994). Don't let them take you to the barn. *The Clearing House, 67*(5), 252-253.

Hansen, J. M. (1974). Discipline: A whole new bag. *High School Journal, 57,* 172-181.

Harper's Magazine. (1985, March). The top problems in schools in 1940 and 1982.

Hart, L. A. (1983). *Human brain and human learning.* New York: Longman.

Jambor, T. (1988). Classroom management and discipline alternatives to corporal punishment: The Norwegian example. *Education, 109*(2), 220-225.

Johns, F. A., & MacNaughton, R. H. (1990). Spare the rod: A continuing controversy. *The Clearing House, 63*(9), 338-392.

Jones, V. F. (1989). Classroom management: Clarifying theory and improving practice. *Education, 109,* 330-339.

Jones, V. F., & Jones, L. S. (1986). *Comprehensive classroom management: Creating positive learning environments* (2nd ed.). Boston: Allyn & Bacon.

Kounin, J. S. (1977). *Discipline and group management in classrooms.* Melbourne, FL: Krieger.

MacNaughton, R. H., & Johns, F. A. (1991, September). Developing a successful schoolwide discipline program. *NASSP Bulletin, 75*(536), 47-57.

Maslow, A. (1954). *Motivation and personality.* New York: Harper and Row.

McDaniel, T. R. (1994). How to be an effective authoritarian: A back-to-basics approach to classroom discipline. *The Clearing House, 67*(5), 254-256.

National Center for Education Statistics (1991). *Education counts.* Washington, DC: U.S. Department of Education.

Oana, R.G. (1993). *Changes in teacher education: Reform, renewal, reorganization. A professional development leave report.* Bowling Green, Ohio: Bowling Green State University.

Phelps, P. H. (1991, March–April). Helping teachers excel as classroom managers. *The Clearing House, 64,* 241-242.

Redl, F., & Wattenberg, W. W. (1959). *Mental hygiene in teaching* (2nd ed.). Orlando, FL: Harcourt Brace Jovanovich.

Rutter, M., Maughan, B., Mortimore, P., & Duston, J. (1979). *Fifteen thousand hours.* Cambridge: Harvard University Press.

Sanders, S. G., & Yarbrough, J. S. (1976). Achieving a learning environment with order. *The Clearing House, 50,* 100-102.

Sapp, G. L., Clough, J. D., Pittman, B., & Toben, C. (1973). Classroom management and student involvement. *High School Journal, 56,* 276-283.

Savage, T. V. (1991). *Discipline for self-control.* Englewood Cliffs, NJ: Prentice-Hall.

Shook, J. (1975). Alternatives for managing disruptive classroom behaviors. *School and Community, 61,* 28-29.

Tanner, L. (1978). *Classroom discipline for effective teaching and learning.* New York: Holt, Rinehart & Winston.

Thompson, G. (1994). Discipline and the high school teacher. *The Clearing House, 67*(5), 261-265.

Vockell, E. L. (1991, March–April). Corporal punishment: The pros and cons. *The Clearing House, 64,* 279-283.

Wasicsko, M. M., & Ross, S. M. (1994). How to create discipline problems. *The Clearing House, 67*(5), 248-251.

Weber, W., Roff, L. A., Crawford, J., & Robinson, C. (1983). Classroom management. In W. A. Weber, L. A. Roff, J. Crawford, & C. Robinson (Eds.), *Classroom management: Reviews of the teacher education and research literature* (pp. 38-39). Princeton: Educational Testing Service.

SUGGESTED READINGS

Buckner, J. H., & Bickel, F. (1991, January). If you want to know about effective teaching, why not ask your middle school kids? *Middle School Journal, 21*(3), 22-29.

Dagley, D. L., & Orso, J. K. (1991, September). Integrating summative and formative modes of evaluation. *NASSP Bulletin, 75,* 72-82.

Johnston, W. J. (1985). *Education on trial.* San Francisco: Institute for Contemporary Studies (ICS) Press.

Katz, L. G., & McClellan, D. (1991). *The teacher's role in social development.* Urbana, IL: ERIC Clearinghouse on Elementary and early Childhood Education.

Moles, O. C. (Ed.). (1989). *Strategies to reduce student misbehavior.* Washington, DC: Office of Educational Research and Improvement, U.S. Department of Education.

part SIX

Tests and Evaluation

Every teacher is responsible for testing and evaluation, terms that are frequently confused and misunderstood. Chapters 14 and 15 will help you understand the many uses of tests and evaluations in the classroom. Most U.S. secondary and middle schools require grades, so you must learn all you can about constructing, administering, and scoring tests and about converting these results, along with other criteria, into grades. Because most teachers underuse formative evaluation and criterion-based evaluation, Chapter 14 explains their advantages for secondary and middle school teachers.

chapter 14

Evaluation

To talk with disdain of "teaching to the test" is to misunderstand how we learn.
Grant Wiggins

OBJECTIVES

Define evaluation.

Differentiate between testing and evaluation.

List three factors a term grade should reflect.

Justify using assignments for extra credit and justify rejecting the practice.

Describe one major limitation of using the bell curve in assigning high school grades.

Determine the stanine scores for a class of students, and transfer stanines into percentages.

Differentiate between formative and summative evaluation.

Design an evaluation system to replace some classroom competition with cooperation.

PRETEST

	Agree	Disagree	Uncertain
1. Evaluation is the same as the sum of a student's test scores.	_____	_____	_____
2. A student's grades should be based only on what the student has learned.	_____	_____	_____
3. The bell curve is appropriate for assigning letter grades in most secondary and middle-level classes.	_____	_____	_____
4. For a group of secondary school students, final course grades should parallel their respective intelligence quotients (IQs).	_____	_____	_____
5. The teacher's judgment should not enter into the grading process.	_____	_____	_____
6. Evaluation is frequently used in secondary and middle schools to promote learning.	_____	_____	_____
7. A student's effort should determine that student's success in class.	_____	_____	_____

PAST USE OF EVALUATION IN SCHOOLS

Research has provided much information that can help teachers effectively use evaluation, but as Parsons and Jones (1990, p. 17) explain: "Unfortunately, the litany of our knowledge about classroom evaluation does not match our usual practices as teachers."

Middle-Level Message

Testing is one thing, evaluation is another. Be careful if you do not know the difference. You may be like the dog that chased the skunk—when he caught it, he didn't know what to do with it. Before giving your first tests, consider what you will do with the results. This process of deciding what to do with the results is called evaluation. Middle-level learners need organization in their lives. You can help provide organization for your students by mastering the concepts in this chapter and coordinating your tests with your more comprehensive evaluation program. Most teachers fail to use the most valuable type of evaluation—formative evaluation. Formative evaluation can help you promote learning. A second important type of evaluation is criterion-referenced evaluation. Most teachers fail to use this type of evaluation too.

　　Begin thinking of evaluation as an important instructional tool. You can even use it to diagnose your own teaching weaknesses. Use this chapter to learn how to use evaluation positively to raise your students' achievement levels.

For decades teachers have misused evaluation. Winton (1991) warns teachers against the temptation of using grades for the wrong ends:

> Teachers sometimes use grading to motivate, punish, or control. In this they frequently have parents as allies. It is assumed that students with poor grades will naturally work harder to achieve better grades. Good marks become the objective of learning. Grades become the currency which students, teachers, and parents may use for different purposes. (p. 40)

Evaluation differs from testing. Testing should be conducted objectively and apart from the teacher's own values. Evaluation demands that you make a qualitative judgment, or set values, on what you measure. As Bloom, Hastings, and Madaus (1981, p. 105) state: "There is no statistical or completely objective method that can be used to assign grades to a student's score or a student's product. Ultimately, a judgment of the worth or value of that score or product must be made by the teacher." Evaluation is also much broader than testing. Testing requires such tasks as selecting or constructing the appropriate examinations, administering them, and scoring the responses, but all this is merely a prerequisite to evaluation.

　　Evaluation begins where testing ends. Once the results are determined and the tests are returned, you must use these results to make the testing worthwhile. How you use test results is evaluation. The list below shows the relationship between measurement and evaluation and their parts.

Relationship between Measurement and Evaluation

Measurement
1. Deciding on type of test
2. Selecting a ready-made test or constructing a teacher-made test

3. Administering the test

4. Scoring the test

Evaluation

1. Formative: using the test to promote learning

2. Summative: using the test (and possibly other criteria) to grade the student, teacher, or program

Note that evaluation is divided into two main categories—formative and summative. As you read the following paragraphs, note the sharp distinction between the two. Your effective use of evaluation depends on your ability to separate the two basic types.

FORMATIVE EVALUATION

Comparatively little use has been made of formative evaluation. Formative evaluation can be defined as the designing and using of tests for only one specific purpose—to promote learning. Formative evaluation enables teachers to monitor their instruction so they can keep it on course (Oliva, 1992).

Dagley and Orso (1991, p. 73) note the purpose of formative evaluation: "Formative evaluation is an ongoing process, designed to improve the teacher's performance." Also, "if any student cannot learn excellently from the original instruction, the student can learn excellently from one or more correctives" (Block & Henson, 1986, p. 24). Put simply, students often need a chance to test their knowledge without penalty so they will know how to adjust their study techniques. According to Markle, Johnston, Geer, and Meichtry (1990), tests can become strong clarifiers of teacher expectations, thereby guiding students toward expected outcomes. Although most teachers agree that going over test answers in class can help some students learn more about the material, they are aware that this is not likely to result in students' total mastery of the material.

Students usually do not see how tests can promote learning. "After a test is finished, it is time to shut down the schema. Teachers are sometimes frustrated because students do not exhibit any interest in reviewing their tests" (Stefanich, 1990, p. 50). There must be a much more systematic use of evaluation, separate from grading and aimed only at promoting learning.

Successful use of formative evaluation requires both teachers and students to change their attitude of equating tests with grades. When using tests for formative purposes, you should:

1. Avoid recording individual scores.

2. Be concerned only with whether the student has mastered the material at an acceptable level.

3. Involve each student in keeping a continuing record of individual progress.

4. Avoid mentioning grades.

5. Assume that, when properly motivated, all students can master the material.

6. Avoid pushing students so fast that they become confused and discouraged.

7. Reassure students that these test results will not count toward their grades.

TABLE 14.1 A Comparison of progressive reporting and traditional evaluation

Traditional Evaluation	Progressive Evaluation
Spot checks understanding	Measures comprehensive understanding
Detached from student	Involves student
Nondescriptive	Descriptive
One-time evaluation	Ongoing evaluation

Since students and teachers usually never perceive evaluation in this way, you must be patient and reassuring if you elect to use tests to help students learn.

Progressive Reporting

Schools are replacing letter grades with progress reports, which can be more insightful than traditional grades. Winton (1991) explains:

> The use of progress reporting is a viable alternative since it imparts information—information about what is being taught, alternative activities the student has completed, and how he or she is coping with the course. No individual letter grade can do this. Direct conferences supplement narrative reports and a portfolio of student work is much more revealing and reliable. (p. 40)

The 26th Gallup Poll (Elam, Rose, & Gallup, 1994, p. 55) found that American parents find written descriptions the most useful of the ways schools inform them of their child's progress. A full 95 percent of parents vote written progress reports as either quite useful or very useful.

Compared with traditional grading practices, progressive reporting is more comprehensive, more specific, more descriptive, and more personal for the student (Table 14.1). Perrone (1994, p. 13) says "on-going assessment is critical."

Take-Home Tests

An example of formative evaluation is the use of take-home tests. These tests give students access to more information sources and more time to internalize that information. According to Parsons and Jones (1990, p. 17): "Take-home tests can provide an answer for teachers who wish to evaluate student progress with longer and more complex problem situations."

SUMMATIVE EVALUATION

Dagley and Orso (1991, p. 73) present one use of summative evaluation: "The purpose of summative evaluation is to decide if the teacher meets minimal accountability standards." Summative evaluation is also used to measure student performance to deter-

TABLE 14.2 A comparison of summative and formative evaluation

Summative Evaluation	Formative Evaluation
Purpose: issue grades	Improve teaching
Time given: following instruction	Before and during instruction
Basis: norm-referenced	Criterion-referenced
Follow-up: seldom	Always

mine such major decisions as grades, passing, and failing. Lindblad (1994, p. 292) reminds us that in most communities parents insist on the use of letter grades. "Although many teachers will indeed use a variety of instructional methods, the vast majority of schools systems still require that grades be assigned to each student."

Because teachers have used tests almost exclusively to determine student grades, you may assume that with all that practice teachers are systematic in the way they convert raw scores into letter grades. But this is not so. Each teacher seems to have an individual system, and many teachers use a different system each grading period. Why? Because most teachers never find a system that satisfies them. No single system is right for all classes. When you become aware of the strengths and weaknesses of various grading systems, you will be in a better position to choose wisely. To compare summative and formative evaluation, see Table 14.2.

COMPETITIVE EVALUATION

All evaluation systems can be grouped into two categories: those that force a student to compete with other students (norm-referenced), and those that do not require competition among students but instead are based on a set of standards of mastery (criterion-referenced). As Clark and Astuto (1994) explain:

> The argument in support of competition is based on the belief that an individual can push beyond current levels of skill and achieve at the highest possible levels when pressed to do so in the heat of competition. . . . The counterargument is that self-motivation is sustained when individuals maintain a sense of their own efficacy and work in a context in which people help one another develop skills, take risks, and challenge standard operating procedures. (p. 516)

Traditionally U.S. schools have required competition among students, and many teachers believe that competition motivates students. Many also believe that competition prepares students for adulthood in a competitive world, especially for getting ahead in their future employment. But others disagree. For example, Winton (1991, pp. 40–41) expresses concern over excessive use of competition: "Over and over again in homes and in schools we set up situations which guarantee that children will feel defeated and inept." He continues: "Evaluation should be for the purpose of promoting further learning. It should be a positive, supportive experience."

Standardized Tests

One test that forces students to compete among themselves is the standardized test, which is very popular in U.S. schools today. Standardized tests have several features in common. First, they are based on norms derived from the average scores of thousands of students who have taken the test. Usually these scores come from students nation-wide, so each student's performance is compared with that of thousands of other students.

Standardized tests are usually used to measure or grade a school's curriculum. Seeking to make teachers more accountable, state officials have forced schools to use standardized tests, given to students to measure teacher success—and yes, they are even used to measure student success. For example, for decades the state of New York administered its Regents examinations to determine student success. By the early 1980s almost all states had legislated minimal learning standards, and tests are presently being developed to determine each student's and each school's level of attainment. Florida, which in July 1980 began testing its teachers for 23 generic competencies (Oliva & Henson, 1980), and Oklahoma are two of the many states that use standardized tests to make their students, teachers, and colleges of education accountable.

The Normal Curve

A second use of tests that requires students to compete with others is the normal curve (also called the normal probability curve or the probability curve). The curve could well be called the natural curve or chance curve, because it reflects the distribution of all sorts of things in nature. This distribution is shown in Figure 14.1.

The normal curve is divided into equal segments. The vertical line through the center (the mean) represents the average of a whole population. Each mark to the right

FIGURE 14.1   Normal probability curve

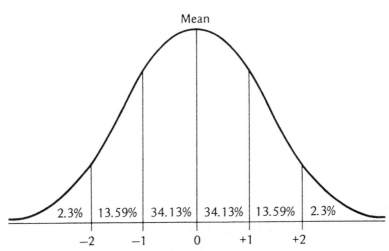

of the mean represents one average, or standard deviation, above the average. Each vertical line to the left of the center represents one standard unit of deviation below the mean. As the figure shows, about 34 percent of the population is within the one standard deviation unit above the mean, and about 34 percent of the population is within the one standard deviation below the mean. Only about 14 percent of the population is in the second deviation range above the mean, and about 14 percent is in the second deviation range below the mean. A very small portion of the population (approximately 2.3 percent) deviates enough from the mean to fall within the third unit of deviation above the mean; an equal portion deviates three standard units below the mean.

To give another example, if the temperature is taken every day at 3 PM from June 15 until August 15 for ten years, and if a mean or average is taken, the individual temperatures are listed vertically from hottest to coldest, and the line is divided into six equal parts, then 34 percent of the temperatures would fall in the section just above the middle, 34 percent would fall within the section just below the middle, 14 percent would fall in the second section above the mean, and 14 percent would fall in the second section below the mean. Only 2.3 percent of the temperature readings would fall in the third section above the mean, and 2.3 percent would fall in the lowest section below the mean.

Some of the many things subject to this type of distribution are the weight and height of animals and plants, the margin of error of both humans and machines, and, of course, the IQs of human beings. Not all phenomena are distributed in the ratios represented by the normal curve. For example, the chronological ages of the human population do not follow this pattern.

The normal curve, as it is often applied to the assigning of grades in a school classroom, makes several bold assumptions. First, like other evaluation schemes based on competition among students, it assumes that the level of a particular student's performance compared with the average of a group of students (usually the student's classmates) is important. Second, it assumes that all students have an equal opportunity to succeed—as though all have equal potential, which is extremely unlikely unless the class has been homogeneously grouped. Third, it assumes that the number of students used as a norm is large enough to reflect the characteristics of all students at the particular grade level. Unless the class size exceeds 100 students, this is a bold assumption indeed. The use of the normal curve assumes that 68 percent of the students will earn Cs, 13.5 percent will earn Bs and another 13.5 percent Ds, and 2.5 percent will earn As and 2.5 percent will fail.

Stanine Scores

Many schools use stanine ("standard nine") scores to determine student performance. This method uses the normal distribution curve to group test scores into nine categories (Figure 14.2). This modification of the bell curve evaluation gets rid of the As, Bs, Cs, Ds, and Fs. Many educators feel that the psychological advantage of escaping the letter grade stigma is important. Also, having nine categories gives the teacher more groups in which to place projects that must be arbitrarily evaluated.

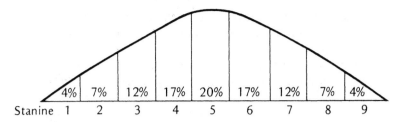

FIGURE 14.2   Normal distribution curve to determine stanine scores

School-wide Standards

Even more popular than the standard curve is the practice of schools' setting their own standards. You are undoubtedly familiar with the following system:

> 90 percent and above = A
> 80–89 percent   = B
> 70–79 percent   = C
> 60–69 percent   = D
> Below 60 percent   = Failure

This type of evaluation makes an important, and often false, assumption. It assumes that the test's level of difficulty fits students' abilities exactly. Student teachers usually realize this error as they begin marking their first set of papers and find that almost everyone failed the test. Although the exact percentage requirements may vary among schools, the system remains a common method of evaluation.

Reflection

The following passage illustrates the magnitude of the standard of error in geology and demonstrates why standardized test scores often have an equally alarming high standard error.* Read the passage, then think about this as you respond to the questions below.

A Very Standard Error

My friend was a geologist. We were in his backyard, awed by the majesty of the Rocky Mountains. The monstrous flat sloping rocks that are the hallmark of Boulder, Colorado, were the subject of our conversation.

"Do you know how old those rocks are?" my friend inquired.
"I have no idea at all," I replied.

"They are about four hundred million years old," he said, "give or take a hundred million years."

1. Do you think the general public is aware of the large standard of error common to many standardized test scores? What evidence can you offer to support your answer?
2. What do educators do that suggests that they do not consider the fallability of standardized test scores?
3. Realizing that standardized tests frequently have large standards of error, how do you think this should affect a teacher's use of standardized test scores? Why?

*The passage is from J. Frymier. (1979). On the way to the Forum: It's a very standard error. *Educational Forum, 36,* 388–391.

NONCOMPETITIVE EVALUATION

Researchers and educators have recently discovered much evidence that shows that grading in the high school should be strictly an individual concern—involving the teacher and the student. "Criterion-referenced tests (which do not force competition among students) contribute more to student . . . progress than [do] norm-referenced tests" (Fantini, 1986, p. 132). Once it was thought that competition for grades was necessary because it motivated students to do their best. This is certainly true for the more-capable students, but forcing the less-capable students to compete with their classmates can discourage them and force them to concentrate on their inadequacies. Competition can also be bad for the more-capable student. You can reduce this damage by not making test scores and grades public.

Many contemporary educators feel that grades should reflect the student's effort, that no one should receive an A without really trying, and that no students exerting themselves to their full potential should receive an F. These teachers believe that grades should not acknowledge high IQs and punish those who do not have high ability, but that each grade should reflect a student's degree of progress relative to his or her ability.

You can improve performance evaluation by using complementary grading systems. Epstein and MacIver (1990, p. 39) recommend blending performance evaluation and progress grades: "A school that officially rewards improvement by using progress grades along with performance grades can expect at least 1.7 percent fewer of its male students to eventually drop out."

Require students to keep a record of their progress in class. According to Pratt (1980, p. 258), "Many schools allow students to write their own self-appraisal. . . . This encourages students to reflect on their own learning." Seek and use students' judgment in determining their grades. A relevant question may be "How do you believe the quality of your work now compares with your previous work? Do you believe this is the best you can do?" Of course this approach requires that the teacher know each student—and not as a face but as a developing, growing person.

Students are now using performance evaluation.

Grading Involves More than Testing

Although the terms *grading* and *testing* are often used synonymously, this is a mistake. And most teachers believe that a student's grade should reflect more than test scores. Fantini (1986, p. 112) states, "No test reveals all there is to know about the learner, and no test should be used as an exclusive measure for any student's capacity." Neither can a single test measure all a student knows about any topic. Some things other than the acquisition of knowledge are important in school. For example, teachers must ensure that each student develops certain behavioral patterns and attitudes, such as honesty, promptness with assignments, the ability to work with others, and respect for others. Therefore a student's grade should reflect each of these traits. Evaluation of these qualities is essentially subjective, and to avoid becoming prejudiced you should decide at the beginning of the year just how much weight this part of the total evaluation carries and take care not to exceed the limits.

Grades should represent all the major activities a student engages in while in your classroom. Daily work and term projects may, and perhaps should, carry as much weight toward the final grade as the tests. If you use several tests (weekly or biweekly), daily assignments, term projects, and daily discussions, you will have more satisfactory material on which to base the final grade. Winton (1991, p. 40) says, "Good middle school philosophy limits competition and substitutes direct conferences and written evaluations for formal grading systems."

Begin with Much Understanding

As a beginning teacher recently exposed to college tests, you will probably grade too firmly. To avoid alienating and discouraging your students, be a little lenient at first.

This does not mean you should always change a grade when a student is unhappy with it, because this often reinforces complaints. Being lenient at first means you should not expect only one particular answer on most types of questions and that you should not expect everyone to score 70 and above. It means that if you believe Jimmy is trying, even though he scores 55 instead of the 60 set as passing, he may receive a C or D rather than an F. Discussions with Jimmy throughout the year will let you assess the degree to which he is applying himself.

Assignments for Extra Credit

To challenge the most capable students, some teachers include a bonus question on every major test. This is fine if those who do not answer it correctly are not penalized. Some teachers offer extra credit to students who come to special sessions and complete extra assignments on problems with which they are having difficulties. This procedure also can be helpful in motivating students.

When a student asks for an assignment for extra credit at the end of the grading period, however, the student may be less interested in learning than in raising a grade. The student may really be asking, "Will you assign me some extra punishment so that my grade can be elevated?" The teacher may respond by assigning the student 40 problems the student already knows how to work, or by assigning the task of copying 2,000 words from an encyclopedia, library book, or magazine without having to learn the content. This practice is most undesirable, because it encourages some students to procrastinate until the last minute and then subject themselves to x amount of punishment rather than attaining x amount of understanding. They also learn to dislike the subject that produces the pain.

When students ask to do extra work for credit, base your decision on whether you believe they will learn from the task. You may ask the students what type of assignment they propose to do and what they expect to learn from it. If they can convince you that they can and will learn from the task, the assignment may be warranted.

GRADING SYSTEMS

The decision on a specific grade is essentially a subjective one. One question may help you each time you assign a grade: What grade will be the best for this student? The student's ability and application will determine your answer. To assign a grade that is higher than deserved is certainly not good for the student, and neither is assigning a grade lower than what the student has earned.

But having a philosophy of grading is not enough. As a teacher, you will make decisions based on available information. And the task is a serious and often thankless one. Pratt (1980, p. 259) explains, "[Grading] is a sensitive area, one in which the teacher can feel uncomfortably exposed and can be subject to powerful pressures to make decisions that are in conflict with the educator's professional judgment."

Too often teachers rely on test scores alone to determine student grades. As Parsons and Jones (1990, p. 20) explain, teachers should use a variety of criteria to assign grades: "In fact, the more diverse and imaginative the evaluation activities used by the teacher, the more all-encompassing and valid the evaluation is likely to be."

So let us begin preparing for that day by examining a typical situation at the end of a grading period. Ideally, you will have a variety of feedback on which to base each grade—for example, some class projects, presentations, classwork, homework, and tests. Following is a list of such feedback that you might have on each of your students at the end of a six-week grading period.

> 6 weekly tests
>
> 1 final examination
>
> 1 term paper
>
> 1 oral presentation or term project
>
> 1 group project
>
> 30 homework assignments
>
> 20 classroom assignments

To arrive at a grade for the six-week period, assign relative values to each item on your list. Be sure to consider the amount of time the student has spent on each activity. You may want to begin by rank-ordering these elements according to the time invested in each, for example:

Activity	*Time Required (Hours)*
Homework 30 × 40 minutes	20
Classwork 20 × 30 minutes	10
Group project	6
6 weekly tests at 50 minutes	5
1 term paper	4
1 presentation of project (including preparation)	3
1 final examination	1

These activities required 49 hours of student time. To simplify the process, you might simply assign an additional hour's credit to class participation. With a new total of 50 points, you may choose to assign 2 percent of the total grade to each hour spent in each activity. Thus the following system would emerge:

Activity	*Percentage of Grade*
Homework =	40
Classwork =	20
Group project =	12
Weekly tests =	10
Term paper =	8
Oral presentation =	6
Final exam =	2
Classroom participation =	20

But suppose you as the teacher of this class are not happy to have the final examination count only 2 percent against 10 percent for classroom participation. This is no problem, because you can now distribute 6 percent to the final examination and 6 percent to participation or 7 percent and 5 percent, and so on. Suppose you discover an error in addition; if these percentages total more than 100 percent, you could reduce the other percentages in proportion to their size, taking off about 10 percent of each of the eight items.

The distribution in your particular system will not be identical to this one. That does not matter, as long as you assign each grade based on your chosen system. But on what criteria other than the time spent on each activity could you base your grading system? How about the emphasis given each topic in class? What about students' cooperation with other students, and so on?

Your school may require a certain percentage for an A, B, C, or D, but if you are free to design your own requirements, do not forget to ask yourself what grade will be most appropriate for and most helpful to each student. The familiar evaluation practices will not meet the needs of future citizens. Smith (1991, p. 21) criticizes traditional evaluation, expressing this concern: "Traditional evaluation, on the other hand, is not likely to provide the clarity and focus students need."

RECAP OF MAJOR IDEAS

1. Report-card grades should reflect a variety of types of student performance, including classwork, homework, reports, projects, and tests.
2. Few secondary or middle-level classes are large enough to support using the bell curve to determine grade distribution.
3. Secondary and middle-level teachers can use formative evaluation to promote learning.
4. Criterion-referenced tests let students compete only with themselves and clearly inform students what is expected of them before they take each test.
5. Competition among students of varying capabilities can damage both less-capable and more-capable students.
6. Consider what is best for each student when you assign a final grade.
7. Unlike the act of measurement, you cannot perform grading and evaluation without reference to your own values.

CASES

As in other aspects of teaching, you will daily encounter new challenges related to evaluation. No list of principles can be comprehensive enough to guide your behavior in all circumstances. The following cases show the complexity of such a seemingly simple task as assigning a student a grade or convincing others of grades' limitations and functions.

CASE 1: A PARENT CONFUSES GRADES WITH SUCCESS

Susie Bates was in the eighth grade when her schoolwork took a rapid decline. From one six-week grading period to the next, her grades fell from B to F. Susie's father, a high school principal, telephoned Susie's principal to discuss the matter—after report cards were passed out. Susie's principal called Susie's homeroom teacher to the telephone. Mr. Bates began with the usual question: "Can you tell me why Susie's grades have fallen so much?" The teacher responded "No." Mr. Bates mentioned that Susie had started playing in a pop band a couple of nights a week and had suddenly become especially interested in boys. Did the teacher think this could have any connection with her low grades? As difficult as it may be to believe, this was how a high school principal responded to the failure of his own child.

The Bates case was typical in that the parent called after the grading period was over to ask what could be done about Susie's low grade. He was really asking, "What are you going to do about it?" but the teacher can do very little after the fact, except help Susie and her father realize that Susie's problem is not that she received an F but that she did not learn enough in a given time and that little can be done to correct the past. We can only try to avoid repeating the mistake. Teachers who are serious about helping students learn to be suspicious of a Bates-type call, much as they learn to appreciate a sign of parent interest that comes early enough to help a child.

The teacher explained to Mr. Bates that he wanted to help Susie achieve and learn, not just get higher grades, and that perhaps together they could do this by encouraging Susie and then rewarding her achievements by letting her know how proud they were of her.

Discussion

1. Should a teacher change a grade at a parents' request?

   Generally not, unless there has been a mistake. To yield to parental pressure will teach the student that force is a satisfactory method for achieving success.

2. Students often come to teachers near the end of a grading period and ask for an extra assignment to pull up a grade. Should this be permitted?

   Only if the student can learn from the assignment—and even then the teacher should avoid allowing this too often. Extra assignments to increase a grade can teach students to procrastinate during the term because they expect they will be allowed to increase their grade at the last moment.

CASE 2: A STUDENT IS GIVEN A BREAK

Linda Eliot was in Mrs. Rolando's ninth-grade math class. She was a delightful girl, always bubbling and happy. Perhaps her lack of seriousness explained the Ds and Fs in all her subjects, or perhaps her Ds and Fs had caused her to become less serious about her schoolwork. At the end of the school year Linda had a D + average. The fact that she had performed higher than usual tempted Mrs. Rolando to give her a C rather than the earned D+, but she decided to talk with Linda before assigning a grade.

Mrs. Rolando began by asking if Linda was aware that she was on the C and D border. Linda responded with enthusiasm. Mrs. Rolando told Linda that the grade was unclear but that she believed Linda was a C student rather than a D student and that if she really wanted to know which she was, there was a plan for finding this out. Linda listened eagerly while her teacher explained that she would assign her a C for the semester if Linda agreed to bring her report card at the end of the first grading period of the next year. At that point they would check her math grade to see if the assumption was correct. Linda happily agreed to these terms. Mrs. Rolando thought the possibility of Linda's remembering the plan throughout the summer vacation and into another school year was remote, but no harm could come of the ploy.

Following a pleasant summer, a new school year began. Mrs. Rolando had a total of 180 new faces to remember and get to know. At the end of the first grading period she was handing out report cards when two girls came rushing through the doorway. Without saying a word, Linda handed over her report card. Mrs. Rolando recalled the agreement they had and scanned the card. She found not only that Linda had a B − in math but also that in all her subjects the lowest grade was a C −. Linda explained that she was now eligible to try out to be a cheerleader. This was obviously an important moment and a triumph for Linda.

Discussion Questions

1. Was the teacher justified in giving Linda a higher grade than she earned?
2. What potential damage is there in telling a student you are assigning a grade that is above his or her average earned grade?

CASE 3: PARENTS' ATTEMPT TO MOTIVATE THEIR CHILD BACKFIRES

Dr. Bough was a reputable physician whose daughter was in Mr. Hammonds' eighth-grade science class. Mr. Hammonds hardly noticed Ann for the first few weeks of the term. She was very quiet, and she never volunteered to answer questions. When asked to respond, she would wait, hoping he would call on another student.

One day Mr. Hammonds received a note from the counselor to return a call to Mrs. Bough. They scheduled an appointment to discuss Ann's performance in school. When the time came, Mr. Hammonds was ready. He had studied Ann's cumulative records and her schoolwork over previous years. He found that the three IQ scores on file were 99, 101, and 102—remarkably consistent and also remarkably average. Ann's grades had consistently been Bs, indicating that she had been performing high in relation to her ability. Ann was currently taking five academic subjects and band, with no study period. Her test scores in Mr. Hammonds's room had steadily declined from B to D−.

Both parents came to the session. As usual, Mr. Hammonds began by letting the parents talk while he listened. Right away he saw that they had two things to say, politely but firmly: Ann was capable of making top grades, and she was doing her best. In fact, often after she had scored a D or an F on Mr. Hammonds' test, her mother would quiz her orally and she would score 100. After the next test, Mr. Hammonds gave Ann an oral examination, asking the same questions. She had failed the written test but scored 90 percent on the oral repeat. Ann studied hard, learned the material, then failed the tests. Why?

Ann's parents saw themselves in her. Both of them had been A students, so why shouldn't Ann make As? They had considered each of Ann's Bs failures. By pressuring her to get As, Ann's parents had turned each test into a trauma that produced mental barriers. The problem carried over into each daily lesson—when a teacher looked at Ann, she froze. Ann had developed real emotional problems. No parents were more interested in their child's success in school, and no parents were more willing to express their concern to the teacher, but one could argue that the Boughs were not trying to help Ann. They were trying to get her to make higher grades, not because they wanted to help her but because they saw themselves in Ann. By making straight As she would reflect the "Bough image" to her teacher and classmates. Perhaps this conclusion is unfairly harsh, but it does point out a common tendency that some parents have, to lose objectivity when trying to help their children.

Mr. Hammonds suggested to Ann's parents that they not discuss grades with her until he could experiment with an idea. He promised that he would call them when the experiment was over, and they agreed to cooperate. For the next few weeks Mr. Hammonds observed Ann, searching for an answer. Several times he caught himself on the verge of reminding the class that they would be held accountable for the material on the next test, but each time he refrained. He soon noticed that Ann and the rest of the class became more confident.

Discussion Question

1. How could the teacher make Ann's parents understand that the ultimate goal should be to have Ann learn, not merely to get a high grade?

ACTIVITIES

As you read this chapter, your mind probably leaped forward to the time when you will be teaching and grading your own classes and the types of activities that would become your criteria for grading. You had an opportunity to examine a grading system for a hypothetical class. Here you have an opportunity to design a system of your own.

1. Suppose you have complete autonomy with regard to grading. (This is very rare in secondary and middle schools.) Decide whether you would use a norm-referenced or criterion-referenced system, and defend your choice.
2. Suppose you are forced to use the A B C D system with 90, 80, 70, and 60

percent intervals. List the criteria you would use for grading, and assign a relative value (percentage) to each.

3. Because formative evaluation is seldom used in secondary and middle schools, research the literature and prepare a report on formative evaluation. Discuss with your professor or classmates the relevance of each characteristic to secondary and middle school classes.

4. Arrange a debate between one team that defends grade competition among classmates and a team that opposes such competition. Ask both teams to limit their remarks to those they can substantiate with a written article. During the debate, have a judge (perhaps the professor) throw out any comments that students cannot defend with written support. Make a list for each point earned by each team. Then, with all the points listed on the board, hold a general discussion (not a debate) on whether and when to hold student competition.

REFERENCES

Block, J. H., & Henson, K. T. (1986). Mastery learning and middle school instruction. *American Middle School Education, 9,* 21–29.

Bloom, B. S., Hastings, J. T., & Madaus, G. F. (1981). *Evaluation to improve learning.* New York: McGraw-Hill.

Dagley, D. L., & Orso, J. K. (1991, September). Integrating summative and formative modes evaluation. *NASSP Bulletin, 75,* 72–82.

Clark, D. L. & Astuto, T. A. (1994). Redirecting reform: Challenges to popular assumptions about teachers and students. *Phi Delta Kappan, 75* (7), 513–520.

Elam, S. M., Rose, L. C., & Gallup, A. M. (1994). The 26th Annual Phi Delta Kappa/Gallup Poll of the Public's Attitudes Toward the Public Schools. *Phi Delta Kappan, 76*(1), 41–64.

Epstein, J. L., & MacIver, D. J. (1990, November). National practices and trends in the middle grades. *Middle School Journal, 22*(2), 36–40.

Fantini, M. D. (1986). *Regaining excellence in education.* Columbus, OH: Merrill.

Lindblad, A. H., Jr. (1994). You can avoid the traps of cooperative learning. *The Clearing House, 67*(5), 291–293.

Markle, G., Johnston, J. H., Geer, C., & Meichtry, Y. (1990, November). Teaching for understanding. *Middle School Journal,* 53–57.

Oliva, P. F. (1992). *Developing the curriculum* (2nd ed.). New York: HarperCollins.

Oliva, P. F., & Henson, K. T. (1980). What are the generic teaching competencies? *Theory into Practice, 19,* 117–121.

Parsons, J., & Jones, C. (1990, September–October). Not another test. *The Clearing House, 64*(1), 17–20.

Perrone, V. (1994). How to engage students in learning. *Educational Leadership, 51*(5), 11–13.

Pratt, D. (1980). *Curriculum design and development.* New York: Harcourt.

Smith, M. W. (1991, January). Evaluation as instruction: Using analytic scales to increase composing ability. *Middle School Journal, 22*(3), 21–25.

Stefanich, G. P. (1990). Cycles of cognition. *Middle School Journal, 22*(2), 47–52.

Winton, J. J. (1991, January). You can win without competing. *Middle School Journal, 22*(3), 40.

SUGGESTED READINGS

Ganz, M. N., & Ganz, B. C. (1990). Linking metacognition to classroom success. *The High School Journal, 73*(3), 180–185.

Wiggins, G. (1989, April). Teaching to the authentic test. *Educational Leadership, 46*(7), 41–47.

Wolf, D. P. (1989, April). Portfolio assessment: Sampling student work. *Educational Leadership, 46*(7), 35–39.

chapter 15

Test Construction, Administration, and Scoring

The bottom line in teaching is always assessment.
Dale R. Phillips and Darrell G. Phillips

OBJECTIVES

List two advantages of objective test questions and two of essay questions.

Develop an objective test that measures different levels of the cognitive domain.

Describe a minimum and a maximum standard teachers can use to determine the appropriate level of difficulty for writing test questions.

List five guidelines for administering a test.

Construct a discussion-type test that will measure students' ability to judge or evaluate.

State two practices that ensure fairness on a discussion-type examination.

Design a system for scoring an essay examination that will justify assigning more value to some questions than to others.

Write a general essay-type question that promotes divergent thinking. Then rewrite the same question, making it more specific.

Write a multiple-choice question with five choices, two of which are viable distracters.

Write a question for each level of the affective and cognitive domains.

Write a simple recall-level test question and rewrite it twice, each time raising the level of behavior required to answer these questions.

PRETEST

	Agree	Disagree	Uncertain
1. Objective questions test only the student's ability to retain facts.	_____	_____	_____
2. Competition among all students is good.	_____	_____	_____
3. Teachers must score essay questions subjectively.	_____	_____	_____
4. Essay questions tend to measure what students know, whereas objective questions measure what they do not know— that is, their learning gaps.	_____	_____	_____
5. Beginning teachers tend to make tests too difficult.	_____	_____	_____
6. Tests should contain both objective and essay questions.	_____	_____	_____
7. Most teachers have an adequate background in testing.	_____	_____	_____

8. Essay tests reveal students' thought processes.   _____   _____   _____

9. Most American students can support their opinions.   _____   _____   _____

10. Give multiple-choice test items only one plausible answer.   _____   _____   _____

11. The more specifically you word essay questions, the better they are.

12. Application level test items require the use of principles.   _____   _____   _____

Middle-Level Message

Teachers often view testing as their most unpleasant responsibility. This occurs when they fail to understand how to use tests appropriately. Middle-level teachers often express a need to know more about classroom management and motivation strategies. Perhaps this accounts for much of their misuse of tests. Middle-level and high school teachers must learn more about the use of tests and their effects on students. In this chapter you will learn how you can use a variety of tests to assess student performance. You will also learn each type of test's major advantages and limitations and how to construct, administer, and score tests to increase student achievement. Help your students realize that test scores are not important terminal goals but important indicators of success.

THE TEACHER'S RESPONSIBILITY

As a teacher, you are responsible for the testing program in your classes. Even teachers who teach in secondary schools that give departmental tests will have to help construct, administer, and score the tests. Therefore, the bulk of this chapter focuses on helping prospective and experienced teachers improve their skills in these areas.

Your responsibility for testing can be the most unpleasant role you will have, or it can be an important, meaningful part of your teaching, depending on your level of expertise in this area. Frankly, few teachers take full advantage of how a good testing program can help their teaching. Fielding and Shaughnessy (1990, p. 90) say, "The gap between the potential of testing as a teaching-learning tool and the reality of current practice is wide." This chapter is concerned with teacher-made tests; Chapter 14 covered standardized tests.

CURRICULUM ALIGNMENT AND AUTHENTIC TESTS

Increased pressures on teachers to have their students score well on standardized tests cause teachers to think about how and what they teach. Accountability for their students' performance on these tests motivates teachers to explore ways of helping students perform better. Paradoxically, those who hold teachers accountable for students' performance are often the same critics who accuse teachers of teaching to the test. What do they expect teachers to do, teach one set of content and activities and test for another? Such behavior is completely illogical.

Faced with the choice between (1) ignoring the tests, thereby risking poor student performance, and (2) feeling guilty about teaching to the test, teachers have another alternative, a very good one. They can plan their curriculum so that it fits the evaluation and then design their learning activities accordingly. Fenwick English (1992) calls this process curriculum alignment. Wiggins (1989) cautions that schools must adjust their graduation requirements to require the same skills state tests require. Wiggins offers an example of a final exhibition of mastery required of seniors at a high school in Racine, Wisconsin (Figure 15.1). Note that these students are required to complete a portfolio. A portfolio is a combination of tangible products that provides evidence of the student's skills. It can serve the prospective teacher much as a commercial artist's portfolio shows the artist's skills in several related areas. Note that this portfolio requires a variety of products such as writing, artwork, and oral performance. Such variety is a common strength of most portfolios. This portfolio requires the same skills as the goals required for high school graduation in Wisconsin. Because a portfolio is part of a student's curriculum, this quality makes this portfolio a good example of curriculum alignment.

Portfolios can serve several functions but only if their purposes are clear to the teacher and students. Barton and Collins (1993) explain the importance of clear portfolio objectives.

FIGURE 15.1   The Rite of Passage Experience (R.O.P.E.) at Walden III, Racine, Wisconsin

From Wiggins G. (1989, April). Teaching to the authentic test. *Educational Leadership, 46*(7), 4–47.

All seniors must complete a portfolio, a study project on U.S. history, and 15 oral and written presentations before a R.O.P.E. committee composed of staff, students, and an outside adult. Nine of the presentations are based on the materials in the portfolio and the project; the remaining six are developed for presentation before the committee. All seniors must enroll in a year long course designed to help them meet these requirements. The eight-part portfolio, developed in the first semester, is intended to be "a reflection and analysis of the senior's own life and times." The requirements include:

- A written autobiography,
- A reflection on work (including a resume)
- An essay on ethics
- A written summary of coursework in science
- An artistic product or a written report on art (including an essay on artistic standards used in judging artwork)

The first characteristic of portfolio development is explicitness of purpose. Teachers by themselves and teachers and learners together must explicitly define purposes of the portfolio so that learners know what is expected of them before they begin developing their evidence file. (p. 202)

The project in Figure 15.1 is a research paper on a topic of the student's choosing in American history. The student is orally questioned on the paper in the presentations before the committee during the second semester.

The presentations include oral tests on the previous work, as well as six additional presentations on the essential subject areas and "personal proficiency" (e.g., life skills, setting and realizing personal goals). The presentations before the committee usually last an hour, with most students averaging about six separate appearances to complete all 15.

A diploma is awarded to those students passing 12 of the 15 presentations and meeting district requirements in math, government, reading, and English.*

This sample portfolio program emphasizes writing: writing about science, writing about history, writing about ethics, and writing about art. Perrone (1994, p. 13) considers the role of writing across the curriculum so important to portfolios that he wrote, "If students are not regularly writing across a variety of topics and in a variety of styles for diverse purposes, then promoting self-evaluation has limited value."

Another example of curriculum alignment is an oral history project for ninth graders designed by Albin Moser at Hope High School, Providence, Rhode Island (Figure 15.2). This project has two outstanding strengths: It requires the student to reflect and to be creative.

Tests designed to help students to develop those skills measured by standardized tests are called authentic tests. "Authentic assessment seeks to engage students by situating problems and tasks in real-world contexts" (Postner & Rudnitsky, 1994, p. 96).

Reflection

Examine the history portfolio project and the oral history project. Make a list of the qualities you like in these projects. Using the qualities, create a project in your discipline. Design some goals and write some test items that are aligned with this project.

This means asking some new types of questions: Are my students' educational needs being met? What information and information-gathering skills will they need to excel when they leave school? How can I put my students in charge of gathering this new information and developing these much-needed information-gathering skills? How can I help them plan their learning and then supervise the process so that they

---

* This summary is paraphrased from both the R.O.P.E. Student Handbook and an earlier draft of Archbald and Newmann's (1988) *Beyond Standardized Testing.*

To the student:
You must complete an oral history based on interviews and written sources and then present your findings orally in class. The choice of subject matter is up to you. Some examples of possible topics include: your family, running a small business, substance abuse, a labor union, teenage parents, and recent immigrants. Create three workable hypotheses based on your preliminary investigations and four questions you will ask to test out each hypothesis.

Criteria for Evaluation of Oral History Project
To the teacher:
Did student investigate three hypotheses?
Did student describe at least one change over time?
Did student demonstrate that he or she had done background research?
Were the four people selected for the interviews appropriate sources?
Did student prepare at least four questions in advance, related to each hypothesis?
Were those questions leading or biased?
Were follow-up questions asked where possible, based on answers?
Did student note important differences between "fact" and "opinion" in answers?
Did student use evidence to prove the ultimate best hypothesis?
Did student exhibit organization in writing and presentation to class?

Note: This example is courtesy of Albin Moser, Hope High School, Providence, Rhode Island. To obtain a thorough account of a performance-based history course, including the lessons used and pitfalls encountered, write to Dave Kobrin, Brown University, Education Department, Providence, RI 02912.

FIGURE 15.2   An oral history project for ninth graders

From Wiggins, G. (1989, April). Teaching to the authentic test. *Educational Leadership, 47*(7), 44.

understand the major concepts throughout and across the disciplines? How can I assess their learning when many of each student's educational goals may be unique? How can I shift much of the responsibility to the students and then shape my new role to let me become a learner again?

Students remain the central foundation for building a curriculum model. Paramount concerns include students' abilities, how they learn, and how they are motivated. Concern for content is as important as ever, but students must learn how to evaluate the information and identify what they must know. These human and subject matter issues must be at least partially resolved before students and teachers can move to the next step and determine how modern technology can help meet these needs. All this is a prerequisite to the selection of hardware and software.

The pie-chart design was chosen because (1) it portrays each part as relatively equal in importance to the others, (2) there is no ideal beginning place; rather, all may be pursued simultaneously, and (3) technology selection is made simultaneously with methodology.

The Special Study Panel on Education Indicators for the National Center for Education Statistics (1991) says "Authentic," "alternative," and "performance" are all terms applied to emerging assessment techniques. Whatever names they go by, their common denominator is that they call on students to apply their thinking and reasoning skills to generate often-elaborate responses to the problems put before them. Successful authentic testing requires teachers to (1) begin planning by examining the types of skills they wish their students to have, (2) design their tests to meet these aims, and (3) teach accordingly.

Through continuous self-assessment or keeping an ongoing record of their own progress, students can fill the gaps in their own learning. Furthermore, by including a variety of self-assessment techniques such as drawings, charts, and diagrams, students can move from concrete to symbolic or abstract thinking (Phillips, Phillips, Melton, & Moore, 1994). Some students find assessing their own performance difficult, yet with their teacher's help, students can learn to evaluate their performance and often enjoy it. Simmons (1994) explains:

> Some students are reluctant to engage in peer and self-assessment because they feel that such activities are the teacher's—the expert's—job and that their own work will ultimately suffer from their own or their peers' assessment. Yet, we have seen in our work that when students and teachers set forth criteria and use them as a basis for reflection on student work, both groups are often surprised at the positive outcomes. (p. 23)

TYPES OF TESTS

Before you begin constructing tests, remember that many types of tests exist and that you have a number of options. For many years American educators have been predisposed to written tests. The practice of using written tests may have been so strongly embedded in your own teachers that when you hear the word "test" you think of a pencil-and-paper exercise.

But there are alternatives. Teachers can choose simply to ask questions orally to solicit oral responses, or they can give a performance test that requires students to perform exercises, such as role playing in a drama class, assembling an engine in an auto mechanics class, or responding in dialogue in a foreign language class. Concern that written tests too frequently measure only the recall of knowledge, ignoring the student's ability to apply it, has prompted greater use of oral and performance options. Most teacher-made tests are of the pencil-and-paper variety. As we examine several types of written tests, keep in mind their potentials and limitations for measuring different student competencies.

Essay versus Objective Tests

When choosing to use a written test, decide whether it will be an objective test or an essay-type test, or possibly a combination. The two types differ drastically in many ways. First, the essay test measures what students know, whereas the objective test is often accused of measuring what student do not know. The essay test does permit students to select from and use their own knowledge in the response. By contrast, the objective test (true-false, matching, and multiple choice) does not provide this freedom. In fact, the objective test can also leave students thinking that they understand the lesson but that the test questions just happened to be from less familiar areas.

Most important, the essay test is flexible enough to give students opportunities to express their own views—to reach beyond the recall level into the application, analysis, synthesis, and evaluation levels and even into the affective domain. In addition, essay questions enable teachers to determine a student's thought processes. As Quellmaiz (1985, p. 32) puts it, "The essay format is especially useful for assessing how students reach and explain their conclusions." The National Assessment of Education Progress (1981) examination, which asked students to interpret or evaluate literary selections in essay form, found that few students could offer even rudimentary support for their opinions. This attests to the need for using essay items in assignments and on tests.

Essay Test Items

Discussion.   Of all types of test items, the essay question is perhaps the most misused. When questions are stated broadly, such as "Discuss Shakespeare's work" or "Discuss the Industrial Revolution," students wonder, "Where should I begin?" and "What issues am I supposed to address?" By carefully restricting the question, you can reduce the ambiguity—for example, "Discuss the types of humor in Shakespeare's *Twelfth Night*" or "Discuss the role of Eli Whitney's cotton gin in the Industrial Revolution." By sharpening essay questions' focus, you also simplify your scoring. The more exactly you state your expectations, the more accountable your students become for including expected content in their answers. By giving an example, you further clarify your expectations—for example, the question "Discuss the role of Eli Whitney's cotton gin in the Industrial Revolution" could be followed by "Address its effect on the labor market."

Explanation.   Good questions on explanation tests focus on a certain process—for example, "Explain the water cycle." Because the water cycle involves a definite sequence of activities (e.g., rain → runoff → evaporation → condensation), students can be held accountable for a specific body of knowledge, plus the sequences involved in the process. When using explanation questions, avoid general questions such as "Explain the civil rights movement of the Sixties." Stated that way, the question is at best just a discussion and would be better worded as such.

Situation.   Situation test items measure a student's response to a certain situation. Students are asked to apply their knowledge, values, and judgment to decide how they would respond to a given set of circumstances. For example, the teacher of a first-aid course might ask, "If you were driving down the road and came to an accident that had left a person lying in the road unconscious and breathing heavily, what would you do?" Like other types of essay questions, situation questions are best when they request a definite body of knowledge. They also require students to apply that knowledge.

Compare or Contrast.   Questions that ask students to compare or contrast force them to sharpen their understanding about similar or dissimilar concepts. In other words, they require students to differentiate between two or more concepts by focusing on particular similar or dissimilar qualities—for example, "Compare and contrast World War I with World War II." You can get more specific answers by adding limits to the question—"Compare and contrast World War I with World War II according to their ground strategies, air strategies, number of casualties, and number of countries involved."

Objective Test Items

Some popular types of questions found on objective tests include true-false, multiple choice, and matching. Less common is the fill-in-the-blank question. Each type calls for a specific, predetermined answer. Objective test items are often criticized for testing what students do not know rather than what they do know. Furthermore, they tend to encourage guessing.

In addition, the advantage of their objectivity and easily accomplished scoring leads to one of their major limitations, namely, the trivialization of the knowledge tested. The concise, clearly delimited response is emphasized; critical thinking, analytical skills, and conceptualization are all but ignored. Multiple-choice and fill-in responses are preferred; exposition and creativity are penalized.

A study for the National Center for Education Statistics—Special Study Panel on Education Indicators for the National Center for Education Statistics (1991)—identifies some weaknesses of traditional tests used to measure schools' success, noting the limitations of multiple-choice tests. Note the differences in trends of future testing:

> The panel wants to point out that most national assessments rely heavily on multiple-choice formats. Obviously, such tests have their uses. However, education and learning are complicated endeavors, and the panel believes the effort to assess the results must be equal to the task. "Authentic," "alternative," and "performance" are all terms applied to emerging assessment techniques. Whatever name they go by, their common denominator is that they call on students to apply their thinking and reasoning skills to generate often-elaborate responses to the problems put before them. In many of these testing situations, there are multiple "correct" answers; in almost none of them is the student forced to select from a list of prespecified multiple-choice alternatives. Extended writing assignments, hands-on science assessments, student portfolios, and group projects over time are the next generation of tests that will assess a new generation of Americans. (pp. 69–70)

Objective tests do have certain advantages over essay tests. First, they are more quickly scored. This is important to today's teachers, who would better invest time in preparing lessons than in scoring tests. Furthermore, objective questions are likely to be more fairly scored because there is no doubt about whether an answer is correct. This too is an important advantage, since most teachers want their students to perceive them as fair and impartial.

THE PURPOSE OF TESTING

Is testing necessary? What are its advantages? Could these advantages be achieved some other way? How does testing assist the instructional program? How can I improve my own testing program? When we think of testing we think of grades. But if we say that the purpose of testing is to determine grades, another good question is, Why do we need grades? Justifying tests merely as grade determiners is not sufficient; many educators are not convinced that grades are necessary.

Testing helps your students determine their general rate of progress in a specific subject. This information is important to both the student and you. And to report a grade—which most school systems require and most parents expect if not demand—you must know the student's general rate of progress. Chapter 12 showed that when students know their rate of achievement they can be motivated or encouraged to achieve even more.

Testing also helps you determine the class's progress as a whole. The rate of progress in teaching is always proportional to the class's learning rate. In other words, your teaching cannot be better than your students' learning. Test results can help you identify areas where you must improve your methodology and clarify misunderstandings in the classroom—that is, where to slow down, where to repeat more, or where to use different methods. Testing also provides a way to diagnose teacher and student strengths and weaknesses. Through testing, you can help students identify areas needing more effort.

Recognize the test as a tool for helping you improve your methodology and for helping your students improve listening and study habits. Then construct, administer, and evaluate tests with these purposes in mind.

TEST CONSTRUCTION

If you experience mild shock when grading your first set of test papers, do not immediately question your teaching ability. Many teachers argue that the topic of test construction has not been addressed sufficiently in undergraduate teacher training programs (Carter, 1983) and that they need programs to help them develop, manage, and provide practice for evaluation (Fluitt & Gifford, 1980). Carter (1984) found that many teachers are unable to recognize what skill a particular test item was testing. Pre-service teacher training often fails to include a course on testing (Coffman, 1983), and assessment is rarely a topic for in-service training (Stiggins, 1985). Realizing that most of the fault is not in the teaching but in the testing, you may ask, How can I construct good tests?

Stating the Directions

Begin each test with a written statement explaining how to complete the test. Like all assignments, make the directions specific. For example:

> Each item on this test is worth one point. Select the single choice you believe is best. Do not leave questions blank, and do not mark more than one choice. If you have questions, please raise your hand and I will come to your desk. When you finish, please turn your paper face down on your desk and begin working quietly on the assignment now written on the board.

Once you write the test, check it for any ambiguity or possible misinterpretation, making changes and clarifying accordingly. Include the maximum time allotted students for taking the test in the directions. Clear directions will prevent unnecessary interruptions during the testing period and will prevent the discomfort students feel when they are not sure what is being asked of them.

State the Value of Each Question

Most teachers find it convenient to specify or assign values to questions in terms of percentages. Assign relative values, asking yourself how much each question is worth in relation to the other questions. Make the value of each question proportional to the amount of class time spent on that topic and the amount of test time required to answer that question.

Often a test will consist of several short-answer questions or short problems that carry equal value. On such tests, do not specify separate values; merely state in the directions that each question has equal value. On tests with questions of varying values, specify the value of each question in the margin alongside the question.

Select a Variety of Questions

Which type of question is best—objective or subjective? Actually, each type offers advantages that the other does not, so most tests should contain both objective and subjective questions. Objective questions require more time to construct, but they require less time to answer and to score, so many objective questions can be included on each test. Subjective questions can measure creativity and allow students to express their feelings and attitudes; they also show how well students can organize their thoughts.

Many testing experts believe multiple-choice questions are the best type of objective questions. True-false questions are seen to be of average value, and fill-in-the-blank questions are the least valuable. Do use several types of objective questions, however, because students who find one type of question especially difficult to answer will not be penalized by having an entire test of that type. Multiple-choice and other types of test questions are discussed later in this chapter.

Include Both Easy and Difficult Questions

Every test should have some questions so easy that almost every student can answer them correctly. Begin the test with the less-difficult questions to encourage each student to go on to the following question. Placing easy questions at the beginning of multiple-choice examinations has increased test scores significantly—almost 10 percent (Savitz, 1985). Remember that tests should measure ability, not tolerance. Avoid placing a 40-point question at the end of the test. Slower students will think it is unfair if they fail the test because time ran out just as they began answering a last question that is worth that many points.

If every question on a test were so easy that every student could answer it correctly, the test would be of little use. Include some questions that challenge even the most capable students. Make each question a little more difficult than the preceding question, but never try to make the question difficult by wording it so it is vague, too general, or tricky. The difficult questions should be difficult because they are especially challenging and involve a complex process, and they should measure students' attainment of important concepts.

Cover Important Material

Most teachers believe it is necessary to test at least once every two weeks. From the large volume of material covered in this time span, what should you include on the test? A good rule is that any test should contain questions about information covered each day of the testing period. In other words, it should begin testing where the previous test stopped and should test right up through the day preceding the test date.

Ideally, the time spent studying various areas of content should be in proportion to the material's importance. Therefore, the percentage of time studying an area should be proportional to the percentage of the test that the particular area comprises. For example, if in a unit on astronomy the class spent a week studying the sun and only one day studying the moon, the total value of test questions about the sun should be about five times as great as the total value of questions about the moon.

Testing the Test

Many teachers insist on taking a test themselves before administering it. In addition to catching typographical errors and ambiguously worded questions, the teacher can at the same time develop a master answer sheet. Without a list of answers when beginning to score a test, a teacher tends to accept the first students' answers and to use these as a standard for judging the accuracy of the answers on the other students' papers.

WRITING TEST QUESTIONS

Selecting the Type of Test

On completing a unit of study—or, as we shall see, even during a unit—the teacher must decide when to give an examination and then either design the right type of questions or select the right type of ready-made examination. Base both decisions—when to measure and what type of test to use—on the test's purpose. Essay questions measure some skills best, while objective questions are more suitable for measuring other skills. Let us look at the more commonly used types of test questions and some advantages and limitations of each. The suggestions for improving the questions should be of particular interest.

Essay Questions

Although all test questions fall into two categories—subjective or objective—the subjective, or essay, question is a type of its own. Essay questions have some important limitations. First, they are difficult to control. Actually, they require the teacher to relinquish some control, because students are free to answer (and actually must do so) in terms of their own perspectives. This leads to another problem—the scoring. You must decide whether to count such variables as:

1. Ability to focus on the teacher's perspective
2. Writing and spelling skills
3. General neatness
4. Comprehensiveness
5. Specific facts and concepts
6. Broad generalizations
7. Creativity
8. Attitudes
9. Logical reasoning
10. Other skills outside the knowledge category, such as the ability to synthesize or evaluate

Resolve these uncertainties before giving the test to avoid potential disagreements between you and your students. To avoid this risk, you may want to avoid essay or discussion tests in favor of more specific, objective tests. But first consider the advantages of essay questions.

Essay-type questions excel in their ability to let students express themselves. In responding to an essay question, students can be as creative, imaginative, and expressive as they wish; furthermore, they can state and evaluate their own beliefs and values. This is especially important for two reasons. First, evaluation is the highest known level of thinking (according to Bloom's *Taxonomy of Educational Objectives,* as seen in Chapter 4). Second, when responding to test questions, students often want to express their own beliefs and justify their responses.

Writing Essay Questions. Structure each essay question to emphasize the ideas the student should address. This will minimize the difference between teacher and student perceptions of expectations. Following are examples of good and bad essay test items.

A. Discuss the causes of the Revolutionary War.

How would you respond to this question? What is wrong with it? You probably would not know where to begin, because the question is far too general. Suppose it were rewritten to read:

B. Name and discuss three main causes of the Revolutionary War.

Now the question lets you know you are expected to cover three main causes, but it is still a monumental and time-consuming task. You could not ask more than two or three questions of this type on any test. A test should reflect the complete range of material covered in class since the previous test. Suppose the question is altered further, as seen in sample C:

C. Name and discuss three economic factors that contributed to the development of the Revolutionary War.

Now the scope of the question has been limited drastically. The student can immediately eliminate the many political and social factors. By making the question more specific, you reduce its ambiguity and limit the scope of responses the question will elicit. But because discussion questions offer the teacher a unique opportunity to stimulate students to think independently and creatively, you probably will want to include at least one question designed for that purpose. An example of such a question is sample D:

> D. Suppose England had won the war. What changes would have occurred in the American lifestyle?

This question gives students the opportunity to use divergent thinking—that is, it requires them to expand their thoughts by using their imaginations. Therefore it is of a higher order than the previous questions. Note, though, that it requires you as teacher to give up much of your ability to regulate or restrict student responses. In a class of 30 students, this question would probably elicit 30 different responses and create problems in scoring the answer. For this reason, before asking such a question, be sure that the question will measure imagination and creativity; these two considerations would count heavily in determining a grade for this question.

Take the time to word questions very carefully so they will achieve their objectives. You will save time in scoring essay answers if you structure questions unambiguously. To be sure, wording and scoring good essay questions is not easy; it requires time and thought. The quality of the responses you get will probably correlate highly with the amount of time you spend on the questions.

Scoring Essay Questions.   A good approach to assigning values to each part of a response is to take the test yourself before administering it. Then you can assign credit for each part of the expected response according to the respective values. For example, take sample question D: "Suppose England had won the war. What changes would have occurred in the American lifestyle?" Assume that the classroom discussion or textbooks and other materials included such concepts as more rigid tariffs, lower prices, and worsening labor conditions. Each concept could receive 2 points' credit. Other reasonable responses could receive 1 point each, making the question's total value 9 or 10 points.

Consider at least two important considerations in determining how much value to assign to each test item. First, consider the amount of time and emphasis given to this item in class and in homework. Does this item reflect one or more class objectives? "The items on the test should be similar to the instructional objectives" (Griswold, 1990, p. 19). Simply stated, test items should be weighted (or assigned a value) according to the importance of the content being measured.

Second, consider the amount of time required to respond to items. The grade value that items are assigned should approximate the percentage of time required to answer the question. Once you have decided how many points to assign each question, sequence the items so that the ones that count the most are at the beginning of the test. Should you place these items near the end of the test, some students might run out of time before getting to them by spending too much time on questions of lesser grade value.

Multiple-Choice Questions

Multiple-choice questions are popular today, partly because machine scoring is increasingly available, but also because the questions themselves have merit. Like the true-false and fill-in-the-blank test, a multiple-choice test enables the teacher to ask many questions and thus cover many topics on the same test. Unlike true-false and fill-in-the-blank tests, however, the multiple-choice test restricts the amount of success derived by guessing. The multiple-choice item seems best suited to bring out the finer distinctions between what is good, what is best, and what represents loose thinking, if not downright error (Mouly, 1970).

But this advantage is realized only when the teacher designs each test question appropriately. Keep in mind also that tests should be used to help students learn. When correctly written, the multiple-choice test can become an excellent learning device.

Like all other types of tests, select the multiple-choice test on its merits—that is, on its ability to achieve specific goals. Then design it to achieve those goals. If its purpose is formative (to promote learning), design it one way; if its purpose is to determine student success (summative), design it differently. We shall look at specific designs for specific purposes, but first let us answer some general questions that you might have about developing multiple-choice tests.

How Many Alternatives Should I Include?   It is wise to include at least four choices, and five may be desirable if the test is intended to promote learning. Should I include among my alternatives "all of the above" and "none of the above"? Because "all of the above" enables one to measure knowledge about the question, it is a legitimate option. Because "none of the above" does not enable the student to relate specifically to the question, avoid it (Ellsworth, Donnell, & Duell, 1990). The bottom space could be more wisely used to include a concept related to the material being tested.

How Should I Phrase the Stem of a Multiple-Choice Question?   First, keep it brief. Avoid using more than one sentence, lest a student trip on the question itself. Second, avoid negatives in the stem. Both unnecessary length and negatives tend to confuse and interrupt the thought process. Write a test question so that it communicates as clearly as possible (see the following examples).

    E. All isosceles triangles
        a. Have at least two equal sides
        b. Have at least two unequal angles
        c. Have at least three equal sides
        d. Have at least three equal angles

Item E could be simplified as follows:

   E. All isosceles triangles have at least
      a. Two equal sides
      b. Two unequal angles
      c. Three equal sides
      d. Three equal angles
   F. Which of the following is not an example of sedimentary rock?
      a. Limestone
      b. Sandstone
      c. Chert
      d. All of the above

Item F should be changed to read as follows:

   F. An example of igneous rock is
      a. Limestone
      b. Sandstone
      c. Chert
      d. All of the above

How Should I Select the Alternatives?   If you are designing the test to promote learning, purposely include several closely related alternatives. If the purpose of the test is grading, reduce the number of near-correct answers to only one or two. To have all answers almost acceptable would be unduly taxing and might result in teacher preference as opposed to student preference. A question with only one attractive answer would be equally poor design. It would not promote learning or thinking and therefore would not discriminate between those who have mastered the material and those who have not. Examine items G, H, and I and for each question identify at least one major flaw. Then rewrite each to eliminate those flaws.

   G. Alexander Graham Bell invented the
      a. Cotton gin
      b. Telegraph
      c. Radio
      d. All of the above
      e. None of the above
   H. Water is not an example of a
      a. Liquid
      b. Solution
      c. Fluid
      d. Compound
      e. Base
   I. The Pilgrims began arriving in America in the early 1630s. Some came by way of Holland; others came directly from the port of Southampton in England. The real reason for their coming was to

    a. Escape persecution
    b. Seek freedom of religion for all
    c. Form a new denomination
    d. All of the above

The obvious error in item G is the alternative "none of the above." Correct the question simply by eliminating the fifth choice. The stem of question H contains a negative. Correct the question by deleting the "not" and changing the choices. The stem of item I is unnecessarily long. Correct it by eliminating the first two sentences.

What Other Common Errors Can I Avoid?   Some multiple-choice questions give the correct answer unintentionally. Items J and K contain questions that make this mistake. See if you can identify which part leads the student to the correct answer. Then rewrite the question to avoid the error.

J. A well-known French psychologist is
    a. Wilburn Smith
    b. Robert O. Williams
    c. Jean Piaget
    d. Warner Hayes
    e. Sam Jones
K. The nickel is an example of an
    a. Alloy
    b. Solution
    c. Compound
    d. Metal
L. The speed of light is
    a. 100 feet/sec
    b. 100 miles/hr
    c. 120 miles/hr
    d. 186,000 miles/sec

Item J leads the student to select an alternative based on grounds other than knowledge about psychologists. In item K, the use of the word "an" suggests the correct answer; incidentally, the alternative being sought in item K is not the only correct alternative provided. In summative tests, take care not to include more than one correct answer. Test item L is poor because it fails to include a strong distracter (a plausible or near-correct choice).

Fill-in-the-Blank Questions

Although the fill-in-the-blank question can boast no real strengths, it has managed to survive throughout the history of U.S. schools. Not only does this type of question limit the teacher to measuring only knowledge (or recall) level information, but it seldom achieves this with any degree of accuracy. The fill-in-the-blank question often puts the student in the impossible position of trying to guess what the teacher wants. Mastering the material does not guarantee success on this type of test.

Nevertheless, the fill-in-the-blank test appeals to many teachers because it can be developed quickly and effortlessly. (This does not reflect the way it should be developed, but merely the way it often is developed.) Some teachers lift sentences right out of the text and print them verbatim on the test, substituting a blank for one or more words. Item M is an example of a typical fill-in-the-blank question. How would you answer it? Can you modify it to eliminate its ambiguity?

M. The Battle of New Orleans was fought in _____.

This type of question unintentionally invites the imagination to run wild. A creative student might respond with New Orleans, the rain, winter, anger, or mud, blood, and beer. An infinite number of correct answers is possible and should be given full credit, but the student need not know anything about the Battle of New Orleans to respond correctly. Other students may become discouraged over the ambiguity and leave the space blank, thereby getting penalized for the teacher's failure to communicate clearly.

Although you would usually be wise to choose another type of question, suppose you want to test for highly technical or specific factual information. When correctly written, the fill-in-the-blank can achieve this. A teacher writing item M to test for the date of the beginning of the battle need only insert "the year of _____"—that is, "The Battle of New Orleans was fought in the year of _____."

N. Tests are more _____ than are _____ tests.

This kind of question can be even more frustrating to students than single completion items.

In conclusion, avoid fill-in-the-blank tests when other types of tests will achieve your objectives. If you do use them, remember that being specific is the key to designing good questions.

Matching Test Items

Most teachers use matching tests at some time or another. This type of test enables you to measure students' ability to make important associations. Its value is apparent from the number of national standardized tests that test for the examinee's ability to make associations, ranging from the picture association game on Sesame Street to the Miller Analogy Test (MAT) many college graduate programs use.

Matching tests are not easy to construct. Take care to avoid using a stimulus that matches with more than one response (Oliva, 1972). An examiner wishing to have students use a stimulus more than once should inform them that they may use the same number or letter in their answers repeatedly. For example, in item O, stimulus number 1 would fit in both responses A and D.

Teachers should always provide feedback on tests.

O. Stimulus   Response

  1. Noun   _____ **A.** Water   _____ **E.** Slowly

  2. Verb   _____ **B.** Blue   _____ **F.** Her

  3. Adjective   _____ **C.** Fishing   _____ **G.** Into

  4. Pronoun   _____ **D.** Moon

  5. Adverb

Note also that in item O the number of responses exceeds the number of stimuli. This is to discourage guessing. Another important precaution in writing multiple-choice items is to avoid giving hints. Item P illustrates such carelessness in item writing.

P. Match the dates with the corresponding events.

  1. 1861   **A.**   Signing of the Magna Charta

  2. 1812   **B.**   Beginning of the Civil War

  3. 1776   **C.**   Storming of the Bastille

  4. 1215   **D.**   Signing of the Declaration of Independence

  5. 1918   **E.**   War of 1812

             F.   Cardinal Principles of Secondary Education

Obviously, "War of 1812" is a dead giveaway. Avoid such matches on matching tests because they fail to measure any level of understanding.

HIGHER LEVEL QUESTIONS: COGNITIVE DOMAIN

Returning to Bloom's *Taxonomy of Educational Objectives* discussed in Chapter 4, we find that the major areas in the cognitive domain are:

Level 1. Knowledge
Level 2. Comprehension
Level 3. Application
Level 4. Analysis
Level 5. Synthesis
Level 6. Evaluation

Most types of objective questions discussed so far have been limited to measuring the retention of information, but this does not mean such test items as multiple-choice and matching cannot be designed to test for higher levels of understanding. Do not conclude that only discussion-type questions can measure higher levels of understanding. Each type of question can be used to measure different levels of all three learning domains. The following examples show prospective teachers, student teachers, and experienced teachers at least one way of designing questions to measure understanding at each level.

Level 1: Knowledge

Since we are all familiar with questions that test only one's ability to recall facts, this first level need not be discussed.

Level 2: Comprehension

Charts, maps, graphs, and tables lend themselves well to measuring learning mastery at the comprehension level. Questions at this level should require the student to translate, interpret, or predict a continuation of trends (Bloom, Hastings, & Madaus, 1971). For example, Figure 15.3 shows the general sales ratio of a textbook during its first three years of publication. If a certain book has sold 10,000 copies in the first year and 30,000 copies by the end of a second year, how many copies can we estimate it will have sold by the end of a third year? Of course, a multiple-choice question could be written to use with this graph—for example: The total accumulated sales projected by the end of the third year are:

a. 10,000
b. 20,000
c. 30,000
d. 40,000

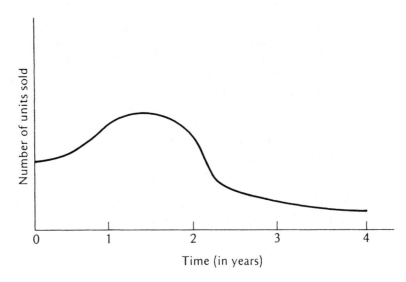

FIGURE 15.3   Sales ratio of textbooks

Level 3: Application

Questions measuring the ability to think at the application level must require students to apply abstractions—such as general ideas, rules, and methods—to concrete situations. In other words, the student must use a principle or generalization to solve a new problem.

When students are taught concepts, they are seldom able to generalize from one situation to another. Stefanich (1990) addresses this concern:

> Students tend to deal with concepts in isolation. They cannot effectively consider a number of isolated examples and apply these to general theory or principle. They cannot effectively apply a general principle to a number of instances or examples. They are unable to cognitively process variable time frames or situations which require simultaneous consideration of multiple characters or events. (p. 48)

The following example (Ward, 1969) is offered to clarify the process of generalizing:

> You enter the old kitchen, in which there is a blazing hearthfire complete with bubbling, boiling teakettle. Oh, it's always there anyway; you've seen it before. Besides, your mind is on something else. Your quaint kitchen is pretty well tuned out by you, or you only perceive it at the (blob) level. Wait, something focuses your attention on the event system that is the boiling kettle. You've noticed. Now you're beginning to operate. You've noticed something, and something is happening. The lid jumps up and down. You won-

der why. Ah, cause, the why sets you to scrutinizing relationships. First you attend, focus, observe, isolate. Next you want the cause of something. Establishing tentative cause gets you to infer a low-level generalization. "That lid will move because steam is pushing it up and down. If that particular kettle is put on that fire and it boils, then its lid will jump up and down" a relatively low level of abstraction because the particulars of the scene are still involved. The next level of abstraction, of generalizations, will take you to a point of thinking, "When a kettle is placed on a fire, the water will boil and cause a loose lid to move." (p. 423)

You have gone from the particular to the general, although you are still involved with the category of tea kettles. Several levels of application are possible here. First, the student can match a principle with its correct corresponding situation, as in item Q.

> **Q.** Match each situation with the principle at play. Each stimulus may be used repeatedly.
>
> **1.** Radiation   **A.** A sea breeze
> **2.** Convection   **B.** An air conditioner
> **3.** Conduction   **C.** A kite
>   **D.** A heater
>   **E.** A hot coffee cup

A second level of application requires the student to restate a problem. For example, in the story of the tea kettle you might say that the problem at hand is to determine why the lid was moving. Given this situation and problem, ask students to state the problem without using the word "steam." Still another level of application would require students to generalize to predict what will happen in a different situation involving the same principles. You might ask students a question, "Suppose the kettle lid were held fast and the spout were stopped up. What would happen when the kettle was placed on the stove?" (Caution: Do not try this experiment!)

There are other levels of application, but these examples show how you can arrange experiences or tasks that force students to perform at the application stage.

Level 4: Analysis

The analysis level requires breaking down generalizations, concepts, and principles to clarify ideas or understand them better. A common type of question for measuring at the analysis level gives the student one or more paragraphs to read and then a list of questions. These questions do not simply ask for retention (knowledge level) and the ability to predict patterns or trends (comprehension level); they require the student to identify the author's underlying assumptions. For example, students might be asked to read the following parable on education taken from Plato's Republic. In the seventh book, which opens with a beautiful description of the nature of man confined in a dark cave, Plato proceeds to show the means and plan for learning true philosophy and how we may attain the serious and sober practice of social life and politics.

Behold men, as it were, in an underground cave-like dwelling, having its entrance open toward the light and extending through the whole cave, and within it persons, who from childhood upwards have had chains on their legs and their necks, so as, while abiding there, to have the power of looking forward only, but not to turn round their heads by reason of their chains, their light coming from a fire that burns above and afar off.

Let us inquire then, said I, as to their liberation from captivity . . . and their cure for insanity, such as it may be, and whether such will naturally fall to their lot; were a person let loose and obliged immediately to rise up, and turn round his neck and walk, and look upwards to the light, and doing all this still feel pained, and be disabled by the dazzling from seeing those things of which he formerly saw the shadows; what would he say, think you, if any one were to tell him that he formerly saw mere empty visions, but now saw more correctly, as being nearer to the real thing, and turned toward what was more real, and then, specially pointing out to him every individual passing thing, should question him and oblige him to answer respecting its nature; think you not he would be embarrassed, and consider that what he before saw was truer than what was just exhibited?

But if, said I, a person should forcibly drag him thence through a rugged and steep ascent without stopping, till he dragged him to the light of the sun, would he not while thus drawn be in pain and indignation, and when he came to the light, having his eyes dazzled with the splendor, be unable to behold even any one thing of what he had just alleged as true?

And consider this, said I, whether, in the case of such as one going down and again sitting in the same place, his eyes would not be blinded in consequence of coming so suddenly from the sun? Quite so, replied he . . . and as for any one that attempted to liberate him and lead him up, they ought to put him to death, if they could get him into their hands? Especially so, said he. (Davis & Burgess, 1901)

The teacher might follow this passage with a series of questions, such as the following:

1. Why does Plato select an underground cave for his location for "mankind"?
2. Why does Plato have his released prisoner look at the blinding firelight and then the blinding sun?
3. Why did Plato choose to have the released prisoner dragged to the outside rather than merely led?
4. On his return to the cave, why might the released prisoner be put to death for telling the truth?

Note that each question focuses on a specific part of the parable. This is important to the analytical process. Note also that the student is required to use the particular passage to solve a problem. If this assignment seems difficult or bizarre, remember the assignments you had in high school poetry class. You probably have had extensive contact with analysis assignments and analysis level test questions. This is only one of several types of analysis questions, but it should help prepare you to introduce your students to analysis tasks.

Level 5: Synthesis

In recent years, students and teachers have come to hold in high esteem assignments that have no single, predetermined, "correct" answer but that require students to apply their unique talents and perceptions to arrive at an acceptable answer. Unfortunately, today's teachers are pressured by community members who want the schools to reject these exercises in divergent thinking and return to the traditional approach to teaching the "Three Rs."

The value of such synthesis tasks is summed up in the concept of gestalt—that is, "The whole is greater than the sum of its parts." The student is given the task of putting together a number of concepts to communicate a uniquely different idea, one that is his or her own. This is the essence of creativity itself, which is known by the artist, painter, songwriter, movie producer, dancer, architect, and others who use their minds, bodies, and talents to express themselves. Rich in aesthetic qualities, it also has practical value, because the synthesis process requires perceiving problems from different perspectives, leading to inventions and to "building a better mousetrap."

Instead of trying to satisfy the demand for exercises that require "the" correct answer, students could better spend the time seeking out relationships that will guide their actions. If this sounds unscientific, today's scientists would not agree that such open-ended exercises requiring divergent, creative thinking are at all unscientific.

> For example, if a layman were to ask a physicist for a definition of light, he would likely be told that light may be considered a wave phenomenon (wave theory) or it may be thought of as having particles (corpuscular theory). If the layman insisted on the correct definition of light, the physicist would probably respond "That isn't a useful question; physicists have stopped asking it" (Conant, 1952). The reason that physicists no longer pursue a "correct" definition of light is that it is irrelevant. One definition, within a limited situation, enables scientists to account for certain phenomena; the other definition, in another set of circumstances, is more useful. (Zais, 1976, p. 14)

We should recognize the value of lower levels of thinking and their importance in the curriculum. What better way is there to master the multiplication tables than by rote memorization? Yet to limit classroom tasks only to those that require memorization would be to keep students from experiencing the types of problems they must be prepared to solve in real life. Such a restriction also robs them of the ability to form new perceptions and express new conceptualizations.

In synthesis tasks, students are asked to take certain material, reorganize it, and assemble it in a new way to give it new meaning. The problem must be new to the students and, when possible, of special interest to them. For this reason, students should be involved in identifying the problem. This does not preclude assigning a particular problem to a group of students or to the entire class.

You are responsible for providing problems for students or for leading them in the selection process. Since there is no single, correct answer, be sure to stipulate exactly what criteria to use in evaluating the work. For example, consider the following problem:

> In many American communities, interest and participation in high school sports is so intense, and the financial support for athletics is so great, that many complain that academic subjects are neglected. Suppose you are captain of the football team at such a school. Furthermore, suppose the classrooms have deteriorated and the school does not have the funds to restore the buildings. To make things worse, suppose your team has just ended another losing season. Prepare a statement to justify continuation of an interscholastic sports program in face of these critical circumstances. Devise a plan that will enable the school to finance the necessary building restorations and still finance the team for coming years.

Or the geology teacher may present a rock for students to examine. Giving each student, or group of students, the materials needed to run tests for color, hardness, and acidity, the students would tell where the rock originated and substantiate this conclusion with logic. The main objective is that the student design a plan for locating the derivative of particular rocks. The location itself is irrelevant. Another example of a synthesis task would be to give each student a box of assorted materials with which to devise a container that will support the fall of a raw egg when dropped from a two-story window.

Studies on creativity (Torrance, 1967) indicate that the mind is usually more creative when the student:

1. Is encouraged to pursue a direction that seems right for him or her even when to others it may seem disorderly
2. Is given the opportunity to work alone, yet is allowed (not forced) to share his or her work with others
3. Works in a pressure-free environment
4. Is protected from peer pressure to conform
5. Works within areas of his or her special interests

When you develop tasks at the synthesis level, consider these conditions and try to provide an atmosphere that is most conducive to creative thinking.

Level 6: Evaluation

Tasks at the evaluation level require students to make judgments based on logical accuracy, consistency, and other given criteria in addition to remembered criteria. An example of a task at this level would be to present students with a politician's election platform and ask them to examine it for accuracy, logic, and consistency. Students would also be expected to compare it with the politician's previous political behav-

TABLE 15.1   Sample activities from the levels of Bloom's Cognitive Taxonomy

Level	
6	Critique two per lessons and describe the qualities that make each lesson superior to the other lesson.
5	Reshape a piece of clay to increase its buoyancy. Explain why the newly formed shape is more buoyant.
4	After reading *The Republic* explain (interpret) Plato's use of the image of the "blinding light."
3	Examine a boiling tea kettle and explain why the lid is bobbing up and down.
2	Interpret the annual rainfall as shown on a chart.
1	Name three types of rocks.

ior or support or rejection of bills involving similar issues—in other words, does he practice what he preaches?

Other levels of evaluation tasks require students to identify values or assumptions on which judgments are made. For example, in your methods classes you may be asked to critique your peers while they teach a mini-lesson. Suppose you were asked to respond to the following questions:

1. The critic found the lesson organized so that the concepts
   a. Flowed smoothly
   b. Were illogically presented
   c. Were arranged in chronological order
   d. Both a and b
   e. Both b and c
2. According to the critic, the delivery of the lesson was
   a. Enhanced by the teacher's poise and self-confidence
   b. Strengthened by the use of good visual aids
   c. Augmented by the absence of unnecessary jargon and technical terms
   d. All of the above

Other types of evaluation questions require the student to judge a particular work based on similar works. Students may even be given an opportunity to form their own lists of criteria to use for evaluation. Table 15.1 shows a sample activity for each level of the cognitive domain. Space limitations do not allow discussion and samples of test items in all the sublevels of the six categories of Bloom's taxonomy, but you can explore further by examining the sources listed at the end of this chapter. Of special help are the Bloom books, the Mager book, and the Stiggins book.

A BALANCE IS NEEDED

Although experts tell us that we should work to raise the level of thinking in our lessons and on our examinations, we risk going overboard. Even if we could manage to raise our instruction and test items to the upper levels of the taxonomy, still we might find

TABLE 15.2 Percentage of individuals in Piagetian stages

Age (Years)	Preoperational	Concrete Onset	Concrete Mature	Formal Onset	Formal Mature
7	35	55	10		
8	25	55	20		
9	15	55	30		
10	12	52	35	1	
11	6	49	40	5	
12	5	32	51	12	—
13	2	34	44	14	6
14	1	32	43	15	9
15	1	14	53	19	13
16	1	15	54	17	13
17	3	19	47	19	12
18	1	15	50	15	19

SOURCE: G. P. Stefanich (1990, November). Cycles of cognition. *Middle School Journal, 22*(2), p. 49. Used with permission from G. P. Stefanich and *Middle School Journal*. Originally taken from H. T. Epstein, "Brain growth and cognitive learning." *Colorado Journal of Educational Research, 3,* 1979.

that major problems exist, since the majority of students in most classes cannot think at these levels of abstraction. Table 15.2 shows the distribution of students across these domains.

AFFECTIVE DOMAIN

The attainment of knowledge and of skills needed to apply that knowledge are what school is all about, but unless students elect to use that knowledge and those skills, a great deal has been wasted. For example, although the ability to read has some intrinsic value, suppose students choose not to read because they do not like to read. Suppose other students master just enough skills in math to pass required courses, but in the meantime develop such fear or contempt toward mathematics that they refuse even to try to keep an accurate checkbook. In a sense the efforts of those students and their teachers have failed, because learning itself is defined as a long-term or even permanent change in behavior. Exactly what have these students failed to learn? They have failed to learn to appreciate what reading can enable them to accomplish; they have failed to realize their own potential in mathematics.

Experience with people who have chosen not to use the knowledge and skills they have shows how important attitude toward knowledge is. The proper attitudes are indispensable for successful, happy living, as the cases of learned people who have become destructive to society or to themselves demonstrate. The greatest lists of aims for American education contain aims that depend on certain attitudes. For example, examine the Seven Cardinal Principles of Secondary Education:

1. Health
2. Command of the fundamental processes
3. Worthy home membership
4. Vocational efficiency
5. Civic participation
6. Worthy use of leisure time
7. Ethical character

Success in any of these areas depends on the development of certain attitudes. Even the aim that may seem most separate from attitudes—vocational efficiency—certain attitudes are necessary for success. More than 85 percent of all jobs lost are lost because workers cannot get along with their supervisors and coworkers.

A national poll of attitudes toward education concluded that "Character education, which is uncommon as a formal subject in public high schools, has as much support as a required subject" (Elam, 1990, p. 49). Teachers must help students develop both necessary skills and certain attitudes.

QUESTIONING TECHNIQUES

In their *Taxonomy of Educational Objectives: The Classification of Educational Goals, Handbook II: Affective Domain,* Krathwohl, Bloom, and Masia (1964) give five levels of internalization of values:

1. Receiving—a willingness to tolerate a phenomenon
2. Responding—voluntarily using the phenomenon
3. Valuing—prizing and acting on the phenomenon
4. Organizing—using values to determine interrelationships between the phenomena
5. Characterizing—organizing values, beliefs, ideas, and attitudes into an internally consistent system

As you consider your expectations of your future students, take time now to list two attitudes you want them to have toward the subject you will teach. Now, using the following examples as models, write a question that will measure student attitudes at each of the four levels: receiving, responding, valuing, and organizing.

Example 1: A math teacher uses the following questions to measure attitudes at each level.

1. Receiving: Would you like to join the math club?
2. Responding: When you play games that involve scorekeeping, do you ever volunteer to keep score?
3. Valuing: Do you plan to take math next year when it becomes an elective?
4. Organizing: Have you ever thought of math as an art?

Example 2: A history teacher covering the Civil War asks the following questions.

1. Receiving: Would you like to own Confederate relics?
2. Responding: If your family or friends planned a vacation that had Vicksburg, Mississippi, on its route, would you suggest visiting the battleground?
3. Valuing: Do you feel excited when seeing a movie on the Civil War?
4. Organizing: While studying this unit on the Civil War, have you ever tried to decide for yourself ways in which each side was wrong?

Using the definition of each level of internalization, and using these examples as models, write a question to test each level of your two statements about attitudes that you want your future students to have.

Your role in the development of students' attitudes will extend into other areas. First, you must help students learn to examine their current attitudes, particularly their values (values clarification), and to understand the basis for their values—that is, the process they use to develop values. To achieve this, you can give students tasks requiring them to analyze their values. Second, you can help students develop their moral values by assessing the level of their moral maturity and then giving them problem situations requiring them to perform at a level slightly above their current maturation level.

Lawrence Kohlberg (1976), formerly a professor at Harvard University, developed a hierarchy of three major stages through which each person must pass in the development of ethical awareness. These are:

Level 1. Preconventional—behavior is determined by rewards and punishment. (What is best for me?)

Level 2. Conventional—behavior is controlled by anticipation of praise or blame. (What will others think?)

Level 3. Postconventional—behavior is regulated by principles embodying generality and comprehensiveness. (What is the right thing to do?)

A familiar example would be why a person obeys a stop sign:

To avoid getting a fine. (Level 1)
To avoid criticism from others and to avoid breaking a law. (Level 2)
To avoid hurting others. (Level 3)

A different version of the same problem might be as follows. In one of our major cities, the fine for violating a stop sign was increased overnight from about $20 to $87.50. Many police officers refused to enforce the law, which they perceived as unreasonable; others enforced it because they had taken an oath to enforce all the laws. At what level did each group of police officers behave?

Not all attitudes are limited to moral behavior. Other important behaviors that the school should foster include learning to appreciate, desire, find interesting, enjoy, and empathize.

TEST ADMINISTRATION

Preliminary Arrangements

For your test to be valid, you must make certain preliminary arrangements. First, see that all students are physically prepared—that they have the necessary materials, such as sharp pencils, paper, reference sources, and measuring instruments. If not, allot time before the test for each student to make these preparations.

Second, be sure everyone is comfortable. The room should not be hot or cold or noisy. Merely closing windows facing a noisy highway or closing the door to a noisy hall can help. Adjusting a room thermostat or radiator controls can help. Each student should have enough room to avoid being cramped. Remind everyone to remove unnecessary books and papers from desktops, lest some students try to balance their paper on top of a stack of books or support books or purses in their laps.

Finally, if test results are to reflect true abilities, students should be mentally relaxed. Many students become so tense during tests that they are unable to show that they know the material.

ACCOUNTABILITY: STANDARDIZED AND ALTERNATIVE TESTS

Harris and Longstreet (1990) raise several critical questions about the standardized testing that has become so rampant in school districts throughout the nation.

> Despite a growing interest in alternative forms of assessment, standardized measures of achievement are more extensively used than ever before. Why? One obvious response that comes quickly to mind is that of accountability. Has education achieved the goals established for it? Standardized tests would appear to offer an objective means for assessing how well teachers, individual schools, and the nation's schools as a whole are functioning. Seduced by the ease with which these tests are administered and the illusory importance of the numbers they yield, we have not sufficiently examined their adequacy as a measure of educational accountability. At best, they reflect only a small portion of what American education is about. What is omitted is everything not subject to the multiple-choice questions typically used in these tests. What kind of accountability is this? . . . The reality is that nothing substantive is gained from standardized testing other than the improvement of some students' test-taking skills. (p. 91)

Anxiety toward taking a test can be further reduced if you explain the test's purpose and permit students to practice taking tests (Griswold, 1990). You can help relieve tension by telling a joke, relating a humorous personal experience, or simply talking for a moment about a ball game, a party, the weather, or another activity unrelated to the test.

Before the test begins, specify how the students should ask questions, if they have any. Do you want them to raise their hands and direct their questions to you at once? Or do you want to go to the student to answer a question? Usually it is better if the students do not ask questions so the whole class can hear, because it disrupts others. Also, tell students in advance what to do when they finish the test. Should they bring it to you? Then should they study another subject, read a library book, or just relax?

Taking the Test

Begin each test by reading the instructions aloud and allowing time for questions. All students should begin at the same time. This provides structure. Also, do not permit students to talk or otherwise disrupt others. Conduct test administration comfortably but uniformly.

Once the test has begun, do not interrupt. If students ask questions, answer them and make a note of each necessary clarification or correction. To avoid interruptions, near the end of the testing period you can inform the entire class of all these corrections at one time. Avoid making disturbing noises during the test, such as rattling papers, talking, or walking around the classroom. Remain in the room at all times during the test.

To end the test in an organized way, take up all remaining papers when time is called. Otherwise, students who feel pressured and do hand in their papers, and then see that a few persistent students are allowed additional time to finish, will feel cheated.

Test Scoring

Whether the test questions are objective, subjective, or both, scoring should always be as objective as possible. Otherwise your judgment will be affected by your likes and dislikes for the students, by the paper's general appearance, and by a force that all teachers experience—a tendency to equalize the scores by subconsciously accepting poor responses from the poorer papers and being overly critical and deducting credit from respectable responses on the better papers. Because this is common among beginning teachers, test scoring leaves them feeling guilty, and many develop a real dislike for testing.

Testing is as much a part of the teacher's role and responsibility as preparing and executing lessons. How, then, can you avoid developing the common distaste for testing? Learning and using the following principles should be of some help.

RECAP OF MAJOR IDEAS

1. Because both objective-type and subjective-type questions have unique advantages and disadvantages, it is usually best to include questions of both types on a test.
2. Objective questions are easily scored and permit the teacher to cover much material by including many questions on a test, but they do not enable the student to be self-expressive or creative.

3. Subjective items permit students to show their knowledge and state their feelings, and they enhance writing and synthesizing skill development; however, they restrict the teacher's ability to test all material covered. Subjective questions are also difficult to score.
4. Grade all tests, including essay-type tests, as objectively as possible.
5. Each test should measure everything covered since the previous test.
6. Assign credit to each item according to the time and emphasis it received in class and the time required to answer it.
7. On discussion-type tests, give partial credit for accurate answers, even though they were unanticipated.
8. Multiple-choice items should contain four or five choices, one or two of which should be strong distracters.
9. To pilot the test, take it before administering it to students.

CASES

All teachers must develop, administer, and score teacher-made tests. Failure to develop expertise in any of these dimensions of testing can lead to serious problems. The following case shows a common problem situation in which teachers find themselves.

CASE 1: A TWELFTH-GRADE CLASS WANTS INFORMATION ABOUT AN UPCOMING TEST

Ms. Wheeler had been teaching physical education for about five years when she noticed a sudden change in student attitudes toward tests. Up until that time she had considered that discussing tests before giving them was unethical and absurd. If an examination was going to be a fair measure of students' knowledge about the subject, would not a previous discussion destroy the test's validity and purpose? The only information she ever gave about a test was when it would be given. Although previous classes had teased, asking questions about what would be on the test, Ms. Wheeler knew that they never expected her to answer their questions.

But this twelfth-grade class was different. When they asked for information about the upcoming test, they expected her to provide it. They never asked about specific content, but they did ask such questions as "How many questions will the test have?" "How much will each question count?" and "How many are true-false questions?" Taking these questions as good-natured teasing, Ms. Wheeler ignored them and went on with the lesson. But it became clear that the students were serious. They became upset when they had no advance notice about how long a test would be and the type of questions it would contain.

Soon after having been confronted by these disgruntled students, Ms. Wheeler changed her policy and began holding a discussion about each test a few days before giving it. This practice was successful. First, the students no longer felt she was trying to trick them with an unfamiliar test, and they could study according to the type of test they were to take. Second, she came to see that answering certain questions about a test did not suggest what content to study as much as it suggested the correct method of study.

Discussion

1. If you reveal the number and type of questions to be included on an upcoming test, will the test be less valid and less reliable?

    No, not if all the students in your class have this information. It may help them identify the important ideas in the unit. It may improve the scores of students who use the information to study for the test, but these students will probably learn more in accordance with their increased scores. If you are afraid to provide information about an objective, factual test you are planning to administer, you can increase the length of the test. It will then be so comprehensive that the student who scores high on it will have to know a majority of the content studied during the unit.

2. Do today's students view tests as less important than did the students of a few years ago?

    Today's students feel tests are important. The main difference is that yesterday's students saw tests as important for one reason only—to determine grades. Today's students see an additional purpose in tests: They want to score well because they know that test scores reflect the quality of their learning. This is why they want to know how to study for each test. They realize that a test that tricks them is not an accurate instrument for measuring their learning progress.

3. How can you make testing more palatable?

    By removing fear from testing, you can make it less distasteful to you and your students. Develop a routine for test administration and return, and always be as pleasant as you can. Your manner will help the students relax, and if you follow the same routine each time you give a test, you can ease feelings of insecurity.

    When returning tests, always go over each question and explain the correct answers. Give partial credit when it is earned.

CASE 2: EDUCATION REFORM AFFECTS ASSESSMENT

Samuel Clemens Middle School is located in a state that takes pride as a national leader of education reform. Jimmy Smith, a May graduate of Regional State University, was delighted to have landed a teaching position at Clemens Middle because he had heard of the school's reputation as a leader in education reform. After all, Regional State had adjusted its mission statement six years ago to include education reform as a major component, and, consequently, Jimmy had been well grounded in all the state's reform practices.

Jimmy's teacher education program had stressed the importance of on-going self-evaluation. The use of portfolios throughout the program was consistent with this emphasis. To promote education reform, Clemens Middle School required each teacher to design an assessment system and present a rationale statement linking the system with education reform. Put simply, his task was to write a convincing statement telling how his new assessment system promoted education reform.

Jimmy began by reviewing his college notes to reaquaint himself with the concepts on education reform that related to assessment. His review turned up such terms as self-assessment, continuous assessment, portfolios, objective-based education, curriculum alignment, alternative testing, authentic tests, and valued outcomes. The number of terms alone was a reminder of how much material he had covered on assessment related to education reform. Although he felt confident that he had mastered most or all of the topics on assessment and education reform that his college curriculum had covered, he mused silently, wondering where to begin the seemingly monumental assignment.

Discussion Questions

1. Which of these topics would be the most useful to assessment system to promote education reform?
2. What major precautions should a teacher take to prepare students for a reform-oriented assessment program?
3. How should education reform change the role and nature of teacher-made tests?
4. How does and how should education reform alter a teacher's emphasis on the affective domain?

ACTIVITIES

In this chapter you have read about good practices for constructing, administering, and scoring tests and examined questions written at different levels of the cognitive and affective domains. Now you have an opportunity to assemble and apply your knowledge and skills on testing.

1. In your major teaching field, develop an objective test containing a combination of true-false, matching, and multiple-choice items. Include questions that measure the higher cognitive levels as well as some that measure in the affective domain.
2. Construct an essay test, then rewrite each question to make it more precise and manageable.
3. Decide exactly how you would prefer to administer a test. Then write a set of instructions to guide student behavior during and immediately following the test. Ask some of your classmates to interpret your instructions. Look for discrepancies in the interpretations and rewrite items that had multiple interpretations.
4. Write a subjective test item. Identify and list the most important points that

students should include in their responses. Now identify and make a list of secondary points that are important but less so than the primary points. Assign 2 points each to the primary points and 1 point each to the secondary points.

5. For the preceding test item, develop three alternative ways of testing that do not use pencil and paper. Try to make each of these alternative tests discriminate between those who understand the primary and secondary points and those who do not.

6. Make a list of unique advantages offered by essay questions and a list of unique advantages offered by objective questions.

REFERENCES

Archbald, D., & Newmann, F. (1988). *Beyond standardized testing: Authentic academic achievement in the secondary school.* Reston, VA: NASSP Publications.

Barton, J., & Collins, A. (1993). Portfolios in teacher education. *The Journal of Teacher Education, 44*(3), 200-210.

Bloom, B. S., Hastings, J., & Madaus, G. F. (1971). *Handbook on formative and summative evaluation of student learning.* New York: McGraw-Hill.

Brown, R. (1989). Testing and thoughtfulness. *Educational Leadership, 46*(7), 31-33.

Carter, K. (1983). *Tackling the testing issue: Testwiseness for teachers and students.* Paper presented at the annual meeting of the American Educational Research Association, Montreal.

Carter, K. (1984). Do teachers understand principles for writing tests? *Journal of Teacher Education, 35,* 59.

Coffman, W. E. (1983). *Testing in the schools: A historical perspective.* Paper presented at the UCLA Center for the Study of Evaluation Conference on Paths to Excellence: Testing and Technology, Los Angeles.

Conant, J. B. (1952). *Modern science and modern men.* Garden City, NY: Doubleday/Anchor.

Davis, H., & Burgess, G. (Trans. 1901). *The republic: The statesman of Plato* (pp. 209-210). New York: Dunne.

Elam, S. M. (1990). The 22nd annual Gallup poll and the public's attitudes toward the public schools. *Phi Delta Kappan, 72*(1), 41-55.

Ellsworth, R. A., Donnell, P., & Duell, O. K. (1990). Multiple-choice test item: What are textbook authors telling teachers? *Journal of Educational Research, 83*(5), 290-293.

English, F. (1992, March). *Curriculum alignment.* Paper presented at an Eastern Kentucky University/Phi Delta Kappa Conference, Richmond, KY.

Fielding, G., & Shaughnessy, J. (1990, November). Improving student assessment: Overcoming the obstacles. *NASSP Bulletin,* pp. 90-98.

Fluitt, J., & Gifford, C. (1980). Who's teaching teachers how to teach test-wiseness? *Contemporary Education, 51*(3), 152-154.

Griswold, P. A. (1990, February). Assessing relevance and reliability to improve the quality of teacher-made tests. *NASSP Bulletin,* pp. 18-23.

Harris, K. H., & Longstreet, W. S. (1990). Alternative testing and national agenda for control. *The Clearing House, 64,* pp. 90-93.

Kohlberg, L. (1976). Moral stages and moralization: The cognitive developmental approach. In T. Lickona (Ed.), *Moral development and behavior: Theory, research, and social issues* (pp. 31-53). New York: Holt, Rinehart & Winston.

Krathwohl, D. R., Bloom, B., & Masia, B. (1964). *Taxonomy of educational objectives: The classification of educational goals. Handbook II: Affective domain.* New York: McKay.

Mager, R. F. (1962). *Preparing instructional objectives.* Belmont, CA: Fearon.

Mouly, G. J. (1970). *The science of educational research* (2nd ed.). New York: Van Nostrand Reinhold.

National Assessment of Educational Progress (1981). *Reading, thinking, and writing: Results from the 1970-1980 National Assessment of Reading and Literature.* Denver, CO.

Oliva, P. F. (1972). *The secondary school today* (2nd ed.) (chap. 18). New York: Harper & Row.

Perrone, V. (1994). How to engage students in learning. *Educational Leadership, 51*(5), 11-13.

Phillips, D. R., Phillips, D. G., Melton, G., & Moore, P. (1994). Beans, blocks, and buttons: Developing thinking. *Educational Leadership, 51*(5), 50-53.

Postner, G.J., & Rudnitsky, A. N. (1994). *Course design: A guide to curriculum development for teachers.* (4th ed). New York: Longman.

Quellmaiz, E. S. (1985). Needed: Better methods for testing higher-order thinking skills. *Educational Leadership, 43,* 29-35.

Savitz, F. R. (1985). Effects of easy questions placed at the beginning of science multiple-choice examinations. *Journal of Instructional Psychology, 12,* 6-10.

Simmons, R. (1994). The horse before the cart: Assessing for understanding. *Educational Leadership, 51*(5), 22-23.

Special Study Panel on Education Indicators for the National Center for Education Statistics (1991). *Education counts.* Washington, DC: United States Department of Education.

Stefanich, G. P. (1990, November). Cycles of cognition. *Middle School Journal, 22*(2), 47-52.

Stiggins, R. J. (1985). Improving assessment where it means the most: In the classroom. *Educational Leadership, 43,* 69-74.

Torrance, E. P. (1967). Creative teaching makes a difference. In J. C. Gowan (Ed.), *Creativity: Its educational implications.* New York: Wiley.

Ward, M. W. (1969). Learning to generalize. *Science Education, 53,* 423-424.

Wiggins, G. (1989, April). Teaching to the authentic test. *Educational Leadership, 46*(7), 41-47.

Zais, R. S. (1976). *Curriculum principles and foundations.* New York: Crowell.

SUGGESTED READINGS

Farris, R. A. (1990, November). Meeting their needs: Motivating middle level learners. *Middle School Journal, 22,* 22-26.

National Educational Goals Panel (1991). *The National Education Goals Report.* Washington, DC: U.S. Government Printing Office.

Popham, W. J., & Hambleton, R. K. (1990, January). Can you pass the test on testing? *Principal,* pp. 38-39.

Wiggins, G. (In press). A true test: Toward authentic and equitable forms of testing. *Phi Delta Kappan.*

Winton, J. J. (1991, January). You can win without competing. *Middle School Journal, 22*(3), 40.

Appendixes

To understand appropriate methodology at any level, one must understand the history of American schools. Middle level education has blossomed during the latter half of the twentieth century. Appendices A and B provide a historical look at the forerunner of the middle school—the junior high school—and the middle school movement. Appendix C discusses the unique demands and opportunities of teaching at the middle level.

This text has emphasized the importance of using simulations and games in the classroom. Appendix D is a directory of simulation and games with a brief description and an address for each. Appendix E is a directory of programs for teaching thinking skills.

Although this text celebrates the contributions made by minority cultural groups, it recognizes the special obstacles that many minority students face daily. Appendix F is a directory of materials designed for use by secondary and middle level teachers to help all students understand the advantages of working with members of cultures other than their own.

The Junior High Movement

As the twentieth century approached, the typical elementary school had grades kindergarten (K) through 8, and the high school included grades 9 through 12. Common knowledge held that the purpose of grades 7 and 8 was to review the content covered in K through 6. Many saw this use of the seventh and eighth grades as a waste of time, but it was difficult to prove because American schools had no nationally accepted goals.

During the next 30 years, several national committees were established to set goals and measure how well schools met them. The first of these was the National Education Association (NEA) Committee of Ten, which reported its conclusions in 1893. The committee set the major purpose of secondary education as preparation for life, not just for college. Accordingly, it recommended that the secondary school's grades 10 through 12 be extended downward to include grades 7 through 12. This would make it possible to teach some secondary school subjects earlier.

In 1895 another major NEA report was issued (see Stinnett & Henson, 1982; Armstrong, Henson, & Savage, 1993). The NEA Department of Superintendents Committee of Fifteen also wanted the secondary school content to be lowered into grades 7 and 8, but it did not recommend changing the 8-12 grade pattern—in fact, it opposed this change. But four years later the NEA Department of Secondary Education issued a report by its Committee on College Requirements suggesting a 6-6 grade pattern. In 1918 the NEA Commission on the Reorganization of Secondary Education, which issued the Cardinal Principles of Secondary Education, also recommended a 6-6 system, but with an added alteration: the upper 6 was to be divided into a 3-3 pattern. This, along with the recommendation of several other committees, recommended a junior high school to meet the instructional needs of seventh-, eighth-, and ninth-graders.

It would be easy to say that junior high school was developed to improve the curriculum for this age-group, but that is an oversimplification. Many factors collectively caused the development of the junior high, and some of them had nothing to do with the quality of curriculum and instruction. In fact, junior high schools were built before goals for junior high were identified.

However, there was some real concern for meeting this age-group's educational needs. The

NEA was quick to warn that merely regrouping the old elementary and secondary grades would not meet adolescent learners' needs, and it provided a list of features needed to make a "real junior high school" (NEA Research Bulletin, 1923):

A building of its own, housing grades 7, 8, and 9 or at least two of these grades

A separate staff of teachers

Recognition of individual differences among students

A reform of the progress of studies traditionally offered these grades

Elective courses to be chosen by the students

Student activities designed for the needs of early adolescents

Research on the nature of adolescence seemed to demand a special school for these students (Hall, 1904).

Practical reasons also gave impetus to the development of the junior high school. These included the need to relieve overcrowded high school classrooms caused by the post–World War I population boom, to reduce the high dropout rate, and to make more efficient use of the time spent in school.

From the start, junior high schools have varied in many ways. About half the earlier schools were located in the high school building, about one-third were housed in elementary schools, and the rest were located in separate buildings. The types of instruction in these schools were equally diverse. Therefore, it is not surprising that a majority of studies found little or no difference in the scholastic attainment of junior high school students and their counterparts in the traditional high schools. The many studies on the effect of the junior high pattern on students' socialization and psychological welfare found little difference between junior high school students and high school students in grades 7 through 9. By the middle of the twentieth century, studies of the junior high school had painted a dismal picture.

SUGGESTED READINGS

Armstrong, D. G., Henson, K. T., & Savage, T. (1993). *Education: An introduction* (4th ed.). New York: Macmillan.

Hall, G. S. (1904). *Adolescence, its psychology, and its relations to physiology, anthropology, sociology, sex, crime, religion, and education.* Vols. I and II. New York: Appleton.

Stinnett, T. M., & Henson, K. T. (1982). *America's public schools in transition: Future trends and issues.* New York: Teachers College Press, Columbia University.

The Middle School Movement

Widespread dissatisfaction with the junior high schools, coupled with several other factors, gave rise to a new kind of school—the middle school. By 1950, many critics of the junior high believed it had lost sight of its original purpose: to serve the adolescent's unique needs and interests. They felt that the junior high school had gradually become a miniature high school. It is important to note that educators were dissatisfied with the junior high school's failure to attain its goals, but not with the goals themselves.

The time was ripe for a new type of school to replace the junior high school. Thus emerged the middle school, defined by Alexander (1981, p. 3) as "a school of some three to five years between the elementary and high school focused on the educational needs of students in these in-between years and designed to promote continuous educational progress for all concerned."

Positive forces contributed to the development of the middle school:

New research found that children in the seventh and eighth grades resembled children in the fifth and sixth grades more than they resembled ninth-graders.

Research showed that preadolescent children have special needs and interests.

Puberty was occurring earlier than ever before; each generation reaches puberty four months earlier than the previous generation (Smart & Smart, 1978).

An educational program could be designed especially for this group.

Curricula for individualizing instruction could be developed.

The middle school could bridge the gap between the elementary and high schools.

Curricula could be designed to serve the whole child, not just the intellect.

Middle schools could have their own counselors.

Teacher education programs could be designed to prepare teachers to meet this age-group's interests and needs.

The middle school could be an exploratory school.

HISTORY AND STATUS OF MIDDLE SCHOOLS

The first middle school was opened in Bay City, Michigan, in 1950. Middle schools grew modestly in number for about 15 years, but by the mid-1960s there was rapid growth. By 1980 there were 5,000 U.S. middle schools. With such rapid expansion, it is not surprising that middle schools vary greatly. Some middle schools encompass grades 5 through 8, some have grades 6 through 8, and some 5 through 7. Some use interdisciplinary team-teaching, but most do not. Less than half the middle schools use flexible scheduling. States' failure to pass legislation defining the middle school's role and local concerns and priorities have undoubtedly contributed to middle schools' failure to reach their goals. Another contributing factor has been the general failure of middle school principals to adjust their own perceptions and concepts of the middle school. Only a small minority have received any special training. Fortunately, middle school teachers have made more progress in adjusting their attitudes toward the middle school student. Unfortunately, the middle school teacher's humanistic attitude has not always changed the middle school teacher's behavior.

Middle school teachers should realize that they are responsible for helping attain the general middle school goals. Some of these goals are:

1. To help students progress intellectually, socially, physically, and emotionally
2. To enhance the student's self-image
3. To provide opportunities for success
4. To promote active learning
5. To encourage exploration
6. To provide security

The teacher who wants to contribute to middle school goals must understand the middle school student. For instance, middle school students are active by nature. Klingele (1979, p. 33), offered the following rationale for involving all middle school students:

1. Middle school students, by their very nature, need and desire a variety of challenging and flexible learning activities.
2. Middle school students both desire and are capable of accepting variable amounts of responsibility for learning.
3. Middle school students learn variable degrees of content, at different rates, and at different times.
4. Middle school students will learn more and better when actively involved in the learning activity.
5. Middle school students learn through various learning styles—no one style is necessarily effective for all students.
6. Middle school students learn best in environments characterized by a respectful, warm, informal, and personalized climate.

Clearly, the middle school teacher must find many and varied ways of involving all students, but this does not always happen. All too often the school practitioners, teachers and administrators both, have strayed from the purposes for which the middle school was originally designed. Lately this has led to considerable criticism of middle schools.

SUGGESTED READINGS

Alexander, W. M. (1981). *The exemplary middle school.* New York: Holt, Rinehart & Winston.
Klingele, W. E. (1979). *Teaching in middle schools.* Boston: Allyn & Bacon.
Smart, M. S., & Smart, R. C. (1978). *Adolescence* (2nd ed.). New York: Macmillan.

appendix C

Teaching in Middle Schools

When polled about their prospective teaching assignments, only a very small percentage of pre-service teachers who are not participating in middle school programs express a desire to teach in the middle or junior high grades. Initially, almost all secondary education majors assume they will teach in the upper secondary grades. But this is before their student-teaching experience. In reality, more than half of all secondary education majors teach in the junior or middle school grades. Attrition alone ensures that there are more grade 7–9 students than grade 10–12 students, excluding the middle schools. The result is that more than half of all students who plan to teach in the upper secondary grades actually become junior high teachers.

An interesting phenomenon occurs when students have an opportunity to student-teach at junior and middle levels. By the end of their student-teaching program, most of these students know if they want to teach at these levels. In fact, most students end their middle and junior high student-teaching program with either a very strong determination to teach early adolescents or an equally strong determination to avoid this age-group at all costs. Because there are these typically strong reactions, and because most of those who will actually teach these age-groups do not do so by choice, it is important to know as much as possible about this age-group and about the teacher's role in working with them.

TRANSESCENCE: AN UNKNOWN STAGE

Middle schools exist in varying grade patterns. Some span grades 5 through 8, while other middle schools include as few as two grades (often 5 and 6, 6 and 7, or 7 and 8). Because most junior highs involve grades 7 through 9, students are usually at the adolescent stage, but most middle schools cater to preadolescents. *Transescence* is a term that refers to the preadolescent to early-adolescent ages.

There is relatively little in the literature about the transescent student; few studies have focused on this age-group. Transescence is difficult to define because it is tied to our history and to our culture. For example, being a 12-year-old in the United States is different from being a 12-year-old in Japan. A few physical characteristics are shared, but these are complicated by the many different expectations of this age-group that come out of different cultural environments. Furthermore, being a 12-year-old in the late 1980s is different from being a 12-year-old in the 1950s. In a sense, it is not possible to discuss adolescence outside a sociohistorical perspective. From a psychological perspective, adolescence is an integration of past experiences, the development of a sense of individuality, and a growing awareness of personal destiny.

As youths enter the preadolescent ages, their goals may become less acute and their attention spans shorter. They often develop a keen sense of interdependence. But as we consider such "typical" characteristics, we must remember that many individual members of this age-group are perfect nonexamples of the stereotype. For instance, we might well think of middle school as a time of change (from child to adolescent and from home guidance to peer guidance), but a study of primarily middle-class suburban students reported that "stability, not change, is the overriding characteristic in the psychological patterns of reaction of these older adolescents" (Offer, 1969, p. 222).

Although the terms *transcence* and *adolescence* are almost impossible to define, teachers of middle and junior high school students are quick to say that there is something unique about the preadolescent and early adolescent. This uniqueness makes teaching this group a real challenge—and extremely satisfying. The young adolescent is sometimes described as lonely and vulnerable (Knopka, 1973). Teachers of this age group will be surprised to learn how important teacher approval is to their students. Many middle and junior high school teachers find it very rewarding to teach this age group because of the opportunity it provides for influencing their students' lives.

Another challenge that comes with the territory is determining how many intellectual demands one can make of these students. Research has shown that only a few individuals develop the ability to function well at the formal operations level (Neimark, 1975).

THE ROLE OF THE TEACHER

Studies show that there is a hiatus in brain growth between the ages of 12 and 14 (Epstein, 1976). One can therefore conclude that the middle school teacher should spend more time giving students opportunities to use the mental skills they have already developed rather than demanding that these students acquire new skills.

Further complicating the role of the middle and junior high teacher is a list of paradoxical demands made on these teachers. For example, in an attempt to make students feel secure and well adjusted, teachers may remove from their students "the springs of their intellectual and artistic productivity" (Hudson, 1966). Another middle school expert notes, "The mercurial nature of the transescent requires a fluid but structured atmosphere. It should provide students with the security of structure, but it should be sufficiently elastic to permit students to explore learning and socialization in a manner consistent with individual needs" (Eichhorn, 1980, p. 67). Since youths in the middle years are seeking greater independence, activities should allow students to accept challenges, and support from the teacher to help them meet those challenges.

Winn, Regan, and Gibson (1991) introduce another challenge that faces middle level teachers, another mercurial quality of transescents: "One main characteristic of the learner during the fifth through the eighth grades is that his or her strategies for learning are unpredictable. Because the move from concrete operations to formal operations occurs during this time, the learning vacillates between the two as the shift is occurring" (p. 265). Student activities are most effective in friendly, personal classrooms. Although proponents of this need offer different packages—for example, core-curriculum versus non-core-curriculum—there are similar elements: personalization, sequential process, and organized knowledge. In other words, middle and junior high teachers should learn how to plan continuous curricula chock-full of activities, each one leading to the next. As for instructional skills, these teachers must know how to relate personally to their students.

A PERSONAL CHALLENGE

As you continue your program, look into the world of middle and junior high school teaching. Consider its advantages and its frustrations. Take every opportunity you get to prepare yourself better for teaching at these levels. Consider the slogan of the U.S. Marines: "We need a few good men." America's middle and junior high schools need many good men and women who are mentally, emotionally, and academically prepared to accept this challenge.

Based on developmental characteristics, certain principles should underline the middle years' curriculum. Winn, Regan, and Gibson (1991) offer the following characteristics, which can be used to ensure middle-level curricula:

1. The learner must be an active participant.
2. Strategies for learning should be taught, modeled, and retaught as necessary.
3. Oral language should be encouraged to allow sharing of the thought process.
4. Transfer of learning strategies should be taught.
5. Vocabulary should be taught orally through regular use of new words as well as activities to enlarge vocabulary.
6. Small learning groups should be a regular part of the classroom organization.
7. Teacher feedback should deal primarily with learning rather than discipline.
8. Learners need to have time to react and share their learning with interested listeners.
9. Learners need to hear excellent readers read.
10. Reading should be viewed as a means to an end, not the end in itself.
11. Learners need to produce their own reading materials.

SUGGESTED READINGS

Eichorn, D. H. (1980). The school. In M. Johnson (Ed.), *Toward adolescence.* 79th Yearbook of the National Society for the Study of Education. Chicago: University of Chicago Press.

Epstein, H. T. (1976). A bibliography based framework for intervention projects. *Mental Retardation, 14,* 26-27.

Henson, K. T. (1986, April). Middle schools: Paradoxes and promises. *The Clearing House, 59,* 345-347.

Hudson, L. (1966). *Contrary imaginations: A psychological study of the English schoolboy.* Middlesex, England: Penguin.

Knopka, G. (1973). Requirements for healthy development of adolescent youth. *Adolescence, 8,* 2.

Neimark, E. (1975). In F. D. Horowitz (Ed.), *Review of child development research* (Vol. 4). Chicago: University of Chicago Press.

Offer, D. (1969). *The psychological world of the teenager.* New York: Basic.

Winn, D. D., Regan, P., & Gibson, S. (1991, March–April). Teaching the middle years learner. *The Clearing House, 64,* 265-267.

Directory of Simulation Materials

Blue Widjet Company

A business simulation about the problems of pollution facing industry.

Requirements	*Designer/Supplier*
25–30 players	Interact
4–6 hours	P.O. Box 1023
	Lakeside, CA 92040

Clug (Community Land Use Game)

A simulation of urban land-use interactions that has been compared with a combined chess-Monopoly and allows for considerable elaboration.

Requirements	*Designer/Supplier*
9 players (minimum)	Systems Gaming Association
3 hours (minimum)	Triphammer Road
Packaged materials and kit	Ithaca, NY 14850

Community Disaster

A simulation of a community hit by a localized natural disaster.

Requirements	*Designer/Supplier*
6–16 players	Western Publishing Co., Inc.
2–6 hours	School and Library Department
Packaged materials	850 Third Avenue
	New York, NY 10022

Conflict (preliminary edition)

A simulation centered on a crisis that erupts in 1999 in a world disarmed by universal agreement and policed by three international councils (based on Waskow's peacekeeping model described in *Keeping the World Disarmed* published by the Centre for the Study of Democratic Institutions).

Requirements	*Designer/Supplier*
24-36 players	World Law fund
2-3 hours	11 West 42nd Street
Packaged materials	New York, NY 10036

Farming

A simulation of farm management in western Kansas at three different time periods. Part of Unit 2 of the High School Geography Project produced by the Association of American Geographers.

Requirements	*Designer/Supplier*
15-30 players	Macmillan Company
40-50 hours	866 Third Avenue
Packaged materials	New York, NY 10022

Galapagos (Evolution)

A simulation of the evolution of Darwin's finches in which players fill a scientific role and are required to predict the evolution rate.

Requirements	*Designer/Supplier*
6-50 players	Abt Associates, Inc.
1-2 hours	14 Concord Lane
Mimeographed materials	Cambridge, MA 02138

Inner City Planning

A role-playing simulation of urban renewal processes involving various community interest groups.

Requirements	*Designer/Supplier*
18-35 players	Project Simile
5-6 hours	P.O. Box 1023
Kit of printed materials	La Jolla, CA 92037

Location of the Metfab Company

A simulation designed as an integral part of Unit 2 of the High School Geography Project produced by the Association of American Geographers. The central feature is a hypothetical metal-fabricating company trying to determine a new site for a company branch.

Requirements	Designer/Supplier
5-10 players per group	Macmillan Company
4-6 hours (40-min. minimum periods)	866 Third Avenue
Packaged materials	New York, NY 10022

Low Bidder

A packaged simulation of contract bidding in the construction industry.

Requirements	Designer/Supplier
2-25 players, with 3-8 preferable	Entelek, Inc.
30 minutes (minimum)	42 Pleasant Street
Packaged materials	Newburyport, MA 01950

Manchester

A simulation of the impact on the agricultural population of major historical and social issues at the advent of the Industrial Revolution in England.

Requirements	Designer/Supplier
8-40 players	Abt Associates, Inc. (for Educational
1-2 hours	Services, Inc.)
Instructional manual	14 Concord Lane
	Cambridge, MA 02138

Marketplace

A simulation of the American economic system at work in a medium-size urban manufacturing community.

Requirements	Designer/Supplier
30-50 players	Joint Council on Economic Education
3-4 hours (minimum)	1212 Avenue of the Americas
Packaged materials	New York, NY 10036

Point Roberts

A simulation of international boundary arbitration procedures that is part of Unit 4 of the High School Geography Project produced by the Association of American Geographers.

Requirements	Designer/Supplier
30 players	Macmillan Company
30-50 hours	866 Third Avenue
Packaged materials	New York, NY 10022

Political

A political crisis simulation set in Latin America and involving major international conflicts.

Requirements	Designer/Supplier
40-80 players	Abt Associates, Inc.
2-4 hours	14 Concord Lane
Mimeographed materials	Cambridge, MA 02138

Portsville

An interactive game designed to simulate the growth of the city of Portsville in three different time periods, produced by the Association of American Geographers as part of Unit 1 of the High School Geography Project.

Requirements	Designer/Supplier
6 players per map board	Macmillan Company
8-10 hours (40 min. minimum periods)	866 Third Avenue
Packaged materials	New York, NY 10022

Rutile and the Beach

A simulation of Australian mining, conservation, and recreation groups in competition for land. Part of Unit 5 of the High School Geography Project, produced by the Association of American Geographers.

Requirements	Designer/Supplier
27 players roles	Macmillan Company
50-60 hours (40 min. minimum periods)	866 Third Avenue
Packaged materials	New York, NY 10022

Section

A simulation designed to provide students with an understanding of conflicts of interest among the sections of a political territory as they are expressed in the political process used in Unit 4 of the American High School Geography Project produced by the Association of American Geographers.

Requirements	Designer/Supplier
Over 30 players	Macmillan Company
5-6 hours	866 Third Avenue
Packaged materials	New York, NY 10022

Simulation of American Government

A simulation of certain hypothetical roles and relationships analogous to those found in various branches of the U.S. government.

Requirements	Designer/Supplier
9 players and above	Dale M. Garvey
2-4 hours	Division of Social Sciences
Mimeographed materials	Kansas State Teachers College
	Emporia, KA 66801

Solution for ACME Metal

A simulation of flood prevention planning designed as an integral part of Unit 5 of the High School Geography Project produced by the Association of American Geographers.

Requirements	*Designer/Supplier*
7-28 players	Macmillan Company
30-40 hours (40 min. minimum periods)	866 Third Avenue
Packaged materials	New York, NY 10022

Steam

A simulation of some of the economic aspects of steam engine development relevant to coal mining in England at the start of the nineteenth century.

Requirements	*Designer/Supplier*
6-15 players	Abt Associates, Inc.
1-2 hours	14 Concord Lane
Mimeographed materials	Cambridge, MA 02138

Venture

A school business game that is a total enterprise simulation covering many of the major decision-making areas of business and management.

Requirements	*Designer/Supplier*
20-35 players	Public Relations Department
4-5 hours	Education Services
Complete kit (available without	P.O. Box 599
charge in the U.S.)	Cincinnati, OH 45201

Yes, But Not Here

A role-playing simulation of an urban locational conflict involving a housing project for the elderly.

Requirements	*Designer/Supplier*
32 roles	Macmillan Company
2-3 hours	866 Third Avenue
Published materials	New York, NY 10022

Directory of Programs for Teaching Thinking Skills

Much is being written about teaching thinking skills. This movement is more than a passing fad; it will continue to expand and we will continue to learn more about how people learn. Walters (1990, p. 57) explains*: "Although there is much debate as to how critical thinking is best taught, . . . the educational establishment is in almost unanimous agreement that it should be taught."

Teachers must know as much as they can about how students learn. Following is information on several of the more widely known programs designed to help teachers teach their students how to improve their thinking skills.

Strategic Reasoning, Edited by John J. Glade

Audience:　Ages 10 to adult. The program has instructional levels appropriate to students from fourth grade through adult education. Most appropriate subjects in which to teach this project: The program is usually taught in English/reading classes but has also been taught in math and social studies classes.

Suggested schedule:　One class period per week.

Total hours required to complete program:　30 hours per instructional level.

Estimated cost of materials:　Classroom Starter Package is one-time cost of $198; additional student materials cost $4.50 per student per school year.

---

* Walters, K. S. (1990, September–October). How critical is critical thinking? *The Clearing House, 64*(1), 57–60.

Address for further information:

> Innovative Sciences, Inc.
> P.O. Box 15129
> Park Square Station
> Stamford, CT 06901-0129
> Tel.: (800) 243-9169

Purpose of goals: To teach the conscious metacognitive and applied-thinking skills students must have to function effectively in school and real life, with an emphasis on the transfer of thinking skills to improving academic performance.

Motivational strategies: By balancing group and individualized instruction, as well as analytical and creative-thinking experiences, the carefully sequenced learning activities guide students to improve their ability to think and demonstrate the benefits this has for enhanced academic achievement and life success.

Theoretical background: The program is based on the "Design for Thinking" theory of Dr. Albert Upton.

Curriculum for training teachers to use the program: Full pre-service and in-service programs are conducted by specially trained consultants.

Evidence of success: A large number of field research studies demonstrate improvements in such areas as academic achievement, problem solving, critical thinking, specific thinking skills, self-concept, and IQ.

Mastering Reading through Reasoning and Analytical Reading and Reasoning, a Two-Book Series, by Dr. Arthur Whimbey

Audience: Ages 12 to adult. Mastering Reading through Reasoning spans reading levels 6–9; Analytical Reading and Reasoning spans reading levels 9–12.

Most appropriate subjects in which to teach this project: English/reading class. The texts are appropriate for remedial, on-level, or advanced instruction. In addition, the texts are often used in special projects such as study skills classes or SAT/ACT examination preparation courses.

Suggested schedule: One or more periods per week over an entire school year or intensive study for one semester.

Total hours required to complete program: Approximately 35 hours per text. Estimated cost of materials: $12.95 per text.

Address for further information:

> Innovative Sciences, Inc.
> P.O. Box 15129
> Park Square Station
> Stamford, CT 06901-0129
> Tel.: (800) 243-9169

Purpose of goals: To improve students' vocabulary, reading comprehension, and cognitive abilities by developing their skills in reasoning with and about words and ideas.

Motivational strategies: Strategies such as "thinking aloud" and "cooperative learning" are used to boost students' ability to develop their reasoning and reading abilities. High-inter materials, relevant to students' schoolwork in many disciplines, engage students' commitment to the program's goals.

Theoretical background: The texts are founded on Dr. Whimbey's theory of precise processing and incorporate The Whimbey Method, an acclaimed instructional methodology reflecting current research in cognitive science and learning.

Curriculum for training teachers to use the program: Full pre-service and in-service program are conducted by specially trained consultants. Evidence of success: Field research studies show gains in such areas as vocabulary, reading comprehension, academic aptitude, specific thinking skills, Scholastic Aptitude Test (SAT) score, and self-concept.

Think: A Thinking Skills Language Arts Program, edited by John J. Glade

Audience: Ages 10 to adult. *Think* is designed to meet the special needs of typical Chapter I students, who may be performing three or more years below grade level. The program has a sequence of instructional reading levels ranging from functional illiteracy through grade 9.

Most appropriate subjects in which to teach this project: The program is best suited to a "learning lab" setting, within English or reading classes.

Suggested schedule: Three or more class periods per week.

Total hours required to complete program: The program provides instruction for an entire school year. Students should continue studying the program over successive school years, progressing through its sequential levels until they no longer require intensive remedial instruction.

Estimated cost of materials: (The following figures are based on 100 students' participating in the program and include all pre-service and in-service consulting expenses.) First year cost is approximately $80 to $100 per student; continuing years' cost is approximately $10 to $12 per student.

Address for further information:

Innovative Sciences, Inc.
P.O. Box 15129
Park Square Station
Stamford, CT 06901-0129
Tel.: (800) 243-9169.

Purpose of goals: To remediate students' word attack, vocabulary, and comprehension language skills by systematically improving thinking skills and reasoning processes. Cognitive development serves as the vehicle for improving language abilities.

Motivational strategies: High-interest materials engage students in the instructional process. Language skills are treated as the application and extension of thinking skills. A balance of group and individualized instruction provides for both the social development of language skills and individual learning progress in language and thinking ability.

Theoretical background: The program is based on the "Design for Thinking" theory of Dr. Albert Upton and incorporates elements of Dr. J. P. Guilford's "Structure of Intellect" theory.

Curriculum for training teachers to use the program: Full pre-service and in-service programs are conducted by specially trained consultants.

Evidence of success: Substantial research evidence supports significant student gains in such areas as word attack skills, vocabulary, comprehension, thinking skills, problem solving, academic aptitude, and self-concept.

Intuitive Math: A Thinking Skills Mathematics Program, edited by Thomas P. Burke

Audience: Ages 10 to adult. Intuitive Math is designed to meet the special needs of typical Chapter I students, who may be performing three or more years below grade level. The program has a sequence of instructional mathematics levels ranging from functional illiteracy through pre-algebra.

Most appropriate subjects in which to teach this project: The program is best suited to a "learning lab" setting within mathematics classes.

Suggested schedule: Three or more class periods per week.

Total hours required to complete program: The program provides instruction for an entire school year. Students should continue studying the program over successive school years, progressing through its sequential levels until they no longer require intensive remedial instruction.

Estimated cost of materials: (The following figures are based on 100 students' participating in the program and include all pre-service and in-service consulting expenses.) First year cost is approximately $80–$100 per student; continuing years' cost is approximately $10–$12 per student.

Address for further information:

LInnovative Sciences, Inc.
P.O. Box 15129
Park Square Station
Stamford, CT 06901-0129
Tel.: (800) 243-9169

Purpose of goals: To intensively remediate students' conceptual, computational, and problem-solving math skills by systematically improving thinking skills and reasoning processes. Cognitive development serves as the vehicle for improving mathematical abilities.

Motivational strategies: High-interest materials engage students in the instructional process. Math skills are treated as the application and extension of thinking skills. Group and individualized instruction provides opportunity for whole-class exploration of mathematics as well as individual learning progress in mathematical and thinking ability.

Theoretical background: The program is based on the "Design for Thinking" theory of Dr. Albert Upton and incorporates elements of Dr. J. P. Guilford's "Structure of Intellect" theory.

Curriculum for training teachers to use the program: Full pre-service and in-service programs are conducted by specially trained consultants.

Evidence of success: Substantial research evidence supports significant student gains in such areas as number concepts, computational abilities, problem solving, thinking skills, academic aptitude, and self-concept.

Odyssey: A Curriculum for Thinking

Audience: Ages 10 to 14, Odyssey can be introduced to students between grades 4 and 8. It is appropriate for all ability groups.

Most appropriate subjects in which to teach this project: Odyssey focuses on fundamental thinking processes—classification, hierarchical classification, sequencing analogical reasoning—which are used in all curriculum areas.

Suggested schedule: Foundations of reasoning should be taught first, then any other course or combination of courses.

Total hours required to complete program: "Foundations of Reasoning": 30-35 hours approx. "Problem Solving": 15-20 hours. All other courses: 15-20 hours.

Estimated cost of materials: "Foundations of Reasoning" student book is $5. All other student books cost $3. All teacher manuals cost $15.

Address for further information:

>Gary Chadwell, Director of Information and Training
>Mastery Education Corporation
>85 Main Street
>Watertown, MA 02171

Purpose of goals: To help students make the most productive use of their intellectual potential through lessons that encompass a broad range of highly productive thinking skills and processes.

Motivational strategies: Because students learn best by doing, Odyssey instruction is highly interactive. It is designed to involve all students to the fullest extent possible in discussions, role-playing, simulations, and other problem-solving activities.

Theoretical background: The Odyssey program approaches thinking as a life skill that involves performance, communication, attitudes, and values.

Curriculum for training teachers to use the program: The Odyssey teacher manual provides detailed instructions for every lesson. This comprehensive support means that teachers can implement the program successfully without special training.

Evidence of success: In controlled field tests of Odyssey, three standardized tests were used: CATTELL, OLSAT, and a battery of General Ability Tests (GATs). The gain of the experimental group was 20 percent greater than the gain of the control group on the CATTELL, 50 percent greater on the OLSAT, and 68 percent greater on the GATs.

Philosophy for Children: Harry Stottlemeier's Discovery (Text); Philosophical Inquiry (Instructional Manual)

Audience: Ages 11 to 12. Most appropriate subjects in which to teach this project: Language arts or as an independent subject.

Suggested schedule: $2\frac{1}{4}$ hours per week.

Total hours required to complete program: 75 hours.

Estimated cost of materials: $10.

Address for further information:

> IAPC
> Montclair State College
> Upper Montclair, NJ 07043

Purpose of goals: Strengthening reasoning, inquiry, concept formation, and translation skills.

Motivational strategies: Classroom discussion, reading of novel (text) so as to form community of inquiry.

Theoretical background: Bruner, Dewey, Vygotsky, Piaget, G. H. Mead.

Curriculum for training teachers to use the program: Teacher education seminars, modeling sessions, and observations by workshop directors.

Evidence of success: After one year, children in experimental classes gained 80 percent more in reasoning, 66 percent more in reading comprehension, and 36 percent more in mathematics proficiency than children not in the program.

Philosophy for Children: Lisa (Text); Ethical Inquiry (Instructional Manual)

Audience: Ages 13 to 14.

Most appropriate subjects in which to teach this project: English, ethics.

Suggested schedule: $2\frac{1}{4}$ hours per week.

Total hours required to complete program: 75 hours.

Estimated cost of materials: $10.

Address for further information:

IAPC
Montclair State College
Upper Montclair, NJ 07043

Purpose of goals: Teaching children strategies of moral reasoning and procedures of ethical inquiry.

Motivational strategies: Converting classroom into a discussion community.

Theoretical background: History of philosophical ethics.

Curriculum for training teachers to use the program: Teaching education seminars (once a week for one year), plus modeling and observations by workshop director.

Philosophy for Children: Suki (Text); Writing: How and Why (Instructional Manual)

Audience: Ages 14 to 16.

Most appropriate subjects in which to teach this project: English, writing.

Suggested schedule: $2\frac{1}{4}$ hours per week for at least one year.

Total hours required to complete programs: 75 hours.

Estimated cost of materials: $10

Address for further information:

IAPC
Montclair State College
Upper Montclair, NJ 07043

Purpose of goals: Stimulating children's writing.

Motivational strategies: Promoting classroom discussion that can then be continued in written form.

Theoretical background: Aesthetics, epistemology.

Curriculum for training teachers to use the program: Teacher education seminars, modeling sessions, and observations by workshop directors.

Philosophy for Children: Mark (Text); Social Inquiry (Instructional Manual)

Audience: Ages 16 to 17

Most appropriate subjects in which to teach this project: Social studies.

Suggested schedule: $2\frac{1}{4}$ hours per week.

Total hours required to complete program: 37–75 hours.

Estimated cost of materials: $10

Address for further information:

IAPC
Montclair State College
Upper Montclair, NJ 07043

Purpose of goals: Encouraging reflection upon nature of society and citizenship.

Motivational strategies: Converting classroom into community of social inquiry.

Theoretical background: Philosophy of social sciences, sociology, contemporary civilization.

Curriculum for training teachers to use the program: Teachers are taught in seminars; workshop directors model and observe in classrooms.

Directory of Materials
for Multicultural Classes*

The Adventures of Billy Bean, Wesley Studies, Cross-Cultural Education Center (P.O. Box 66, Park Hill, OK 74451), 1982.

> Produced by the Cherokee Bilingual Education Program, this collection of stories was published as a response to problems that Cherokee children have faced because of language deficiency and culture gap. These stories portray Billy Bean in such a way that he promotes the Native American culture and its value system as a priceless heritage.

The Girl on the Outside, Mildred Pitts Walker, Lothrop, Lee & Shepard, 1982.

> Written against the background of the September 1957 desegregation in Little Rock, Arkansas, this book presents an interesting comparison between the poor, black teenage girl who will desegregate the school and the rich white teenage girl who already attends the school. Black characters argue on valid grounds, and white characters reveal the struggles of conscience as life in this country changed.

Tic Tac Toe and Other Three-in-a-Row Games from Ancient Egypt to the Modern Computer, Claudia Zaslavsky, T. Y. Crowell, 1982.

> Games from China, the Philippines and Kenya, such as Nine-Men's Morris, Five Square, and Shisima, are explained with diagrams. These games are suitable for children and many for adults. The African and Asian origins of the games are given as historical context.

Count on Your Fingers African Style, Claudia Zaslavsky, T. Y. Crowell, 1980.

> This book has been recognized by the National Council of Christians and Jews and has received awards as a notable Social Studies and Outstanding Science Book.

My Mama Needs Me, Mildred Pitts Walker, illustrated by Pat Cummings, Lothrop, Lee & Shepard, 1983.

> The illustrations in this book reveal that Jason lives in a neighborhood that is both black and white. This story deals with an older child's adjustment to the new baby in the family. It is a

---

* Grace R. Bishop. (1986, Fall). The identification of multicultural materials for the middle school library: Annotations and sources, American Middle School Education, 9.

positive book with a simple text in which Jason grows to love his sister and support his mother with the new baby.

Home Boy, Joyce Hansen, Clarion/Houghton Mifflin, 1982.
A youth and his family move to New York City from the Caribbean. The boy learns to fit into his new environment despite difficulties of time and place.

In Neuva York, Nicholosa Mohr, Dial, 1977.
A set of interrelated short stories provides good reading for young adults. The setting is a Puerto Rican community in New York's lower east side.

Just My Luck, Emily Moore, Dutton, 1983.
The story of a middle-class black family provides humorous and refreshing reading for middle school teenagers.

Music, Music for Everyone, Vera B. Williams, Greenwillow, 1984.
This book is the third in a series about Rosa, her mother, grandmother, and friends. The beautiful illustrations add to the positive message, and this book includes not only interracial friendship but family affection and community cooperation.

Sweet Whispers, Brother Rush, Virginia Hamilton, Philomel, 1982.
A Newbery Honor Book for 1983 and recipient of the Coretta Scott King Award for that year, this book centers on a brother-sister relationship and a relationship with a helpful ghost named Brother Rush.

Friends Till the End, Todd Strasser, Delacorte, 1981.
David visits a newcomer, Howie, who has leukemia; they develop a very close friendship. Through his relationship with Howie, David gains an understanding of the meaning and value of life. An excellent book for any young person who has faced or may have to face a friend's death.

All the Colors of the Race. Arnold Adoff, Lothrop, Lee & Shepard, 1982.
This collection of poems pictures an interracial family through the daughter's eyes. It emphasizes both the richness of cultural difference and the confusion of outsiders. The poems are beautiful in their vision of racial harmony.

She Was There: Stories of Pioneering Women Journalists, Jean E. Collins, Messner, 1980.
Collins interviews 15 women journalists who were pioneers in their fields. These stories include excerpts from their lives as well as short biographical accounts. The book leaves the reader wanting to learn more. A good book for teenagers, especially girls.

The Balancing Girl, Berniece Rabe, Dutton, 1981.
The touching story of a handicapped child who works toward acceptance from her peers in a "regular" classroom situation. This book has a positive tone.

Don't You Turn Back, Lee Bennett Hopkins, Alfred A. Knopf, 1969.
A collection of Langston Hughes' poetry that can be used to create student posters—art to celebrate poetry. (There is also a recording by Spoken Arts—"Langston Hughes Reads and Talks about His Poems").

The Golda Meir Story, Margaret Davidson, Scribners, 1981.
The story of Golda Meir, the former prime minister of Israel, is a fascinating one. It focuses upon her experience as an American immigrant and her part in the founding of Israel. This book is suitable for more mature readers and for teachers to use in introducing the accomplishments of a famous world figure, in this case a woman.

Julie of the Wolves, Jean George, Harper & Rowe, 1972.
A fascinating story of an Eskimo girl set against the sparsely populated, expansive territory of Alaska.

The New Wind Has Wings: Poems from Canada, Oxford/Merrimack, 1975.
This prize-winning collection includes poems about Canada, its history, its early settlers, and its cultural blend of English- and French-speaking people.

American Indians: A Bibliography of Sources, American Library Association, 50 East Huron St., Chicago, IL 60611.
A list of many sources.

Asia: A Guide to Basic Books, Asia Society, 112 East 64th St., New York, NY 10021.
A list of basic books on Asia.

The Black Experience in Children's Books, Augusta Baker, Office of Children's Services, New York Public Library, 8 East 40th St., New York, NY 10016.
A revision that includes 400 titles.

American Negro in Contemporary Society, California Library Association, 1741 Solano Ave., Berkeley, CA 94707.
An annotated list of 121 titles.

Children's Books from Mexico, Centro Mexicano de Escritores, Apartodo Postal 1298, Mexico. 1. D.F., Mexico.
A list of books for children in Spanish.

Multi-ethnic Media: Selected bibliographies, David Cohen, Chairman, American Association of School Librarians, 50 East Huron St., Chicago, IL 60611.

To Be Black in America, Free Library of Philadelphia, 19th and Vine Sts., Philadelphia, PA 19103.
A bibliographic essay arranged in broad categories: materials included suitable for use by junior and senior high school students.

Children's Interracial Fiction, Barbara Jean Glancy, American Federation of Teachers, AFL-CIO. 1012 14th St. NW., Washington, DC 20036.
An annotated unselected bibliography identifying 328 books with black characters.

The National Assessment and Dissemination Center for Bilingual Bicultural Education (385 High St., Fall River, MA 02720) has Spanish, Portuguese, Oriental, native American, Greek, Italian, and French materials.

The Dissemination Center for Bilingual/Bicultural Education (6504 Tracor Lane, Austin, TX 78721) has Spanish, Navajo, Portuguese, and French materials.
Another center funded by the National Institute of Education (NIE) and the Educational Products Exchange Institute (EPIE) has published informative volumes (EPIE Institute, 453 West St., New York, NY 10014).

Child of UNICEF, Eight children, each from a different country, tell of their experiences with UNICEF in separate booklets.

Africa: An Annotated List of Printed Materials Suitable for Children, Information Center on Children's Cultures, United States Committee for UNICEF, 331 East 38th St., New York, NY 10016.
An evaluation of all in-print English-language materials for children on the subject of Africa.

Glossary

Accountability in Instructional Management (AIM). Mississippi's educational reform program.

Achievement test. Standardized test designed to measure how much has been learned about a particular subject.

Acronym. Word made up of the first letter of a set of several words.

Action zone. The area in classrooms, arranged in rows and columns, that includes the front row and center columns. Students seated in this area tend to interact more with the teacher and to be higher achievers.

Advance organizers. Concepts within which learners can subsume the new material and relate it to what they already know.

Affective domain. The part of human learning that involves changes in interests, attitudes, and values.

Affective objectives. Instructional objectives that stress attitudes, feelings, and values.

Aims. Aspirations that are so general that they can never be attained.

Algorithm. Step-by-step procedure for solving a problem.

Alignment. Matching learning activities with desired outcomes, or matching what is taught to what is tested.

Allotted time. The amount of time given to a subject in a curriculum plan; also called assigned time.

Alternative testing. Testing methods that do not rely on a pencil and paper.

Assertive discipline. An approach to classroom management developed by Canter and Canter that stresses the rights of teachers to teach and the rights of students to learn; teachers respond to students in a clear, firm, unhostile way.

Axiom. Universally recognized truth.

Balanced curriculum. Equal emphasis on disciplines: for example, the arts and sciences, or vocational courses and college preparatory courses.

BASIC. (Beginner's All-Purpose Symbolic Instruction Code) A versatile and popular computer language used extensively by educators.

Behavior contracts. An agreement between teacher and students that specifies behaviors that earn specified rewards (e.g., free time out).

Behavior modification. Techniques of shaping behavior by reinforcing desirable responses and ignoring undesirable responses.

Behavioral objective. Objective that requires students to perform at specified level under specified conditions; also called performance objectives.

Behavioral psychology. School of thought that embraces basing all decisions on observation of actual behavior.

Behavioral disordered students. Emotionally disturbed students.

Binary digits. (One and Zero) Used to code information and store it electronically in a computer.

Cardinal Principles of Secondary Education, Seven. The National Education Association's aims for secondary schools.

Child-centered education. Curricula that involve students in planning and participating in learning activities.

Chip. An integrated circuit.

Classic conditioning. Repeatedly pairing a neutral stimulus with a stimulus that elicits a response until the previously neutral stimulus alone elicits the response.

Classroom management. Maintaining a healthy learning environment, relatively free of behavioral problem.

COBOL. (Common Business Oriented Language) A higher-level programming language developed for use in business.

Cognitive domain. The part of human learning that involves changes in intellectual skills, such as assimilation of information.

Cognitive objectives. Instructional objectives that stress knowledge and intellectual abilities and skills.

Cognitive psychology. A branch of psychology devoted to the study of how individuals acquire, process, and use information.

Compendium. An abridgement or a complete summary.

Computer. An electronic machine that performs rapid, complex calculations or compiles and correlates data.

Computer Assisted Instruction (CAI). Use of computers to present programs or otherwise facilitate or evaluate learning.

Computer literacy. Knowledge of a computer's basic operation, potential, and limitation: recently expanded to include such skills as the ability to write simple programs, use data bases, and use spread sheets.

Computer Managed Instruction (CMI). The use of a computer system to manage information about learner performance.

Concepts. Those major understandings within each discipline characterized by recurring patterns such as common physical characteristics or common utility.

Concrete operations. Stage in Piaget's learning that precedes the ability to think abstractly; roughly includes the elementary school years.

Constructism. A philosophy of curriculum as connected concepts.

Content generalization. General categories of ideas, objects, and experiences with recurring patterns; example: concepts, principles, and theories.

Contracts. A written agreement signed by the teacher and the student.

Control group. In an experiment, a group of subjects that receives no special treatment and serves as basis for comparison.

Convergent question. Question with only one correct answer.

Convergent thinking. Thinking that uses the deductive processes.

Cooperative learning. Students working in pairs or small groups helping each other reach the class objectives.

Creativity. An individual's capacity to produce imaginative, original products or solutions to problems.

Criterion-referenced evaluation. Evaluation that measures success by the attainment of established levels of performance; individual success is based wholly on the individual's performance without regard for others' performance.

Criterion-referenced test. Measure of student's performance with reference to specified criteria or to that individual's previous level of performance.

Cultural pluralism. Cultural diversity; the existence of several different cultures within a group; encouraging each group to keep its individual qualities within the larger society.

Curriculum. The total experiences planned for a school or student.

Curriculum alignment. Matching learning activities with desired outcomes, or matching what is taught to what is tested.

Curriculum guide. A written statement of objectives, content, and activities to be used with a particular subject at specified grade levels; usually produced by state department of education or local education agencies.

Data base. A collection of related information organized for quick access to specific items of information.

Data-based instruction. Selection and implementation of teaching methods proven effective by research.

Debugging. The process of locating and removing errors from a program.

Delphi method. A systematic problem-solving process that uses deductive reasoning.

Diagnostic test. Test designed to identify specific academic strengths and weaknesses.

Direct instruction. Teacher-directed instruction based on clear objectives, engaged time, and mastery of content.

Discovery learning. Form of instruction in which a teacher arranges the learning environment so that students can find their own answers by forming hypotheses, gathering information, and testing hypotheses.

Discrimination. Teachers' attempt to identify students who master learning assignments and those who do not.

Disequilibration. In Piaget's theory, the learner searches for a balance between what is being learned and what the learner already knows.

Diskette. See floppy disk.

Distractors. Attractive but wrong answers to a multiple-choice question on a test.

Divergent question. Question for which there is no single, correct answer.

Divergent thinking. Thinking that uses the inductive processes.

Downlink. The reception end of a satellite transmission; entails a satellite dish with a decoder and display screen.

Downtime. A period of time when a computer is not functioning properly.

Education for All Handicapped Children Act. A 1977 legislative act that requires each state to provide special services for its handicapped students at public expense and under public supervision and direction.

Educational domain. Three broad categories of learning: affective, cognitive, and psychomotor.

Effective schools. Those schools whose students are high academic achievers.

Effective teachers. Those teachers whose students are high academic achievers.

Efficacy studies. Studies of the effect of the teacher and students' self-confidence on educational success.

Eight-Year Study. A study from 1933 to 1941 conducted by Harvard University to compare the success of child-centered education with the success of traditional education.

Emotionally disturbed students. Students with a chronic inability to learn, relate to others, or overcome depression.

Empathy. The ability to feel an emotion as another experiences it.

Engaged time. The time students actually spend learning as opposed to the time assigned or allotted for studying.

EPROM. Erasable Programmable Read Only Memory.

Equilibration. Tendency for individuals to make newly learned knowledge agree with what they already know.

Evaluation. Making measurements plus providing value judgements.

Execute. To perform the operations specified by a computer instruction or program.

Expository teaching. Lecturing.

Extinction. Tendency for a conditional response to disappear if not reinforced.

Extrinsic motivation. Doing something to earn a reward or because it is required.

Faculty psychology. Early twentieth century branch of psychology that perceived the brain as a muscle, the growth of which required exercising with unpleasant and repetitious tasks.

Floppy disk. A flexible disk used widely by microcomputers.

Formal operations. Piaget's highest level of thinking involving abstractions.

Formative evaluation. Evaluation before or during instruction aimed at improving learning and teaching.

FORTRAN. (FORmula TRANslation) A high-level programming language designed for scientific studies.

Free time. Time that students earn to use as they prefer; usually requires completing an assignment; also called earned free time.

Freudian psychology. A school of thought instigated by Sigmund Freud to explain behavior by breaking the personality into three parts: the ego, superego, and id.

Gallup Poll of Public Attitudes toward the Schools. A national annual survey of the public's attitudes toward the schools.

Generalizations. The broad understandings required to master any given field of study; also called content generalizations.

GIGO. (Garbage In, Garbage Out) Bad or faulty input leads to bad results.

Goals for 2000. A list of six goals set by the president and governors in 1990, to be reached by all American schools by the year 2000.

Grade contract. An agreement between teacher and student that specifies behaviors that will earn specified grades.

Guided discovery learning. Discovery learning where the teacher uses questions to guide the students. Also called inquiry learning.

Hardware. The machines or equipment of a computer system.

Heuristics. Methods or techniques of problem solving.

Hidden curriculum. Messages that a school or teacher unintentionally gives by the procedures used.

High-level language. A language that, when translated into machine language, produces many machine language instructions. A language that is more English-like than machine-like.

Histrionics. The use of humor in teaching, often using exaggerated body movement.

Houses. Groups of students of varying abilities who work together and compete with groups of near equal ability.

Humanistic education. Approach to education that stresses attitudes, values, personal fulfillment, and relationships with others.

Hypothesis. A statement of predicted outcomes.

Individualized Education Program (IEP). A curriculum designed especially for a student with special needs.

Individualized Instruction. Instruction that has been designed to meet each student's needs, interests, and abilities.

Inductive learning. The formulation of general principles based on knowledge of specific examples and details.

Inquiry learning. Discovery learning where the teacher uses questions to guide the students; also called guided discovery learning.

Information-processing theory. Study of the ways sensory input is transformed, stored, recovered, and used.

In-service teachers. Teachers who have graduated and are teaching full time.

Insight. Learning that occurs when an individual perceives new relationships.

Instruction. A statement that specifies an operation.

Instructional unit. A curriculum plan that covers 1 or 2 weeks of elementary study or 6 to 18 weeks of high school.

Intrinsic learning. Learning for its own sake.

Integrated circuit. A solid-state electronic circuit on a single layer of silicon.

Interface. An electronic go-between used to connect the computer to another device, such as a disk drive.

Interpreter. A computer program that translates and executes expressions one at a time.

Invitational learning. Form of humanistic education in which teachers communicate to students that they (students) are responsible, able, and valuable.

Keyboard. A typewriter-like instrument for putting information into a computer; replaces the earlier keypunch machine.

Knowledge base. The research-derived knowledge that supports practices of a profession.

Lau v. Nichols [Supreme Court case] A law that requires any school with as many as 20 students who speak a common non-English first language to offer all subjects in that language.

Learning. More or less permanent change in behavior as a result of experiences.

Learning disability. Discrepancy between achievement and ability in one or more of several areas of school performance.

Learning for Mastery (LMF). A special category of teacher-directed, group-centered mastery learning.

Learning strategy. Integrated system for improving one's ability to learn.

Line printer. An instrument that prints computer output in the form of letters, numbers, and other symbols.

Load. To enter data into a program or to enter a stored program into memory.

Locus of control. Perception of where the responsibility for one's successes and failures lie.

Long-term memory (LTM). Storehouse of permanently recorded information in one's memory.

Loop. A sequence of program instructions that is repeated until an exit command is given or a predetermined completion is reached.

Low-level language. Computer-programming language that is closely related to machine language.

Machine language. The instructions that a computer can recognize and execute without translation, usually expressed in ones and zeros.

Mainstreaming. Moving handicapped students into classrooms with nonhandicapped students.

Management classroom. Management of students and resources to ensure learning.

Maslow's Hierarchy of Needs. A list of human needs ranked from the lowest (physical needs) to the highest (self-actualization needs)

Mastery learning. Technique of instruction whereby pupils are given multiple opportunities to learn using criterion-based objectives, flexible time, and instruction that matches the learner's style preference.

Melting pot. The idea that immigrants should blend their cultural characteristics into one society.

Meta-analysis. A statistical technique that searches for consistencies and inconsistencies in studies of a common problem.

Metacognition. Knowledge of how one's mind works; thinking about ways to improve one's ability to memorize and learn.

Microcomputer. Microprocessor, memory, and auxiliary hardware, such as video units and printers, connected in a single unit.

Microprocessor. The memory unit of a computer, often called a chip.

Middle-level education. Usually grades from 4 or 5 to 7 or 8.

Mild desists. Private explanations of the need for a rule.

Minicomputer. A small computer that has peripheral equipment attached to it. Together with its equipment, it is larger than the microcomputer but smaller than the general-purpose computer.

Modeling. The influence of one's behavior on another's behavior.

Motivation. Arousal, selection, direction, and continuation of behavior.

Multicultural education. Education goals and methods that teach students the value of cultural diversity.

NMSA. National Middle School Association.

National at Risk. The first (1983) and most widely publicized of over 400 reports on the public schools.

Norm-referenced evaluation. Evaluation that compares the individual's performance with classmates' performance to determine the individual's success.

Norm-referenced grading. A student's performance is evaluated by comparing it with others' performance.

Normal learning curve. A symmetrical, bell-shaped curve that shows the distribution of learners' abilities.

On-task behavior. Students involved in lesson activities or assignments.

Open education. Form of instruction stressing student activity, learning areas, multi-age grouping, self-selection, and individualized teaching, also called open classroom.

Operational objective. Objective written with active verb and specified criteria; also called behavioral objective and performance objective because it requires the student to perform specific behaviors.

Pacing. Adjusting a lesson's tempo to students' ability.

Pall level. A state of physical, program-related fatigue caused by presentations being too short, too long, too simple, or too complicated.

Pascal. A higher-level language used extensively with microcomputers.

Perception. Interpretation of sensory information.

Performance objective. Objective that requires students to perform at specified levels under specified conditions; also called behavioral objective or instructional objective.

Personal computer. An inexpensive microcomputer designed for the home or small business.

Phenomenology. A branch of psychology that studies strategies for getting people to change their own behavior.

Portfolio. A collection of teaching methods.

Pretest. A formative test given before instruction to promote learning.

Process evaluation. Evaluation that measures success by focusing on the performer's behavior.

Product evaluation. Evaluation that measures success by examining the product.

Progressive Education Era. From the early 1920s to the early 1940s, when the curriculum was student-centered.

PROM. (Programmable Read Only Memory) ROM that is programmed by the user, not the manufacturer.

Proximity control. Controlling students' behavior by standing closer to them.

Psychomotor domain. The part of human learning that involves motor skills.

Pygmalion effect. Tendency for individuals who are treated as capable (or incapable) to act that way (same as self-fulfilling prophecy).

RAM. (Random Access Memory, also called read-write memory.) A high-speed memory to which the user can have access in about one-millionth of a second.

Regents examination. A state-wide achievement examination used annually by the state of New York.

Reinforcement. Using consequences to strengthen behavior.

Reliability tests. How consistent scores are if the same test is given to the same students a second time.

Repertoire of teaching methods. A collection of teaching methods.

Research-based teaching. Using methods that are research-validated.

Restructuring. Changing a school's entire program or procedure, as opposed to changing only one part of the curriculum.

Rhetorical questions. Questions without solicited or intended answers.

Rogerian psychology. Founded by Carl Rogers, a counseling system that lets clients talk out their problems to gain a clearer perception of their problems.

Role model. The use of one's own behavior to shape the behavior of others.

ROM. (Read Only Memory) Memory produced by the manufacturer to which the user cannot store or write additional information.

Saber-Tooth Curriculum. A 1939 satire on education, written by Harold Benjamin.

Salient content. Content that teachers consider very important.

Self-concept. How people view themselves on those characteristics they consider most important.

Self-efficacy. Feeling that one can successfully achieve a particular outcome.

Self-fulfilling prophesy. Tendency for individuals to behave in ways they are expected to behave (same as Pygmalion effect).

Sensorimotor. Piaget's earliest stage of development, 0–2 years.

Sensory-deprived students. Students with such handicaps as loss of hearing or vision.

Sensory register. Memory structure that holds information for possible processing.

Set induction. Teacher strategies for capturing student attention; most commonly used at the onset of a lesson.

Shaping. Reinforcement of actions that move progressively closer to the desired behavior.

Short-term memory (STM). "Working" memory, or information temporarily stored in one's memory.

Simulations. Games that involve students in lifelike roles.

Site-based decision making. The governance of a school by a local team, usually consisting of one or more administrators and two or more teachers and parents. Also called school-based decision making or local decision making.

Socratic teaching method. The method used by Socrates, which involved asking a series of questions of one student while classmates observed; each question changed the student's course until the student eventually totally disagreed with his or her own earlier answers.

Software. Computer program control instructions and accompanying documentation, stored on diskettes or cassettes when not being used.

Solid state. Electronic components, such as diodes, resistors, transistor, that are made of solid materials, as opposed to tube-type components.

Standard deviations. The degree a particular score deviates (or varies) from the mean distribution of a group of scores.

Standardized test. Test prepared for nation-wide use by a testing corporation that establishes norms by presenting a carefully selected set of items to a representative sample of students.

Stanine score. Score that indicates a pupil's position in a distribution divided into nine one-half standard deviation units.

Stimulus. Any event in the environment that activates behavior.

Stimulus-response psychology. The study and practice of learning how to vary individuals' behavior by varying their stimuli.

Stimulus variation. Changing the classroom environment and lesson delivery to increase student motivation.

Style flex. A student's ability to learn from a variety of teaching style.

Summative evaluation. Evaluation that occurs following instruction and is used to determine grades and promotion.

Taba's Inverted Model. A curriculum model that begins with teachers who design learning units; considered opposite or inverted from traditional top-down models.

Table of specifications. Chart to ensure coverage of varying levels of desired knowledge and skills.

Tabula rasa. Seventeenth-century-philosopher John Locke's idea that at birth the mind is a blank slate.

Tactile instruction. Instruction that involves hands-on activities.

Taxonomy of educational objectives. Comprehensive classification scheme with learning objectives arranged in hierarchical order.

Teaching strategy. Integrated system for improving one's teaching, using a combination of methods.

Tempo. The rate of speed at which a lesson is delivered.

Test validity. The degree to which a test measures what it is intended to measure.

Time-out. Behavior modification technique in which undesirable behavior is weakened by temporarily removing positive reinforcement.

Time-sharing. The distribution of computer processing time among many users simultaneously.

Transescence. Preadolescent development stage.

Tutoring. Providing learning assistance to individual students.

Underachievers. Students who consistently perform below their ability.

Unit plan. A planned study unit, usually 1 to 2 weeks long for elementary students and 3 to 12 weeks long for secondary students.

Unobtrusive. Not readily noticeable.

Uplink. A ground station that transmits a signal to a satellite for transmission to other ground stations.

User-friendly. A subjective measure of how easy an item of hardware or software is to use.

Values clarification. Techniques of humanistic education designed to help students understand the basis of their beliefs and choose, prize, and act on their beliefs.

Videodisc. A video recording and storage system in which audiovisual signals are recorded on plastic discs, as opposed to magnetic tape.

Wait time. The time teachers provide students to respond to questions.

Author Index

Subject Index